S P[illegible]
COMPREH[illegible]VE
RAILROAD ATLAS
OF NORTH AMERICA

NORTHEAST

MIKE WALKER

Published in England by
Ian Andrews
SPV, Dawes Road, Dunkirk, Faversham, Kent ME13 9UU U.K.

ISBN 1 874745 10 2
First Published 1993
Completely revised & updated 1998

SYMBOLS & ABBREVIATIONS

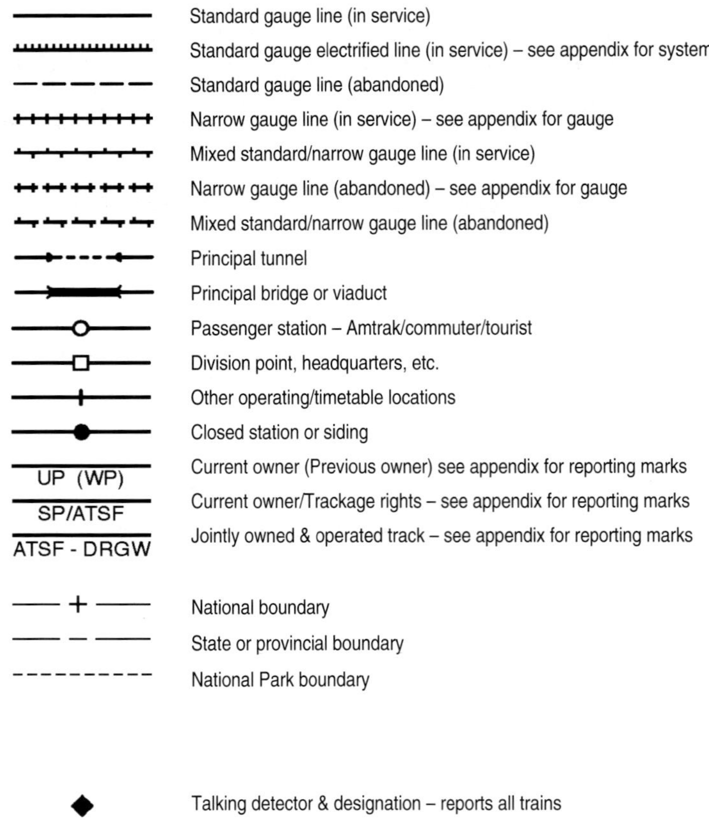

◆	Talking detector & designation – reports all trains
◇	Talking director & designation – reports on defect only
▲	Summit (elevation in feet a.s.l.)
+	Passenger station – scheduled regular service
⧺	Passenger station – tourist or museum operation

A	Automatically controlled interlocking	n	Northbound
B	General or bulletin office	e	Eastbound
C	Passenger car yard	s	Southbound
D	Draw, lift or swing bridge	w	Westbound
E	Engine facility	m	Mileage
G	Railroad crossing at grade with gate or gate on line	CP	Control point
L	DTC block limits	DTC	Direct traffic control
M	Manually controlled interlocking (may be remotely controlled)	Bch	Branch
P	Passing siding	Br	Bridge
R	Register station	Jct	Junction
S	Railroad crossing at grade with stop sign protection	Stn	Station
T	Turning facility (turntable or wye)	Tnl	Tunnel
U	Railroad crossing unprotected	Twr	Tower
W	Water tank	Vdt	Viaduct
X	Crossover on multiple track	Yd	Yard
Y	Yard		

INTRODUCTION

This all-new edition of the NORTH EAST volume SPV's COMPREHENSIVE RAILROAD ATLAS OF NORTH AMERICA has been prepared to coincide with the take over of Conrail by CSX and Norfolk Southern. The opportunity has also been taken to include additional enlargements of complex areas and to include many early lines which were omitted from the earlier edition and bring the style of presentation into line with later volumes of the series. Due to space considerations, the New England states are no longer included and will appear in a separate volume, along with the Canadian Maritime provinces, to be published in the winter of 1999/2000.

The Atlas shows all currently operated common carrier, tourist and major industrial railroads along with abandoned routes. The electric interurbans are generally not shown except where they incorporated part of, or later became part of a 'steam' railroad or are still extant. Lines shown as narrow gauge are shown only as such when they are currently so laid or were at abandonment. Lines built as narrow or broad gauge and subsequently regauged are shown as standard gauge. It should be noted that some lines shown as 'in service' may see very infrequent use whilst some 'abandoned' lines may, if the tracks remain in place, be reactivated for a special movement.

Every effort has been made to show all current operating locations as defined in railroad operating timetables. Letter and symbol codes adjacent to locations give an indication of what facilities may be found there. The approximate location of 'talking defect detectors' along with their identification, together with 'Controlled Points' (which may be heard over the radio), major bridges and tunnels are also identified.

In the case of former Conrail trackage, the lines are marked CSXT or NS as appropriate but those 'Shared Asset Areas' which will be jointly operated by CSX and NS under the Conrail title are identified by the mark CSAO (Conrail Shared Asset Operation) to distinguish them from the original CR. The operating points and designations reflect the final days of Conrail, once CSX and NS assume full operations, expected on March 1, 1999, these may change - for example defect detectors may be changed to mileage based identifications.

It should be noted that not all former stations and mines are shown due to their great number. For example, in the late 1920's the Pennsylvania Railroad alone served more than a thousand mines in its home state. For clarity, only the end points of some minor branches are shown.

The Atlas does not show roads, as this would be confusing. For detail of road access to lines the DeLorme topographic atlases are recommended. The author and publisher remind readers that the contents on this Atlas are for information only and do not imply any right of public access. Railroads and much of the property surrounding them are private and should be respected as such.

Sources used in the compilation of this Atlas include old and current timetables, railroad documents, magazine articles, books on the region's railroads, topographic, county and railroad maps and field surveys. Whilst every care has been taken in the preparation of this volume, cross checking various sources, it is accepted that there may be some errors or omissions. In addition the continuing process of mergers, regional and shortline spin-offs and abandonments within the North American railroad industry will affect the accuracy of this Atlas. The author welcomes corrections and updated information via the publisher. The information herein is compiled to late 1998.

ACKNOWLEDGEMENTS: *Finally, in any work such as this, numerous individuals both in the UK and USA have helped to provide information. In particular, thanks should be given to Ralph Balfoort, Dick Carpenter, Richard Cossey, Patrick Lane, Peter Mosse, C. H. 'Corky' Price Sr., John Riegel, John Sears, Gary Shrey, Reggie Tonry and Thomas L. Underwood Jr. who all spent many hours on research, checking, acting as guides, answering questions and loaning or donating materials. Without their help this volume would not be have been possible. I would also like to take the opportunity of thanking all those who wrote offering comments and encouragement following the publication of the first edition. All correspondence was read and wherever possible your comments have been incorporated in this new edition.*

Mike Walker

Marlow, Bucks., December 1998

TABLE OF CONTENTS

ITEM	PAGE
SYMBOLS AND ABBREVIATIONS	2
INTRODUCTION	3
TABLE OF CONTENTS	4
MAP GRID	5
MAPS	6-74
APPENDIX	75-78
INDEX	79-104

KEY TO MAPS

Code	Page	Map
DE-1	6	Wilmington
DE-2a	7	Delaware North
DE-2b	7	Delaware South
MD-1	8	Cumberland
MD-1a	8	Westernport
MD-2	9	Maryland West
MD-3	10	Maryland Central
MD-3a	10	Hagerstown
MD-4	11	Maryland East
MD-5	12	Baltimore
MD-6	13	Aberdeen
MD-7	14	Maryland South
MD-7a	14	Washington
MD-8	15	Delmarva Peninsular
NJ-1a	16	Sparta Mountain
NJ-1b	16	Delaware Water Gap
NJ-2	17	New Jersey North
NJ-2a	17	Dover
NJ-3	18	New Jersey Central
NJ-4	19	New Jersey South
NJ-4a	19	Atlantic City
NJ-5	20	Perth Amboy
NJ-6	21	Morristown
NJ-7	22	Newark
NY-1	23	New York
NY-2	24	Nassau County
NY-3	25	Bronx - Yonkers
NY-4	26	Croton-Harmon
NY-4a	26	Beacon
NY-4b	26	Brewster
NY-5	27	Middletown
NY-6	28	Adirondacks North
NY-7	29	Adirondacks South
NY-7a	29	Ticonderoga
NY-8	30	Hudson & Mohawk
NY-9	31	Upper Hudson
NY-10a	32	Schenectady
NY-10b	32	Albany
NY-11	33	Ravena - Hudson
NY-12	34	Lower Hudson
NY-12a	34	Kingston
NY-12b	34	Poughkeepsie
NY-13	35	Long Island
NY-14	36	St. Lawrence
NY-14a	36	Syracuse
NY-14b	36	Binghamton
NY-15	37	Watertown
NY-15a	37	Oswego
NY-16	38	Syracuse - Utica
NY-17	39	Ithaca - Binghamton
NY-18	40	Rochester - Geneva
NY-19	41	Hornell - Corning
NY-20	42	Niagara Frontier
NY-20a	42	Niagara Falls
NY-21	43	Dunkirk - Salamanca
NY-22	44	Rochester
NY-23	45	Batavia - Retsof
NY-24	46	Buffalo
PA-1	47	Erie
PA-1a	47	Sharon
PA-1b	47	Greenville
PA-1c	47	Mahoning
PA-2	48	Meadville - Oil City
PA-3	49	Lower Allegheny
PA-4	50	Southwest Pennsylvania
PA-5a	51	New Castle
PA-5b	51	Freeport
PA-6	52	Pittsburgh West
PA-7	53	Pittsburgh East
PA-8	54	Brownsville
PA-9	55	Connellsville
PA-10	56	Bradford
PA-11	57	DuBois - Tyrone
PA-12	58	Clearfield
PA-13a	59	Altoona
PA-13b	59	Mahaffey
PA-13c	59	Patton
PA-14	60	Southern Allegheníes
PA-15	61	Sayre - Williamsport
PA-16	62	Upper Susquehanna
PA-17	63	Lower Susquehanna
PA-18a	64	Johnstown
PA-18b	64	Harrisburg
PA-18c	64	Reading
PA-18d	64	Lancaster
PA-18e	64	Columbia
PA-19a	65	Scranton
PA-19b	65	Wilkes-Barre
PA-20a	66	Mount Carmel
PA-20b	66	Hazleton
PA-20c	66	Sunbury
PA-21	67	Pottsville
PA-22	68	Northeast Pennsylvania
PA-23	69	Lehigh Valley
PA-23a	69	Jim Thorpe
PA-23-b	69	Lehigh Gap
PA-24	70	Southeast Pennsylvania
PA-24a	70	Phoenixville
PA-24b	70	Downington
PA-25	71	Allentown
PA-26	72	Philadelphia West
PA-27	73	Philadelphia East
PA-28	74	Morrisville - Trenton

MAP GRID

Continued in SPV's NEW ENGLAND & MARITIMES Atlas
Continued in SPV's GREAT LAKES EAST Atlas
Continued in SPV's APPALACHIA & PIEDMONT Atlas
Rouses Pt.
Massena
Plattsburgh
NY-6
NY-14
Watertown
NY-7
NY-15
Whitehall
Oswego
Syracuse
Utica
NY-8
Niagara Falls
Rochester
NY-20
NY-16
Schenectady
Buffalo
NY-18
Geneva
Albany
Ithaca
Dunkirk
NY-21
Hornell
Coming
NY-17
NY-9
Hudson
PA-1
Salamanca
Jamestown
Olean
NY-19
Elmira
Binghamton
Kingston
Erie
Bradford
Sayre
Corry
Warren
Monroeton
Poughkeepsie
PA-22
NY-12
Meadville
PA-2
PA-10
Emporium
PA-15
Pt. Jervis
Oil City
Scranton
Greenville
Driftwood
Williamsport
Wilkes-Barre
Sharon
Brookville
Du Bois
Clearfield
NJ-2
PA-23
Punxsutawney
New Castle
Newark
NY-13
Sunbury
New York
Butler
PA-3
PA-11
PA-16
Pottsville
Eastern Long Island NY-13b
Allentown
Lewistown
Altoona
Long Beach
Pittsburgh
Harrisburg
Reading
Trenton
Mt Union
Johnstown
PA-24
NJ-3
Bay Head
PA-14
PA-17
Philadelphia
York
Brownsville
Connellsville
Somerset
Chambersburg
Lancaster
PA-4
Wilmington
Cumberland
DE-2a
Hagerstown
NJ-4
Atlantic City
Martinsburg
Baltimore
MD-2
MD-3
Dover
MD-4
Washington
DE-2b
MD-7
MD-8

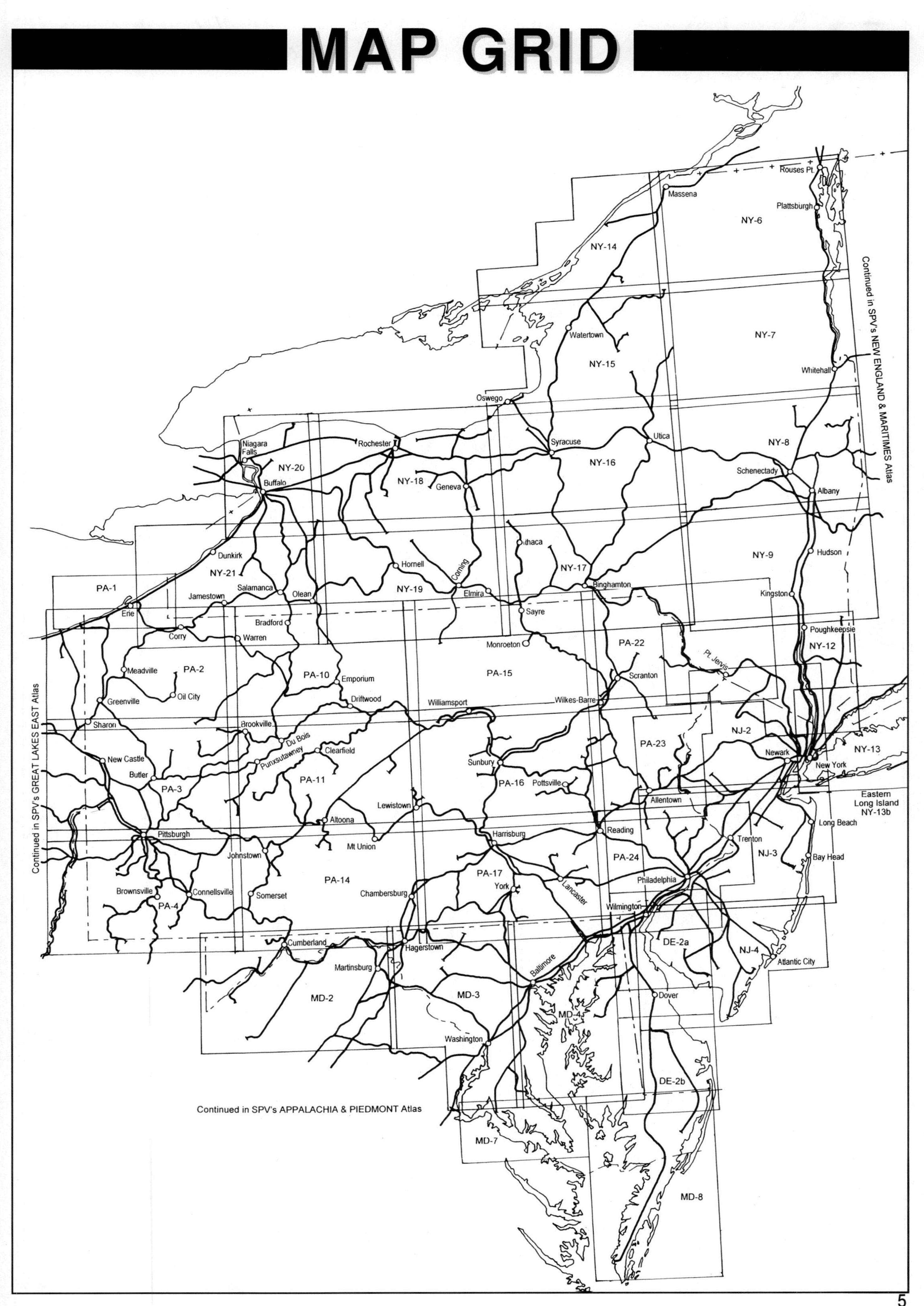

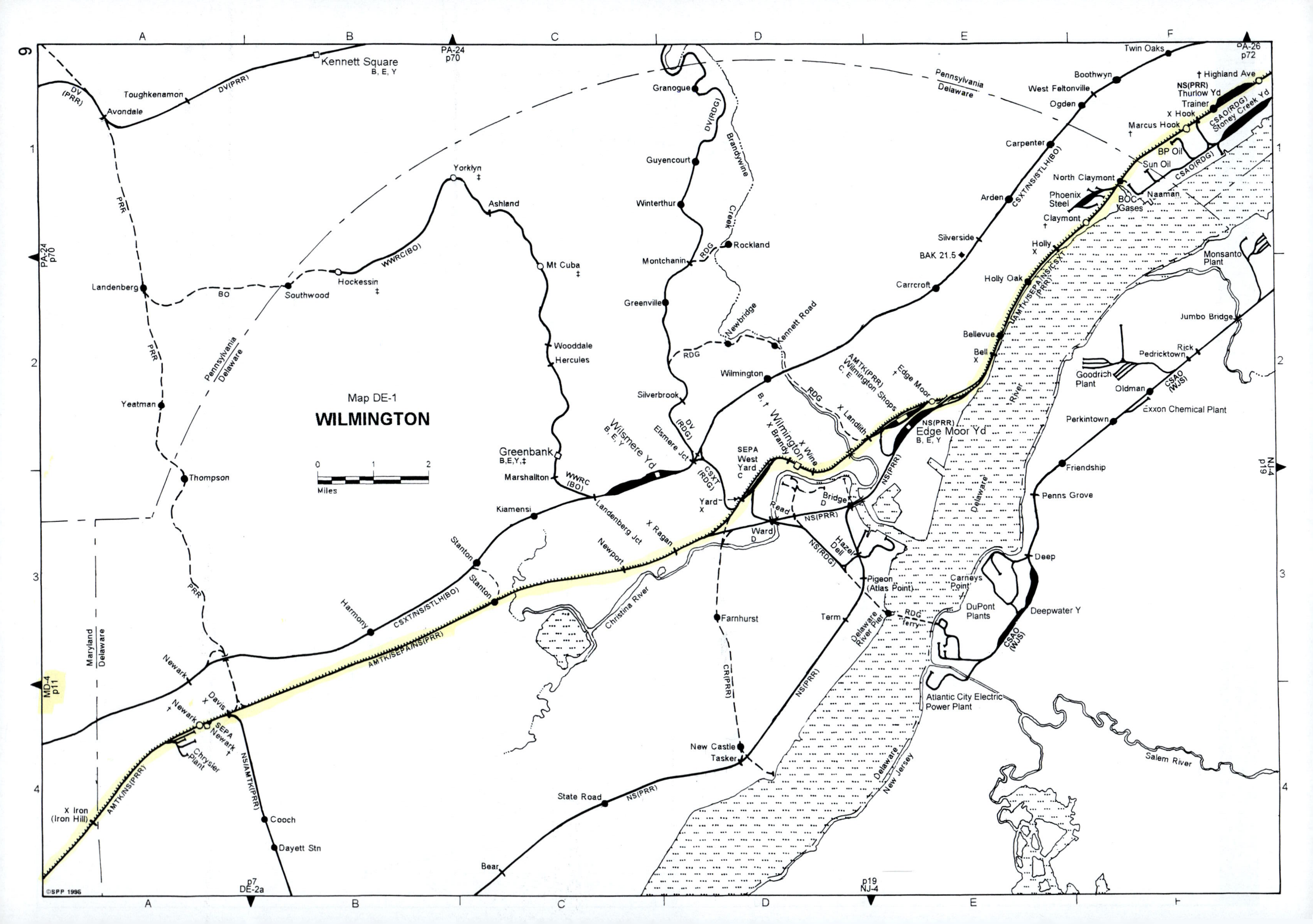
Map DE-1
WILMINGTON
Miles
Pennsylvania
Delaware
Maryland
New Jersey
Delaware River
Christina River
Brandywine Creek
Salem River
Stoney Creek Yd
Twin Oaks
Boothwyn
West Feltonville
Ogden
Carpenter
Arden
Silverside
BAK 21.5
Carrcroft
Marcus Hook
x Hook
Trainer
Thurlow Yd
Highland Ave
BP Oil
Sun Oil
Naaman
BOC Gases
North Claymont
Phoenix Steel
Claymont
Holly
Holly Oak
Bellevue
Bell
Edge Moor
Edge Moor Yd
AMTK(PRR) Wilmington Shops
Landlith
Kennett Road
Newbridge
Rockland
Wilmington
Wine
Brandy
SEPA West Yard
Bridge
Read
Ward
Hazel Dell
Pigeon (Atlas Point)
Delaware River Pier
RDG Ferry
Term
Farnhurst
New Castle
Tasker
State Road
Bear
Granogue
Guyencourt
Winterthur
Montchanin
Greenville
Silverbrook
Elsmere Jct
Yard
Wilsmere Yd
Ragan
Newport
Landenberg Jct
Marshallton
Greenbank
Kiamensi
Stanton
Harmony
Davis
Newark
Chrysler Plant
Cooch
Dayett Stn
Iron (Iron Hill)
Wooddale
Hercules
Mt Cuba
Ashland
Yorklyn
Hockessin
Southwood
Kennett Square
Toughkenamon
Avondale
Landenberg
Yeatman
Thompson
Monsanto Plant
Jumbo Bridge
Rick
Pedricktown
Exxon Chemical Plant
Oldman
Goodrich Plant
Perkintown
Friendship
Penns Grove
Deep
Deepwater Y
Carneys Point
DuPont Plants
Atlantic City Electric Power Plant
NJ-4 p19
PA-26 p72
PA-24 p70
MD-4 p11
p7 DE-2a
©SPP 1996

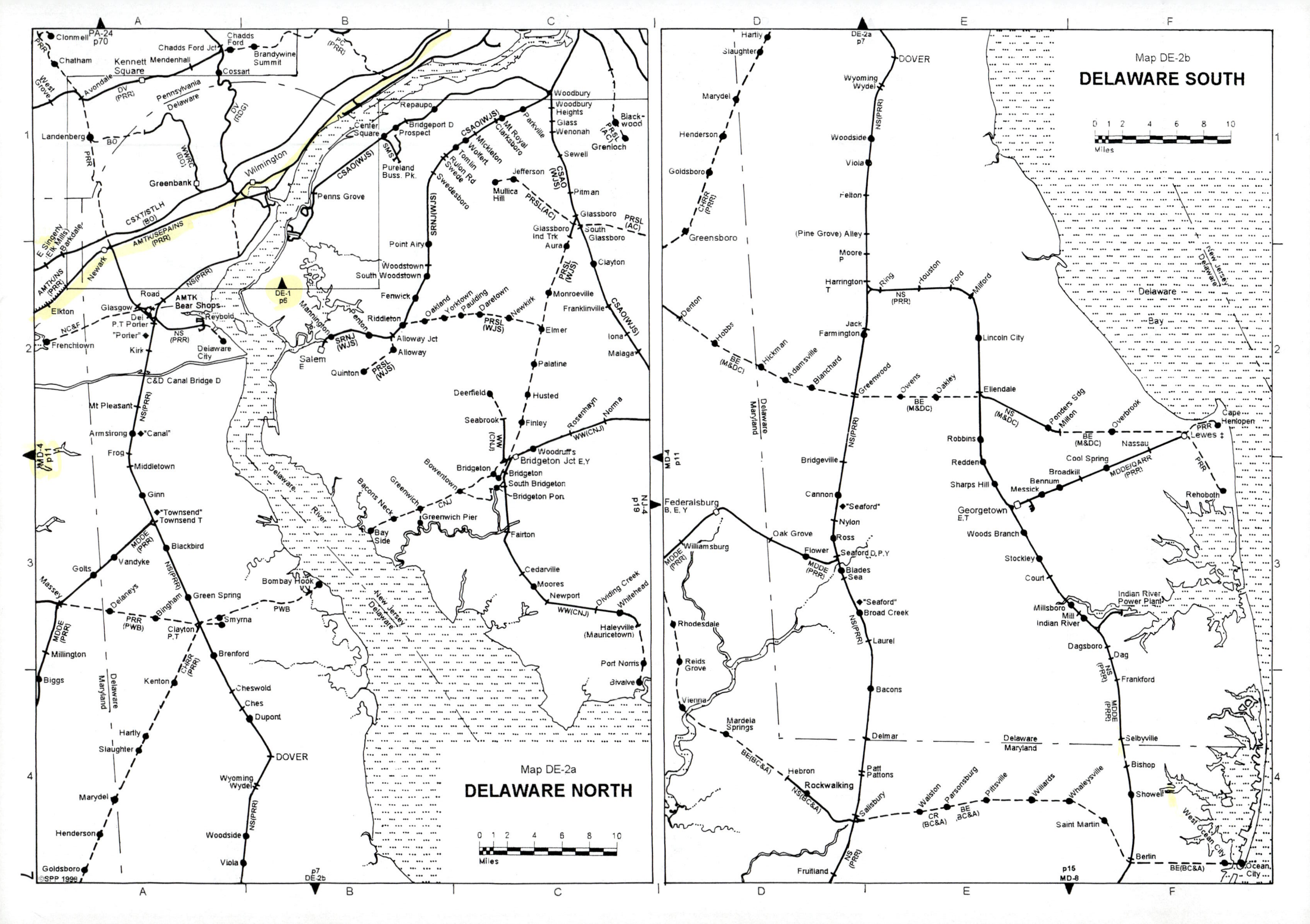
Map DE-2a
DELAWARE NORTH
Map DE-2b
DELAWARE SOUTH
Miles
0 1 2 4 6 8 10
PA-24 p70
DE-1 p6
MD-4 p11
NJ-4 p19
DE-2a p7
p7 DE-2b
p15 MD-8
Wilmington
Newark
Elkton
Kennett Square
Chadds Ford
Chadds Ford Jct
Brandywine Summit
Cossart
Mendenhall
Clonmell
Chatham
West Grove
Avondale
Landenberg
Greenbank
Pennsylvania
Delaware
New Jersey
Maryland
Delaware River
Delaware Bay
Penns Grove
Woodbury
Glassboro
Salem
Bridgeton
Bridgeton Jct
Delaware City
C&D Canal Bridge D
AMTK Bear Shops
Reybold
Glasgow
Frenchtown
Kirk
Mt Pleasant
Armstrong
"Canal"
Frog
Middletown
Ginn
"Townsend"
Townsend T
Blackbird
Green Spring
Smyrna
Bombay Hook
Clayton P.T
Brenford
Cheswold
Ches
Dupont
DOVER
Wyoming
Wydel
Woodside
Viola
Massey
Golts
Vandyke
Delaneys
Bingham
Millington
Biggs
Kenton
Hartly
Slaughter
Marydel
Henderson
Goldsboro
Greensboro
Denton
Hobbs
Hickman
Adamsville
Blanchard
Greenwood
Owens
Oakley
Ellendale
Felton
(Pine Grove) Alley
Moore P
Harrington T
Ring
Houston
Ford
Milford
Jack
Farmington
Lincoln City
Ponders Sdg
Milton
Overbrook
Lewes
Cape Henlopen
Nassau
Cool Spring
Broadkill
Bennum
Messick
Rehoboth
Robbins
Redden
Sharps Hill
Georgetown E.T
Woods Branch
Stockley
Court
Millsboro
Mill
Indian River
Indian River Power Plant
Dagsboro
Dag
Frankford
Selbyville
Bishop
Showell
West Ocean City
Ocean City
Berlin
Saint Martin
Whaleysville
Willards
Pittsville
Parsonsburg
Walston
Salisbury
Fruitland
Rockwalking
Hebron
Mardela Springs
Vienna
Reids Grove
Rhodesdale
Federalsburg B, E, Y
Williamsburg
Oak Grove
Flower
Seaford D, P, Y
Blades
Sea
"Seaford"
Broad Creek
Laurel
Bacons
Delmar
Patt
Pattons
Bridgeville
Cannon
Nylon
Ross
©SPP 1998

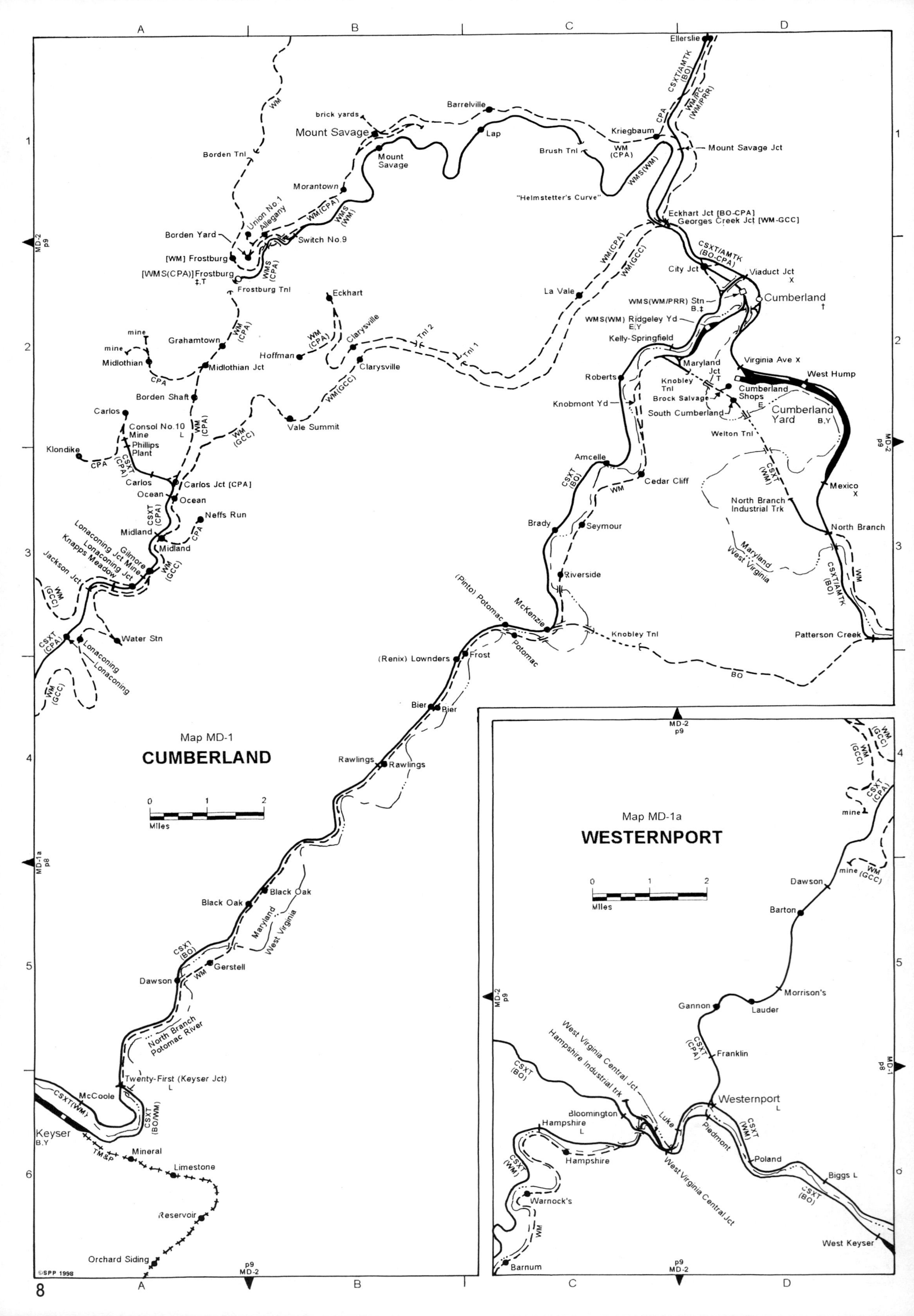

Map MD-1
CUMBERLAND
Map MD-1a
WESTERNPORT
0 1 2
Miles
Ellerslie
Barrelville
brick yards
Mount Savage
Lap
Brush Tnl
Kriegbaum
Mount Savage Jct
Borden Tnl
Morantown
"Helmstetter's Curve"
Union No.1
Allegany
Borden Yard
Switch No.9
Eckhart Jct [BO-CPA]
Georges Creek Jct [WM-GCC]
[WM] Frostburg
[WMS(CPA)] Frostburg
Frostburg Tnl
City Jct
Viaduct Jct
Cumberland
La Vale
WMS(WM/PRR) Stn
WMS(WM) Ridgeley Yd
Kelly-Springfield
Eckhart
Clarysville
Hoffman
Tnl 2
Tnl 1
Grahamtown
Midlothian
Midlothian Jct
mine
Maryland Jct
Virginia Ave
West Hump
Roberts
Knobley Tnl
Cumberland Shops
Brock Salvage
Borden Shaft
Knobmont Yd
South Cumberland
Cumberland Yard
Carlos
Consol No.10 Mine
Phillips Plant
Vale Summit
Welton Tnl
Klondike
Amcelle
Cedar Cliff
Mexico
Carlos Jct [CPA]
Ocean
Neffs Run
North Branch Industrial Trk
Brady
Seymour
North Branch
Midland
Lonaconing
Gilmore Mine
Lonaconing Jct
Knapps Meadow
Jackson Jct
Maryland
West Virginia
Riverside
(Pinto) Potomac
McKenzie
Knobley Tnl
Patterson Creek
Water Stn
(Renix) Lowndes
Frost
Potomac
Bier
Rawlings
Black Oak
Gerstell
Dawson
North Branch Potomac River
Twenty-First (Keyser Jct)
McCoole
Keyser
Mineral
Limestone
Reservoir
Orchard Siding
©SPP 1998
mine
Dawson
Barton
Morrison's
Gannon
Lauder
Franklin
West Virginia Central Jct
Hampshire Industrial trk
Westernport
Bloomington
Hampshire
Luke
Piedmont
Poland
Biggs
Warnock's
West Keyser
Barnum

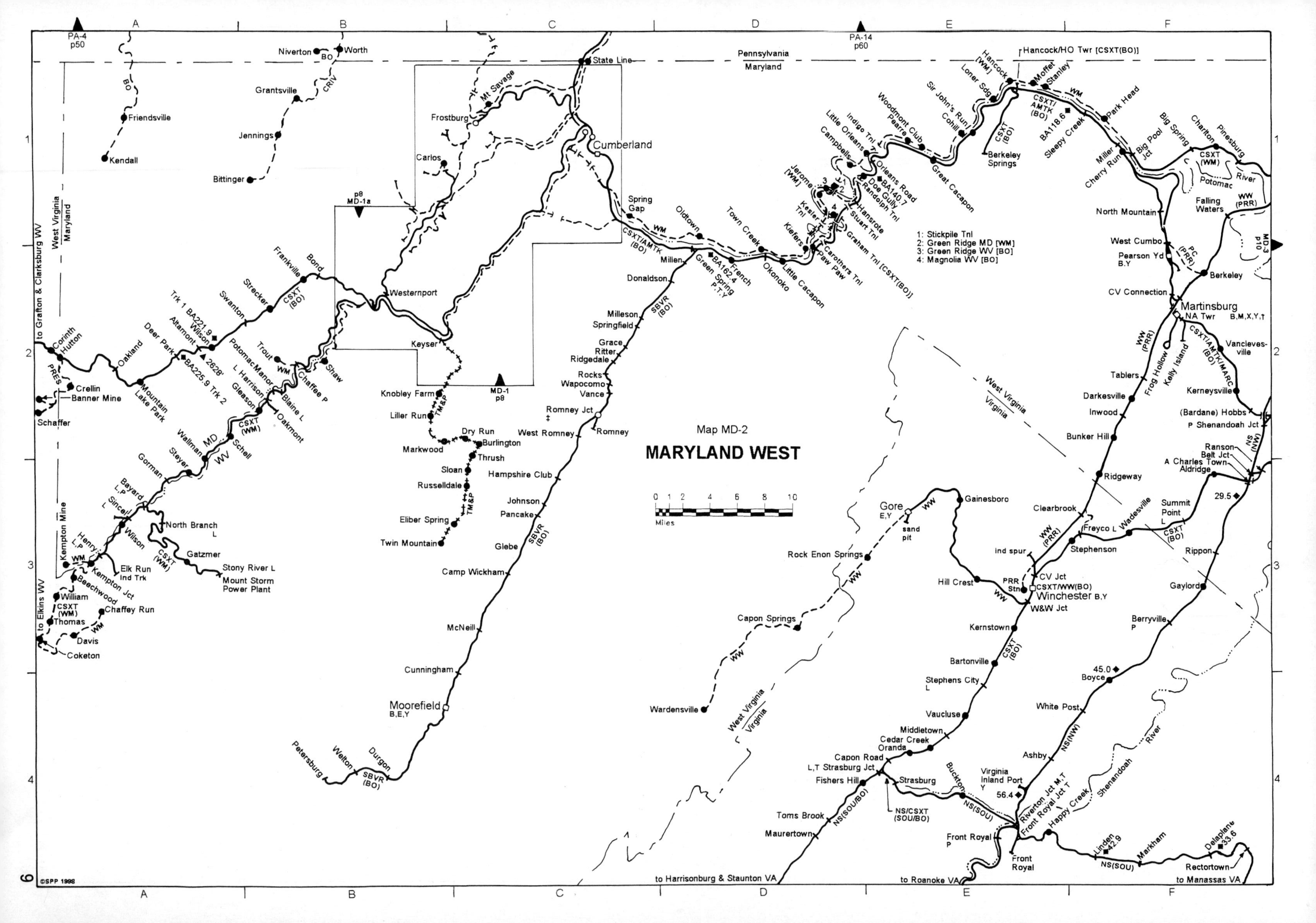
MARYLAND WEST
Map MD-2
Miles
0 1 2 4 6 8 10
1: Stickpile Tnl
2: Green Ridge MD [WM]
3: Green Ridge WV [BO]
4: Magnolia WV [BO]
Pennsylvania
Maryland
West Virginia
Virginia
PA-4 p50
PA-14 p60
MD-3 p10
MD-1 p8
p8 MD-1a
Niverton
Worth
BO
CRIV
Grantsville
Friendsville
Jennings
Kendall
Bittinger
State Line
Mt Savage
Frostburg
Carlos
Cumberland
Spring Gap
WM
CSXT/AMTK (BO)
Oldtown
Town Creek
Millen
Green Spring P,T,Y
BA162.4
French
Okonoko
Little Cacapon
Kiefers
Paw Paw
Carothers Tnl
Graham Tnl [CSXT(BO)]
Kesler Tnl
Jerome [WM]
Stuart Tnl
Hansrote
Campbells
Little Orleans
Indigo Tnl
Randolph Tnl
Doe Gully
BA140.7
Orleans Road
Woodmont Club
Pearre
Great Cacapon
Sir John's Run
Cohill
Loner Sdg
Hancock [WM]
Hancock/HO Twr [CSXT(BO)]
Moffet
Stanley
CSXT/AMTK (BO)
BA118.6
Sleepy Creek
CSXT (BO)
Berkeley Springs
Park Head
Miller
Cherry Run
Big Pool Jct
Big Spring
Charlton
Pinesburg
CSXT (WM)
Potomac River
Falling Waters
WW (PRR)
North Mountain
West Cumbo
Pearson Yd B,Y
PC (PRR)
Berkeley
CV Connection
Martinsburg
NA Twr
B,M,X,Y,T
CSXT/AMTK/MARC (BO)
Vanclevesville
Frog Hollow
Kelly Island
Tablers
Darkesville
Inwood
Kerneysville
(Bardane) Hobbs
P Shenandoah Jct
NS (NW)
Bunker Hill
Ranson
Belt Jct
A Charles Town
Aldridge
Ridgeway
29.5
Clearbrook
Wadesville
Summit Point L
CSXT (BO)
Freyco L
Stephenson
WW (PRR)
ind spur
Rippon
CV Jct
PRR Stn
CSXT/WW(BO)
Winchester B,Y
W&W Jct
Hill Crest
Gaylord
Gainesboro
Gore E,Y
sand pit
Rock Enon Springs
Capon Springs
Wardensville
Kernstown
Berryville P
Bartonville
45.0
Boyce
Stephens City L
White Post
NS(NW)
Vaucluse
Middletown
Cedar Creek
Oranda
Capon Road
L,T Strasburg Jct
Fishers Hill
Strasburg
Buckton
NS(SOU)
NS/CSXT (SOU/BO)
NS(SOU/BO)
Toms Brook
Maurertown
Ashby
Virginia Inland Port Y
56.4
Riverton Jct M,T
Front Royal Jct T
Happy Creek
Shenandoah River
Front Royal P
Front Royal
Linden
42.9
Markham
Delaplane
33.6
Rectortown
NS(SOU)
to Harrisonburg & Staunton VA
to Roanoke VA
to Manassas VA
Westernport
Keyser
Knobley Farm
Liller Run
TM&P
Dry Run
Burlington
Markwood
Thrush
Sloan
Russelldale
Eliber Spring
Twin Mountain
Romney Jct
West Romney
Romney
Donaldson
SBVR (BO)
Milleson
Springfield
Grace
Ritter
Ridgedale
Rocks
Wapocomo
Vance
Hampshire Club
Johnson
Pancake
Glebe
Camp Wickham
McNeill
Cunningham
Moorefield B,E,Y
Durgon
Welton
Petersburg
to Grafton & Clarksburg WV
Corinth
Hutton
PRES
Crellin
Banner Mine
Schaffer
Oakland
Mountain Lake Park
Deer Park
BA225.9 Trk 2
Altamont
2628'
Trk 1 BA221.9
Wilson
Swanton
Strecker
CSXT (BO)
Frankville
Bond
Trout
WM
Chaffee P
Shaw
Potomac Manor
L Harrison
Gleason
Blaine L
Oakmont
CSXT (WM)
Schell
MD
WV
Wallman
Steyer
Gorman
Bayard L,P
Sincell L
North Branch L
Wilson
Gatzmer
Stony River L
Mount Storm Power Plant
Kempton Mine
Henry L,P
Elk Run Ind Trk
Kempton Jct
Beechwood
William
CSXT (WM)
Thomas
Chaffey Run
Davis
Coketon
to Elkins WV
©SPP 1998

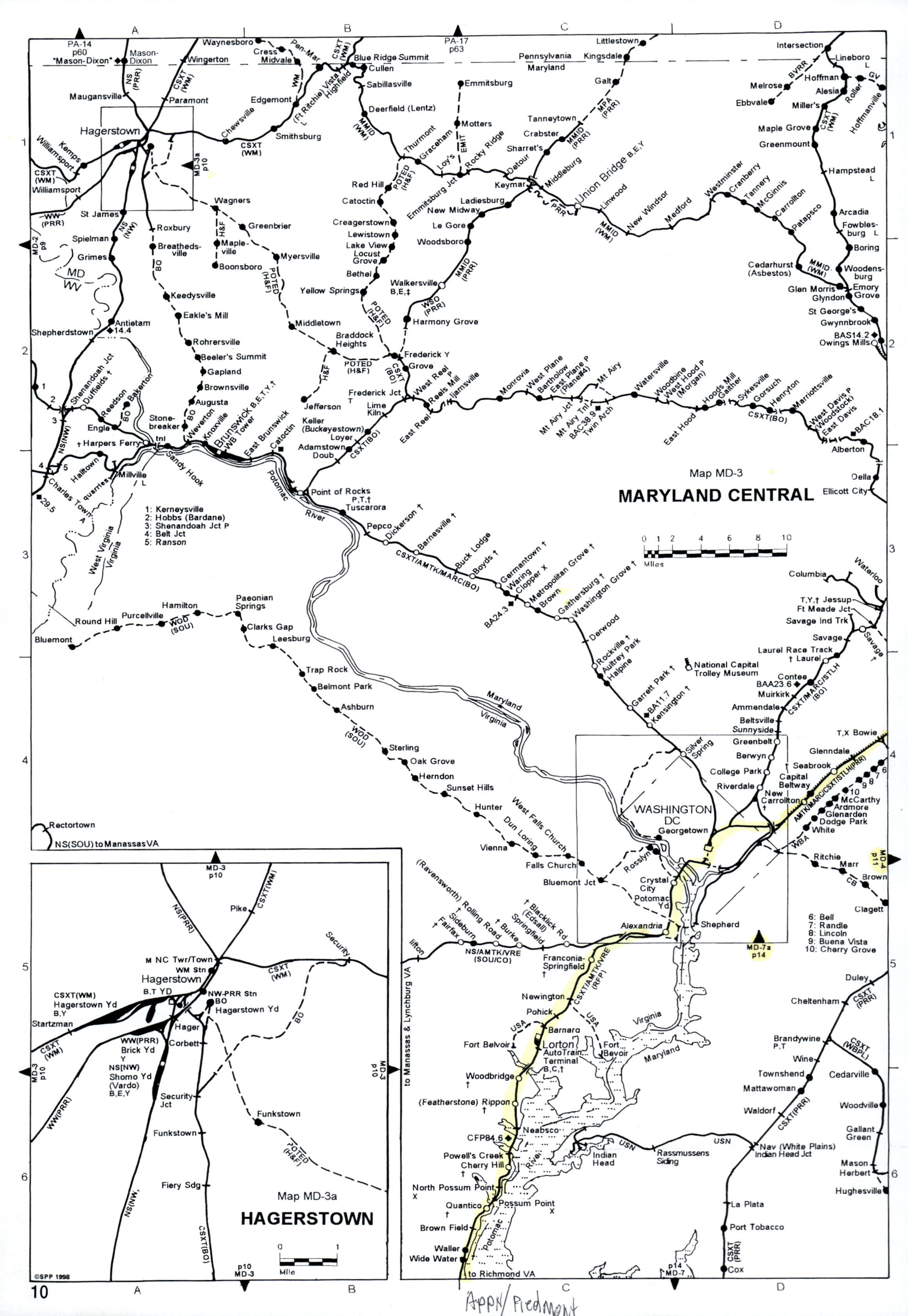

Appn/Piedmont

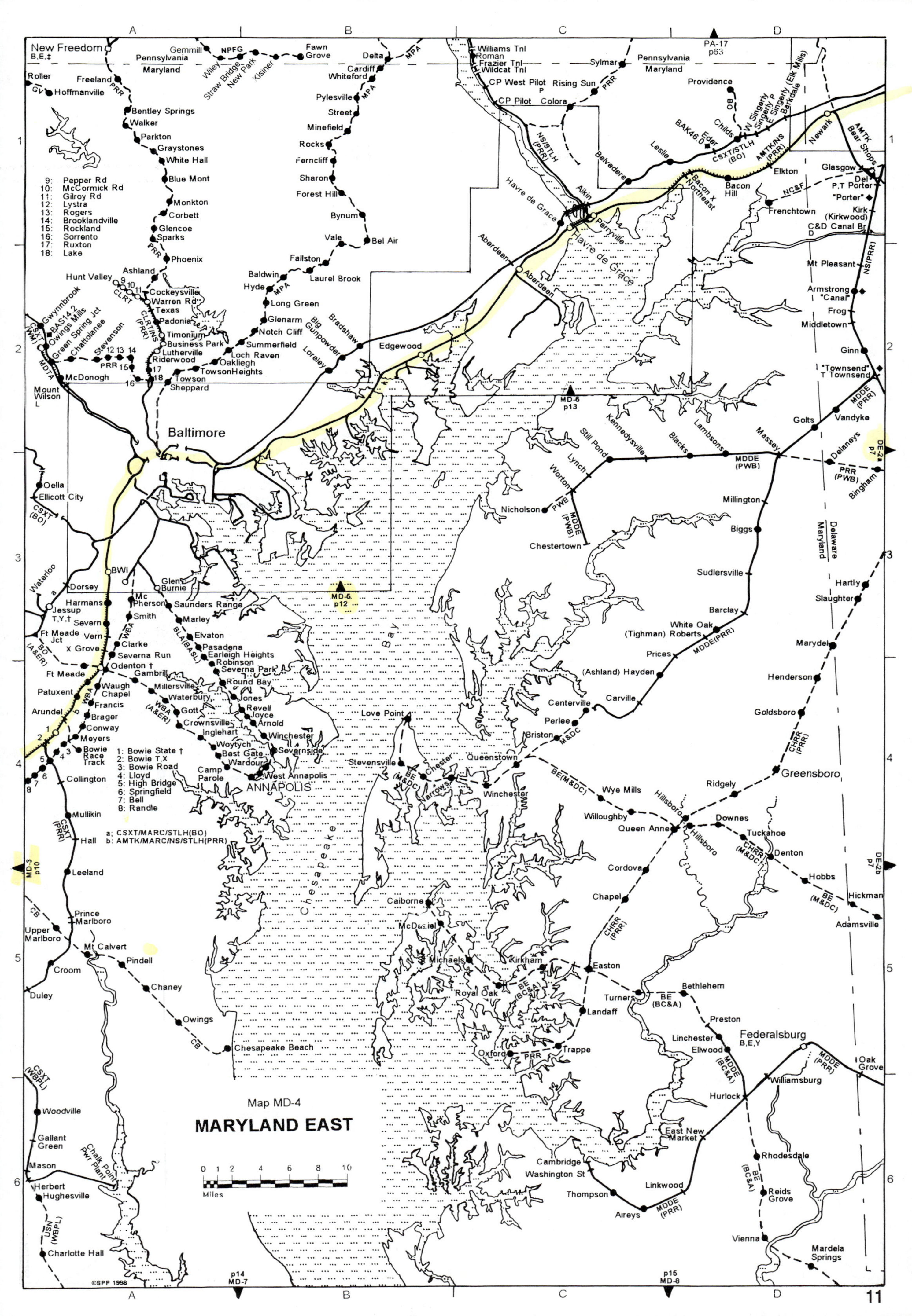
Map MD-4
MARYLAND EAST
Miles
0 1 2 4 6 8 10
©SPP 1998
New Freedom
B,E,‡
Pennsylvania
Maryland
Gemmill
NPFG
Wiley
Straw Bridge
New Park
Kisiner
Fawn Grove
Delta
MPA
Cardiff
Whiteford
Pylesville
Street
Minefield
Rocks
Ferncliff
Sharon
Forest Hill
Bynum
Vale
Bel Air
Fallston
Laurel Brook
Baldwin
Hyde
Long Green
Glenarm
Notch Cliff
Summerfield
Loch Raven
Oakliegh
TowsonHeights
Towson
Sheppard
Roller
GV
Hoffmanville
Freeland
PRR
Bentley Springs
Walker
Parkton
Graystones
White Hall
Blue Mont
Monkton
Corbett
Glencoe
Sparks
Phoenix
Ashland
Hunt Valley
Cockeysville
Warren Rd
Texas
Padonia
Timonium
Business Park
Lutherville
Riderwood
CLRT
CLRT/NS (PRR)
9: Pepper Rd
10: McCormick Rd
11: Gilroy Rd
12: Lystra
13: Rogers
14: Brooklandville
15: Rockland
16: Sorrento
17: Ruxton
18: Lake
Gwynnbrook
BAS14.2
Owings Mills
Green Spring Jct
Chattolanee
Stevenson
CSXT (WM)
MDTA
McDonogh
Mount Wilson
L
Baltimore
Oella
Ellicott City
CSXT (BO)
Waterloo
Dorsey
Harmans
Jessup
T,Y,†
Severn
Ft Meade Jct
Vern
X Grove
BO (A&ER)
Ft Meade
Odenton †
BWI
Glen Burnie
Mc Pherson
Saunders Range
Smith
Marley
WBA
BLA(BAS)
Elvaton
Clarke
Severna Run
Pasadena
Earleigh Heights
Robinson
Severna Park
Gambrill
Round Bay
Millersville
Waterbury
Jones
Patuxent
Waugh Chapel
Francis
Brager
Conway
Meyers
Bowie Race Track
Arundel
Gott
Revell
Joyce
Arnold
Crownsville
Inglehart
Winchester
Woytych
Best Gate
Severnside
Wardour
West Annapolis
ANNAPOLIS
Camp Parole
Collington
1: Bowie State †
2: Bowie T,X
3: Bowie Road
4: Lloyd
5: High Bridge
6: Springfield
7: Bell
8: Randle
a; CSXT/MARC/STLH(BO)
b: AMTK/MARC/NS/STLH(PRR)
Mullikin
CSXT (PRR)
Hall
Leeland
MD-3 p10
CB
Prince Marlboro
Upper Marlboro
Mt Calvert
Pindell
Croom
Duley
Chaney
Owings
Chesapeake Beach
CSXT (WBPL)
Woodville
Gallant Green
Mason
Chalk Point Pwr Plant
Herbert
Hughesville
USN (WBPL)
Charlotte Hall
p14 MD-7
Williams Tnl
Roman
Frazier Tnl
Wildcat Tnl
CP West Pilot
Rising Sun
P
CP Pilot
Colora
Sylmar
Pennsylvania
Maryland
PA-17 p53
Providence
BO
NS/STLH (PRR)
Havre de Grace
Aikin
Perryville
Aberdeen
Edgewood
Big Gunpowder
Bradshaw
Loreley
Belvedere
Leslie
BAK46.0
Eder
Childs
W Singerly
Singerly P
E Singerly (Elk Mills)
Barksdale
CSXT/STLH (BO)
AMTK/NS (PRR)
Newark
AMTK Bear Shops
Elkton
Bacon Hill
Bacon X
Northeast
Glasgow
Del
P,T Porter
"Porter"
NC&F
Frenchtown
Kirk (Kirkwood)
C&D Canal Br
D
Mt Pleasant
NS(PRR)
Armstrong "Canal"
Frog
Middletown
Ginn
"Townsend"
T Townsend
MD-6 p13
Still Pond
Kennedysville
Blacks
Lambsons
Massey
Golts
Vandyke
MDDE (PRR)
MDDE (PWB)
Delaneys
DE-2a p7
PRR (PWB)
Bingham
Lynch
Worton
PWB
MDDE (PWB)
Nicholson
Chestertown
Millington
Biggs
Delaware
Maryland
Sudlersville
Hartly
Slaughter
Barclay
White Oak
(Tighman) Roberts
MDDE(PRR)
Prices
Marydel
(Ashland) Hayden
Henderson
Carville
Centerville
Perlee
Goldsboro
Briston
M&DC
CHRR (PRR)
Greensboro
MD-5 p12
Bay
Chesapeake
Love Point
Stevensville
BE (M&DC)
Chester
Narrows
Queenstown
Winchester
BE(M&DC)
Wye Mills
Ridgely
Willoughby
Hillsboro
Queen Anne
Downes
Tuckahoe
CHRR (M&DC)
Denton
DE-2b p7
Cordova
Hobbs
Chapel
Hickman
BE (M&DC)
Adamsville
Caiborne
McDaniel
St Michaels
Kirkham
Easton
Royal Oak
BE (BC&A)
Turners
Bethlehem
Landaff
Preston
Federalsburg
B,E,Y
Linchester
Ellwood
MDDE (BC&A)
Oxford
PRR
Trappe
MDDE (PRR)
Oak Grove
Williamsburg
Hurlock
East New Market
Rhodesdale
Cambridge
Washington St
Thompson
Linkwood
BE (BC&A)
Reids Grove
Aireys
Vienna
Mardela Springs
p15 MD-8
A
B
C
D
1
2
3
4
5
6

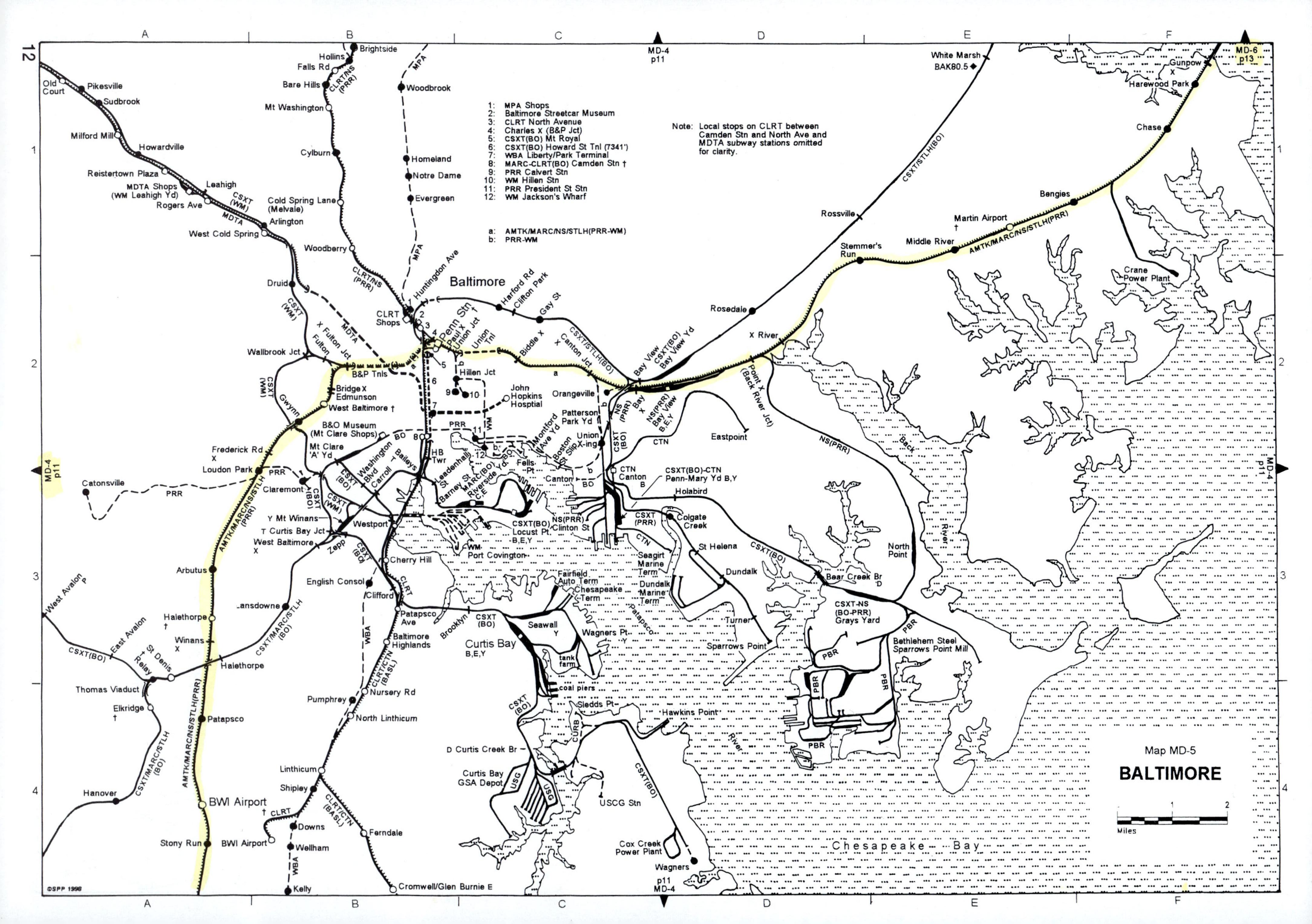
Map MD-5
BALTIMORE
Miles
1
2
1: MPA Shops
2: Baltimore Streetcar Museum
3: CLRT North Avenue
4: Charles X (B&P Jct)
5: CSXT(BO) Mt Royal
6: CSXT(BO) Howard St Tnl (7341')
7: WBA Liberty/Park Terminal
8: MARC-CLRT(BO) Camden Stn †
9: PRR Calvert Stn
10: WM Hillen Stn
11: PRR President St Stn
12: WM Jackson's Wharf
a: AMTK/MARC/NS/STLH(PRR-WM)
b: PRR-WM
Note: Local stops on CLRT between Camden Stn and North Ave and MDTA subway stations omitted for clarity.
MD-4
p11
MD-6
p13
White Marsh
BAK80.5
Gunpow
Harewood Park
Chase
Bengies
Martin Airport
Middle River
Stemmer's Run
Rossville
Rosedale
X River
Point X (Back River Jct)
Crane Power Plant
CSXT/STLH(BO)
AMTK/MARC/NS/STLH(PRR)
Bay View
CSXT(BO) Bay View Yd
NS(PRR) Bay View B,E,Y
Eastpoint
NS(PRR)
Back River
North Point
Holabird
CSXT(BO)-CTN Penn-Mary Yd B,Y
Colgate Creek
St Helena
Dundalk
Bear Creek Br
Turner
Sparrows Point
CSXT-NS (BO-PRR) Grays Yard
Bethlehem Steel Sparrows Point Mill
PBR
Hawkins Point
Patapsco River
Chesapeake Bay
Cox Creek Power Plant
Wagners
USCG Stn
Curtis Bay GSA Depot
Curtis Creek Br
USG
CURB
Sledds Pt
coal piers
tank farm
Wagners Pt
Seawall
Curtis Bay B,E,Y
Brooklyn
Fairfield Auto Term
Chesapeake Term
Seagirt Marine Term
Dundalk Marine Term
CTN
Canton
Union X-ing
Boston St Slip
Montford Ave Yd
Patterson Park Yd
Orangeville
Canton Jct
Biddle X
Gay St
Clifton Park
Harford Rd
Baltimore
Huntingdon Ave
Penn Stn
Paul X
Union Jct
Union Tnl
Hillen Jct
John Hopkins Hospital
Fells Pt
Leadenhall St
Barney St
MARC(BO) Riverside Yd C,E
CSXT(BO) Locust Pt B,E,Y
NS(PRR) Clinton St
Port Covington
HB Twr
Baileys
Carroll
Washington Blvd
B&O Museum (Mt Clare Shops)
Mt Clare 'A' Yd
West Baltimore
Edmunson
Bridge X
B&P Tnls
Fulton
Fulton Jct
Wallbrook Jct
Gwynn
Frederick Rd
Loudon Park
Claremont
Mt Winans
Curtis Bay Jct
West Baltimore
Westport
Zepp
Cherry Hill
English Consol
Clifford
Patapsco Ave
Baltimore Highlands
Nursery Rd
North Linthicum
Pumphrey
Linthicum
Shipley
Downs
Wellham
Kelly
Ferndale
Cromwell/Glen Burnie E
BWI Airport
Stony Run
Patapsco
Halethorpe
Winans
Lansdowne
Arbutus
Catonsville
PRR
St Denis
Relay
Thomas Viaduct
Elkridge
East Avalon
West Avalon
Hanover
CSXT/MARC/STLH (BO)
CLRT/CTN (BASL)
WBA
CLRT
MDTA
MPA
Druid
CSXT (WM)
Woodberry
Arlington
West Cold Spring
Cold Spring Lane (Melvale)
Rogers Ave
MDTA Shops (WM Leahigh Yd)
Leahigh
Reistertown Plaza
Howardville
Milford Mill
Sudbrook
Pikesville
Old Court
Mt Washington
Bare Hills
Falls Rd
Hollins
Brightside
Cylburn
CLRT/NS (PRR)
CLRT Shops
Woodbrook
Homeland
Notre Dame
Evergreen
©SPP 1998

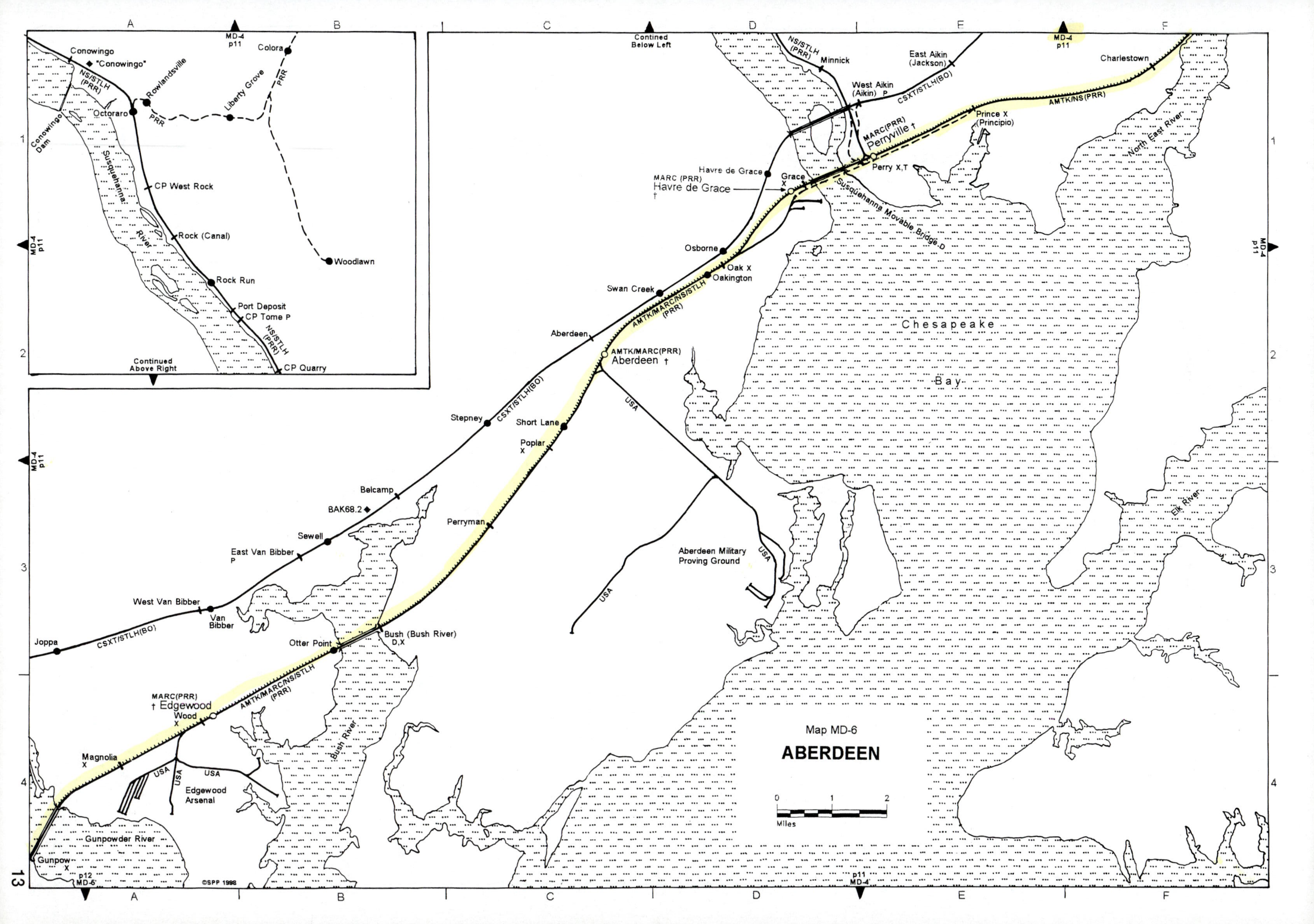
Map MD-6
ABERDEEN
0 1 2
Miles
Conowingo
"Conowingo"
NS/STLH (PRR)
Conowingo Dam
Octoraro
Rowlandsville
PRR
Liberty Grove
Colora
Woodlawn
CP West Rock
Susquehanna River
Rock (Canal)
Rock Run
Port Deposit
CP Tome P
CP Quarry
Continued Above Right
Contined Below Left
MD-4 p11
Minnick
East Aikin (Jackson)
West Aikin (Aikin) P
CSXT/STLH(BO)
Charlestown
AMTK/NS(PRR)
Prince X (Principio)
North East River
MARC(PRR) Perryville †
Perry X,T
Havre de Grace
MARC (PRR) Havre de Grace †
Grace X
Susquehanna Movable Bridge D
Osborne
Oak X
Oakington
Swan Creek
Chesapeake Bay
AMTK/MARC/NS/STLH (PRR)
Aberdeen
AMTK/MARC(PRR) Aberdeen †
USA
Stepney
Short Lane
Poplar X
Belcamp
BAK68.2
Perryman
Sewell
East Van Bibber P
Aberdeen Military Proving Ground
Elk River
West Van Bibber
Van Bibber
Joppa
Otter Point
Bush (Bush River) D,X
MARC(PRR) † Edgewood
Wood X
Magnolia X
Edgewood Arsenal
Bush River
Gunpowder River
Gunpow X
p12 MD-6
p11 MD-4
©SPP 1998

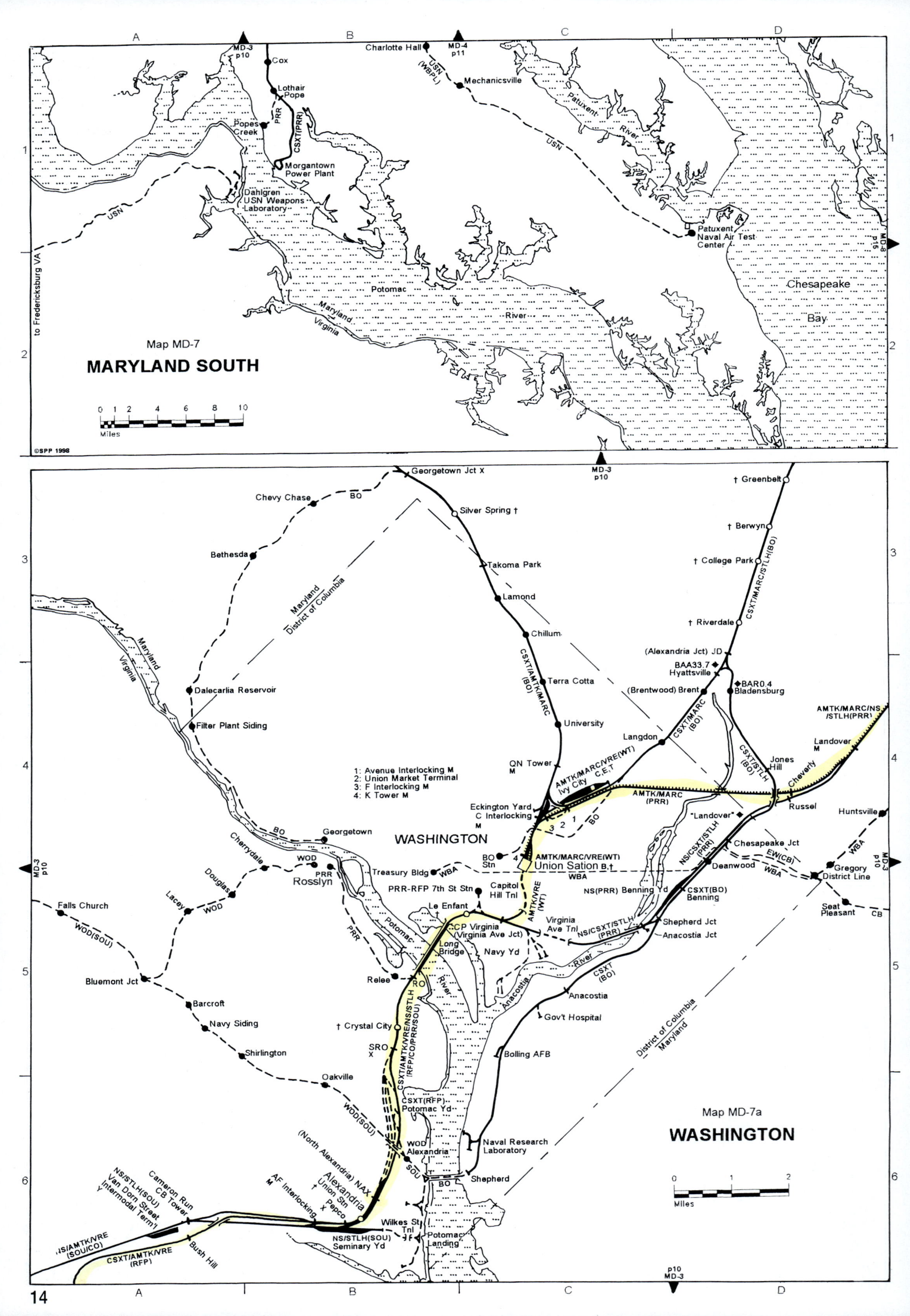

Map MD-7
MARYLAND SOUTH
Miles
©SPP 1998
MD-3 p10
MD-4 p11
MD-8 p15
Cox
Lothair
Pope
Popes Creek
PRR
CSXT(PRR)
Morgantown Power Plant
Dahlgren USN Weapons Laboratory
USN
to Fredericksburg VA
Charlotte Hall
USN (WBPL)
Mechanicsville
Patuxent River
Patuxent Naval Air Test Center
Potomac River
Maryland
Virginia
Chesapeake Bay
Map MD-7a
WASHINGTON
Miles
MD-3 p10
Georgetown Jct X
Silver Spring †
Chevy Chase
BO
Bethesda
Takoma Park
Lamond
Chillum
CSXT/AMTK/MARC (BO)
Terra Cotta
University
Maryland
District of Columbia
Dalecarlia Reservoir
Filter Plant Siding
† Greenbelt
† Berwyn
† College Park
CSXT/MARC/STLH(BO)
† Riverdale
(Alexandria Jct) JD
BAA33.7
Hyattsville
BAR0.4
Bladensburg
(Brentwood) Brent
CSXT/MARC (BO)
Langdon
QN Tower M
AMTK/MARC/VRE(WT)
Ivy City C,E,T
AMTK/MARC (PRR)
CSXT/STLH (BO)
Jones Hill
Cheverly
Landover M
AMTK/MARC/NS /STLH(PRR)
Russel
Huntsville
"Landover"
1: Avenue Interlocking M
2: Union Market Terminal
3: F Interlocking M
4: K Tower M
Eckington Yard
C Interlocking M
WASHINGTON
Georgetown
BO Stn
AMTK/MARC/VRE(WT)
Union Sation B,†
NS/CSXT/STLH (PRR)
Chesapeake Jct
Deanwood
EW(CB)
WBA
Gregory
District Line
Seat Pleasant
CB
Cherrydale
WOD
PRR
Rosslyn
Treasury Bldg
WBA
Douglas
Lacey
Falls Church
WOD(SOU)
PRR-RFP 7th St Stn
Capitol Hill Tnl
AMTK/VRE (WT)
NS(PRR) Benning Yd
CSXT(BO) Benning
Le Enfant †
CP Virginia (Virginia Ave Jct)
Virginia Ave Tnl
NS/CSXT/STLH (PRR)
Shepherd Jct
Anacostia Jct
Long Bridge
Navy Yd
Potomac
Anacostia
River
CSXT (BO)
Bluemont Jct
Relee
RO
Anacostia
Barcroft
Gov't Hospital
Navy Siding
† Crystal City
CSXT/AMTK/VRE/NS/STLH (RFP/CO/PRR/SOU)
SRO X
Shirlington
Bolling AFB
District of Columbia
Maryland
Oakville
CSXT(RFP) Potomac Yd
WOD(SOU)
WOD Alexandria
SOU
Naval Research Laboratory
(North Alexandria) NAX
Alexandria Union Stn †
Pepco X
BO
Shepherd
Cameron Run CB Tower
NS/STLH(SOU) Van Dorn Street Intermodal Term'l Y
AF Interlocking M
Wilkes St Tnl
NS/STLH(SOU) Seminary Yd
Potomac Landing
NS/AMTK/VRE (SOU/CO)
CSXT/AMTK/VRE (RFP)
Bush Hill
p10 MD-3

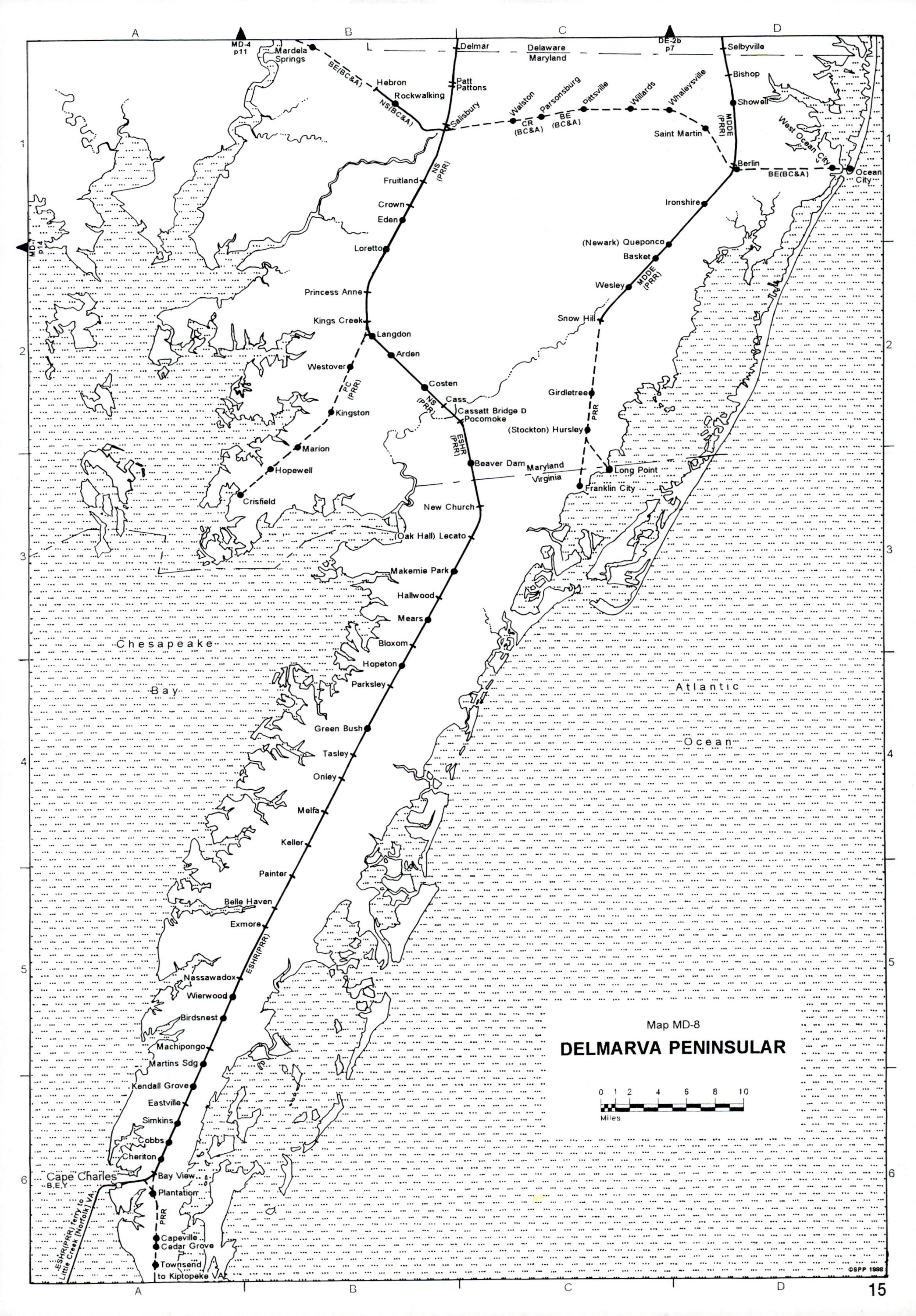
Map MD-8
DELMARVA PENINSULAR
Delaware
Maryland
Virginia
Chesapeake
Bay
Atlantic
Ocean
Mardela Springs
Hebron
Rockwalking
Delmar
Patt
Pattons
Salisbury
Walston
Parsonsburg
Pittsville
Willards
Whaleysville
Selbyville
Bishop
Showell
Saint Martin
Berlin
West Ocean City
Ocean City
Fruitland
Crown
Eden
Loretto
Princess Anne
Kings Creek
Langdon
Arden
Westover
Kingston
Marion
Hopewell
Crisfield
Costen
Cass
Cassatt Bridge D
Pocomoke
Beaver Dam
Ironshire
(Newark) Queponco
Basket
Wesley
Snow Hill
Girdletree
(Stockton) Hursley
Long Point
Franklin City
New Church
(Oak Hall) Lecato
Makemie Park
Hallwood
Mears
Bloxom
Hopeton
Parksley
Green Bush
Tasley
Onley
Melfa
Keller
Painter
Belle Haven
Exmore
Nassawadox
Wierwood
Birdsnest
Machipongo
Martins Sdg
Kendall Grove
Eastville
Simkins
Cobbs
Cheriton
Cape Charles
B,E,Y
Bay View
Plantation
Capeville
Cedar Grove
Townsend
to Kiptopeke VA
ESHR(PRR) ferry to Little Creek (Norfolk) VA
BE(BC&A)
NS(BC&A)
NS (PRR)
CR (BC&A)
BE (BC&A)
MDDE (PRR)
PC (PRR)
ESHR (PRR)
PRR
MD-4 p11
DE-2b p7
MD-7 p14
L
0 1 2 4 6 8 10
Miles
©SPP 1998

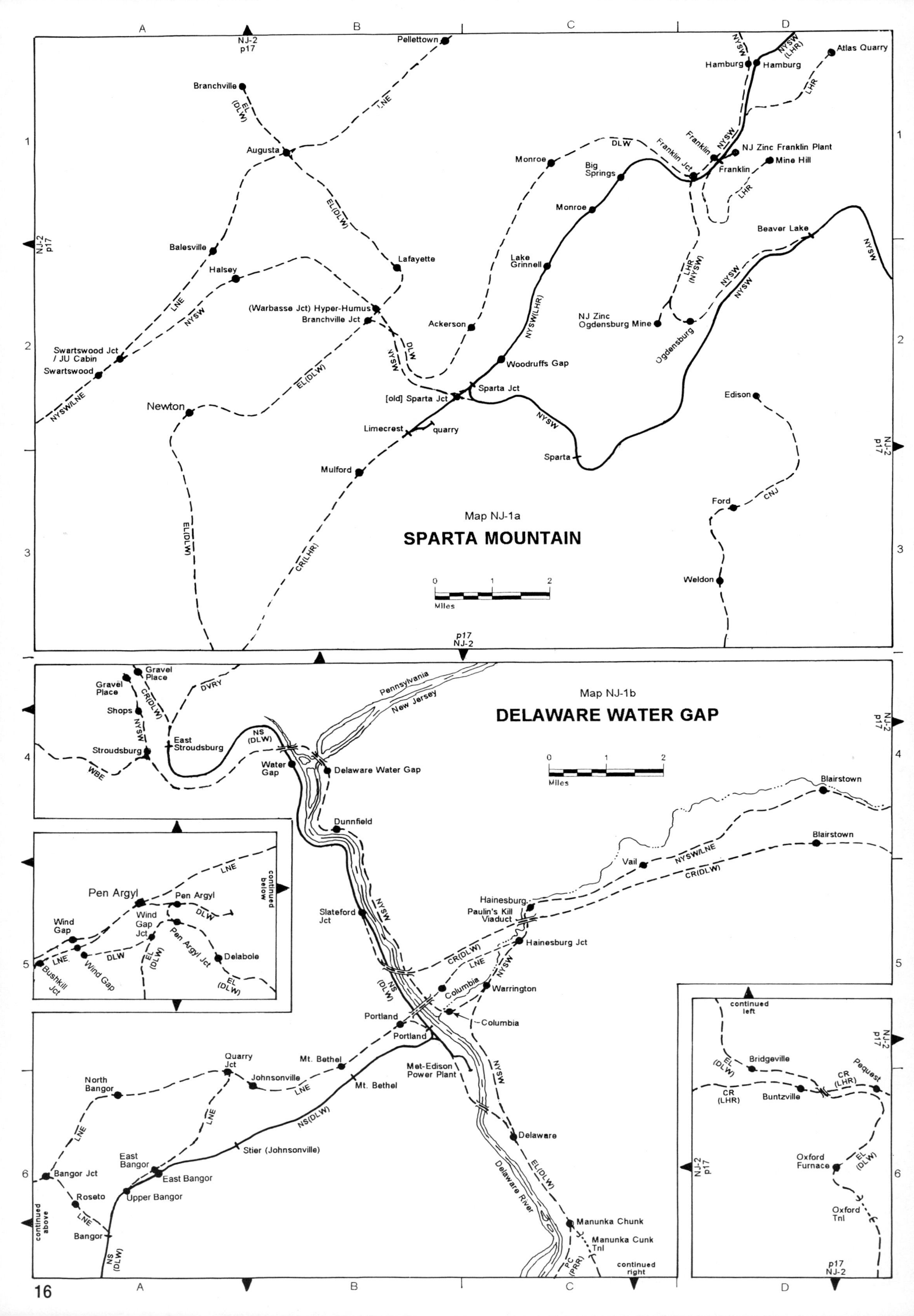
Map NJ-1a
SPARTA MOUNTAIN
Pellettown
Branchville
Augusta
Balesville
Halsey
Lafayette
(Warbasse Jct) Hyper-Humus
Branchville Jct
Swartswood Jct / JU Cabin
Swartswood
Newton
Mulford
Limecrest
quarry
[old] Sparta Jct
Sparta Jct
Sparta
Woodruffs Gap
Ackerson
Lake Grinnell
Monroe
Big Springs
Franklin Jct
Franklin
NJ Zinc Franklin Plant
Mine Hill
Hamburg
Atlas Quarry
Beaver Lake
NJ Zinc Ogdensburg Mine
Ogdensburg
Edison
Ford
Weldon
LNE
NYSW
EL(DLW)
DLW
LHR
NYSW(LHR)
CR(LHR)
CNJ
NYSW/LNE
Miles
Map NJ-1b
DELAWARE WATER GAP
Gravel Place
Shops
Stroudsburg
East Stroudsburg
DVRY
WBE
Water Gap
Delaware Water Gap
Pennsylvania
New Jersey
Dunnfield
Slateford Jct
Blairstown
Vail
Hainesburg
Paulin's Kill Viaduct
Hainesburg Jct
Warrington
Columbia
Portland
Met-Edison Power Plant
Mt. Bethel
Quarry Jct
Johnsonville
North Bangor
East Bangor
Stier (Johnsonville)
Bangor Jct
Roseto
Upper Bangor
Bangor
Delaware
Delaware River
Manunka Chunk
Manunka Cunk Tnl
Pen Argyl
Wind Gap
Wind Gap Jct
Pen Argyl Jct
Delabole
Bushkill Jct
Bridgeville
Buntzville
Pequest
Oxford Furnace
Oxford Tnl
NS(DLW)
CR(DLW)
PC (PRR)
continued below
continued above
continued left
continued right
NJ-2 p17
p17 NJ-2

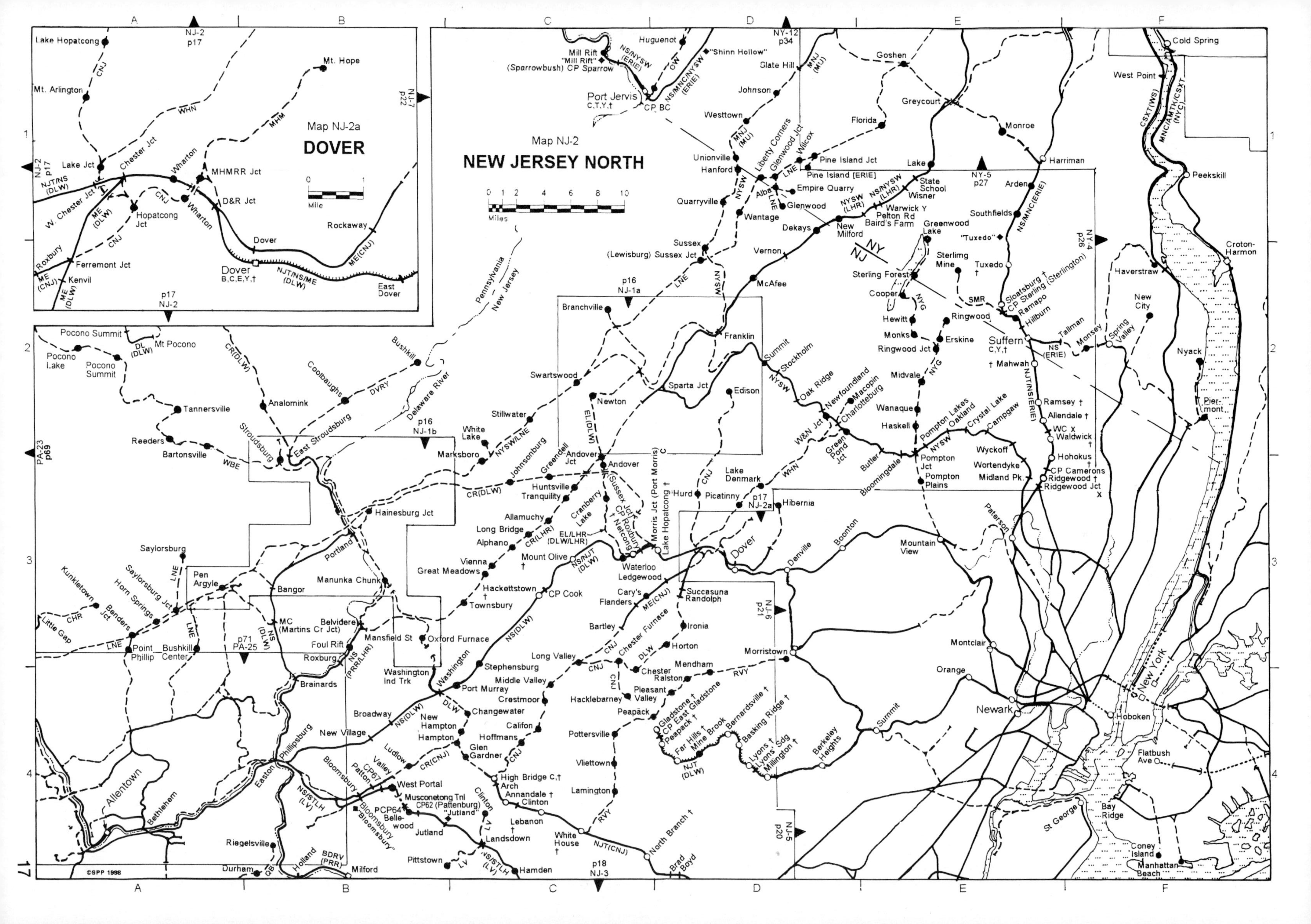
Map NJ-2a
DOVER
Mile
Lake Hopatcong
Mt. Hope
Mt. Arlington
Lake Jct
Chester Jct
Wharton
MHMRR Jct
D&R Jct
Hopatcong Jct
Rockaway
Dover
Dover B,C,E,Y,†
Roxbury
Ferremont Jct
Kenvil
East Dover
W. Chester Jct
Map NJ-2
NEW JERSEY NORTH
Miles
Pennsylvania
New Jersey
Delaware River
NY
NJ
Port Jervis C,T,Y,†
Mill Rift
"Mill Rift"
(Sparrowbush) CP Sparrow
Huguenot
"Shinn Hollow"
Slate Hill
Johnson
Westtown
Unionville
Hanford
Liberty Corners
Glenwood Jct
Wilcox
Pine Island Jct
Pine Island [ERIE]
Empire Quarry
Glenwood
Quarryville
Wantage
Dekays
Sussex
(Lewisburg) Sussex Jct
Vernon
McAfee
Goshen
Greycourt
Florida
Monroe
Harriman
Lake
State School
Wisner
Warwick Y
Pelton Rd
Baird's Farm
New Milford
Arden
Southfields
Greenwood Lake
"Tuxedo"
Tuxedo
Sterling Forest
Cooper
Hewitt
Monks
Ringwood Jct
Ringwood
Erskine
Midvale
Wanaque
Haskell
Suffern C,Y,†
Mahwah
Ramsey †
Allendale †
Waldwick
Hohokus
CP Camerons
Ridgewood †
Ridgewood Jct
Hillburn
Ramapo
Tallman
Monsey
Spring Valley
New City
Haverstraw
Nyack
Piermont
Croton-Harmon
Peekskill
Cold Spring
West Point
Branchville
Newton
Franklin
Summit
Stockholm
Oak Ridge
Newfoundland
Macopin
Charlotteburg
Green Pond Jct
Butler
Bloomingdale
Pompton Lakes
Oakland
Crystal Lake
Campgaw
Wyckoff
Wortendyke
Midland Pk.
Pompton Jct
Pompton Plains
Paterson
Mountain View
Boonton
Denville
Hibernia
Sparta Jct
Edison
Swartswood
Stillwater
White Lake
Marksboro
Johnsonburg
Greendell
Andover Jct
Andover
Lake Denmark
Hurd
Picatinny
Dover
Huntsville
Tranquility
Allamuchy
Long Bridge
Alphano
Vienna
Great Meadows
Hackettstown
Townsbury
CP Cook
Mount Olive
Waterloo
Ledgewood
Cary's
Flanders
Succasuna
Randolph
Ironia
Horton
Bartley
Morristown
Montclair
Orange
Newark
Hoboken
New York
Flatbush Ave
Bay Ridge
St George
Coney Island
Manhattan Beach
Summit
Berkeley Heights
Pocono Summit
Mt Pocono
Pocono Lake
Tannersville
Reeders
Bartonsville
Analomink
Coolbaughs
Bushkill
Stroudsburg
East Stroudsburg
Hainesburg Jct
Saylorsburg
Pen Argyle
Bangor
Portland
Manunka Chunk
Belvidere
Mansfield St
Oxford Furnace
Foul Rift
Roxburg
Brainards
Washington
Washington Ind Trk
Stephensburg
Port Murray
Long Valley
Middle Valley
Crestmoor
Changewater
Califon
Hoffmans
Glen Gardner
New Hampton
Hampton
Broadway
New Village
Phillipsburg
Easton
Allentown
Bethlehem
Riegelsville
Durham
Holland
Milford
Pittstown
Hamden
Landsdown
Jutland
West Portal
Musconetong Tnl
CP62 (Pattenburg)
"Jutland"
Bloomsbury
"Bloomsbury"
Ludlow
Valley
Patton
High Bridge C,†
Arch
Annandale †
Clinton
Lebanon †
White House †
North Branch †
Brad Boyd
Lamington
Vliettown
Pottersville
Hacklebarney
Pleasant Valley
Peapack
Chester
Ralston
Mendham
Gladstone †
CP East Gladstone
Far Hills †
Mine Brook
Bernardsville †
Basking Ridge †
Lyons †
Lyons' Sdg
Millington †
Kunkletown
Benders Jct
Horn Springs
Saylorsburg Jct
Little Gap
Point Phillip
Bushkill Center
©SPP 1998

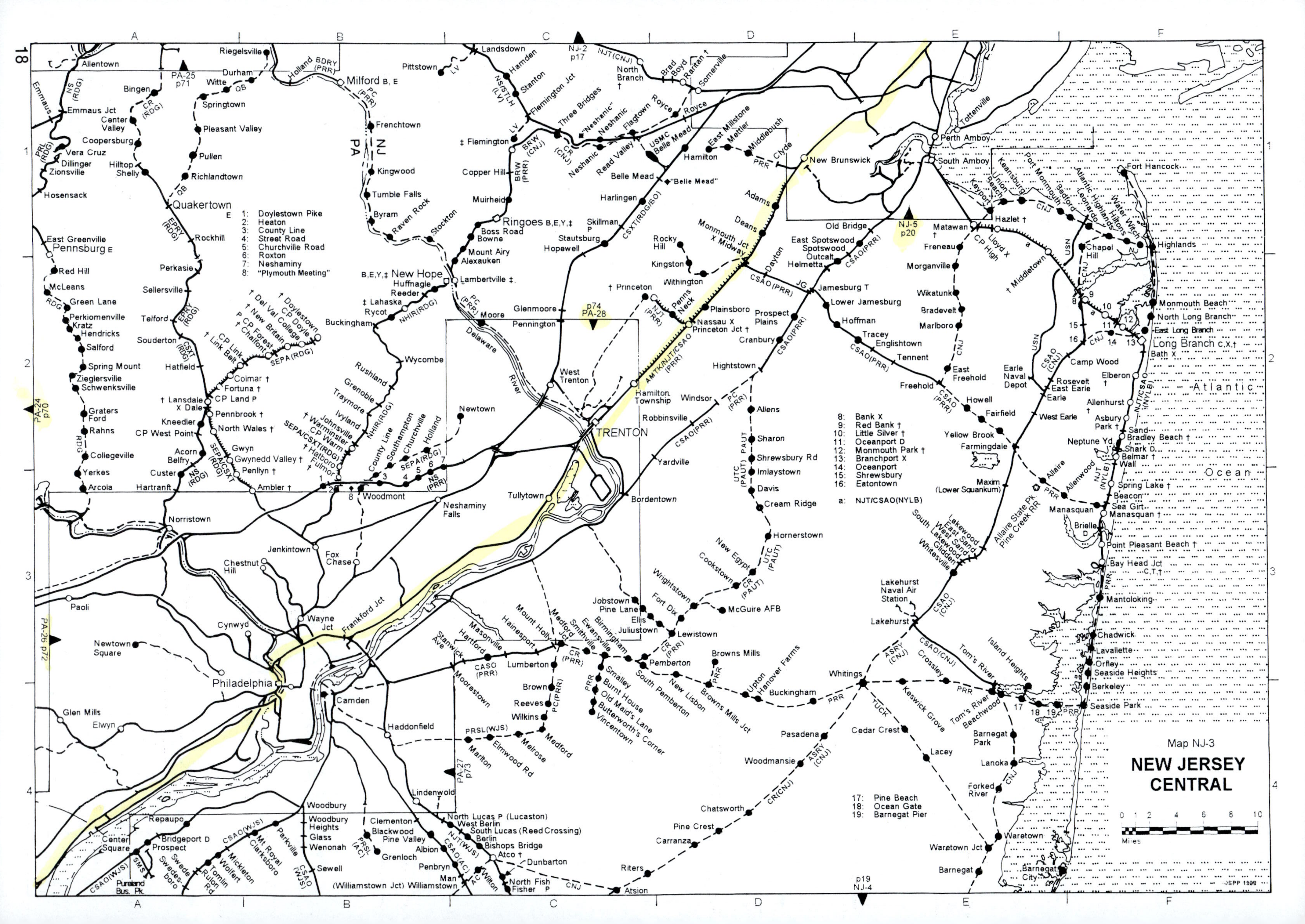
Map NJ-3
NEW JERSEY CENTRAL
Miles
1: Doylestown Pike
2: Heaton
3: County Line
4: Street Road
5: Churchville Road
6: Roxton
7: Neshaminy
8: "Plymouth Meeting"
8: Bank X
9: Red Bank †
10: Little Silver †
11: Oceanport D
12: Monmouth Park †
13: Branchport X
14: Oceanport
15: Shrewsbury
16: Eatontown
a: NJT/CSAO(NYLB)
17: Pine Beach
18: Ocean Gate
19: Barnegat Pier
Atlantic
Ocean
TRENTON
Philadelphia
Delaware River

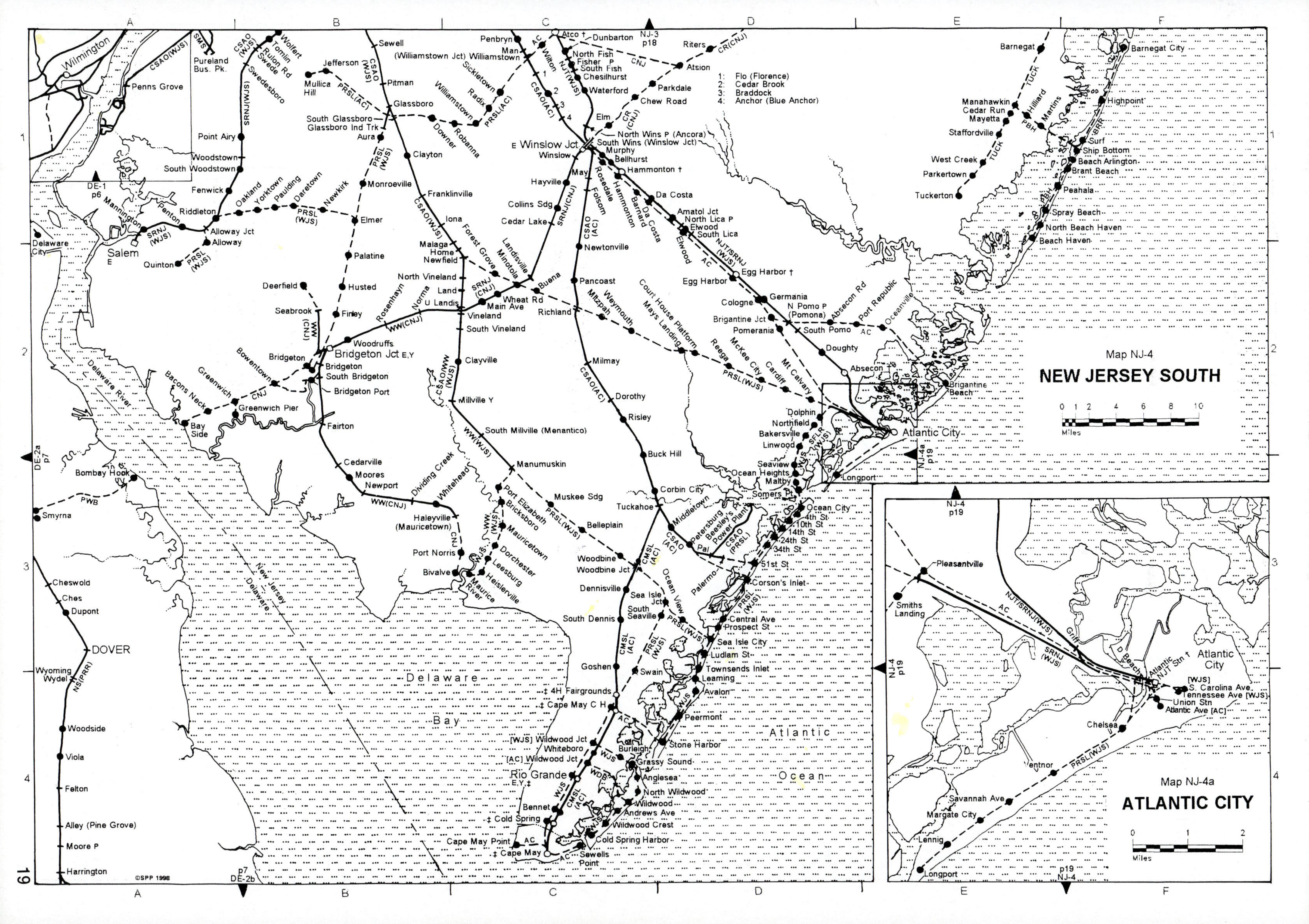
Map NJ-4
NEW JERSEY SOUTH
Miles
1: Flo (Florence)
2: Cedar Brook
3: Braddock
4: Anchor (Blue Anchor)
Map NJ-4a
ATLANTIC CITY
Wilmington
Penns Grove
Pureland Bus. Pk.
Salem
Delaware City
Bombay Hook
Smyrna
DOVER
Cheswold
Dupont
Woodside
Viola
Felton
Alley (Pine Grove)
Harrington
Bridgeton Jct
Vineland
Winslow Jct
Glassboro
Millville Y
Tuckahoe
Atlantic City
Cape May
Rio Grande
Absecon
Egg Harbor
Hammonton
Ocean City
Sea Isle City
Wildwood
Stone Harbor
Barnegat
Tuckerton
Beach Haven
Delaware Bay
Atlantic Ocean
Delaware River
©SPP 1998

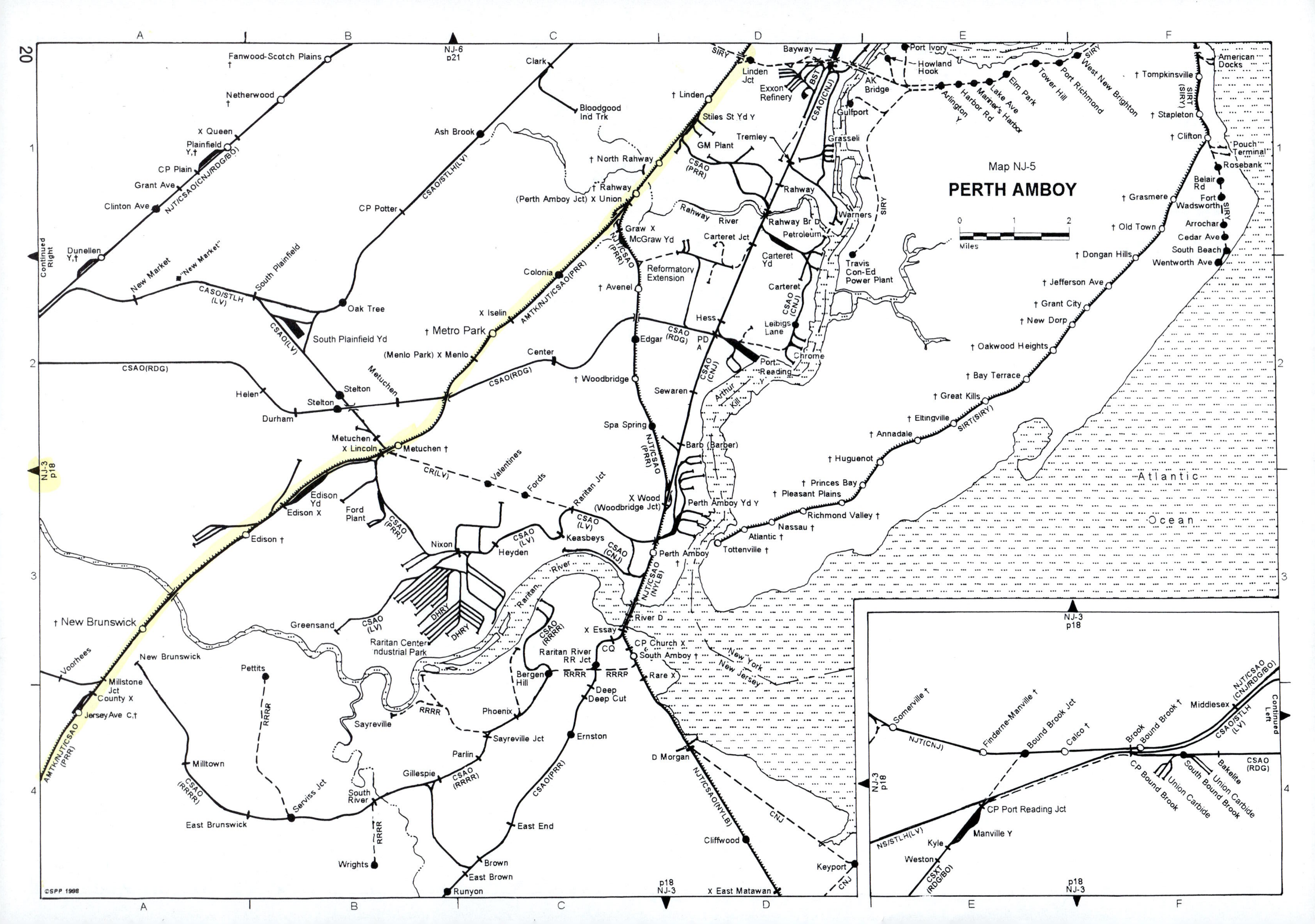

Map NJ-5
PERTH AMBOY
Miles
Atlantic
Ocean
Continued Right
Continued Left
NJ-6 p21
NJ-3 p18
p18 NJ-3
Fanwood-Scotch Plains †
Netherwood †
X Queen
Plainfield Y,†
CP Plain
Grant Ave
Clinton Ave
Dunellen Y,†
NJT/CSAO(CNJ/RDG/BO)
New Market
"New Market"
South Plainfield
CASO/STLH (LV)
CSAO(LV)
Oak Tree
South Plainfield Yd
CSAO(RDG)
Helen
Durham
Stelton
Metuchen
X Lincoln
Metuchen †
(Menlo Park) X Menlo
† Metro Park
X Iselin
Center
Clark
Bloodgood Ind Trk
Ash Brook
CP Potter
CSAO/STLH(LV)
Colonia
AMTK/NJT/CSAO(PRR)
† North Rahway
† Rahway
(Perth Amboy Jct) X Union
Graw X McGraw Yd
NJT/CSAO (PRR)
† Avenel
Edgar
† Woodbridge
Spa Spring
X Wood (Woodbridge Jct)
Reformatory Extension
Carteret Jct
Rahway River
Hess
PD A
CSAO (RDG)
CSAO (CNJ)
Sewaren
Arthur Kill
Barb (Barber)
Perth Amboy Yd Y
Perth Amboy †
SIRY
Linden Jct
† Linden
Stiles St Yd Y
GM Plant
CSAO (PRR)
Tremley
Rahway
Rahway Br D
Petroleum
Carteret Yd
Carteret
Leibigs Lane
Port Reading Y
Chrome
Bayway
BST
Exxon Refinery
CSAO(CNJ)
AK Bridge
Gulfport
Grasseli
Warners
Travis Con-Ed Power Plant
Port Ivory
Howland Hook
Arlington Y
Harbor Rd
Mariner's Harbor
Lake Ave
Elm Park
Tower Hill
Port Richmond
West New Brighton
† Tompkinsville
SIRT (SIRY)
† Stapleton
† Clifton
American Docks
Pouch Terminal
Rosebank
Belair Rd
Fort Wadsworth
Arrochar
Cedar Ave
South Beach
Wentworth Ave
† Grasmere
† Old Town
† Dongan Hills
† Jefferson Ave
† Grant City
† New Dorp
† Oakwood Heights
† Bay Terrace
† Great Kills
† Eltingville
SIRT(SIRY)
† Annadale
† Huguenot
† Princes Bay
† Pleasant Plains
Richmond Valley †
Nassau †
Atlantic †
Tottenville †
Edison Yd
Edison X
Edison †
Ford Plant
CSAO (PRR)
CR(LV)
Valentines
Fords
Raritan Jct
CSAO (LV)
Keasbeys
CSAO (CNJ)
Nixon
Heyden
DHRY
Greensand
Raritan Center Industrial Park
Raritan River
NJT/CSAO (NYLB)
River D
X Essay
CQ
CP Church X
South Amboy †
New York
New Jersey
Rare X
CSAO (RRRR)
Raritan River RR Jct
Bergen Hill
RRRR
Deep
Deep Cut
Phoenix
Sayreville
Sayreville Jct
Ernston
Parlin
Gillespie
CSAO (RRRR)
South River
CSAO(PRR)
East End
Brown
East Brown
Runyon
Wrights
D Morgan
NJT/CSAO(NYLB)
CNJ
Cliffwood
Keyport
X East Matawan
† New Brunswick
Voorhees
Millstone Jct
County X
Jersey Ave C,†
AMTK/NJT/CSAO (PRR)
New Brunswick
Pettits
Milltown
CSAO (RRRR)
East Brunswick
Serviss Jct
Somerville †
NJT(CNJ)
Finderne-Manville †
Bound Brook Jct
Calco †
Brook
Bound Brook †
Middlesex
NJT/CSAO (CNJ/RDG/BO)
CSAO/STLH (LV)
CSAO (RDG)
Bakelite
Union Carbide
South Bound Brook
Union Carbide
CP Bound Brook
CP Port Reading Jct
Manville Y
NS/STLH(LV)
Kyle
Weston
CSXT (RDG/BO)
©SPP 1998

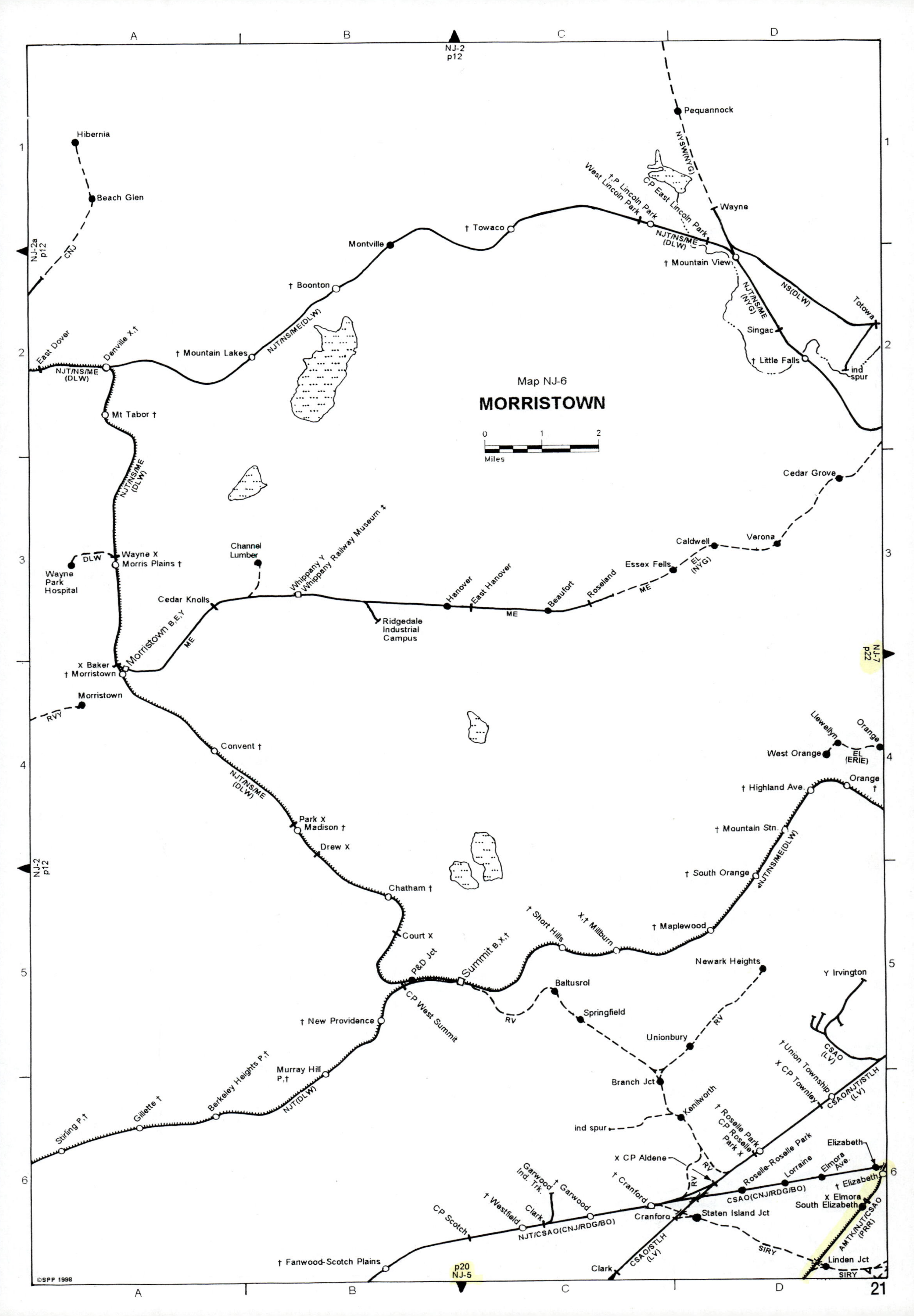

Map NJ-6
MORRISTOWN
0 1 2
Miles
Hibernia
Beach Glen
CNJ
Pequannock
NYSW(NYG)
Wayne
West Lincoln Park
†,P Lincoln Park
CP East Lincoln Park
NJT/NS/ME (DLW)
† Mountain View
NS(DLW)
NJT/NS/ME (NYG)
Totowa
Singac
† Little Falls
ind spur
† Towaco
Montville
† Boonton
NJT/NS/ME(DLW)
† Mountain Lakes
East Dover
Denville X,†
NJT/NS/ME (DLW)
Mt Tabor †
NJT/NS/ME (DLW)
Cedar Grove
Caldwell
Verona
Essex Fells
EL (NYG)
ME
Wayne X
Morris Plains †
DLW
Wayne Park Hospital
Channel Lumber
Whippany Y
Whippany Railway Museum †
Cedar Knolls
Hanover
East Hanover
Beaufort
Roseland
ME
Ridgedale Industrial Campus
Morristown B,E,Y
ME
X Baker
† Morristown
Morristown
RVY
Llewellyn
Orange
West Orange
EL (ERIE)
Convent †
NJT/NS/ME (DLW)
Orange †
† Highland Ave.
† Mountain Stn.
NJT/NS/ME(DLW)
† South Orange
Park X
Madison †
Drew X
Chatham †
† Short Hills
X,† Millburn
† Maplewood
Court X
P&D Jct
Summit B,X,†
CP West Summit
Newark Heights
Y Irvington
Baltusrol
Springfield
RV
RV
Unionbury
† New Providence
CSAO (LV)
† Union Township
X CP Townley
CSAO/NJT/STLH (LV)
Murray Hill P,†
NJT(DLW)
Branch Jct
Berkeley Heights P,†
Gillette †
Stirling P,†
Kenilworth
ind spur
† Roselle Park
CP Roselle Park X
Roselle-Roselle Park
Lorraine
Elmora Ave.
Elizabeth
X CP Aldene
RV
RV
† Elizabeth
Garwood Ind. Trk.
† Garwood
† Cranford
CSAO(CNJ/RDG/BO)
X Elmora
South Elizabeth
AMTK/NJT/CSAO (PRR)
† Westfield
Clark
Cranford
Staten Island Jct
CP Scotch
NJT/CSAO(CNJ/RDG/BO)
SIRY
CSAO/STLH (LV)
Linden Jct
SIRY
† Fanwood-Scotch Plains
Clark
NJ-2 p12
NJ-2a p12
NJ-2 p12
NJ-7 p22
p20 NJ-5
A B C D
1 2 3 4 5 6

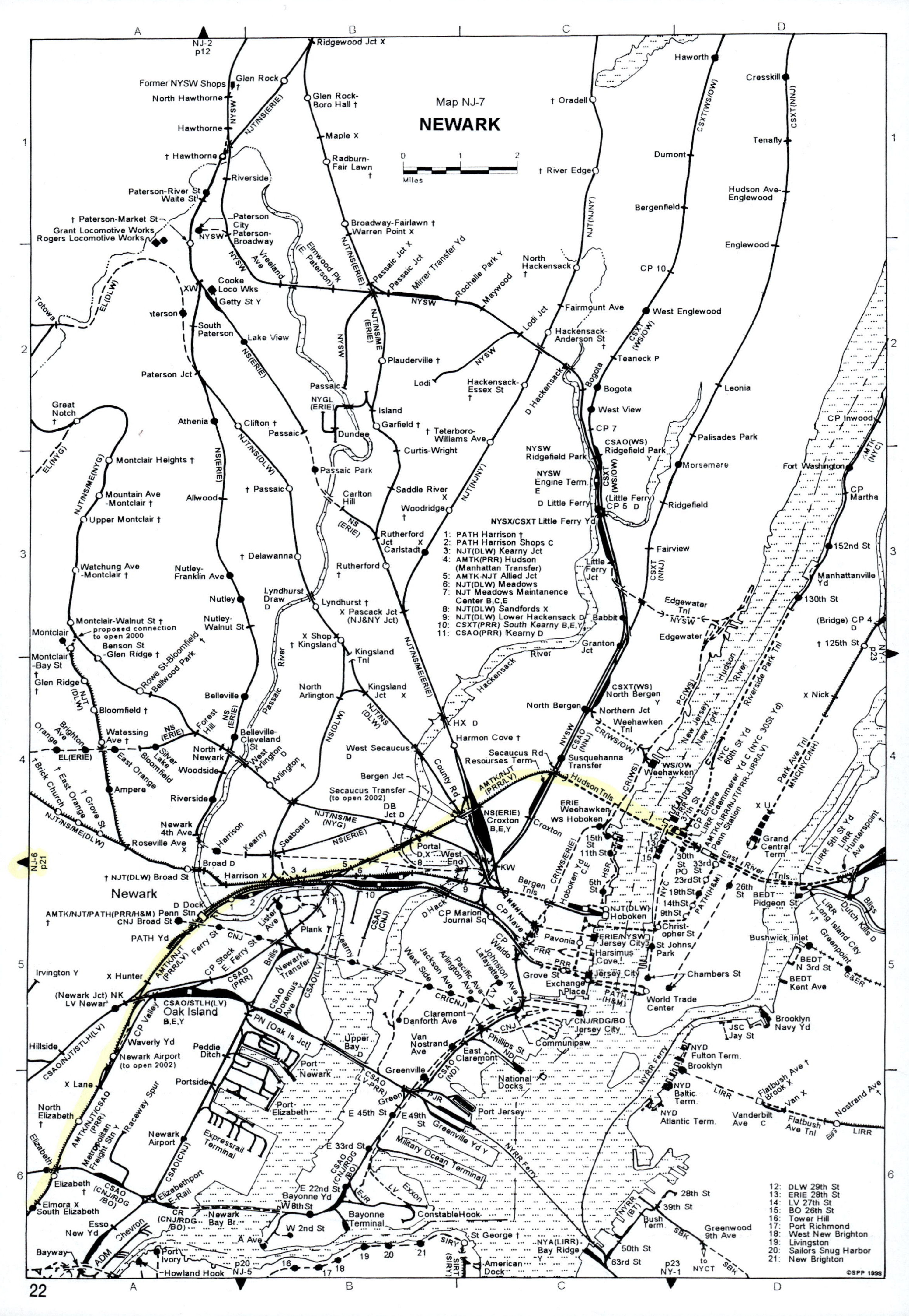

Map NJ-7
NEWARK
0 1 2
Miles
A
B
C
D
1
2
3
4
5
6
NJ-2
p12
Ridgewood Jct X
Glen Rock
Former NYSW Shops
North Hawthorne
Glen Rock-
Boro Hall †
Hawthorne
† Hawthorne
Maple X
Radburn-
Fair Lawn
†
Riverside
Paterson-River St
Waite St
† Paterson-Market St
Grant Locomotive Works
Rogers Locomotive Works
Paterson
City
Paterson-
Broadway
Broadway-Fairlawn †
Warren Point X
Elmwood Pk
(E. Paterson)
Vreeland
Ave
Passaic Jct X
Passaic Jct
Mirrer Transfer Yd
Rochelle Park Y
Maywood
North
Hackensack
†
Cooke
Loco Wks
Getty St Y
XW
Totowa
EL(DLW)
South
Paterson
Lake View
NS(ERIE)
Plauderville †
Lodi
Lodi Jct
Fairmount Ave
Hackensack-
Anderson St
†
Hackensack-
Essex St
†
D Hackensack
Bogota
Paterson Jct
Passaic
NYGL
(ERIE)
Island
Dundee
Garfield †
† Teterboro-
Williams Ave
Curtis-Wright
Great
Notch
†
Athenia
Clifton †
Passaic
Passaic Park
EL(NYG)
NJT/NS/ME(NYG)
Montclair Heights †
Mountain Ave
-Montclair †
Upper Montclair †
Watchung Ave
-Montclair †
Montclair-Walnut St †
proposed connection
to open 2000
Montclair
Montclair
-Bay St
†
Glen Ridge
†
Benson St
-Glen Ridge †
Allwood
† Passaic
Carlton
Hill
Saddle River
X
Woodridge
†
NJT(NJNY)
Rutherford
Jct X
Carlstadt
Rutherford
†
† Delawanna
Nutley-
Franklin Ave
Nutley
Nutley-
Walnut St
Lyndhurst
Draw
D
Lyndhurst †
X Pascack Jct
(NJ&NY Jct)
X Shop
X Kingsland
Kingsland
Tnl
Kingsland
Jct X
North
Arlington
Rowe St-Bloomfield
Bellwood Park
Bloomfield †
Belleville
Belleville-
Cleveland
St
North
Newark
Forest
Hill
Watessing
Ave †
Brighton
Ave
Orange
EL(ERIE)
Silver
Lake
Bloomfield
East Orange
Ampere
Woodside
Riverside
West
Arlington
D
Arlington †
West Secaucus
D
† Brick Church
† East Orange
† Grove St
NJT/NS/ME(DLW)
Roseville Ave
X
Newark
4th Ave
Harrison
Kearny
Seaboard
NJT/NS/ME
(NYG)
NS(ERIE)
Broad D
† NJT(DLW) Broad St
Newark
Harrison X
NJ-6
p21
HX D
Harmon Cove †
County Rd
Bergen Jct
Secaucus Transfer
(to open 2002)
DB
Jct D
Portal
D,X
West
End
AMTK/NJT
(PRR/LV)
NS(ERIE)
Croxton
B,E,Y
Croxton
KW
Secaucus Rd
Resourses Term
Susquehanna
Transfer
Hudson Tnls
1: PATH Harrison †
2: PATH Harrison Shops C
3: NJT(DLW) Kearny Jct
4: AMTK(PRR) Hudson
(Manhattan Transfer)
5: AMTK-NJT Allied Jct
6: NJT(DLW) Meadows
7: NJT Meadows Maintanence
Center B,C,E
8: NJT(DLW) Sandfords X
9: NJT(DLW) Lower Hackensack D
10: CSXT(PRR) South Kearny B,E,Y
11: CSAO(PRR) Kearny D
Hackensack
River
NYSW
Ridgefield Park
NYSW
Engine Term.
E
D Little Ferry
NYSX/CSXT Little Ferry Yd
Little
Ferry
Jct
Babbit
Granton
Jct
North Bergen
CSXT(WS)
North Bergen
Y
Northern Jct
Weehawken
Tnl
CR(WS/OW)
WS/OW
Weehawken
ERIE
Weehawken
WS Hoboken
15th
St
11th St
5th
St
Hoboken Yd
C,E
HSR
NJT(DLW)
Hoboken
Christ-
opher St
ERIE/NYSW
Jersey City
St Johns
Park
Harsimus
Cove
Jersey City
Pavonia
Grove St
Exchange
Place
PATH
(H&M)
World Trade
Center
Chambers St
Haworth
† Oradell
† River Edge
Dumont
Bergenfield
CSXT(WS/OW)
Cresskill
CSXT(NNJ)
Tenafly
Hudson Ave-
Englewood
Englewood
CP 10
West Englewood
CSXT
(WS/OW)
Teaneck P
Leonia
Bogota
West View
CP 7
CSAO(WS)
Ridgefield Park
Y
Palisades Park
Morsemare
(Little Ferry)
CP 5 D
Ridgefield
Fairview
CSXT
(NNJ)
Edgewater
Tnl
NYSW
Edgewater
CP Inwood
AMTK
(NYC)
Fort Washington
CP
Martha
152nd St
Manhattanville
Yd
130th St
(Bridge) CP 4
D
† 125th St
NY-1
p23
X Nick
Riverside Park Tnl
Hudson
River
New Jersey
New York
NYC 60th St Yd
NYC 30St Yd
Park Ave Tnl
MNC(NYC/NH)
CP Empire
LIRR Caemmerer Yd C (NYC 30th St Yd)
AMTK/LIRR/NJT(PRR-LIRR/LV)
Penn Station
X U
Grand
Central
Term
LIRR 5th St Yd
LIRR
Hunterspoint
Ave
East
River
Tnls
30th
St
33rd
PO
St
23rdSt
19thSt
14thSt
9thSt
PATH(H&M)
26th
St
BEDT
Pidgeon St
LIRR
Long Island City
Y,I
Dutch Kills D
Bliss
Bushwick Inlet
Greenpoint
BEDT
N 3rd St
G&ER
BEDT
Kent Ave
D Dock
Penn
Stn
AMTK/NJT/PATH(PRR/H&M)
†
CNJ Broad St
PATH Yd
Lister
Ave
Plank
CSAO
(CNJ)
D Hack
CP Marion
Journal Sq
CP Nave
CP
Waldo
Ferry St
CNJ
E. Ferry St
Brills
Newark
Transfer
Kearny
West Side
Jackson Ave
Arlington Ave
Pacific Ave
Johnston
Ave
Lafayette
LV
CR(CNJ)
PRR
Irvington Y
X Hunter
CP Stock
CSAO
(PRR)
(Newark Jct) NK
LV Newark
CSAO/STLH(LV)
Oak Island
B,E,Y
CP Valley
CSAO/NJT/STLH(LV)
Waverly Yd
PN [Oak Is Jct]
CSAO
Doremus
Ave
CSAO(LV)
Claremont
Danforth Ave
Upper
Bay
D
Hillside
Newark Airport
(to open 2002)
Peddie
Ditch
Van
Nostrand
Ave
East
Claremont
Phillips St
ND
CNJ/RDG/BO
Jersey City
Communipaw
National
Docks
X Lane
Portside
Port
Newark
Greenville
CSAO
(ND)
CSAO
(LV-PRR)
Green
PJR
North
Elizabeth
†
AMTK/NJT/CSAO
(PRR)
Metropolitan
Freight Stn Y
Raceway Spur
Port
Elizabeth
E 45th St
E 49th
St
Port Jersey
Greenville Yd Y
Newark
Airport
Expressrail
Terminal
CSAO(CNJ)
E 33rd St
Military Ocean Terminal
NYRR Ferry
Elizabeth
Elizabeth
CSAO
(CNJ/RDG
/BO)
Elizabethport
E-Rail
CSAO
(CNJ/RDG
/BO)
E 22nd St
Bayonne Yd
EJR
LV
Exxon
Elmora X
South Elizabeth
CR
(CNJ/RDG
/BO)
Newark
Bay Br.
W 8th St
Bayonne
Terminal
Constable Hook
Esso
New Yd
Chevron
W 2nd St
A Ave
St George †
SIRY
SIRT
(SIRY)
Bayway
ADM
Port
Ivory
Howland Hook
p20
NJ-5
16
17
18
19
20
21
American
Dock
NYA(LIRR)
Bay Ridge
Y
50th St
63rd St
NYRR
(BT)
Bush
Term.
28th St
39th St
SBK
Greenwood
9th Ave
to
NYCT
p23
NY-1
NYD
Fulton Term.
Brooklyn
NYRR Ferry
JSC
Jay St
Brooklyn
Navy Yd
NYD
Baltic
Term.
LIRR
Flatbush Ave †
Brook X
Van X
Nostrand Ave
NYD
Atlantic Term.
Vanderbilt
Ave
C
Flatbush
Ave Tnl
LIRR
12: DLW 29th St
13: ERIE 28th St
14: LV 27th St
15: BO 26th St
16: Tower Hill
17: Port Richmond
18: West New Brighton
19: Livingston
20: Sailors Snug Harbor
21: New Brighton
©SPP 1998

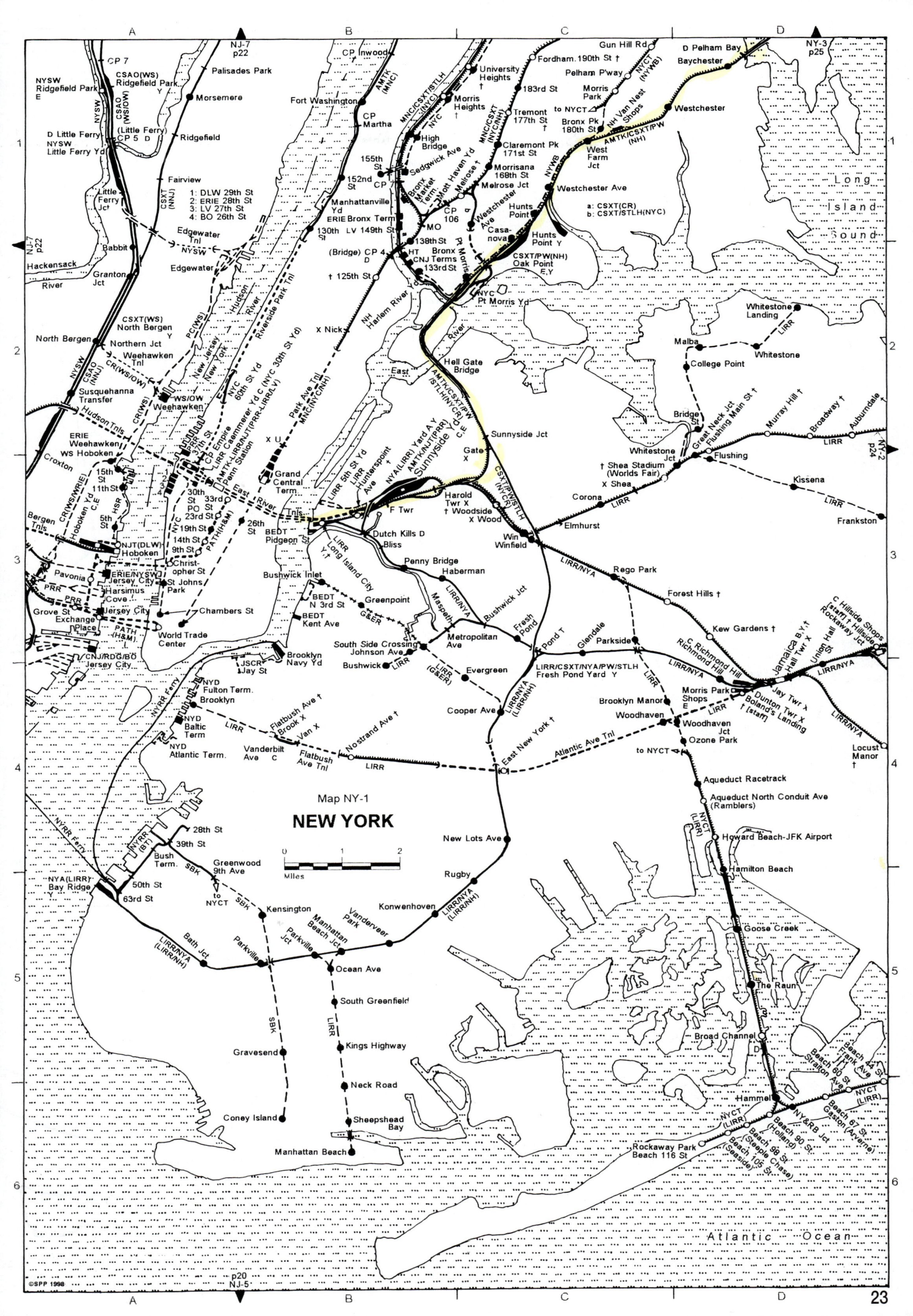
Map NY-1
NEW YORK
Long Island Sound
Atlantic Ocean
Hudson River
East River
Harlem River
Hackensack River
Penn Station
Grand Central Term.
Sunnyside Yd
Hell Gate Bridge
Jamaica
Flushing
Coney Island
Manhattan Beach
Bay Ridge
Hoboken
Jersey City
Weehawken
North Bergen
Fresh Pond
Atlantic Ave Tnl
Flatbush Ave Tnl
Broad Channel
Howard Beach-JFK Airport
Rockaway Park Beach 116 St
1: DLW 29th St
2: ERIE 28th St
3: LV 27th St
4: BO 26th St
a: CSXT(CR)
b: CSXT/STLH(NYC)
NJ-7 p22
NY-3 p25
NY-2 p24
p20 NJ-5
©SPP 1998

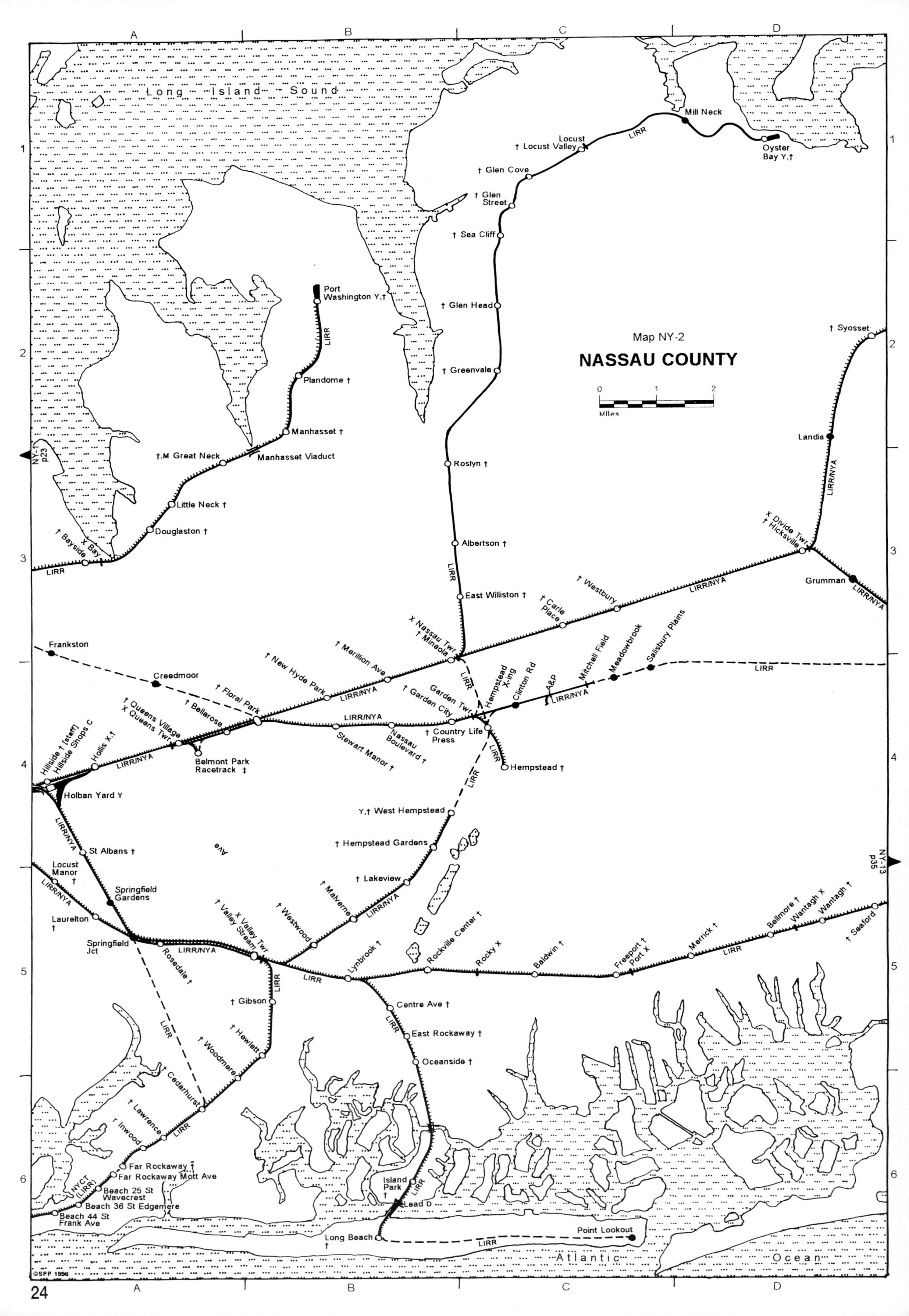
Map NY-2
NASSAU COUNTY
Long Island Sound
Atlantic Ocean
Mill Neck
Locust
† Locust Valley
Oyster Bay Y,†
† Glen Cove
† Glen Street
† Sea Cliff
Port Washington Y,†
† Glen Head
† Greenvale
Plandome †
Manhasset †
†,M Great Neck
Manhasset Viaduct
Little Neck †
Douglaston †
† Bayside
X Bay
Roslyn †
Albertson †
East Williston †
† Syosset
Landia
X Divide Twr
† Hicksville
Grumman
† Westbury
† Carle Place
X Nassau Twr
† Mineola
† Merillion Ave
† New Hyde Park
† Floral Park
† Bellerose
† Queens Village
X Queens Twr
Belmont Park Racetrack ‡
Frankston
Creedmoor
Garden Twr
† Garden City
Hempstead X-ing
Clinton Rd
A&P
Mitchell Field
Meadowbrook
Salisbury Plains
† Country Life Press
Hempstead †
Stewart Manor †
Nassau Boulevard †
Hillside † [staff]
Hillside Shops C
Hollis X,†
Holban Yard Y
St Albans †
Locust Manor †
Springfield Gardens
Laurelton †
Springfield Jct
Y,† West Hempstead
† Hempstead Gardens
† Lakeview
† Malverne
† Westwood
X Valley Twr
† Valley Stream
Rosedale †
† Gibson
† Hewlett
† Woodmere
† Cedarhurst
† Lawrence
† Inwood
Far Rockaway †
Far Rockaway Mott Ave
Beach 25 St Wavecrest
Beach 36 St Edgemere
Beach 44 St Frank Ave
NYCT (LIRR)
Lynbrook †
Rockville Center †
Rocky X
Baldwin †
Freeport †
Port X
Merrick †
Bellmore †
Wantagh X
Wantagh †
† Seaford
Centre Ave †
East Rockaway †
Oceanside †
Island Park †
Lead D
Long Beach †
Point Lookout
LIRR
LIRR/NYA
NY-1 p23
NY-13 p35
Miles
0
1
2
A
B
C
D
1
2
3
4
5
6
©SPP 1998

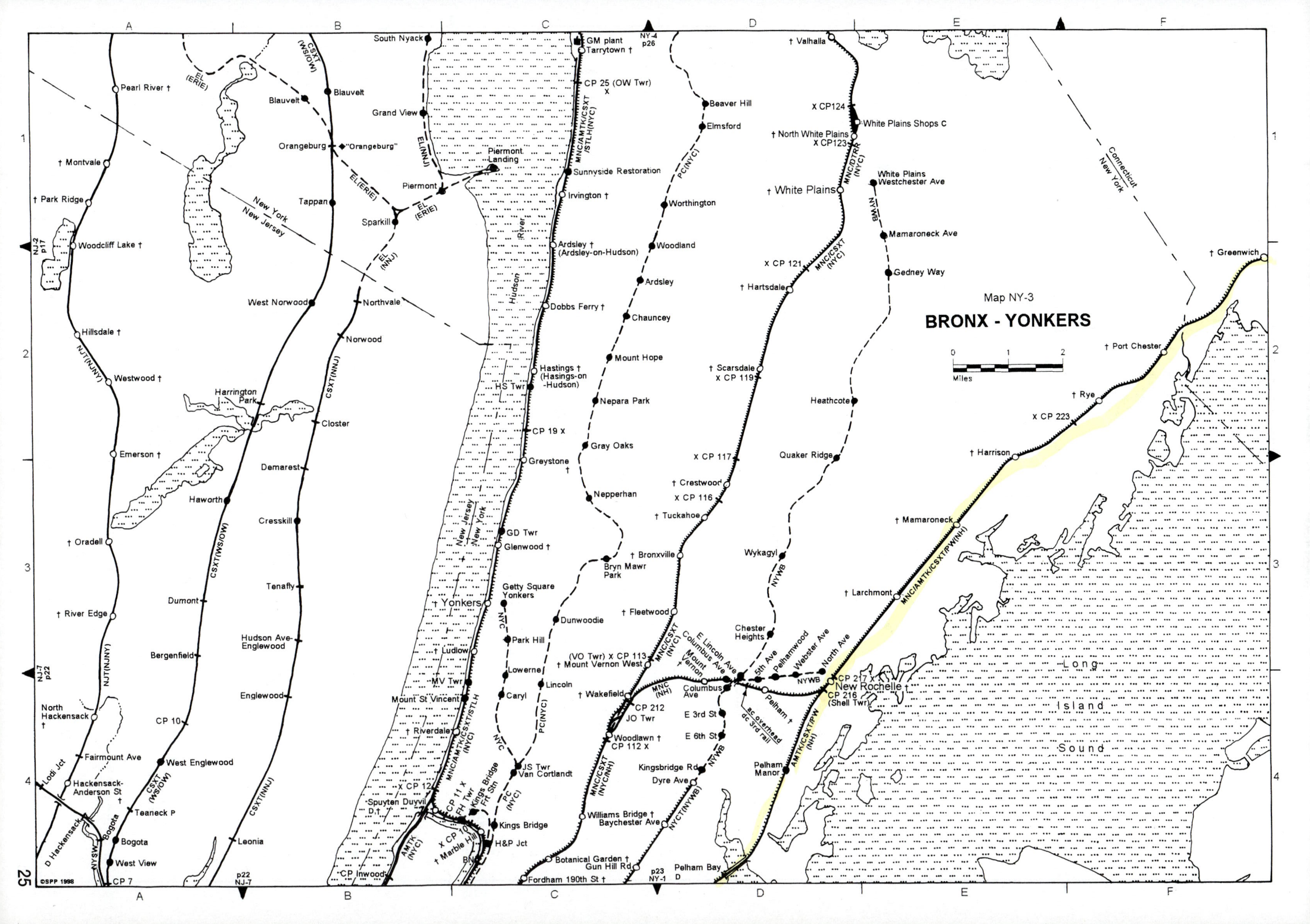

Map NY-3
BRONX - YONKERS
0
1
2
Miles
Connecticut
New York
New York
New Jersey
New Jersey
New York
Hudson River
Long Island Sound
South Nyack
Blauvelt
Blauvelt
Grand View
Orangeburg
"Orangeburg"
EL (ERIE)
EL(ERIE)
EL(NNJ)
Piermont Landing
Piermont
Tappan
Sparkill
EL (ERIE)
EL (NNJ)
CSXT (WS/OW)
Pearl River
Montvale
Park Ridge
Woodcliff Lake
NJ-2 p17
West Norwood
Northvale
Norwood
Hillsdale
NJT(NJNY)
Westwood
Harrington Park
CSXT(NNJ)
Closter
Emerson
Demarest
Haworth
Cresskill
Oradell
CSXT(WS/OW)
Tenafly
Dumont
River Edge
Hudson Ave- Englewood
Bergenfield
NJ-7 p22
NJT(NJNY)
Englewood
North Hackensack
CP 10
Fairmount Ave
West Englewood
Lodi Jct
Hackensack- Anderson St
CSXT (WS/OW)
Teaneck P
CSXT(NNJ)
D Hackensack
Bogota
Bogota
Leonia
NYSW
West View
CP 7
©SPP 1998
p22 NJ-7
GM plant
Tarrytown
NY-4 p26
CP 25 (OW Twr) x
MNC/AMTK/CSXT /STLH(NYC)
Sunnyside Restoration
Irvington
Ardsley (Ardsley-on-Hudson)
Dobbs Ferry
Hastings (Hasings-on -Hudson)
HS Twr
CP 19 x
Greystone
GD Twr
Glenwood
Yonkers
Getty Square Yonkers
NYC
Park Hill
Ludlow
Lowerre
MV Twr
Caryl
Mount St Vincent
Riverdale
MNC/AMTK/CSXT/STLH (NYC)
x CP 12
Spuyten Duyvil D
CP 11 x
FH Twr
Kings Bridge Frt Stn
x CP 10
Marble Hill
AMTK (NYC)
CP Inwood
Kings Bridge
H&P Jct
PC (NYC)
JS Twr
Van Cortlandt
Beaver Hill
Elmsford
PC(NYC)
Worthington
Woodland
Ardsley
Chauncey
Mount Hope
Nepara Park
Gray Oaks
Nepperhan
Bryn Mawr Park
Dunwoodie
Lincoln
PC(NYC)
Valhalla
x CP124
White Plains Shops C
North White Plains
x CP123
MNC/DTRR (NYC)
White Plains
White Plains Westchester Ave
NYWB
Mamaroneck Ave
Gedney Way
x CP 121
MNC/CSXT (NYC)
Hartsdale
Scarsdale
x CP 119
Heathcote
x CP 117
Quaker Ridge
Crestwood
x CP 116
Tuckahoe
Bronxville
Wykagyl
Fleetwood
MNC/CSXT (NYC)
(VO Twr) x CP 113
Mount Vernon West
Chester Heights
E Lincoln Ave
Columbus Ave
Mount Vernon
5th Ave
Pelhamwood
Webster Ave
North Ave
NYWB
Wakefield
MNC (NH)
Columbus Ave
CP 212
JO Twr
Pelham
ac overhead dc 3rd rail
E 3rd St
E 6th St
Woodlawn
CP 112 x
MNC/CSXT (NYC/NH)
Kingsbridge Rd
Dyre Ave
NYCT(NYWB)
Williams Bridge
Baychester Ave
Botanical Garden
Gun Hill Rd
Fordham 190th St
p23 NY-1
Pelham Bay D
Pelham Manor
AMTK/CSXT/PW (NH)
CP 217 x
New Rochelle
CP 216 (Shell Twr)
Larchmont
MNC/AMTK/CSXT/PW(NH)
Mamaroneck
Harrison
x CP 223
Rye
Port Chester
Greenwich
A
B
C
D
E
F
1
2
3
4

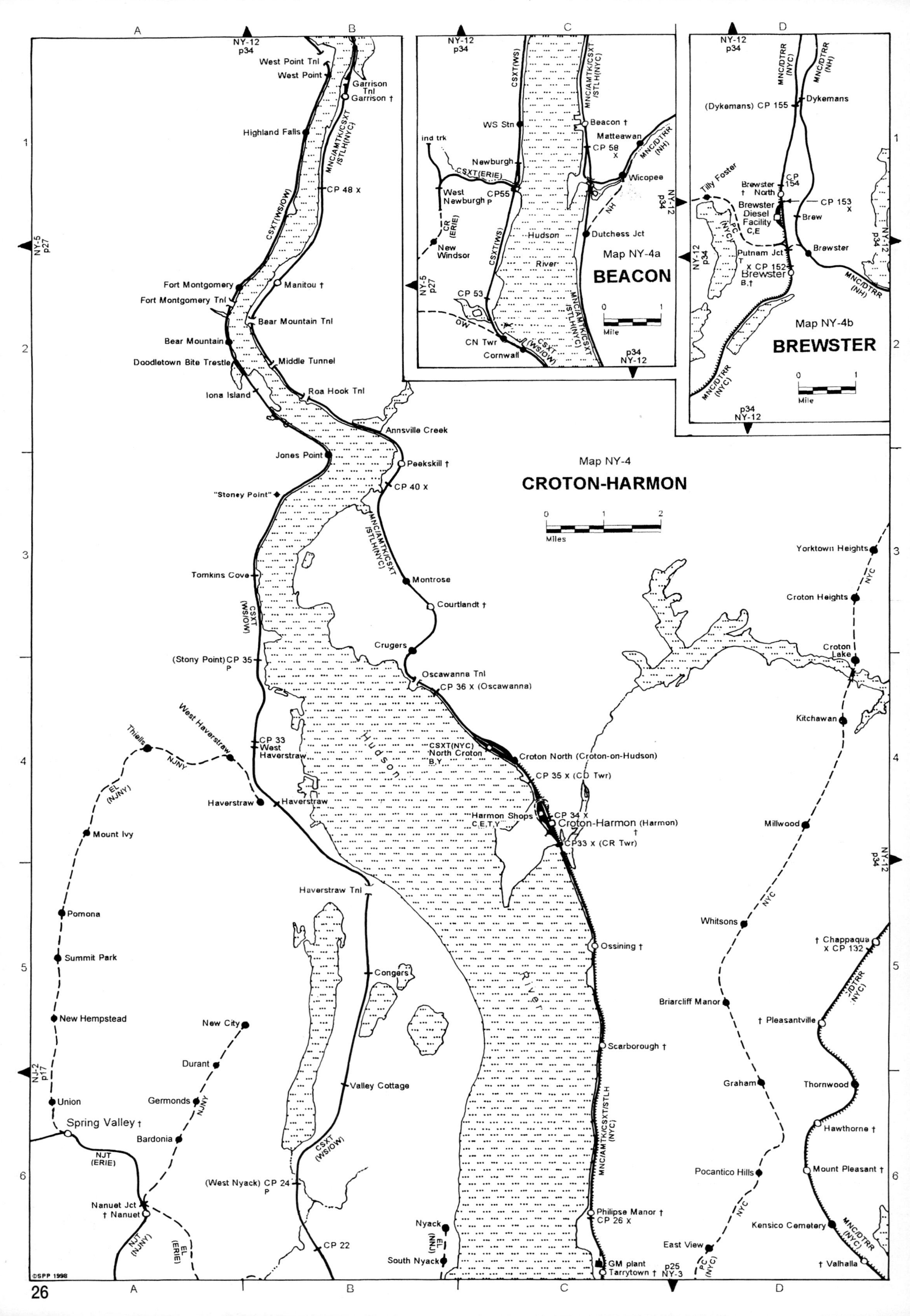
Map NY-4
CROTON-HARMON
Map NY-4a
BEACON
Map NY-4b
BREWSTER
West Point Tnl
West Point
Garrison Tnl
Garrison †
Highland Falls
CP 48 X
Fort Montgomery
Manitou †
Fort Montgomery Tnl
Bear Mountain Tnl
Bear Mountain
Doodletown Bite Trestle
Middle Tunnel
Iona Island
Roa Hook Tnl
Annsville Creek
Jones Point
Peekskill †
CP 40 X
"Stoney Point"
Tomkins Cove
Montrose
Courtlandt †
Crugers
(Stony Point) CP 35
Oscawanna Tnl
CP 36 X (Oscawanna)
CP 33
West Haverstraw
Thiells
West Haverstraw
Haverstraw
Mount Ivy
CSXT(NYC) North Croton B,Y
Croton North (Croton-on-Hudson)
CP 35 X (CD Twr)
Harmon Shops C,E,T,Y
CP 34 X
Croton-Harmon (Harmon) †
CP33 X (CR Twr)
Haverstraw Tnl
Pomona
Summit Park
New Hempstead
New City
Durant
Germonds
Union
Spring Valley †
Bardonia
Congers
Valley Cottage
(West Nyack) CP 24
Nanuet Jct
† Nanuet
CP 22
Nyack
South Nyack
Ossining †
Scarborough †
Philipse Manor †
CP 26 X
GM plant
Tarrytown †
Hudson
River
Yorktown Heights
Croton Heights
Croton Lake
Kitchawan
Millwood
Whitsons
Briarcliff Manor
Graham
Pocantico Hills
East View
† Chappaqua
X CP 132
† Pleasantville
Thornwood
Hawthorne †
Mount Pleasant †
Kensico Cemetery
† Valhalla
WS Stn
Beacon †
Matteawan
CP 58 X
Newburgh
West Newburgh
CP55
Wicopee
Dutchess Jct
New Windsor
CP 53
CN Twr
Cornwall
(Dykemans) CP 155
Dykemans
Tilly Foster
Brewster North
CP 154
Brewster Diesel Facility C,E
CP 153 X
Brew
Putnam Jct
X CP 152
Brewster
Brewster B,†
Miles
Mile
©SPP 1998

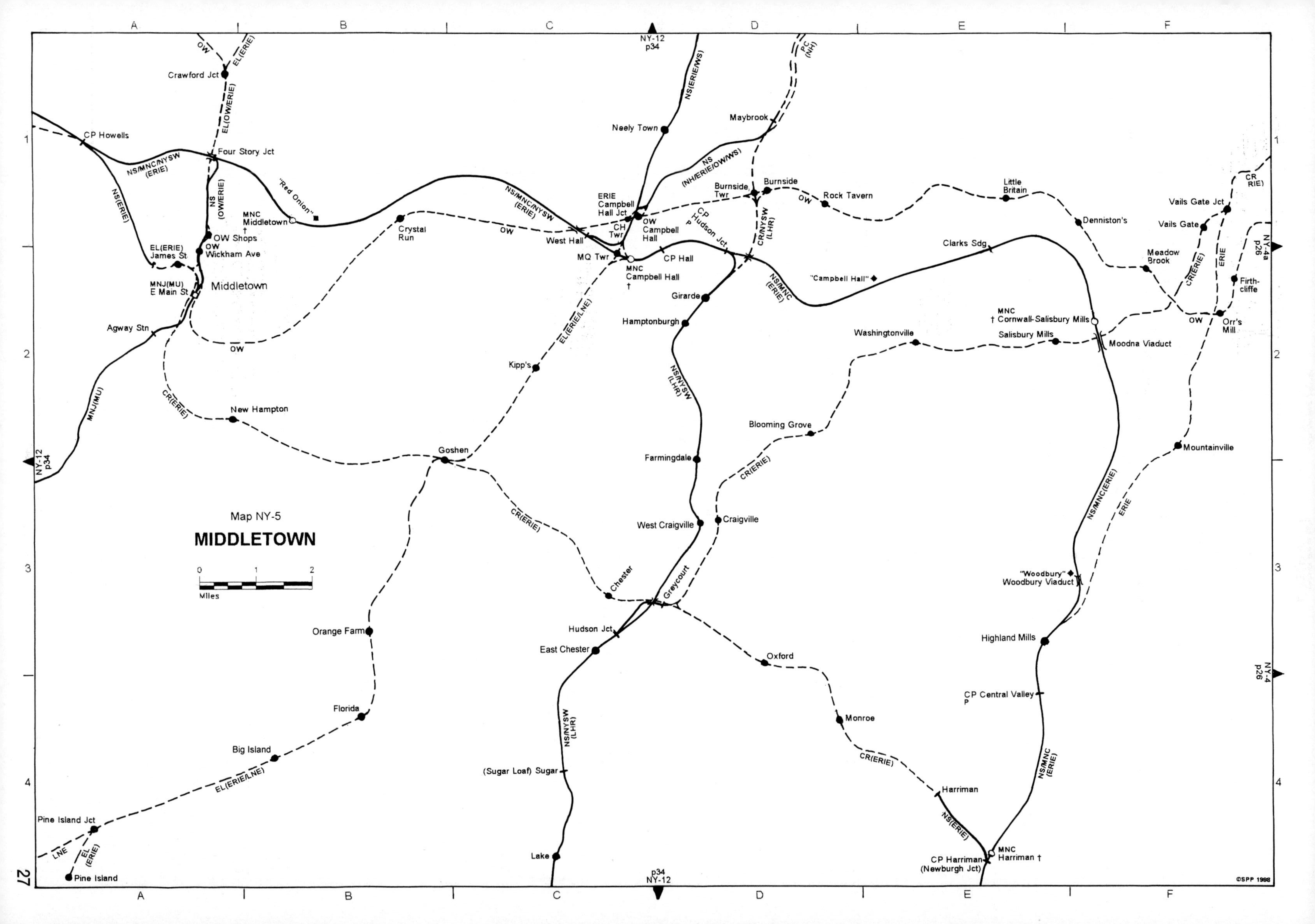
Map NY-5
MIDDLETOWN
0
1
2
Miles
NY-12
p34
NY-4a
p26
NY-4
p26
©SPP 1998
Crawford Jct
CP Howells
Four Story Jct
"Red Onion"
MNC
Middletown
†
OW Shops
OW
Wickham Ave
EL(ERIE)
James St
MNJ(MU)
E Main St
Middletown
Agway Stn
New Hampton
Crystal
Run
West Hall
MQ Twr
ERIE
Campbell
Hall Jct
CH
Twr
OW
Campbell
Hall
MNC
Campbell Hall
†
CP Hall
CP
Hudson Jct
Neely Town
Maybrook
Burnside
Twr
Burnside
Rock Tavern
Little
Britain
Denniston's
Vails Gate Jct
Vails Gate
Meadow
Brook
Firth-
cliffe
Orr's
Mill
Clarks Sdg
"Campbell Hall"
Girarde
Hamptonburgh
Kipp's
Goshen
Washingtonville
MNC
† Cornwall-Salisbury Mills
Salisbury Mills
Moodna Viaduct
Blooming Grove
Mountainville
Farmingdale
West Craigville
Craigville
Chester
Greycourt
Hudson Jct
East Chester
Orange Farm
Florida
Big Island
Pine Island Jct
Pine Island
(Sugar Loaf) Sugar
Lake
Oxford
Monroe
Harriman
CP Harriman
(Newburgh Jct)
MNC
Harriman †
CP Central Valley
"Woodbury"
Woodbury Viaduct
Highland Mills
OW
EL(ERIE)
EL(OW/ERIE)
NS/MNC/NYSW
(ERIE)
NS(ERIE)
NS
(OW/ERIE)
MNJ(MU)
CR(ERIE)
EL(ERIE/LNE)
NS(ERIE/WS)
NS
(NH/ERIE/OW/WS)
PC
(NH)
CR/NYSW
(LHR)
NS/MNC
(ERIE)
NS/NYSW
(LHR)
NS/MNC(ERIE)
ERIE
CR
RIE)
LNE
A
B
C
D
E
F
1
2
3
4

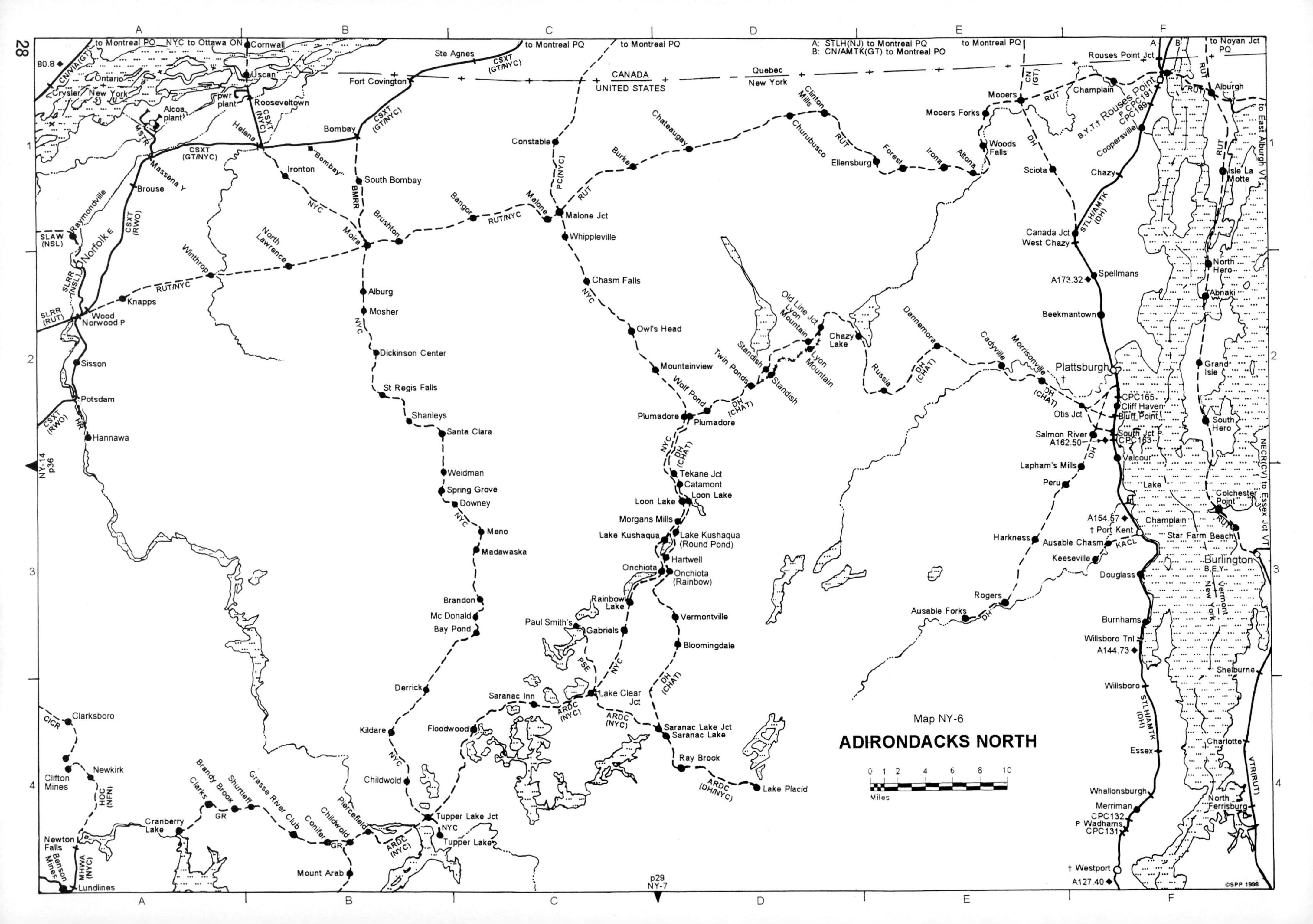

Map NY-6
ADIRONDACKS NORTH
0 1 2 4 6 8 10
Miles
A: STLH(NJ) to Montreal PQ
B: CN/AMTK(GT) to Montreal PQ
CANADA
UNITED STATES
Quebec
New York
Vermont
New York
©SPP 1998
to Montreal PQ
NYC to Ottawa ON
to Noyan Jct PQ
to East Alburgh VT
NECR(CV) to Essex Jct VT
80.8
CN/VIA(GT)
Ontario
New York
Crysler
Cornwall
Uscan
pwr plant
Alcoa plant
Rooseveltown
MSTR
Helena
CSXT (NYC)
CSXT (GT/NYC)
Massena Y
Brouse
Ironton
Bombay
Ste Agnes
Fort Covington
South Bombay
BMRR
Moira
Brushton
Bangor
RUT/NYC
Malone
Malone Jct
Whippleville
Constable
PC(NYC)
Burke
Chateaugay
Churubusco
Clinton Mills
Ellensburg
Forest
Irona
Altona
Woods Falls
Mooers Forks
Mooers
CN (GT)
Champlain
Rouses Point Jct
Rouses Point
CPC191
CPC189
B.Y.T.
Coopersville
Chazy
Sciota
STLH/AMTK (DH)
Canada Jct
West Chazy
Spellmans
A173.32
Beekmantown
Alburgh
Isle La Motte
North Hero
Abnaki
Grand Isle
South Hero
Raymondville
Norfolk
SLAW (NSL)
SLRR (NSL)
SLRR (RUT)
CSXT (RWO)
Wood
Norwood
Knapps
Winthrop
North Lawrence
Alburg
Mosher
Dickinson Center
St Regis Falls
Shanleys
Santa Clara
Weidman
Spring Grove
Downey
Meno
Madawaska
Brandon
Mc Donald
Bay Pond
Derrick
Kildare
Childwold
Sisson
Potsdam
HR
Hannawa
NY-14 p36
Chasm Falls
Owl's Head
Mountainview
Wolf Pond
Plumadore
Twin Ponds
Standish
Old Line Jct
Lyon Mountain
Chazy Lake
Dannemora
Russia
DH (CHAT)
Cadyville
Morrisonville
Plattsburgh
CPC165
Cliff Haven
Bluff Point
Otis Jct
Salmon River
A162.50
South Jct
CPC163
Valcour
Lapham's Mills
Peru
Lake
Champlain
A154.57
Port Kent
Ausable Chasm
KACL
Star Farm Beach
Colchester Point
Burlington
B.E.Y.
Keeseville
Harkness
Douglass
Rogers
Ausable Forks
Burnhams
Willsboro Tnl
A144.73
Willsboro
Essex
Shelburne
Charlotte
VTR(RUT)
Whallonsburgh
Merriman
CPC132
Wadhams
CPC131
North Ferrisburg
Westport
A127.40
Tekane Jct
Catamont
Loon Lake
Morgans Mills
Lake Kushaqua
Lake Kushaqua (Round Pond)
Hartwell
Onchiota
Onchiota (Rainbow)
Rainbow Lake
Paul Smith's
Gabriels
PSE
Vermontville
Bloomingdale
Lake Clear Jct
Saranac Inn
ARDC (NYC)
Saranac Lake Jct
Saranac Lake
Ray Brook
ARDC (DH/NYC)
Lake Placid
Floodwood
Tupper Lake Jct
Tupper Lake
Piercefield
Conifer
Grasse River Club
Shurtleff
Brandy Brook
Clarks
GR
Cranberry Lake
Mount Arab
Clarksboro
CICR
Newkirk
Clifton Mines
HOC (NFN)
Newton Falls
Benson Mines
MHWA (NYC)
Lundlines
p29 NY-7

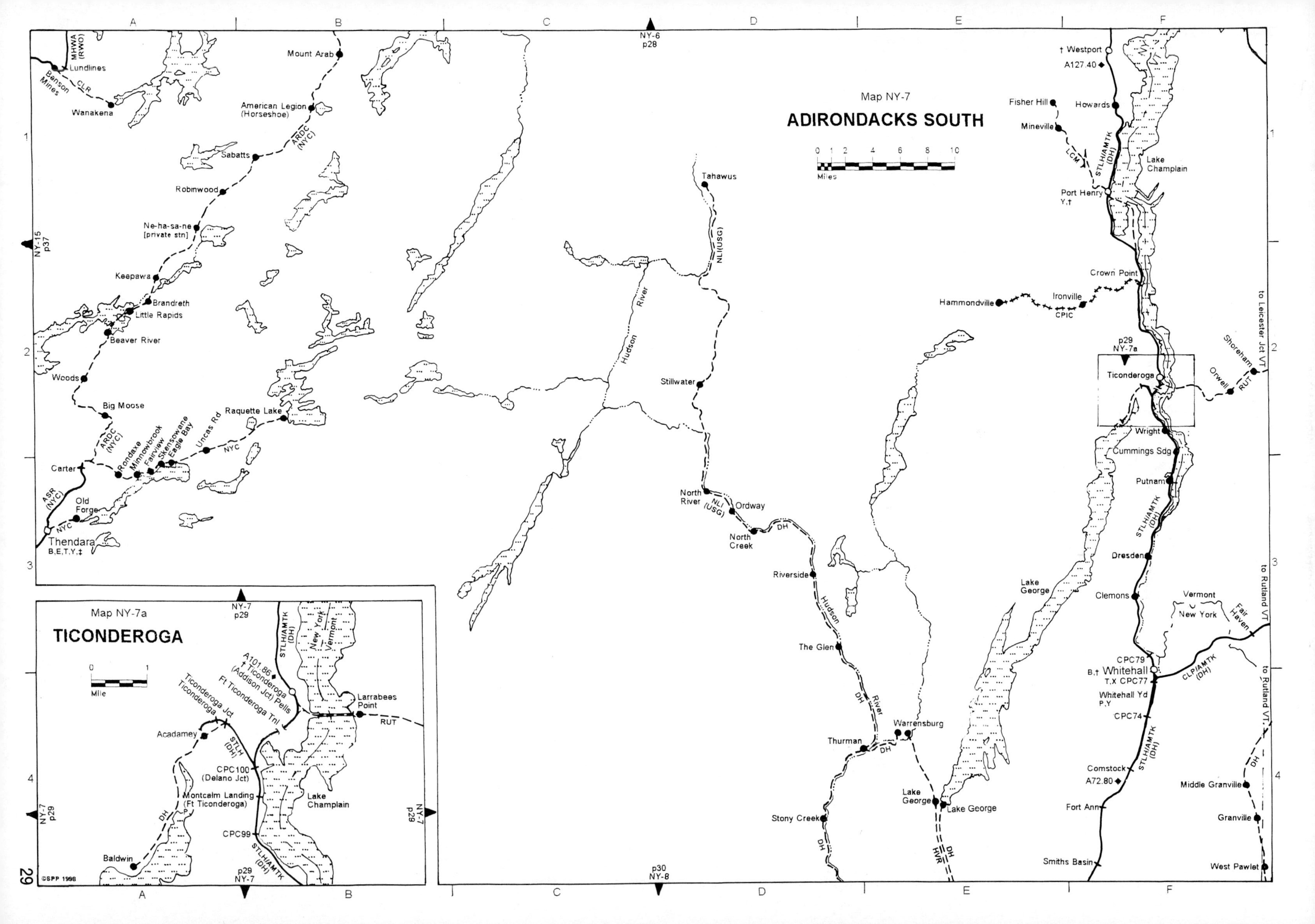

Map NY-7
ADIRONDACKS SOUTH
0 1 2 4 6 8 10
Miles
NY-6 p28
NY-15 p37
p30 NY-8
to Leicester Jct VT
to Rutland VT
to Rutland VT.
MHWA (RWO)
Lundlines
Benson Mines
CLR
Wanakena
Mount Arab
American Legion (Horseshoe)
ARDC (NYC)
Sabatts
Robinwood
Ne-ha-sa-ne [private stn]
Keepawa
Brandreth
Little Rapids
Beaver River
Woods
Big Moose
Raquette Lake
Uncas Rd
NYC
Eagle Bay
Skensowane
Fairview
Minnowbrook
Rondaxe
Carter
ASR (NYC)
Old Forge
Thendara
B,E,T,Y,‡
Tahawus
NLI(USG)
Hudson River
Stillwater
North River
NLI (USG)
Ordway
North Creek
DH
Riverside
The Glen
Thurman
Warrensburg
Stony Creek
Lake George
HVR
Hammondville
Ironville
CPIC
Crown Point
† Westport
A127.40 ◆
Fisher Hill
Mineville
LCM
Howards
STLH/AMTK (DH)
Lake Champlain
Port Henry
Y,†
p29 NY-7a
Ticonderoga
Shoreham
Orwell
RUT
Wright
Cummings Sdg
Putnam
Dresden
Clemons
Vermont
New York
Fair Haven
CPC79
B,† Whitehall
T,X CPC77
Whitehall Yd
P,Y
CPC74
CLP/AMTK (DH)
Comstock
A72.80 ◆
Fort Ann
Smiths Basin
Middle Granville
Granville
West Pawlet
Map NY-7a
TICONDEROGA
0 1
Mile
NY-7 p29
STLH/AMTK (DH)
New York
Vermont
A101.86 ◆
† Ticonderoga (Addison Jct) Pells
Ft Ticonderoga Tnl
Larrabees Point
Ticonderoga Jct
Ticonderoga
Acadamey
STLH (DH)
CPC100 (Delano Jct)
Montcalm Landing (Ft Ticonderoga)
P
CPC99
Baldwin
©SPP 1998

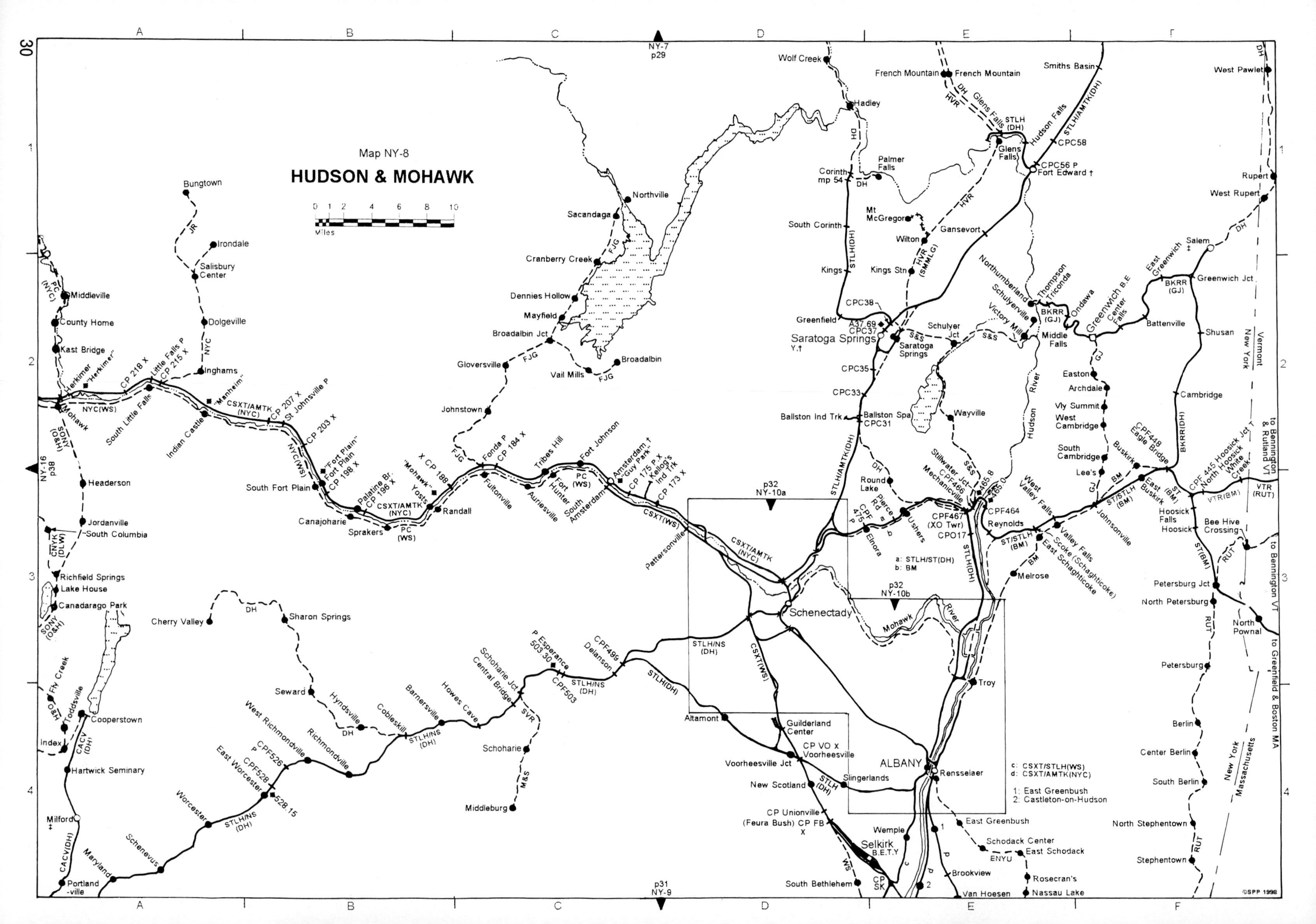
Map NY-8
HUDSON & MOHAWK
0 1 2 4 6 8 10
Miles
©SPP 1998
Vermont
New York
Massachusetts
to Bennington & Rutland VT
to Bennington VT
to Greenfield & Boston MA
West Pawlet
Rupert
West Rupert
Salem
East Greenwich
Greenwich Jct
Shusan
Cambridge
Battenville
Greenwich B.E
Center Falls
CPF449 Eagle Bridge
Buskirk
East Buskirk
Hoosick Falls
Hoosick
Bee Hive Crossing
CPF 445 Hoosick Jct
North Hoosick
White Creek
Petersburg Jct
North Petersburg
North Pownal
Petersburg
Berlin
Center Berlin
South Berlin
North Stephentown
Stephentown
Johnsonville
Easton
Archdale
Vly Summit
West Cambridge
South Cambridge
Lee's
Valley Falls
West Valley Falls
Scoke (Schaghticoke)
East Schaghticoke
Melrose
Smiths Basin
Hudson Falls
CPC58
CPC56 P
Fort Edward
Thompson
Triconda
Ondawa
Middle Falls
Northumberland
Schuylerville
Victory Mill
Hudson River
Glens Falls
French Mountain
Wolf Creek
Hadley
Gansevort
Wilton
Mt McGregor
Kings Stn
Palmer Falls
Corinth mp 54
South Corinth
Kings
Greenfield
CPC38
A37.69
CPC37
Saratoga Springs
Schuyler Jct
Wayville
Ballston Spa
CPC31
CPC33
CPC35
Ballston Ind Trk
Round Lake
Pierce Rd
CPF 475
Elnora
Ushers
Stillwater Jct
CPF466
Mechanicville
CPF464
Reynolds
CPF467 (XO Twr)
CPO17
a: STLH/ST(DH)
b: BM
Troy
Rensselaer
ALBANY
Schenectady
Mohawk River
c: CSXT/STLH(WS)
d: CSXT/AMTK(NYC)
1: East Greenbush
2: Castleton-on-Hudson
East Greenbush
Schodack Center
East Schodack
Rosecran's
Nassau Lake
Brookview
Van Hoesen
Wemple
Selkirk
B.E.T.Y
CP SK
Slingerlands
Guilderland Center
CP VO X Voorheesville
Voorheesville Jct
New Scotland
CP Unionville (Feura Bush) CP FB
South Bethlehem
Altamont
Northville
Sacandaga
Cranberry Creek
Dennies Hollow
Mayfield
Broadalbin Jct
Broadalbin
Vail Mills
Gloversville
Johnstown
Pattersonville
Amsterdam
"Guy Park"
CP 175 P X
Kellogg's Ind Trk
CP 173 X
South Amsterdam
Fort Johnson
Fort Hunter
Tribes Hill
Auriesville
Fultonville
Fonda P
CP 184 X
X CP 188
"Mohawk"
Yosts
Randall
Sprakers
Canajoharie
Palatine Br.
CP 196 X
"Fort Plain"
Fort Plain
CP 198 X
South Fort Plain
CP 203 X
CP 207 X
St Johnsville P
CPF495
Delanson
P Esperance 503.30
CPF503
Schoharie Jct
Central Bridge
Schoharie
Middleburg
Howes Cave
Barnerville
Cobleskill
Hyndsville
Richmondville
West Richmondville
CPF526 P
CPF528
528.15
Seward
Sharon Springs
Cherry Valley
East Worcester
Worcester
Schenevus
Maryland
Portland-ville
Milford
Cooperstown
Hartwick Seminary
Index
Toddsville
Fly Creek
Canadarago Park
Lake House
Richfield Springs
South Columbia
Jordanville
Headerson
Mohawk
Herkimer
"Herkimer"
South Little Falls
Little Falls P
CP 215 X
CP 218 X
Indian Castle
"Manheim"
Inghams
Dolgeville
Salisbury Center
Irondale
Bungtown
Middleville
County Home
Kast Bridge
NY-7 p29
NY-9 p31
p32 NY-10a
p32 NY-10b
NY-16 p38

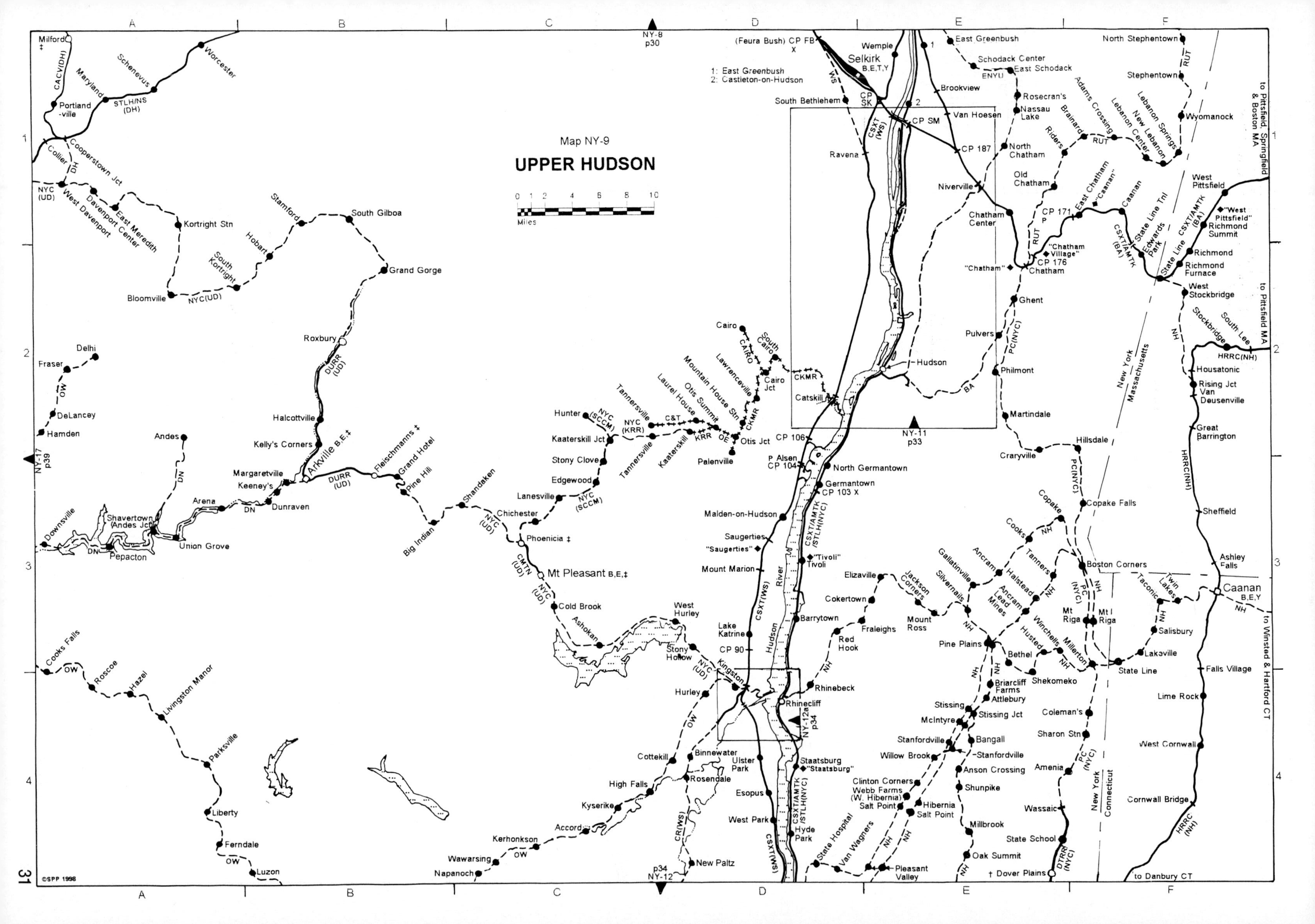
Map NY-9
UPPER HUDSON
0 1 2 4 6 8 10
Miles
1: East Greenbush
2: Castleton-on-Hudson
NY-8 p30
NY-11 p33
NY-12a p34
p34 NY-12
NY-17 p39
to Pittsfield, Springfield & Boston MA
to Pittsfield MA
to Winsted & Hartford CT
to Danbury CT
New York
Massachusetts
New York
Connecticut
Hudson River
Milford ‡
Worcester
Schenevus
Maryland
Portland -ville
STLH/NS (DH)
CACV(DH)
Cooperstown Jct
Collier
DH
NYC (UD)
West Davenport
Davenport Center
East Meredith
Kortright Stn
Stamford
Hobart
South Kortright
Bloomville
NYC(UD)
South Gilboa
Grand Gorge
Roxbury
DURR (UD)
Halcottville
Kelly's Corners
Arkville B.E.‡
Margaretville
Keeney's
Dunraven
Andes
Arena
DN
Shavertown (Andes Jct)
Union Grove
Pepacton
Downsville
Delhi
Fraser
OW
DeLancey
Hamden
Fleischmanns ‡
Grand Hotel
Pine Hill
Big Indian
Shandaken
Chichester
Phoenicia ‡
CMTN (UD)
Mt Pleasant B.E.‡
Cold Brook
Ashokan
Lanesville
Edgewood
Stony Clove
Kaaterskill Jct
Hunter
NYC (SCCM)
Tannersville
NYC (KRR)
C&T
Laurel House
Otis Summit
Mountain House Stn
Lawrenceville
Cairo
South Cairo
CAIRO
Cairo Jct
CKMR
Catskill
Otis Jct
OE
KRR
Kaaterskill
Palenville
Cooks Falls
Roscoe
Hazel
Livingston Manor
Parksville
Liberty
Ferndale
Luzon
Napanoch
Wawarsing
Kerhonkson
Accord
Kyserike
High Falls
Rosendale
Cottekill
Binnewater
Hurley
West Hurley
Stony Hollow
Kingston
CP 90
Lake Katrine
Mount Marion
"Saugerties"
Saugerties
Malden-on-Hudson
CP 104
P Alsen
CP 106
New Paltz
CR(WS)
Ulster Park
Esopus
West Park
CSXT(WS)
(Feura Bush) CP FB X
Wemple
Selkirk B.E.T.Y
South Bethlehem
CP SK
Ravena
CP SM
Van Hoesen
CP 187
Brookview
Niverville
Chatham Center
"Chatham"
Hudson
BA
Pulvers
Philmont
Martindale
Craryville
Hillsdale
PC(NYC)
Copake Falls
Ghent
CP 176
Chatham
"Chatham Village"
CP 171
East Chatham
"Caanan"
Caanan
State Line Tnl
Edwards Park
State Line
CSXT/AMTK (BA)
Richmond
Richmond Furnace
"West Pittsfield"
Richmond Summit
West Pittsfield
West Stockbridge
Stockbridge
South Lee
HRRC(NH)
Housatonic
Rising Jct
Van Deusenville
Great Barrington
Sheffield
Ashley Falls
Caanan B.E.Y
Falls Village
Lime Rock
West Cornwall
Cornwall Bridge
Old Chatham
North Chatham
Riders
Brainard
Adams Crossing
Lebanon Center
New Lebanon
Lebanon Springs
Wyomanock
Stephentown
North Stephentown
RUT
Rosecran's
Nassau Lake
Schodack Center
East Schodack
ENYU
East Greenbush
North Germantown
Germantown
CP 103 X
CSXT/AMTK /STLH(NYC)
"Tivoli"
Tivoli
Barrytown
Red Hook
Rhinebeck
Rhinecliff
Staatsburg
"Staatsburg"
Hyde Park
State Hospital
Van Wagners
Pleasant Valley
Elizaville
Cokertown
Fraleighs
Jackson Corners
Mount Ross
Silvernails
Gallatinville
Ancram
Ancram Lead Mines
Halstead
Tanners
Cooks
Copake
Boston Corners
Mt Riga
Mt I Riga
Taconic
Twin Lakes
Salisbury
Lakeville
State Line
Millerton
Winchells
Husted
Bethel
Shekomeko
Pine Plains
Briarcliff Farms
Attlebury
Stissing
Stissing Jct
McIntyre
Bangall
Stanfordville
Willow Brook
Anson Crossing
Shunpike
Clinton Corners
Webb Farms (W. Hibernia)
Salt Point
Hibernia
Millbrook
Oak Summit
Coleman's
Sharon Stn
Amenia
Wassaic
State School
DTRR (NYC)
† Dover Plains
©SPP 1998

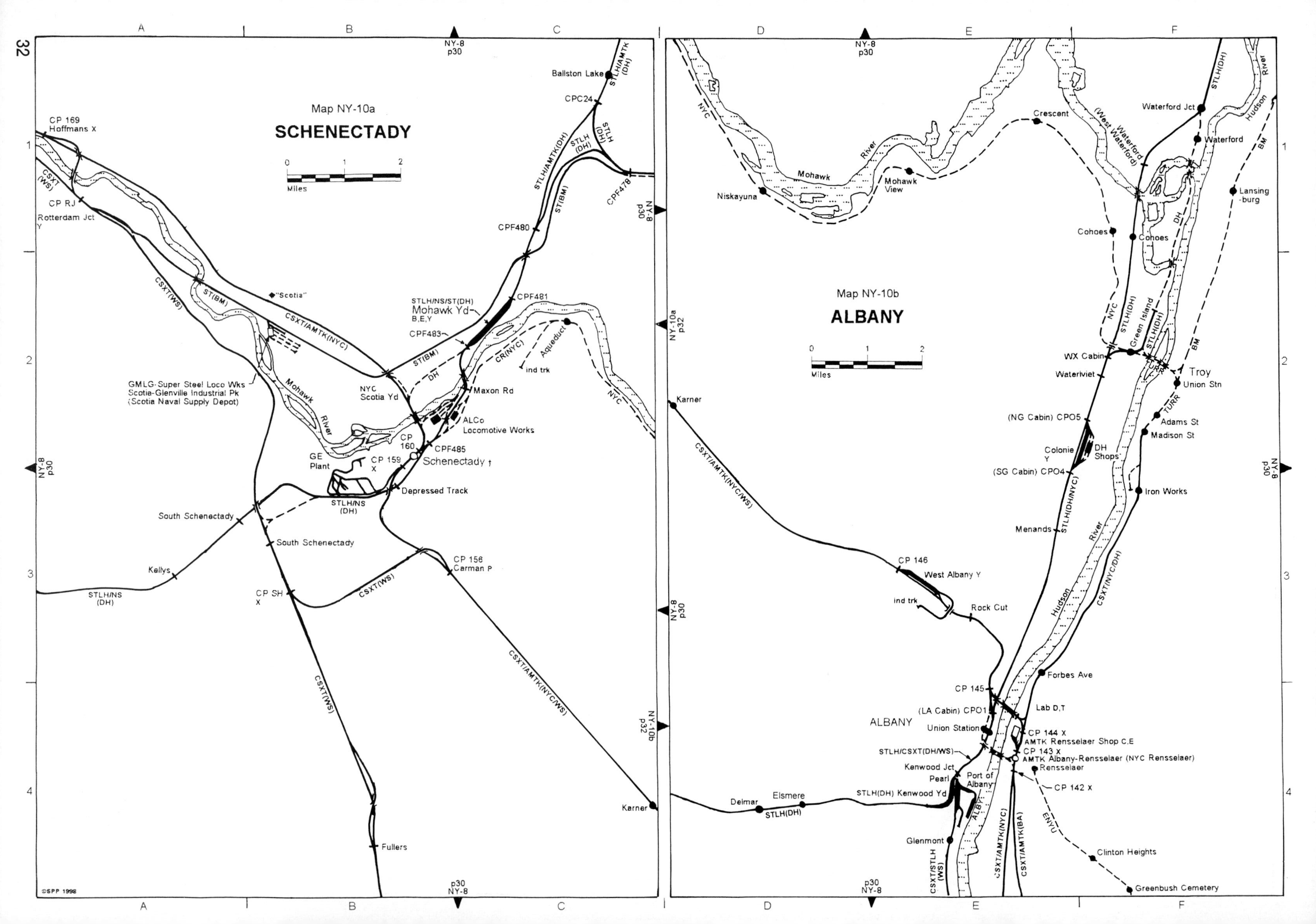
Map NY-10a
SCHENECTADY
0 1 2
Miles
CP 169
Hoffmans X
CSXT (WS)
CP RJ
Rotterdam Jct
Y
Ballston Lake
STLH/AMTK (DH)
CPC24
STLH (DH)
STLH (DH)
STLH/AMTK(DH)
ST(BM)
CPF478
CPF480
CPF481
STLH/NS/ST(DH)
Mohawk Yd
B,E,Y
CPF483
ST(BM)
DH
CR(NYC)
Aqueduct
ind trk
NYC
"Scotia"
ST(BM)
CSXT(WS)
CSXT/AMTK(NYC)
GMLG-Super Steel Loco Wks
Scotia-Glenville Industrial Pk
(Scotia Naval Supply Depot)
Mohawk
River
NYC
Scotia Yd
Maxon Rd
ALCo
Locomotive Works
CP
160
CPF485
Schenectady †
GE
Plant
CP 159
X
Depressed Track
STLH/NS
(DH)
South Schenectady
South Schenectady
Kellys
STLH/NS
(DH)
CP SH
X
CSXT(WS)
CP 156
Carman P
CSXT(WS)
CSXT/AMTK(NYC/WS)
Karner
Fullers
NY-8
p30
NY-10a
p32
NY-10b
p32
©SPP 1998
Map NY-10b
ALBANY
0 1 2
Miles
NYC
Mohawk
River
Niskayuna
Mohawk
View
Crescent
(West Waterford)
West Waterford
Waterford Jct
Waterford
STLH(DH)
Hudson
River
BM
Lansing
-burg
Cohoes
Cohoes
DH
NYC
STLH(DH)
Green Island
STLH(DH)
BM
WX Cabin
Watervliet
Troy
Union Stn
TURR
Adams St
Madison St
Karner
(NG Cabin) CPO5
Colonie
Y
DH
Shops
(SG Cabin) CPO4
STLH(DH/NYC)
Iron Works
Menands
River
Hudson
CSXT(NYC/DH)
CSXT/AMTK(NYC/WS)
CP 146
West Albany Y
ind trk
Rock Cut
Forbes Ave
CP 145
Lab D,T
(LA Cabin) CPO1
ALBANY
Union Station
CP 144 X
AMTK Rensselaer Shop C,E
CP 143 X
AMTK Albany-Rensselaer (NYC Rensselaer)
STLH/CSXT(DH/WS)
Rensselaer
Kenwood Jct
Pearl
Port of
Albany
CP 142 X
Elsmere
Delmar
STLH(DH)
STLH(DH) Kenwood Yd
ALBY
ENYU
Glenmont
Clinton Heights
Greenbush Cemetery
CSXT/STLH
(WS)
CSXT/AMTK(NYC)
CSXT/AMTK(BA)

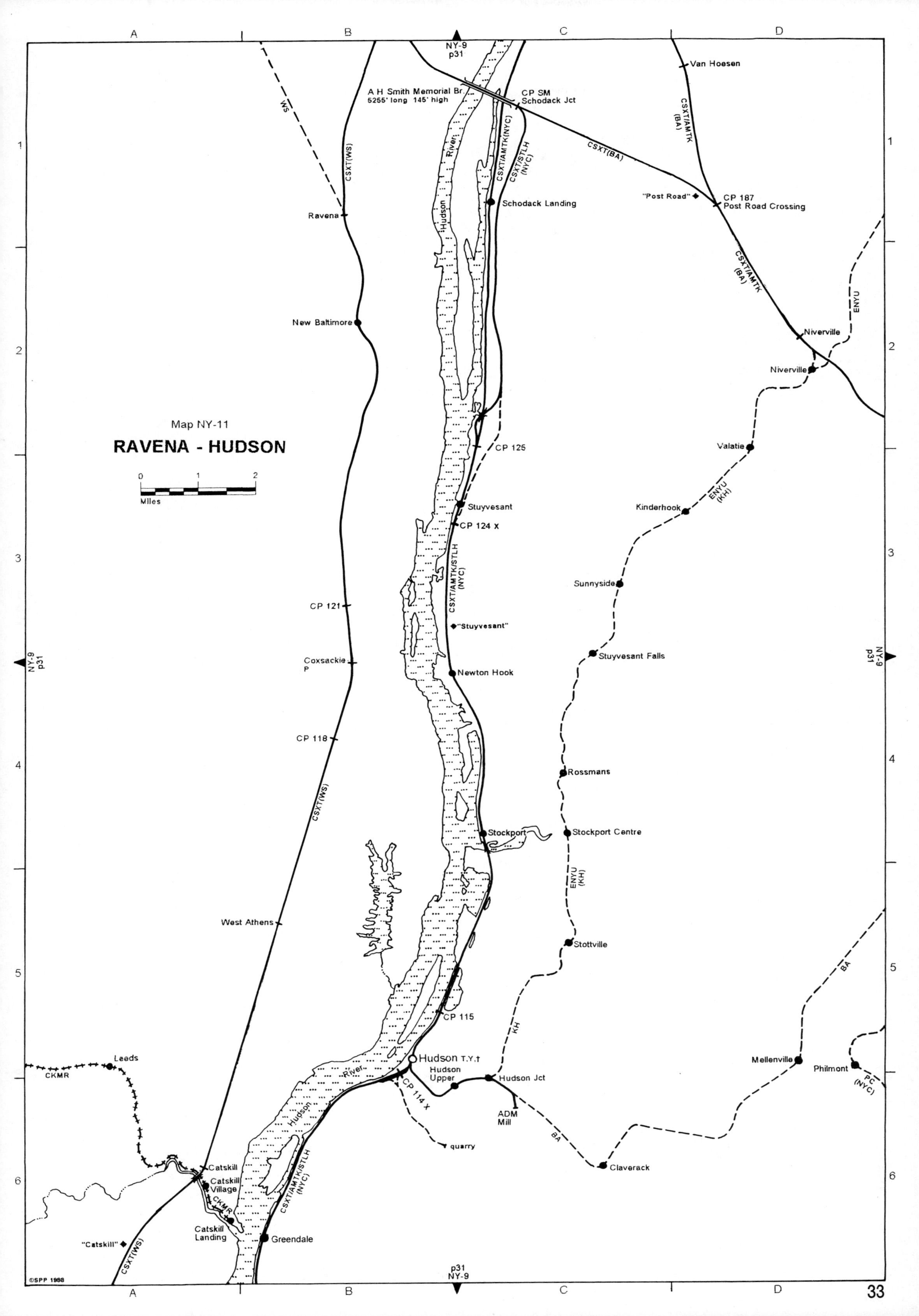

Map NY-11
RAVENA - HUDSON
0
1
2
Miles
NY-9
p31
A H Smith Memorial Br.
5255' long 145' high
CP SM
Schodack Jct
Van Hoesen
CSXT/AMTK
(BA)
CSXT(BA)
WS
CSXT(WS)
Hudson River
CSXT/AMTK(NYC)
CSXT/STLH
(NYC)
Schodack Landing
"Post Road"
CP 187
Post Road Crossing
Ravena
New Baltimore
Niverville
Niverville
ENYU
CP 125
Valatie
Stuyvesant
CP 124 x
Kinderhook
ENYU
(KH)
CSXT/AMTK/STLH
(NYC)
Sunnyside
CP 121
"Stuyvesant"
Coxsackie
P
Newton Hook
Stuyvesant Falls
CP 118
Rossmans
Stockport
Stockport Centre
West Athens
Stottville
CP 115
KH
BA
Leeds
CKMR
Hudson T.Y.†
Hudson
Upper
Hudson Jct
CP 114 x
ADM
Mill
quarry
Mellenville
Philmont
PC
(NYC)
Claverack
Catskill
Catskill
Village
CKMR
Catskill
Landing
"Catskill"
Greendale
Hudson River
CSXT(WS)
©SPP 1988
p31
NY-9

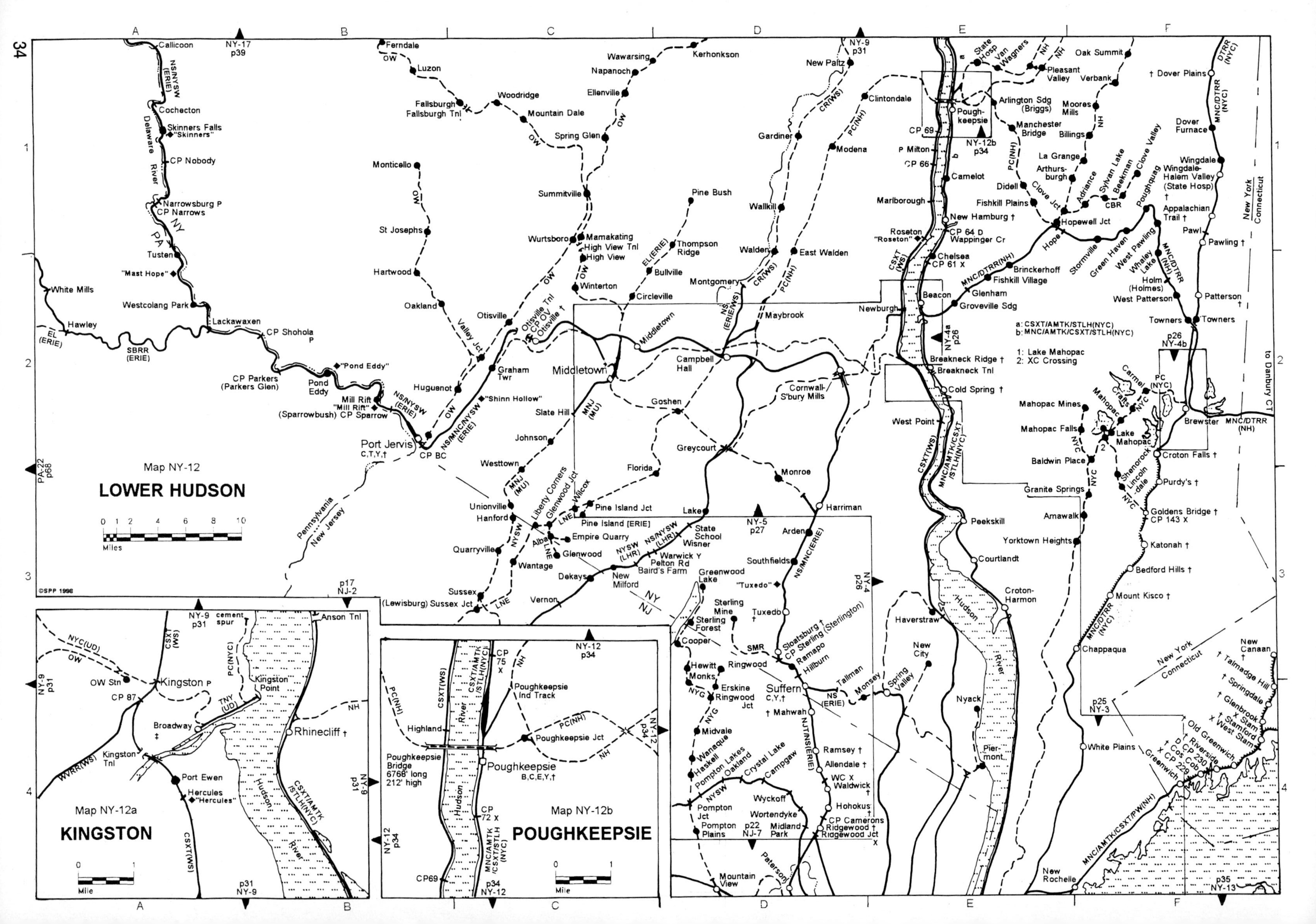
Map NY-12
LOWER HUDSON
0 1 2 4 6 8 10
Miles
Map NY-12a
KINGSTON
Map NY-12b
POUGHKEEPSIE
Mile
a: CSXT/AMTK/STLH(NYC)
b: MNC/AMTK/CSXT/STLH(NYC)
1: Lake Mahopac
2: XC Crossing
to Danbury CT
New York
Connecticut
Pennsylvania
New Jersey
NY
PA
NY
NJ
Delaware River
Hudson River
Callicoon
Cochecton
Skinners Falls
"Skinners"
CP Nobody
Narrowsburg P
CP Narrows
Tusten
"Mast Hope"
White Mills
Westcolang Park
Hawley
Lackawaxen
CP Shohola
CP Parkers
(Parkers Glen)
Pond Eddy
"Pond Eddy"
Mill Rift
"Mill Rift"
(Sparrowbush) CP Sparrow
Port Jervis
C,T,Y,†
CP BC
Ferndale
Luzon
Fallsburgh
Fallsburgh Tnl
Woodridge
Mountain Dale
Spring Glen
Ellenville
Napanoch
Wawarsing
Kerhonkson
Monticello
St Josephs
Hartwood
Oakland
Valley Jct
Otisville
Otisville Tnl
CP OV
Summitville
Wurtsboro
Mamakating
High View Tnl
High View
Winterton
Graham Twr
"Shinn Hollow"
Huguenot
Middletown
Slate Hill
Johnson
Westtown
Unionville
Hanford
Quarryville
Sussex
(Lewisburg) Sussex Jct
Vernon
Dekays
New Milford
Wantage
Glenwood
Empire Quarry
Liberty Corners
Glenwood Jct
Wilcox
Pine Island Jct
Pine Island [ERIE]
Florida
Goshen
Campbell Hall
Greycourt
Monroe
Harriman
Arden
Southfields
Lake
State School
Wisner
Warwick Y
Pelton Rd
Baird's Farm
Greenwood Lake
"Tuxedo"
Tuxedo
Sterling Mine
Sterling Forest
Cooper
Hewitt
Monks
Erskine
Ringwood Jct
Ringwood
Sloatsburg
CP Sterling (Sterlington)
Ramapo
Hillburn
Suffern
C,Y,†
Mahwah
Tallman
Monsey
Spring Valley
New City
Midvale
Wanaque
Haskell
Pompton Lakes
Oakland
Crystal Lake
Campgaw
Wyckoff
Wortendyke
Midland Park
Pompton Jct
Pompton Plains
Mountain View
Paterson
Ramsey
Allendale
WC X
Waldwick
Hohokus
CP Camerons
Ridgewood
Ridgewood Jct
Circleville
Bullville
Thompson Ridge
Pine Bush
Montgomery
Maybrook
Walden
East Walden
Wallkill
Gardiner
Modena
New Paltz
Clintondale
Newburgh
Beacon
Cornwall-
S'bury Mills
West Point
Breakneck Ridge
Breakneck Tnl
Cold Spring
Groveville Sdg
Glenham
Fishkill Village
Brinckerhoff
Chelsea
CP 61 X
CP 64 D
Wappinger Cr
New Hamburg
Roseton
"Roseton"
Marlborough
Camelot
CP 66
P Milton
CP 69
Pough-
keepsie
Arlington Sdg
(Briggs)
Manchester Bridge
State Hosp
Van Wagners
Pleasant Valley
Oak Summit
Verbank
Moores Mills
Billings
La Grange
Arthursburgh
Didell
Clove Jct
Fishkill Plains
Hopewell Jct
Adriance
Sylvan Lake
Beekman
CBR
Clove Valley
Poughquag
Hope
Stormville
Green Haven
West Pawling
Whaley Lake
Holm
(Holmes)
West Patterson
Towners
Patterson
Pawl
Pawling
Appalachian Trail
Wingdale
Wingdale-
Halem Valley
(State Hosp)
Dover Furnace
Dover Plains
Brewster
Croton Falls
Purdy's
Carmel
Crafts
Mahopac
Lake Mahopac
Mahopac Mines
Mahopac Falls
Baldwin Place
Shenorock
Lincoln-dale
Goldens Bridge
CP 143 X
Katonah
Bedford Hills
Mount Kisco
Chappaqua
Granite Springs
Amawalk
Yorktown Heights
Peekskill
Courtlandt
Croton-Harmon
Haverstraw
Nyack
Pier-
mont
White Plains
New Rochelle
Greenwich
Cos Cob
CP 229
CP 230
Riverside
Old Greenwich
Stamford
West Stam
Glenbrook
Springdale
Talmadge Hill
New Canaan
MNC/DTRR (NH)
MNC/DTRR (NYC)
MNC/AMTK/CSXT/PW(NH)
MNC/AMTK/CSXT/STLH(NYC)
CSXT(WS)
NS/NYSW (ERIE)
NS/MNC/NYSW (ERIE)
NS/MNC(ERIE)
NJT/NS(ERIE)
NYSW (LHR)
SBRR (ERIE)
EL (ERIE)
Kingston P
OW Stn
CP 87
Broadway
Kingston Point
Kingston Tnl
Port Ewen
Hercules
"Hercules"
Rhinecliff
Anson Tnl
cement spur
CSXT/AMTK/STLH(NYC)
WRR(WS)
TNY (UD)
NYC(UD)
PC(NYC)
Highland
Poughkeepsie Ind Track
Poughkeepsie Jct
Poughkeepsie
B,C,E,Y,†
Poughkeepsie Bridge
6768' long
212' high
CP 75 X
CP 72 X
CP69
PC(NH)
©SPP 1998

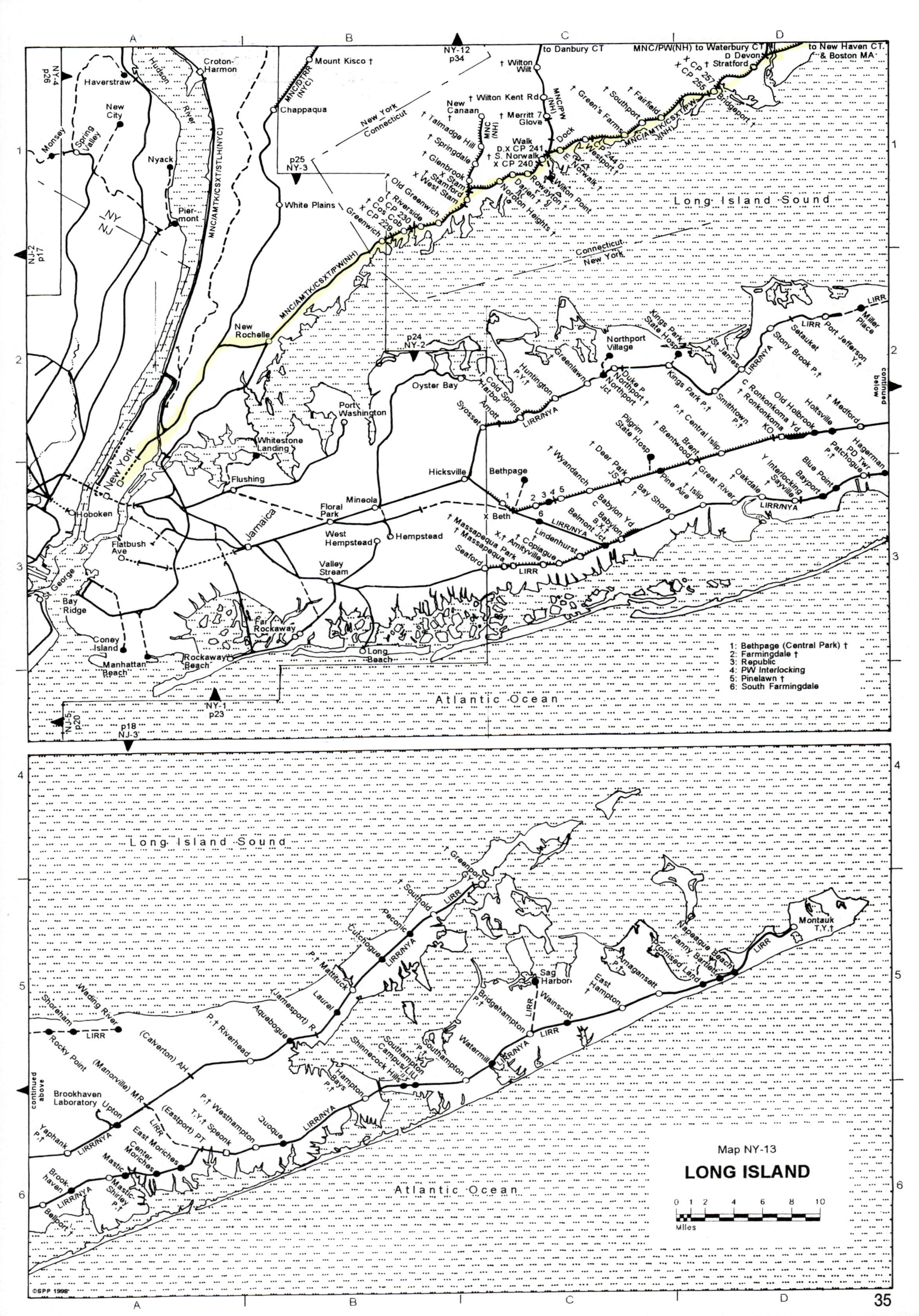
A
B
C
D
NY-4 p26
Haverstraw
Croton-Harmon
Hudson River
New City
Monsey
Spring Valley
Nyack
Piermont
NY
NJ
NJ-2 p17
MNC/AMTK/CSXT/STLH(NYC)
Mount Kisco †
MNC/D/TRR (NYC)
Chappaqua
White Plains
NY-12 p34
p25 NY-3
New York
Connecticut
to Danbury CT
MNC/PW(NH) to Waterbury CT
to New Haven CT. & Boston MA
D Devon
† Stratford
X CP 257
X CP 255
Bridgeport †
† Wilton Wilt
New Canaan †
† Wilton Kent Rd
MNC/PW (NH)
† Merritt 7 Glove
MNC (NH)
Walk
D.X CP 241
† S. Norwalk
X CP 240
Dock
† Green's Farms
† Southport
† Fairfield
MNC/AMTK/CSXT/PW (NH)
CP 244 D
Westport †
E. Norwalk †
Wilton Point
Rowayton †
Darien † g
Noroton Heights †
† Talmadge Hill
† Springdale
† Glenbrook
X Stam
† Stamford
X West Stam
Old Greenwich
† Riverside
D Cos Cob
X CP 229
CP 230
Greenwich
Long Island Sound
Connecticut
New York
MNC/AMTK/CSXT/PW(NH)
New Rochelle
New York
Whitestone Landing
Flushing
Hoboken
Flatbush Ave
St George
Bay Ridge
Coney Island
Manhattan Beach
Rockaway Beach
Far Rockaway
Jamaica
Port Washington
Oyster Bay
p24 NY-2
Cold Spring Harbor
Syosset
Amott
Huntington P,Y,†
Greenlawn
Northport Village
Duke P
Northport †
Northport Jct
Kings Park State Hosp
St James
Kings Park P,†
Smithtown P,†
LIRR/NYA
LIRR
Setauket
Stony Brook P,†
Port Jefferson Y,†
Miller Place
continued below
C Ronkonkoma
† Ronkonkoma Yd
KO
Old Holbrook
Holtsville
† Medford
P,† Central Islip
† Brentwood
Brent
Pilgrim State Hosp
† Wyandanch
† Deer Park
JS
Pine Aire
† Islip
Great River
Oakdale
Y Interlocking
Sayville
Bayport
Blue Point
Patchogue P,†
Hagerman PD Twr
Hicksville
Bethpage
1 2 3 4 5
x Beth
6
LIRR/NYA
Mineola
Floral Park
West Hempstead
Hempstead
Valley Stream
Long Beach
† Massapequa Park
† Massapequa
Seaford
x,† Amityville
† Copiague
Lindenhurst
Babylon Yd
Babylon B,†
Belmont Jct
C
Bay Shore
LIRR
1: Bethpage (Central Park) †
2: Farmingdale †
3: Republic
4: PW Interlocking
5: Pinelawn †
6: South Farmingdale
Atlantic Ocean
NY-1 p23
NJ-5 p20
p18 NJ-3
Long Island Sound
† Greenport
† Southold
Peconic
Cutchogue
LIRR/NYA
P,† Mattituck
Laurel
(Jamesport) R
Aquebogue
P,† Riverhead
(Calverton) AH
Wading River
Shoreham
Rocky Point
LIRR
(Manorville) MR
Brookhaven Laboratory
Upton
Yaphank P,†
LIRR/NYA
LIRR
(Eastport) PT
East Moriches
Center Moriches
Mastic
Mastic-Shirley P,†
Brookhaven
Bellport †
P,† Westhampton
T,Y,† Speonk
Quogue
Hampton Bays P,†
Shinnecock Hills
Southampton Campus/LIU
† Southampton
Bridgehampton P,†
Watermill
Sag Harbor
Wainscott
East Hampton †
Amagansett P,†
Promised Land
Fanny Bartlett
Napeague Beach
Montauk T,Y,†
continued above
Atlantic Ocean
Map NY-13
LONG ISLAND
0 1 2 4 6 8 10
Miles
©SPP 1998

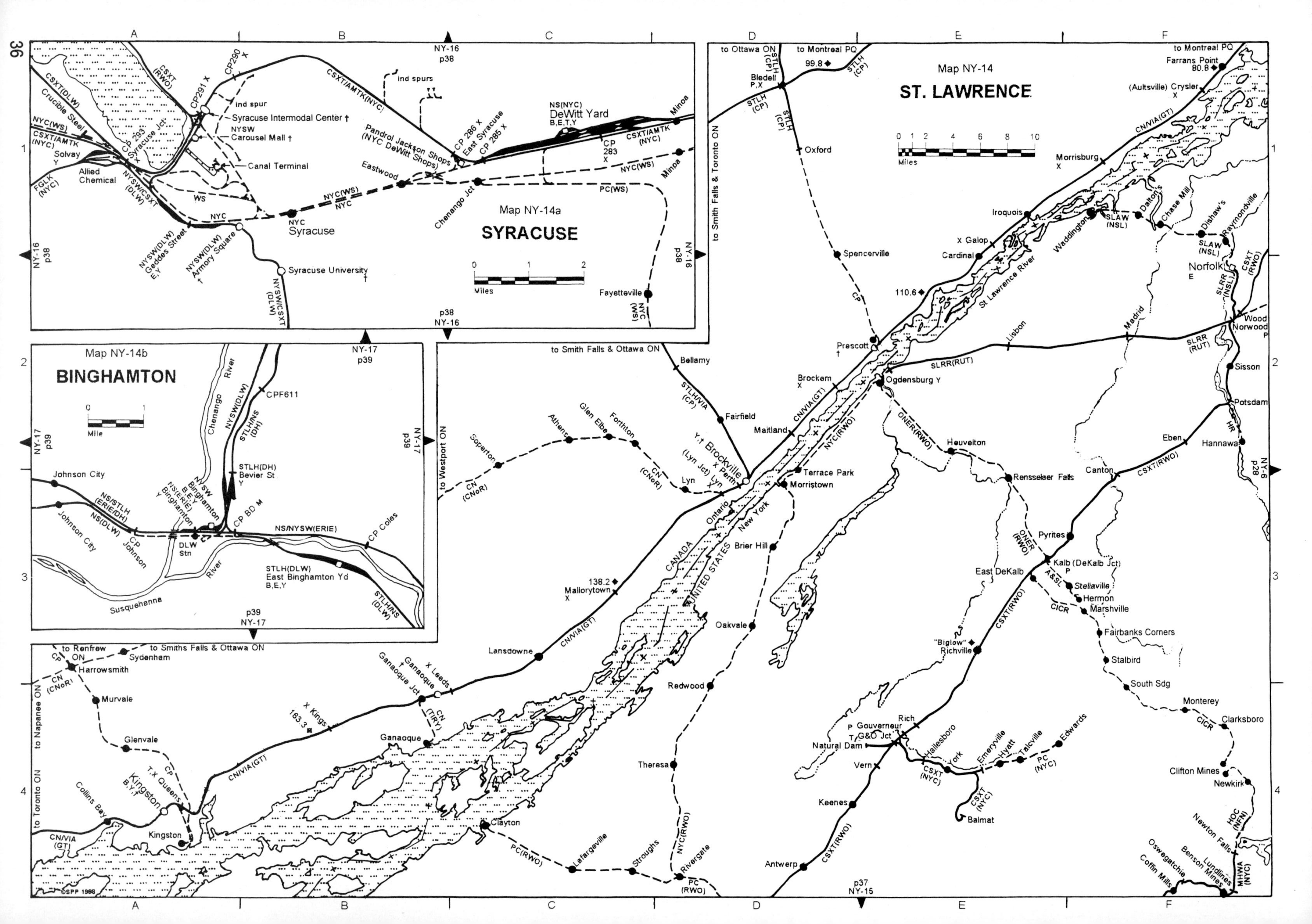
Map NY-14
ST. LAWRENCE
Miles
0 1 2 4 6 8 10
to Ottawa ON
to Montreal PQ
99.8
Bledell P,X
STLH (CP)
Oxford
Spencerville
CP
Prescott
110.6
Cardinal
X Galop
Iroquois
Morrisburg X
(Aultsville) Crysler X
Farrans Point 80.8
to Montreal PQ
CN/VIA(GT)
St Lawrence River
Waddington
SLAW (NSL)
Dalton's
Chase Mill
Dishaw's
Raymondville
Norfolk E
SLRR (NSL)
CSXT (RWO)
Wood
Norwood P
Madrid
Lisbon
SLRR (RUT)
Sisson
Potsdam
HR
Hannawa
Eben
NY-6 p28
Canton
CSXT(RWO)
Ogdensburg Y
ONER(RWO)
Heuvelton
Rensselaer Falls
Pyrites
Kalb (DeKalb Jct) P
East DeKalb
A&SL
Stellaville
Hermon
Marshville
CICR
Fairbanks Corners
Stalbird
South Sdg
Monterey
Clarksboro
Clifton Mines
Newkirk
HOC (NFN)
Newton Falls
Lundlines
Benson Mines
Oswegatchie
Coffin Mills
MHWA (NYC)
"Biglow" Richville
P Gouverneur T G&O Jct
Natural Dam
Rich
Hailesboro
York
Emeryville
Hyatt
Talcville
Edwards
PC (NYC)
CSXT (NYC)
Balmat
Vern
Keenes
Antwerp
p37 NY-15
to Smith Falls & Ottawa ON
Bellamy
STLH/VIA (CP)
Fairfield
Brockem X
Maitland
Terrace Park
Morristown
NYC(RWO)
Y,† Brockville
x Perth
(Lyn Jct)
Lyn
CN (CNoR)
Forthton
Glen Elbe
Athens
Soperton
to Westport ON
CANADA
UNITED STATES
Ontario
New York
Brier Hill
Oakvale
Redwood
Theresa
Rivergate
PC (RWO)
Stroughs
Lafargeville
PC(RWO)
Clayton
138.2
Mallorytown X
Lansdowne
x Leeds
Ganaoque †
Ganaoque Jct
CN (TIRY)
Ganaoque
X Kings
163.3
to Renfrew ON
to Smiths Falls & Ottawa ON
Sydenham
Harrowsmith
Murvale
Glenvale
to Napanee ON
to Toronto ON
T,X Queens
Kingston B,Y,†
Kingston
Collins Bay
©SPP 1988
Map NY-14a
SYRACUSE
Miles
0 1 2
NY-16 p38
CSXT (RWO)
CP290 X
CP291 X
ind spur
ind spurs
Syracuse Intermodal Center †
NYSW Carousel Mall †
Canal Terminal
CSXT/AMTK(NYC)
CSXT(DLW)
Crucible Steel
NYC(WS)
CSXT/AMTK (NYC)
Solvay Y
Allied Chemical
FGLK (NYC)
CP 293 X
Syracuse Jct
NYSW/CSXT (DLW)
WS
NYC
NYSW(DLW) Geddes Street E,Y
NYSW(DLW) Armory Square †
NYC Syracuse
Syracuse University †
NYSW/CSXT (DLW)
Pandrol Jackson Shops (NYC DeWitt Shops)
Eastwood
CP 286 X
East Syracuse
CP 285 X
NS(NYC) DeWitt Yard B,E,T,Y
CP 283 X
CSXT/AMTK (NYC)
Minoa
NYC(WS)
Chenango Jct
PC(WS)
Fayetteville
NYC (WS)
Map NY-14b
BINGHAMTON
Mile
0 1
NY-17 p39
Chenango River
NYSW(DLW)
STLH/NS (DH)
CPF611
STLH(DH) Bevier St Y
Johnson City
NS/STLH (ERIE/DH)
NS(DLW)
CP Johnson
Johnson City
NYSW Binghamton B,E,Y
NS(ERIE) Binghamton Y
CP BD
DLW Stn
NS/NYSW(ERIE)
CP Coles
STLH(DLW) East Binghamton Yd B,E,Y
STLH/NS (DLW)
Susquehanna River

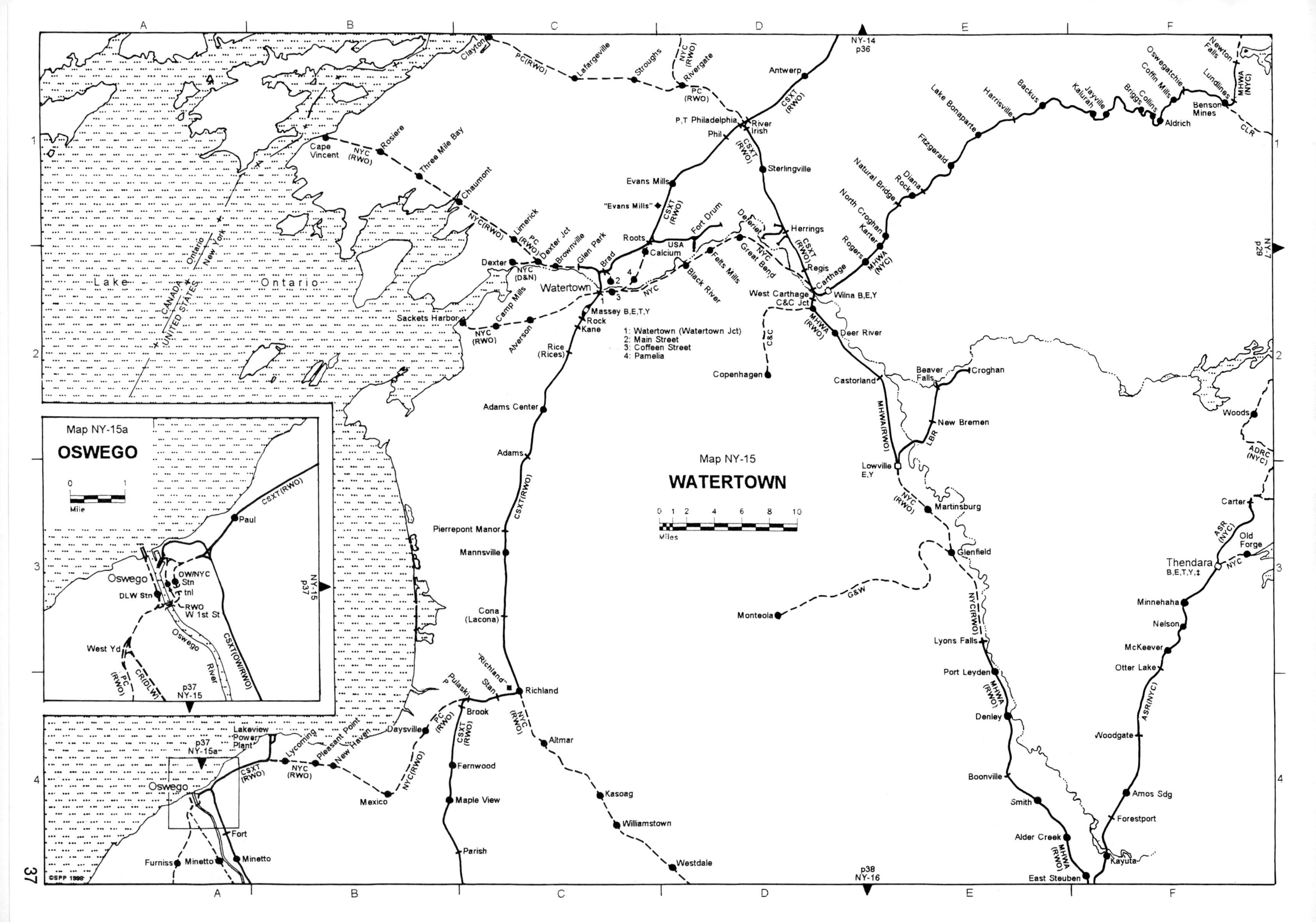

Map NY-15
WATERTOWN
0 1 2 4 6 8 10
Miles
Map NY-15a
OSWEGO
0 1
Mile
NY-14
p36
NY-7
p29
p38
NY-16
NY-15
p37
p37
NY-15
p37
NY-15a
Lake Ontario
Ontario
New York
CANADA
UNITED STATES
1: Watertown (Watertown Jct)
2: Main Street
3: Coffeen Street
4: Pamelia
Clayton
Lafargeville
Stroughs
Rivergate
PC(RWO)
NYC (RWO)
Antwerp
CSXT (RWO)
P,T Philadelphia
River
Irish
Phil
Sterlingville
Cape Vincent
Rosiere
Three Mile Bay
Chaumont
NYC(RWO)
Limerick
Evans Mills
"Evans Mills"
Fort Drum
Herrings
Deferiet
Great Bend
Roots
USA
Calcium
Felts Mills
Black River
Regis
Carthage
Wilna B,E,Y
West Carthage
C&C Jct
Dexter
NYC (D&N)
Dexter Jct
Brownville
Glen Park
Brad
Watertown
Massey B,E,T,Y
Rock
Kane
Sackets Harbor
Camp Mills
Alverson
Rice (Rices)
Deer River
MHWA (RWO)
C&C
Copenhagen
Castorland
Beaver Falls
Croghan
New Bremen
LBR
MHWA(RWO)
Lowville E,Y
Martinsburg
Glenfield
G&W
Monteola
Adams Center
Adams
CSXT(RWO)
Pierrepont Manor
Mannsville
Cona (Lacona)
Richland
"Richland"
Stan
Pulaski P
Brook
Altmar
Kasoag
Williamstown
Westdale
Fernwood
Maple View
Parish
Daysville
Mexico
New Haven
Pleasant Point
Lycoming
Lakeview Power Plant
Oswego
Fort
Minetto
Furniss
Lake Bonaparte
Harrisville
Backus
Kaluarh
Jayville
Briggs
Collins
Coffin Mills
Oswegatchie
Aldrich
Newton Falls
Lundlines
Benson Mines
MHWA (NYC)
CLR
Fitzgerald
Diana
Rock
Natural Bridge
North Croghan
Karter
Rogers
Woods
ADRC (NYC)
Carter
ASR (NYC)
Old Forge
Thendara
B,E,T,Y,‡
Minnehaha
Nelson
McKeever
Otter Lake
ASR(NYC)
Woodgate
Amos Sdg
Forestport
Kayuta
NYC(RWO)
Lyons Falls
Port Leyden
Denley
Boonville
Smith
Alder Creek
East Steuben
Paul
CSXT(OW/RWO)
OW/NYC
Stn
tnl
DLW Stn
RWO
W 1st St
Oswego River
West Yd
CR(DLW)
©SPP 1998

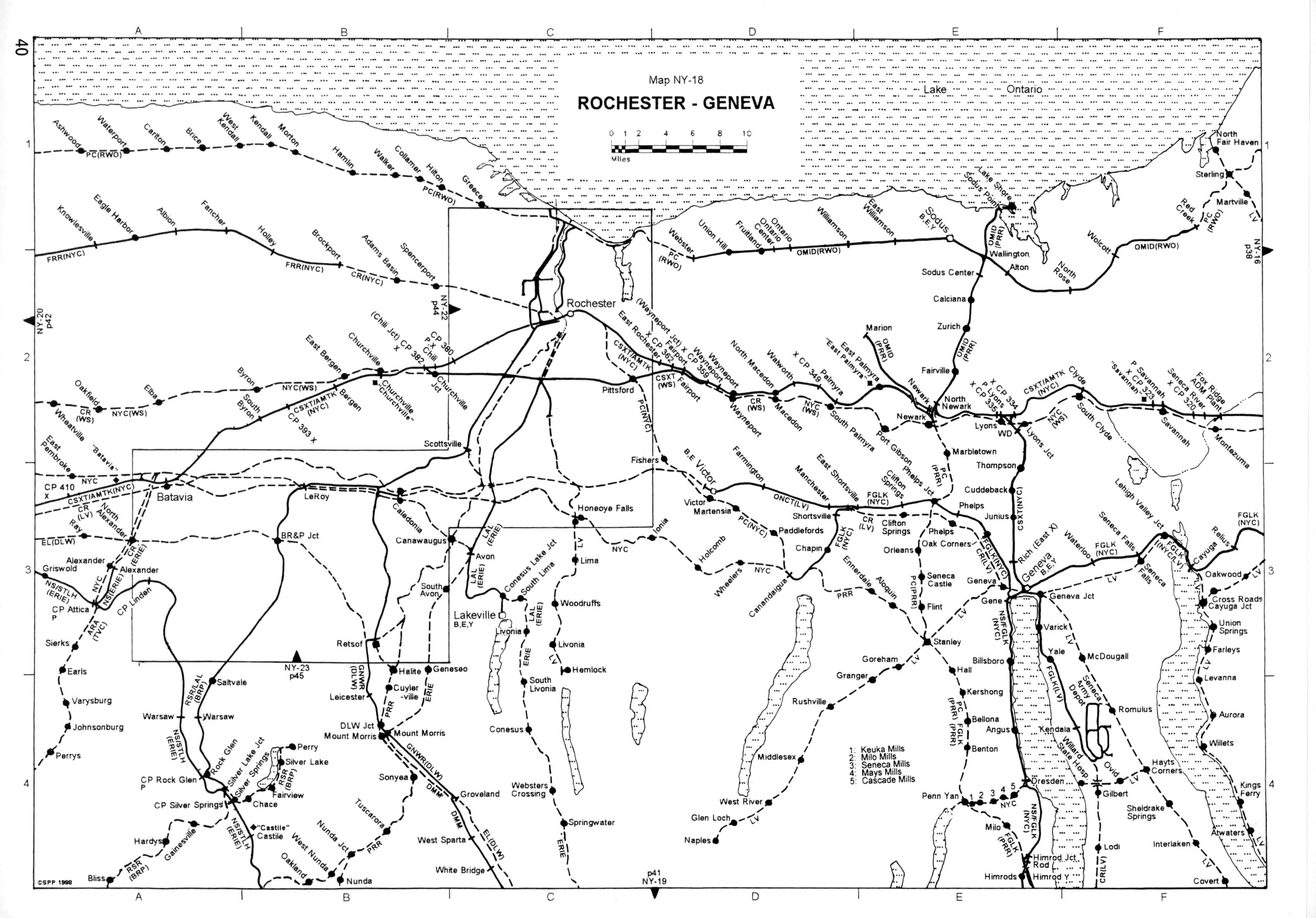
Map NY-18
ROCHESTER - GENEVA
0 1 2 4 6 8 10
Miles
Lake Ontario
NY-16 p38
NY-19 p41
NY-20 p42
NY-22 p44
NY-23 p45
1: Keuka Mills
2: Milo Mills
3: Seneca Mills
4: Mays Mills
5: Cascade Mills
North Fair Haven
Sterling
Martville
Red Creek
Wolcott
North Rose
Alton
Wallington
Sodus Point
Lake Shore
Sodus B,E,Y
Sodus Center
Calciana
Zurich
Fairville
North Newark
Newark
Marion
East Williamson
Williamson
Ontario
Ontario Center
Fruitland
Union Hill
Webster
OMID(RWO)
OMID (PRR)
PC (RWO)
Montezuma
Fox Ridge ADM Plant
Seneca River x CP 320
P Savannah x CP 323
"Savannah"
Savannah
South Clyde
Clyde
Lyons Jct
x CP 334
P Lyons
x CP 335
Lyons WD
Marbletown
Thompson
Cuddeback
Junius
Phelps
Phelps Jct
Port Gibson
East Palmyra
"East Palmyra"
Palmyra
x CP 349
South Palmyra
Walworth
Macedon
North Macedon
Wayneport
(Wayneport Jct) x CP 359
Fairport
x CP 362
East Rochester
CSXT/AMTK (NYC)
CSXT (WS)
Pittsford
PC(NYC)
Rochester
Greece
Hilton
Collamer
Walker
Hamlin
Morton
Kendall
West Kendall
Brice
Carlton
Waterport
Ashwood
PC(RWO)
Spencerport
Adams Basin
Brockport
Holley
Fancher
Albion
Eagle Harbor
Knowlesville
FRR(NYC)
CR(NYC)
Churchville Jct
CP 380
P,x Chili
(Chili Jct) CP 382
Churchville
"Churchville"
East Bergen
Bergen
CP 393 x
Byron
South Byron
Elba
Oakfield
Wheatville
"Batavia"
East Pembroke
CP 410
Batavia
NYC(WS)
Scottsville
Fishers
B,E Victor
Farmington
Manchester
East Shortsville
Shortsville
Paddlefords
Chapin
Canandaigua
Victor
Martensia
Ionia
Holcomb
Wheelers
Honeoye Falls
Lima
Woodruffs
Livonia
Hemlock
South Lima
Conesus Lake Jct
South Livonia
Conesus
Websters Crossing
Springwater
Lakeville B,E,Y
Livonia
Avon
Canawaugus
South Avon
Geneseo
Halite
Cuyler-ville
Mount Morris
DLW Jct
Retsof
Leicester
Caledonia
LeRoy
BR&P Jct
Saltvale
Warsaw
Groveland
West Sparta
White Bridge
Sonyea
Tuscarora
Nunda
Nunda Jct
West Nunda
Oakland
Perry
Silver Lake
Fairview
Chace
"Castile"
Castile
Silver Lake Jct
Silver Springs
Rock Glen
CP Rock Glen
CP Silver Springs
Gainesville
Hardys
Bliss
North Alexander
Alexander
Alexander Griswold
CP Linden
CP Attica
Ray
Sierks
Earls
Varysburg
Johnsonburg
Perrys
Seneca Falls
Lehigh Valley Jct
Waterloo
Geneva Jct
Geneva B,E,Y
Rich (East X)
Gene
Oak Corners
Seneca Castle
Flint
Orleans
Clifton Springs
Aloquin
Ennerdale
Stanley
Goreham
Granger
Rushville
Middlesex
West River
Glen Loch
Naples
Hall
Kershong
Bellona
Benton
Billsboro
Penn Yan
Milo
Himrods
Himrod Jct
Himrod Y
Dresden
Kendaia
Willard State Hosp
Seneca Army Depot
Varick
Yale
McDougall
Romulus
Ovid
Gilbert
Lodi
Sheldrake Springs
Interlaken
Hayts Corners
Covert
Atwaters
Kings Ferry
Willets
Aurora
Levanna
Farleys
Union Springs
Cross Roads Cayuga Jct
Oakwood
Relius
Cayuga
FGLK (NYC)
NS/FGLK (NYC)
©SPP 1998

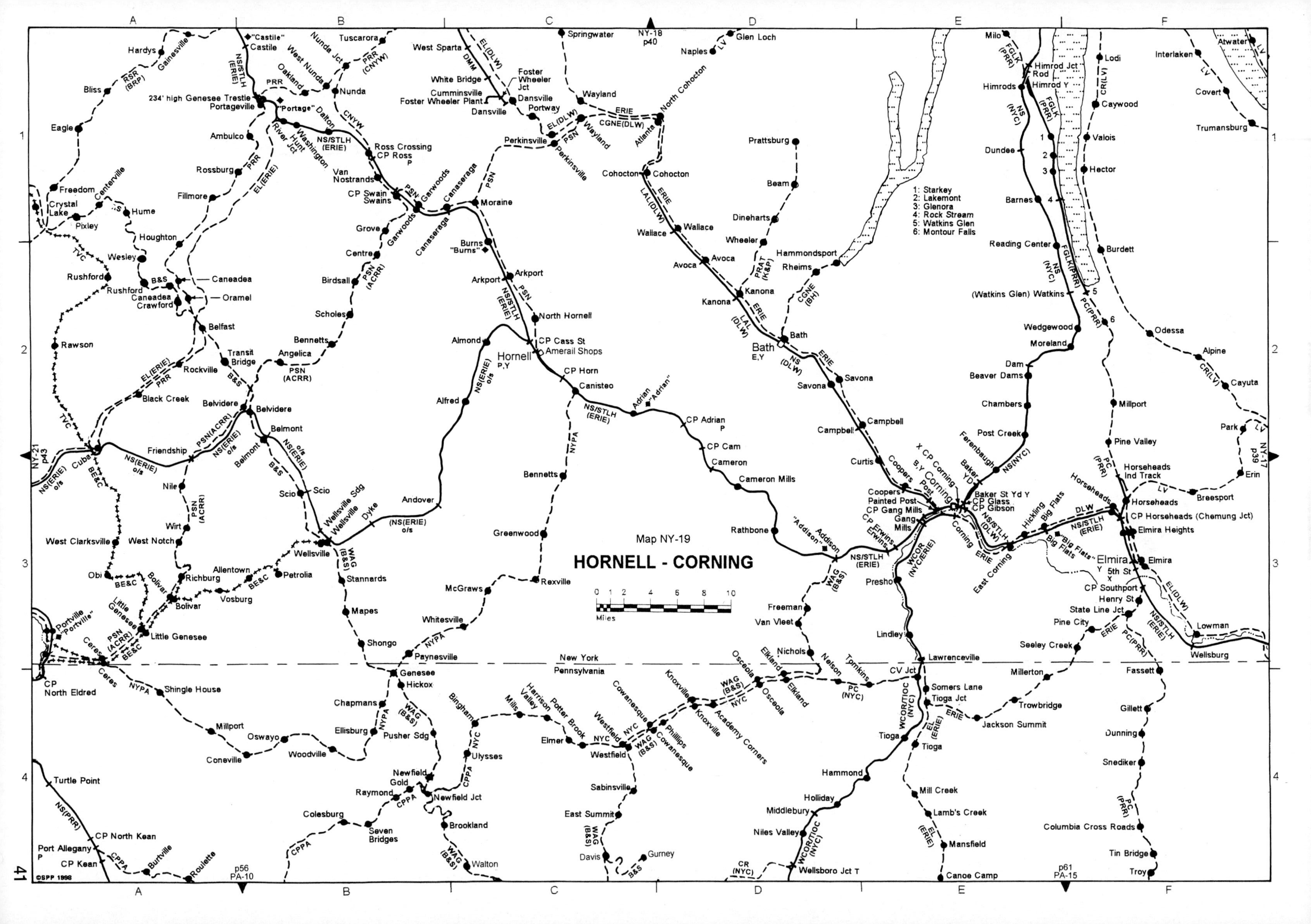

Map NY-19
HORNELL - CORNING
0 1 2 4 6 8 10
Miles
1: Starkey
2: Lakemont
3: Glenora
4: Rock Stream
5: Watkins Glen
6: Montour Falls
New York
Pennsylvania
NY-18
p40
NY-17
p39
NY-21
p43
p56
PA-10
p61
PA-15
Hornell
Corning
Elmira
Bath
Castile
Portageville
234' high Genesee Trestle
Dansville
Wayland
Cohocton
North Cohocton
Avoca
Kanona
Savona
Campbell
Canisteo
Addison
Wellsville
Cuba
Belvidere
Friendship
Watkins
Horseheads
Wellsboro Jct
Tioga
Lawrenceville
Westfield
©SPP 1998

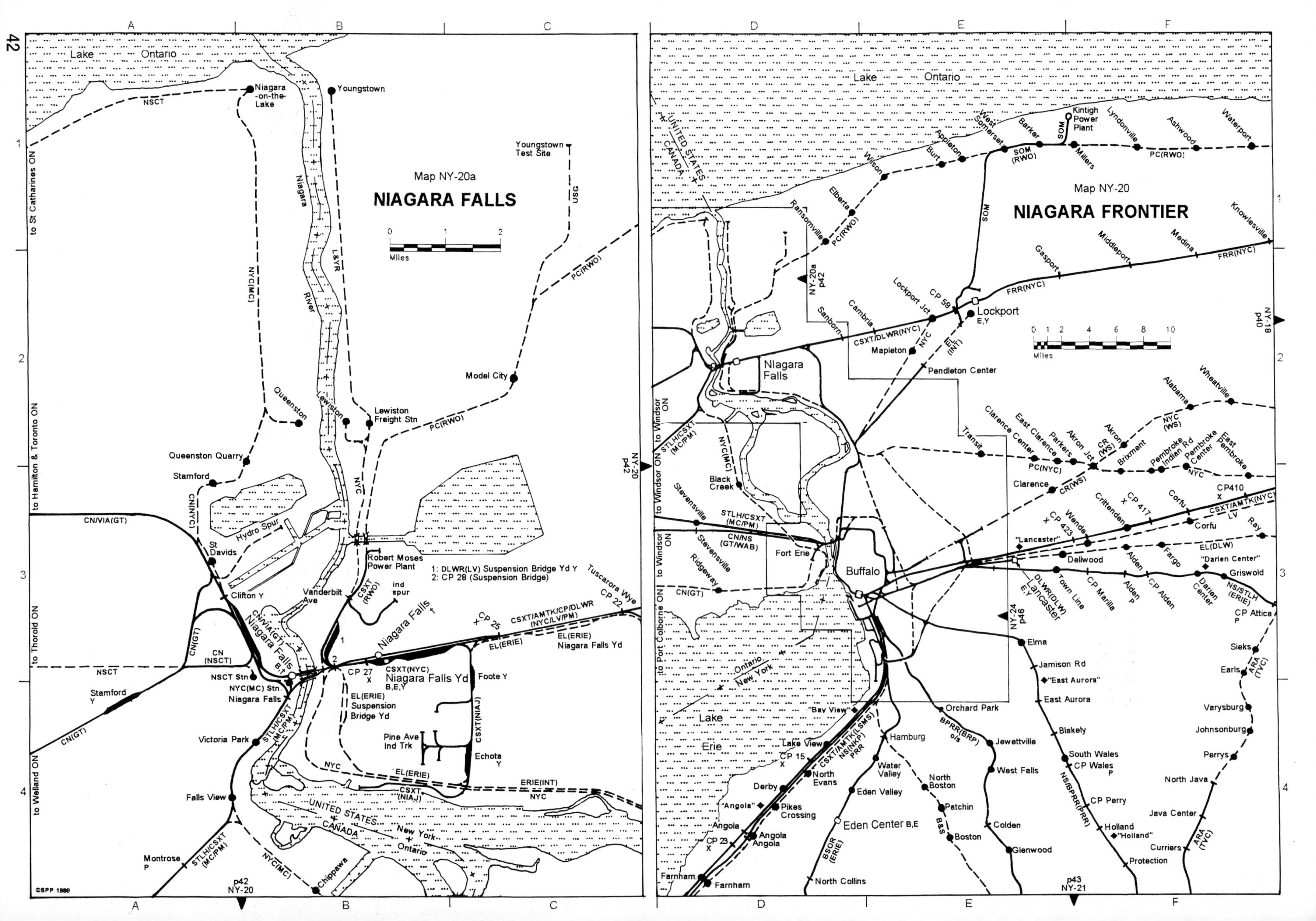
Map NY-20a
NIAGARA FALLS
0 1 2
Miles
Lake Ontario
Niagara-on-the-Lake
Youngstown
Youngstown Test Site
USG
NSCT
NYC(MC)
Niagara River
L&YR
PC(RWO)
Model City
Queenston
Lewiston
Lewiston Freight Stn
Queenston Quarry
Stamford
CN(NYC)
Hydro Spur
St Davids
Robert Moses Power Plant
1: DLWR(LV) Suspension Bridge Yd Y
2: CP 28 (Suspension Bridge)
Tuscarora Wye
CP 22
CSXT/AMTK/CP/DLWR (NYC/LV/PM)
CP 25
EL(ERIE)
Niagara Falls Yd
CN/VIA(GT)
Clifton Y
Vanderbilt Ave
CSXT (RWO)
ind spur
Niagara Falls
CN (NSCT)
CN(GT)
NSCT Stn
NYC(MC) Stn. Niagara Falls
CP 27
CSXT(NYC) Niagara Falls Yd B,E,Y
Foote Y
EL(ERIE) Suspension Bridge Yd
Pine Ave Ind Trk
CSXT(NIAJ)
Echota Y
ERIE(INT)
NYC
Stamford Y
Victoria Park
STLH/CSXT (MC/PM)
Falls View
UNITED STATES
CANADA
New York
Ontario
Montrose P
Chippawa
p42 NY-20
to St Catharines ON
to Hamilton & Toronto ON
to Thorold ON
to Welland ON
©SPP 1988
Map NY-20
NIAGARA FRONTIER
0 1 2 4 6 8 10
Miles
Lake Ontario
Kintigh Power Plant
West Somerset
Barker
SOM
SOM (RWO)
Millers
Lyndonville
Ashwood
Waterport
PC(RWO)
Appleton
Burt
Wilson
Elberta
Ransomville
Knowlesville
Medina
Middleport
Gasport
FRR(NYC)
CP 59
Lockport E,Y
Lockport Jct
Cambria
Sanborn
CSXT/DLWR(NYC)
Mapleton
EL (INT)
Pendleton Center
NY-20a p42
NY-18 p40
Niagara Falls
Transit
Clarence Center
East Clarence
Parkers
Akron Jct
Akron
CR (WS)
Brixment
Pembroke Indian Rd
Pembroke Center
East Pembroke
Alabama
Wheatville
NYC (WS)
PC(NYC)
Clarence
CR(WS)
CP410
CP 417
CP 423
Wende
Crittenden
Corfu
CSXT/AMTK(NYC) LV
Ray
"Lancaster"
Dellwood
Alden
Fargo
EL(DLW)
"Darien Center"
Griswold
Darien Center
NS/STLH (ERIE)
CP Attica P
Town Line
CP Marilla
Alden P
CP Alden
DLWR(DLW) Lancaster E,Y
NY-24 p46
Black Creek
STLH/CSXT (MC/PM)
Stevensville
CN/NS (GT/WAB)
Fort Erie
Buffalo
Ridgeway
CN(GT)
to Windsor ON
to Port Colborne ON
Ontario
New York
Lake Erie
Elma
Jamison Rd
"East Aurora"
East Aurora
Orchard Park
BPRR(BRP) o/s
Blakely
South Wales
CP Wales P
NS/BPRR(PRR)
CP Perry
Holland
"Holland"
Protection
Sieks
Earls
ARA (TVC)
Varysburg
Johnsonburg
Perrys
North Java
Java Center
Curriers
"Bay View"
Hamburg
Lake View
CP 15
CSXT/AMTK(LSMS) NS(NKP) PRR
North Evans
Derby
"Angola"
Pikes Crossing
Angola
CP 23
Farnham
Water Valley
Eden Valley
North Boston
Patchin
B&S
Boston
Eden Center B,E
BSOR (ERIE)
North Collins
Jewettville
West Falls
Colden
Glenwood
p43 NY-21

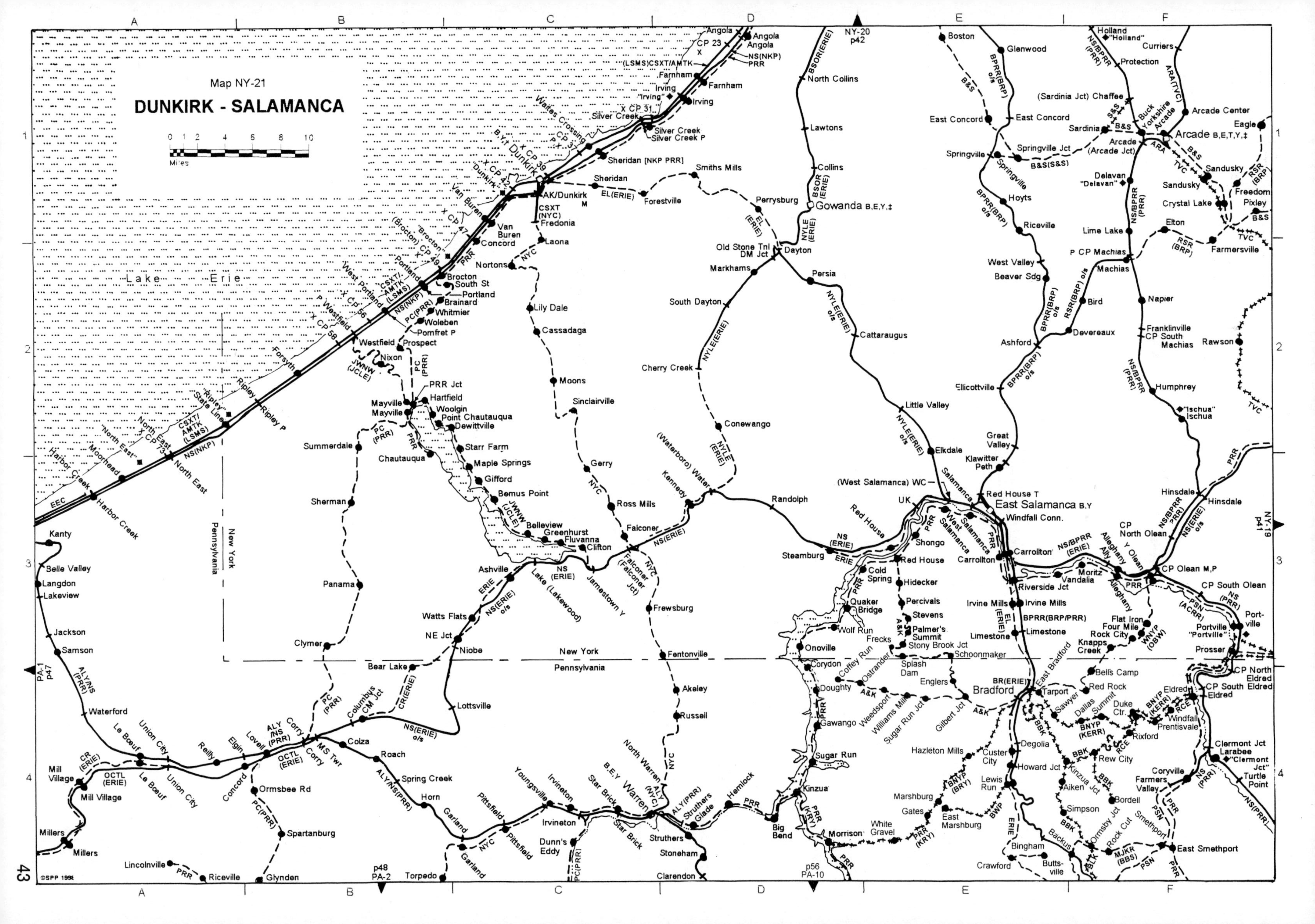
Map NY-21
DUNKIRK - SALAMANCA
Miles
0 1 2 4 6 8 10
Lake Erie
New York
Pennsylvania
NY-20 p42
NY-19 p41
PA-1 p47
p48 PA-2
p56 PA-10
Angola
Farnham
Irving
Silver Creek
Sheridan
Dunkirk
Fredonia
Laona
Forestville
Smiths Mills
Perrysburg
Gowanda B,E,Y,‡
North Collins
Lawtons
Collins
Dayton
Old Stone Tnl
DM Jct
Markhams
South Dayton
Persia
Cattaraugus
Cherry Creek
Conewango
Little Valley
Elkdale
Salamanca
East Salamanca B,Y
Windfall Conn.
Red House T
Great Valley
Klawitter Peth
Ellicottville
Ashford
Devereaux
Bird
West Valley
Beaver Sdg
Riceville
Hoyts
Springville
Springville Jct
East Concord
Glenwood
Boston
Holland
Protection
Curriers
Chaffee
Sardinia
Arcade B,E,T,Y,‡
Arcade Center
Eagle
Sandusky
Freedom
Pixley
Crystal Lake
Elton
Farmersville
Delavan
Lime Lake
Machias
Napier
Franklinville
CP South Machias
Rawson
Humphrey
Ischua
Hinsdale
CP North Olean
CP Olean M,P
CP South Olean
Portville
Prosser
CP North Eldred
CP South Eldred
Eldred
Clermont Jct
Larabee
Turtle Point
Coryville
Farmers Valley
East Smethport
Bradford
Tarport
Custer City
Degolia
Howard Jct
Lewis Run
Kinzua Jct
Bordell
Simpson
Backus
Bingham
Crawford
Butts-ville
Hazleton Mills
Marshburg
East Marshburg
Gates
White Gravel
Morrison
Kinzua
Sugar Run
Gawango
Doughty
Corydon
Onoville
Wolf Run
Quaker Bridge
Cold Spring
Red House
Shongo
Carrollton
Riverside Jct
Irvine Mills
Limestone
Vandalia
Allegheny
Steamburg
Randolph
Kennedy
Ross Mills
Falconer
Frewsburg
Fentonville
Akeley
Russell
Jamestown Y
Gerry
Sinclairville
Moons
Cassadaga
Lily Dale
Nortons
Van Buren
Concord
Brocton
Portland
Westfield
Prospect
Nixon
Mayville
Hartfield
PRR Jct
Chautauqua
Dewittville
Point Chautauqua
Maple Springs
Gifford
Bemus Point
Belleview
Greenhurst
Fluvanna
Clifton
Lake (Lakewood)
Ashville
Watts Flats
NE Jct
Niobe
Bear Lake
Clymer
Panama
Sherman
Summerdale
Forsyth
Ripley
State Line
North East
Moorhead
Harbor Creek
Kanty
Belle Valley
Langdon
Lakeview
Jackson
Samson
Waterford
Le Boeuf
Union City
Mill Village
Millers
Lincolnville
Riceville
Glynden
Spartanburg
Ormsbee Rd
Concord
Elgin
Reilly
Lovell
Corry
MS Twr
Columbus
CM Jct
Colza
Lottsville
Roach
Spring Creek
Horn
Garland
Torpedo
Pittsfield
Youngsville
Irvineton
Dunn's Eddy
Star Brick
Warren
North Warren
Struthers
Stoneham
Clarendon
Glade
Hemlock
Big Bend
©SPP 1996

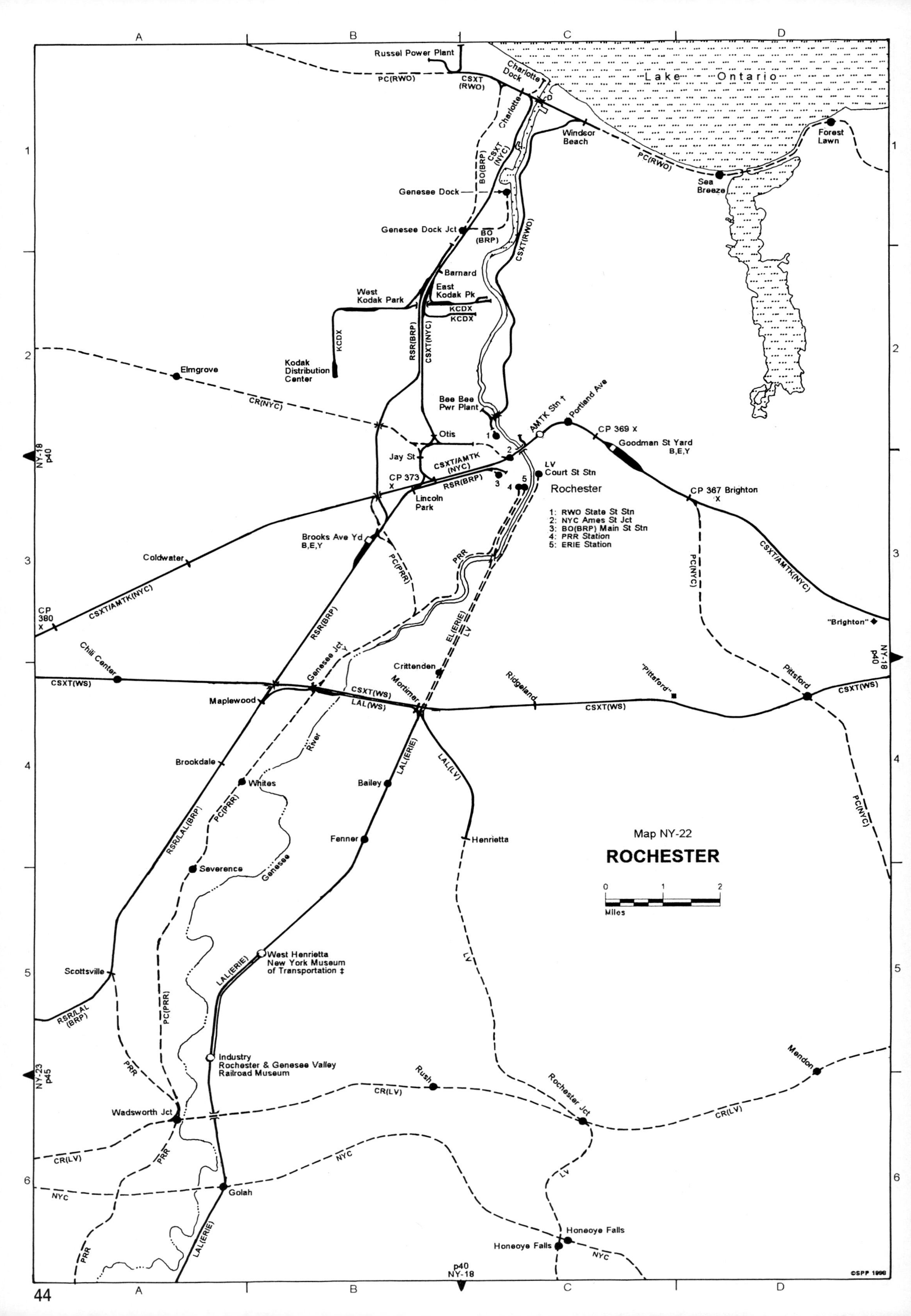
Map NY-22
ROCHESTER
Lake Ontario
Russel Power Plant
PC(RWO)
CSXT (RWO)
Charlotte Dock
Charlotte
Windsor Beach
Forest Lawn
Sea Breeze
Genesee Dock
Genesee Dock Jct
BO (BRP)
CSXT(RWO)
Barnard
West Kodak Park
East Kodak Pk
KCDX
Kodak Distribution Center
Elmgrove
CR(NYC)
Bee Bee Pwr Plant
AMTK Stn †
Portland Ave
CP 369 X
Goodman St Yard B,E,Y
Otis
Jay St
CSXT/AMTK (NYC)
CP 373 X
RSR(BRP)
Lincoln Park
LV Court St Stn
Rochester
1: RWO State St Stn
2: NYC Ames St Jct
3: BO(BRP) Main St Stn
4: PRR Station
5: ERIE Station
CP 367 Brighton X
Brooks Ave Yd B,E,Y
Coldwater
CSXT/AMTK(NYC)
CP 380 X
PC(PRR)
PRR
EL(ERIE) LV
PC(NYC)
"Brighton"
Chili Center
CSXT(WS)
Genesee Jct
Crittenden
Mortimer
LAL(WS)
Ridgeland
"Pittsford"
Pittsford
Maplewood
Brookdale
Whites
River
Bailey
LAL(ERIE)
LAL(LV)
Henrietta
Fenner
RSR/LAL(BRP)
Severence
Genesee
0 1 2
Miles
West Henrietta New York Museum of Transportation ‡
Scottsville
RSR/LAL (BRP)
Industry Rochester & Genesee Valley Railroad Museum
Rush
CR(LV)
Mendon
Rochester Jct
Wadsworth Jct
NYC
Golah
Honeoye Falls
NY-18 p40
NY-23 p45
p40 NY-18
©SPP 1996

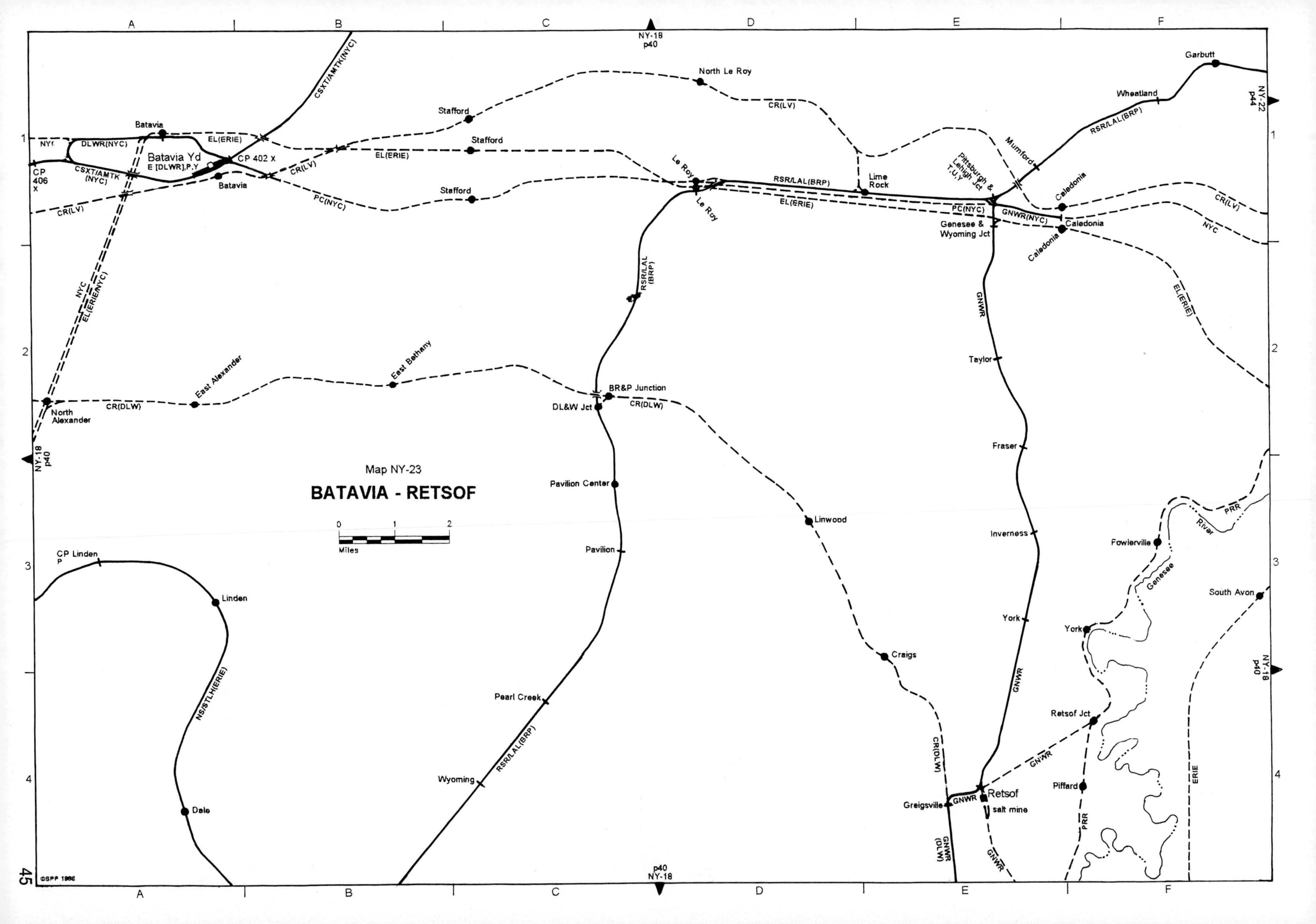

Map NY-23
BATAVIA - RETSOF
0
1
2
Miles
Batavia
Batavia Yd
E [DLWR],P,Y
CP 402 X
Batavia
CP
406
X
NYC
DLWR(NYC)
CSXT/AMTK
(NYC)
CSXT/AMTK(NYC)
EL(ERIE)
CR(LV)
PC(NYC)
NYC
EL(ERIE/NYC)
Stafford
Stafford
Stafford
North Le Roy
Le Roy
Le Roy
Lime
Rock
RSR/LAL(BRP)
EL(ERIE)
Pittsburgh &
Lehigh Jct
T,U,Y
Mumford
Wheatland
Garbutt
Caledonia
Caledonia
Caledonia
GNWR(NYC)
Genesee &
Wyoming Jct
NY-22
p44
NY-18
p40
North
Alexander
CR(DLW)
East Alexander
East Bethany
BR&P Junction
DL&W Jct
RSR/LAL
(BRP)
Pavilion Center
Pavilion
Linwood
Craigs
Taylor
Fraser
Inverness
York
GNWR
Fowlerville
River
Genesee
PRR
York
South Avon
ERIE
Retsof Jct
Piffard
Retsof
salt mine
Greigsville
GNWR
(DLW)
CP Linden
P
Linden
NS/STLH(ERIE)
Dale
Pearl Creek
Wyoming
©SPP 1992

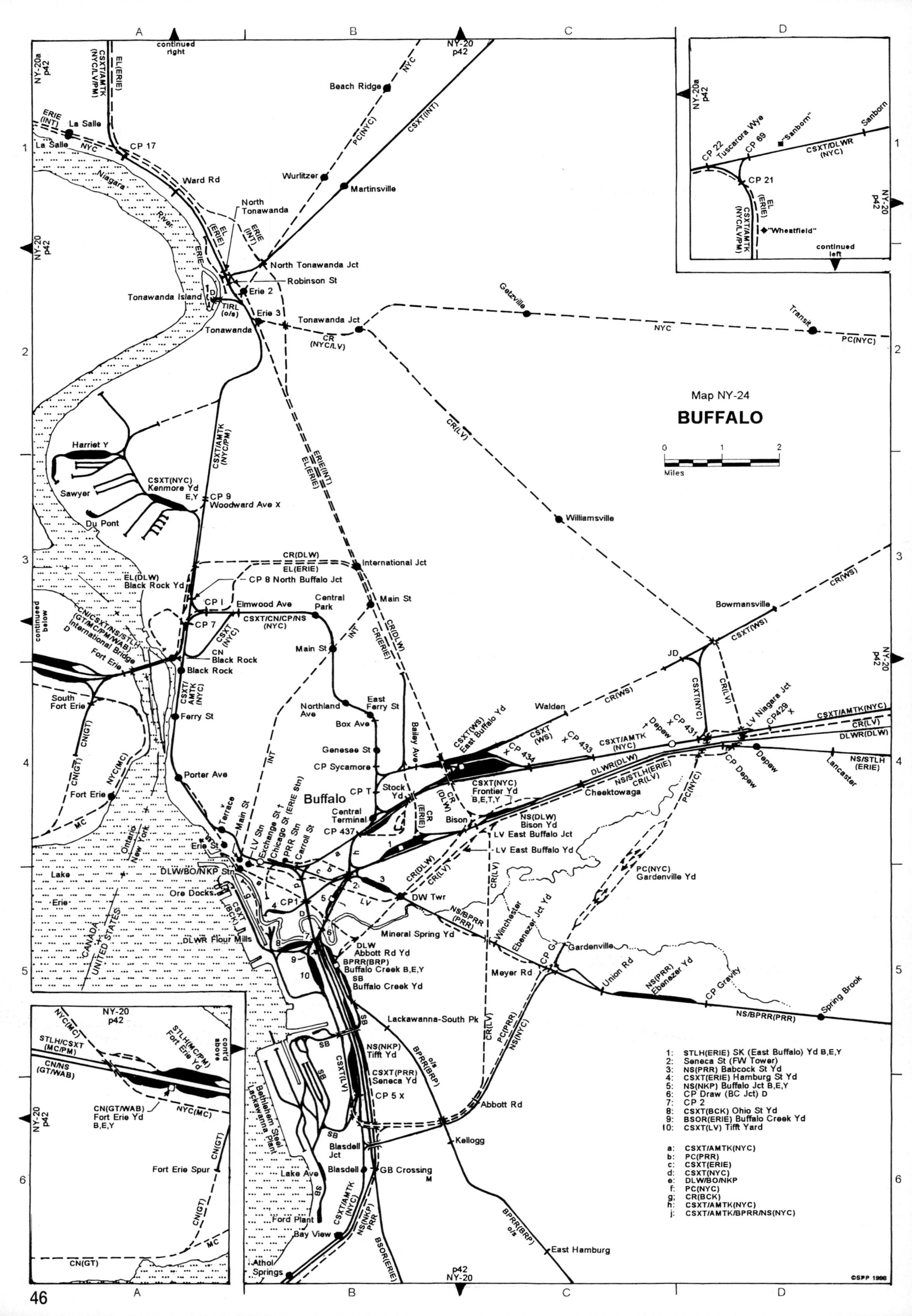

Map NY-24
BUFFALO
0 1 2
Miles
La Salle
CP 17
Ward Rd
Beach Ridge
Wurlitzer
Martinsville
North Tonawanda
North Tonawanda Jct
Robinson St
Erie 2
Erie 3
Tonawanda Island
TIRL (o/s)
Tonawanda
Tonawanda Jct
CR (NYC/LV)
Getzville
NYC
Transit
PC(NYC)
CR(LV)
ERIE(INT)
EL(ERIE)
Niagara River
Harriet Y
Sawyer
Du Pont
CSXT(NYC) Kenmore Yd E,Y
CP 9 Woodward Ave X
CSXT/AMTK (NYC/PM)
Williamsville
CR(DLW)
EL(ERIE)
International Jct
EL(DLW) Black Rock Yd
CP 8 North Buffalo Jct
CP I
Elmwood Ave
Central Park
Main St
CP 7
CSXT/CN/CP/NS (NYC)
CN Black Rock
Black Rock
CN/CSXT/NS/STLH (GT/MC/PM/WAB) D International Bridge
Fort Erie
South Fort Erie
CN(GT)
Ferry St
Northland Ave
East Ferry St
Box Ave
Genesee St
CP Sycamore
CP T
Stock Yd
Bailey Ave
Porter Ave
NYC(MC)
Fort Erie
MC
Buffalo
Central Terminal
CP 437
Terrace
Main St
LV Stn
Exchange St
Chicago St (ERIE Stn)
PRR Stn
Carroll St
Erie St
Ontario
New York
Lake Erie
DLW/BO/NKP Stn
Ore Docks
CP1
DLWR Flour Mills
CANADA
UNITED STATES
Bowmansville
CR(WS)
CSXT(WS)
JD
Walden
CSXT(WS) East Buffalo Yd
CP 434
CP 433
CSXT/AMTK (NYC)
Depew
CP 431
LV Niagara Jct
CP429
CSXT/AMTK(NYC)
CR(LV)
DLWR(DLW)
CP Depew
Depew
NS/STLH (ERIE)
Lancaster
CSXT(NYC) Frontier Yd B,E,T,Y
Bison
NS(DLW) Bison Yd
DLWR(DLW)
NS/STLH(ERIE) CR(LV)
Cheektowaga
LV East Buffalo Jct
LV East Buffalo Yd
PC(NYC) Gardenville Yd
DW Twr
NS/BPRR (PRR)
Winchester
Ebenezer Jct Yd
Gardenville
CP G
Mineral Spring Yd
DLW Abbott Rd Yd
BPRR(BRP) Buffalo Creek B,E,Y
SB Buffalo Creek Yd
Meyer Rd
Union Rd
NS(PRR) Ebenezer Yd
CP Gravity
Spring Brook
NS/BPRR(PRR)
Lackawanna-South Pk
NS(NKP) Tifft Yd
CSXT(PRR) Seneca Yd
CP 5 X
BPRR(BRP) o/s
Abbott Rd
Kellogg
PC(PRR)
NS(NYC)
Bethlehem Steel Lackawanna Plant
Blasdell Jct
Blasdell
GB Crossing
Lake Ave
Ford Plant
Bay View
Athol Springs
BSOR(ERIE)
East Hamburg
1: STLH(ERIE) SK (East Buffalo) Yd B,E,Y
2: Seneca St (FW Tower)
3: NS(PRR) Babcock St Yd
4: CSXT(ERIE) Hamburg St Yd
5: NS(NKP) Buffalo Jct B,E,Y
6: CP Draw (BC Jct) D
7: CP 2
8: CSXT(BCK) Ohio St Yd
9: BSOR(ERIE) Buffalo Creek Yd
10: CSXT(LV) Tifft Yard
a: CSXT/AMTK(NYC)
b: PC(PRR)
c: CSXT(ERIE)
d: CSXT(NYC)
e: DLW/BO/NKP
f: PC(NYC)
g: CR(BCK)
h: CSXT/AMTK(NYC)
j: CSXT/AMTK/BPRR/NS(NYC)
CP 22
Tuscarora Wye
CP 69
"Sanborn"
Sanborn
CSXT/DLWR (NYC)
CP 21
EL (ERIE)
CSXT/AMTK (NYC/LV/PM)
"Wheatfield"
continued left
continued right
continued below
cont'd above
NY-20 p42
NY-20a p42
STLH/CSXT (MC/PM)
CN/NS (GT/WAB)
STLH(MC/PM) Fort Erie Yd
CN(GT/WAB) Fort Erie Yd B,E,Y
NYC(MC)
Fort Erie Spur
CN(GT)
©SPP 1996

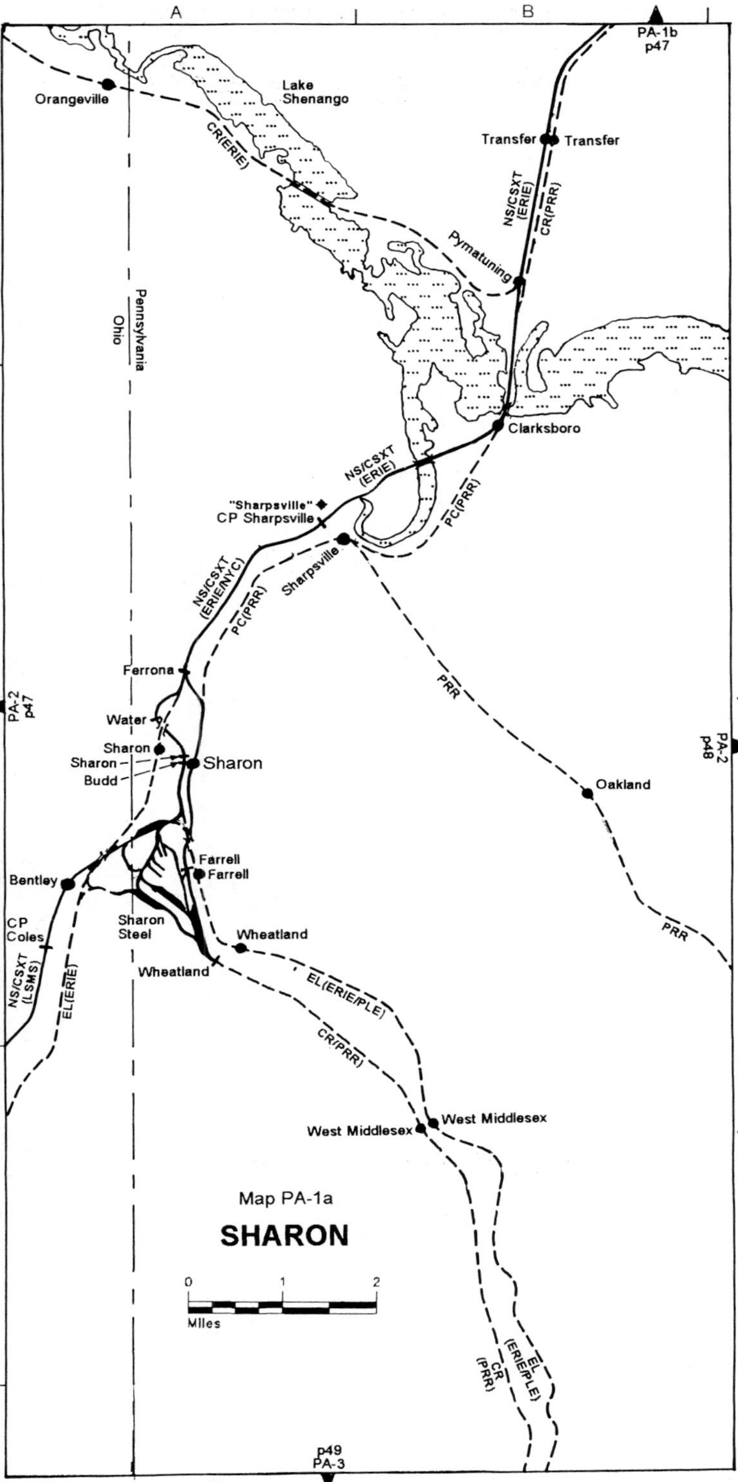

Map PA-1a
SHARON
0
1
2
Miles
Orangeville
Lake Shenango
CR(ERIE)
Transfer
Transfer
NS/CSXT (ERIE)
CR(PRR)
Pymatuning
Pennsylvania
Ohio
Clarksboro
NS/CSXT (ERIE)
PC(PRR)
"Sharpsville"
CP Sharpsville
Sharpsville
NS/CSXT (ERIE/NYC)
PC(PRR)
Ferrona
Water
Sharon
Sharon
Budd
Sharon
PRR
Oakland
Bentley
Farrell
Farrell
CP Coles
Sharon Steel
Wheatland
Wheatland
NS/CSXT (LSMS)
EL(ERIE)
EL(ERIE/PLE)
CR/PRR)
PRR
West Middlesex
West Middlesex
CR (PRR)
EL (ERIE/PLE)
PA-1b
p47
PA-2
p47
PA-2
p48
p49
PA-3

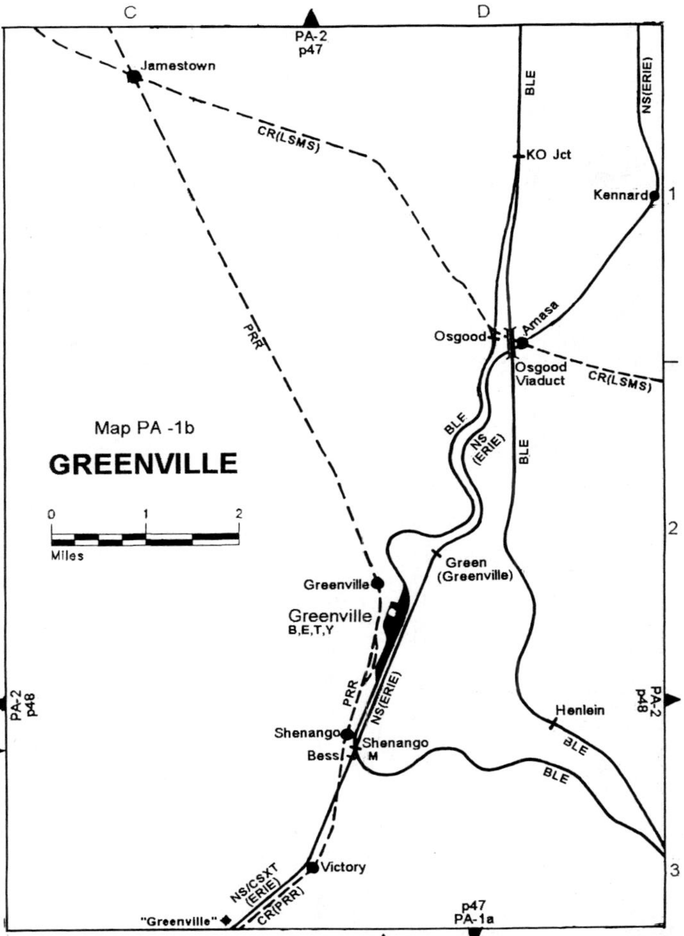

Map PA -1b
GREENVILLE
0
1
2
Miles
PA-2
p47
Jamestown
CR(LSMS)
BLE
NS(ERIE)
KO Jct
Kennard
PRR
Osgood
Amasa
Osgood Viaduct
CR(LSMS)
BLE
NS (ERIE)
BLE
Green (Greenville)
Greenville
Greenville
B,E,T,Y
PRR
NS(ERIE)
Henlein
BLE
BLE
Shenango
Shenango
Bess
M
Victory
NS/CSXT (ERIE)
CR(PRR)
"Greenville"
PA-2
p48
p47
PA-1a

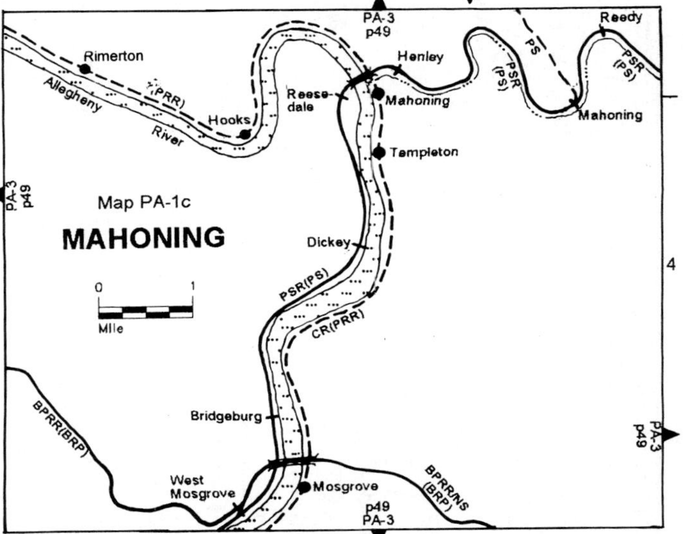

Map PA-1c
MAHONING
0
1
Mile
PA-3
p49
Rimerton
Allegheny
River
(PRR)
Hooks
Reese-dale
Henley
Mahoning
Templeton
PS
PSR (PS)
Reedy
PSR (PS)
Mahoning
Dickey
PSR(PS)
CR(PRR)
Bridgeburg
BPRR(BRP)
West Mosgrove
Mosgrove
BPRR/NS (BRP)
p49
PA-3

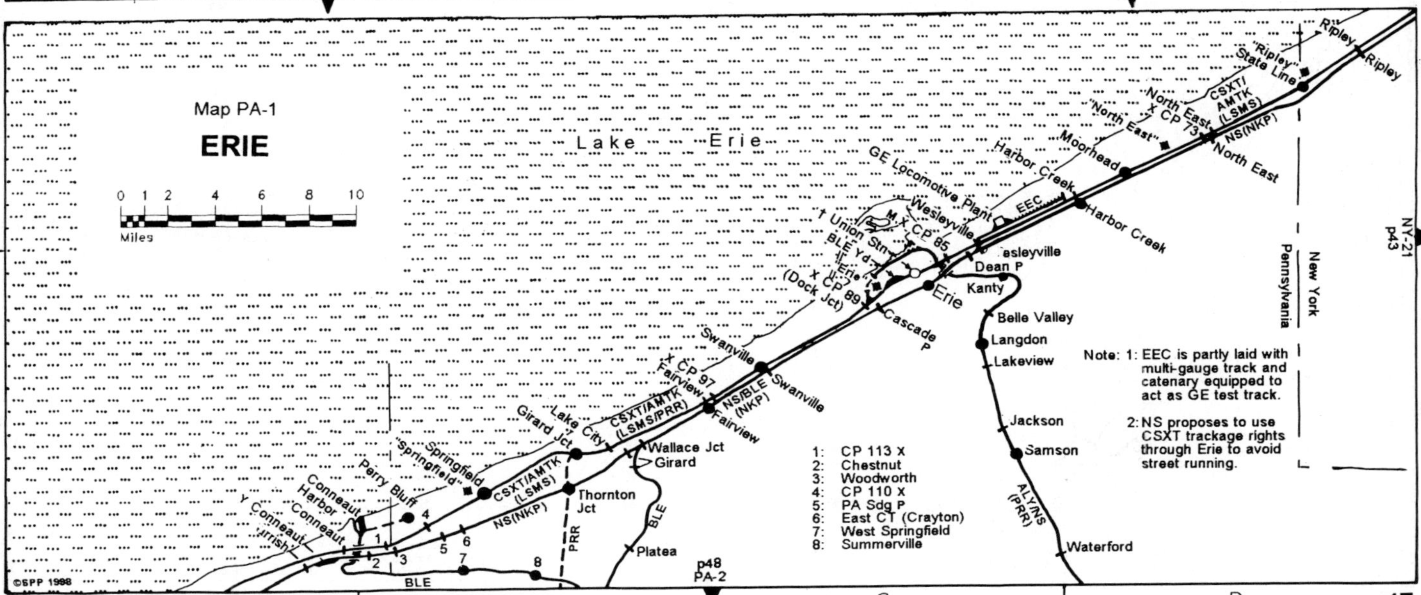

Map PA-1
ERIE
0
1
2
4
6
8
10
Miles
Lake Erie
"Ripley"
Ripley
"Ripley" State Line
Ripley
CSXT/ AMTK (LSMS)
North East
X CP 73
"North East"
NS(NKP)
North East
Moorhead
Harbor Creek
GE Locomotive Plant
EEC
Harbor Creek
Wesleyville
X CP 85
Union Stn
BLE Yd
Erie
X CP 89
(Dock Jct)
Cascade P
Erie
Dean P
Kanty
Belle Valley
Langdon
Lakeview
Jackson
Samson
ALY/NS (PRR)
Waterford
New York
Pennsylvania
Swanville
Swanville
X CP 97
Fairview
Fairview
NS/BLE (NKP)
CSXT/AMTK (LSMS/PRR)
Lake City
Girard Jct
Wallace Jct
Girard
Springfield
"Springfield"
CSXT/AMTK (LSMS)
Thornton Jct
PRR
BLE
Platea
Perry Bluff
Conneaut Harbor
Conneaut
NS(NKP)
BLE
1: CP 113 X
2: Chestnut
3: Woodworth
4: CP 110 X
5: PA Sdg P
6: East CT (Crayton)
7: West Springfield
8: Summerville
Note: 1: EEC is partly laid with multi-gauge track and catenary equipped to act as GE test track.
2: NS proposes to use CSXT trackage rights through Erie to avoid street running.
NY-21
p43
p48
PA-2
©SPP 1988

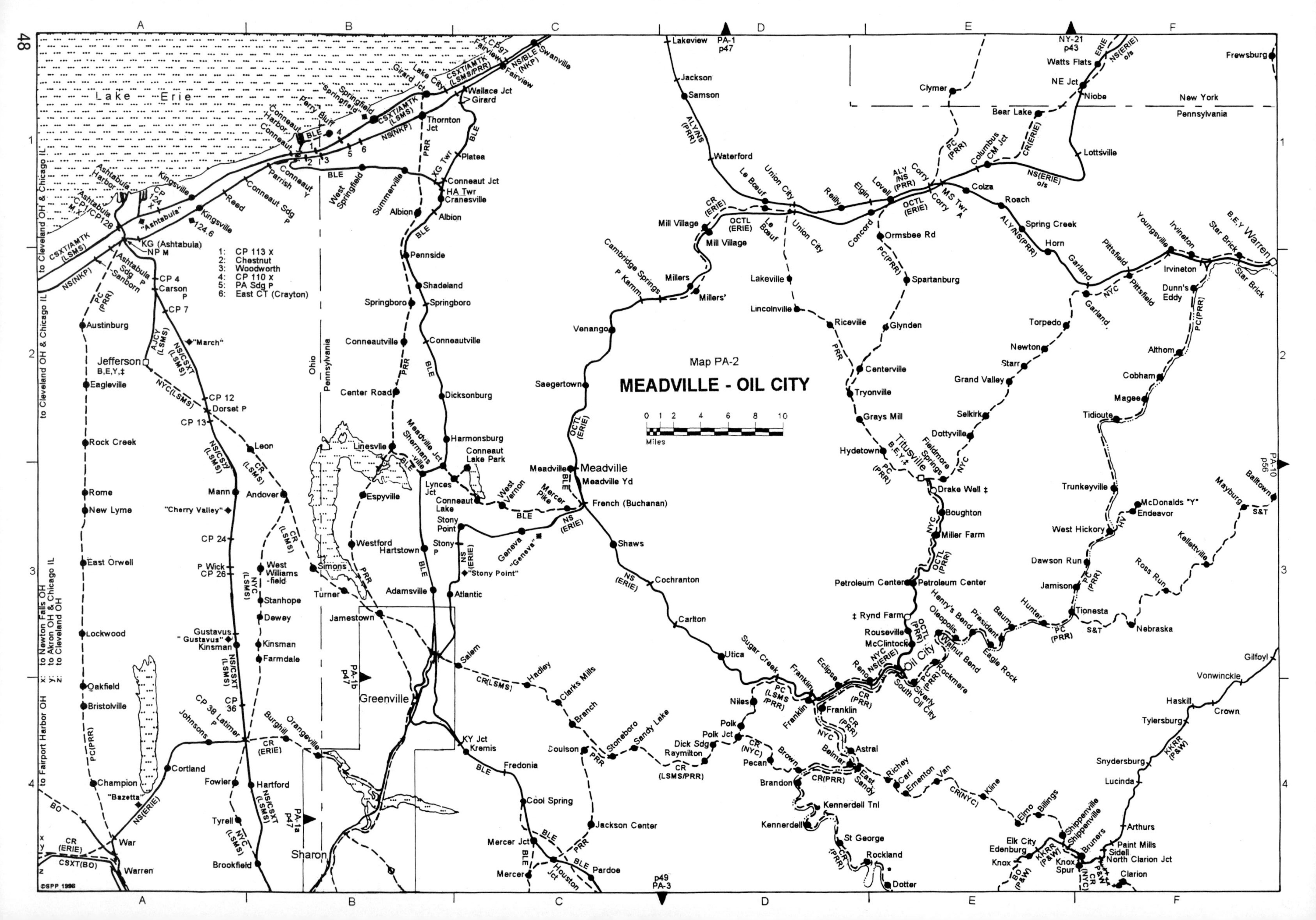

Map PA-2
MEADVILLE - OIL CITY
0 1 2 4 6 8 10
Miles
1: CP 113 X
2: Chestnut
3: Woodworth
4: CP 110 X
5: PA Sdg P
6: East CT (Crayton)
x: to Newton Falls OH
y: to Akron OH & Chicago IL
z: to Cleveland OH
to Cleveland OH & Chicago IL
to Fairport Harbor OH
Lake Erie
New York
Pennsylvania
Ohio
PA-1 p47
PA-1a p47
PA-1b p47
PA-3 p49
PA-10 p56
NY-21 p43
Meadville
Meadville Yd
French (Buchanan)
Titusville
Oil City
South Oil City
Franklin
Warren
Corry
Union City
Greenville
Sharon
Jamestown
Conneaut
Ashtabula
Jefferson
Cambridge Springs
Kingsville
Girard
©SPP 1996

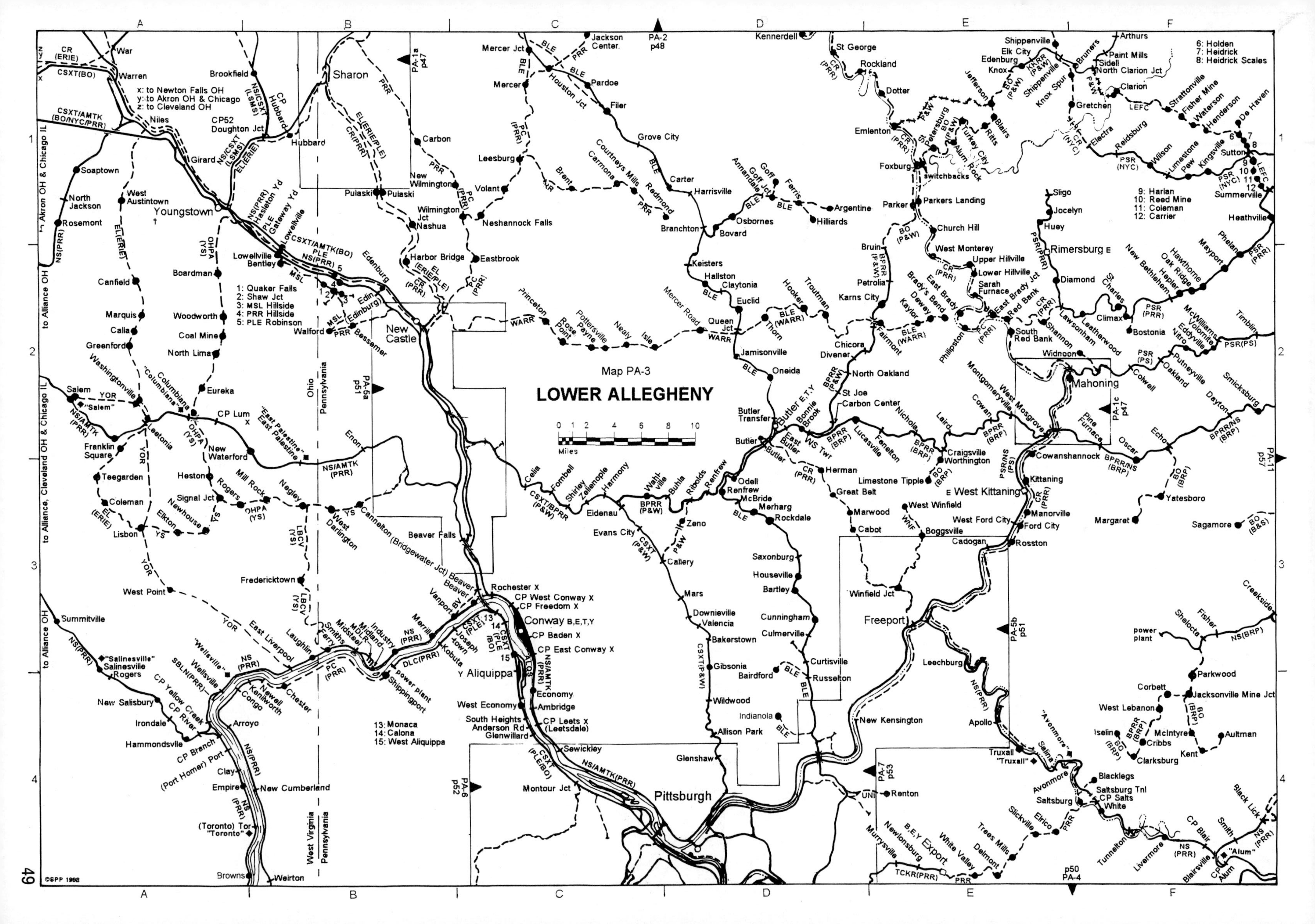
Map PA-3
LOWER ALLEGHENY
0 1 2 4 6 8 10
Miles
x: to Newton Falls OH
y: to Akron OH & Chicago
z: to Cleveland OH
1: Quaker Falls
2: Shaw Jct
3: MSL Hillside
4: PRR Hillside
5: PLE Robinson
6: Holden
7: Heidrick
8: Heidrick Scales
9: Harlan
10: Reed Mine
11: Coleman
12: Carrier
13: Monaca
14: Calona
15: West Aliquippa
PA-2 p48
PA-1a p47
PA-5a p51
PA-1c p47
PA-11 p57
PA-5b p51
PA-7 p53
PA-6 p52
p50 PA-4
Ohio
Pennsylvania
West Virginia
to Akron OH & Chicago IL
to Alliance OH
to Alliance, Cleveland OH & Chicago IL
Youngstown
Warren
Niles
Sharon
New Castle
Butler
Pittsburgh
Freeport
Aliquippa
Conway B,E,T,Y
Beaver Falls
Salem
Leetonia
East Liverpool
Wellsville
Weirton
Kittaning
West Kittaning
Mahoning
Rimersburg
Emlenton
Foxburg
Clarion
Grove City
Mercer
Harrisville
Leechburg
New Kensington
Saltsburg
Blairsville
Export
Evans City
Mars
©SPP 1998

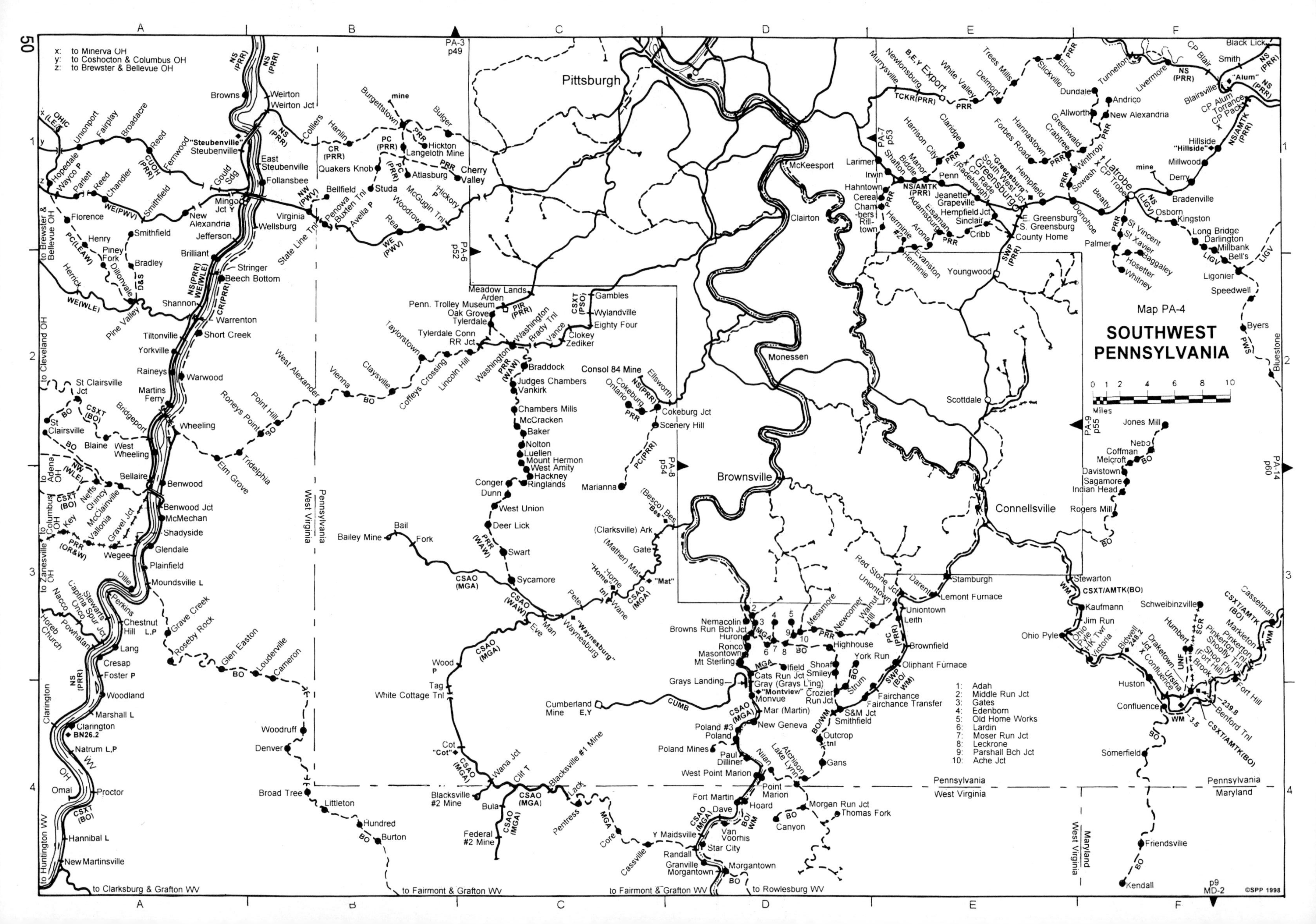
Map PA-4
SOUTHWEST PENNSYLVANIA
0 1 2 4 6 8 10
Miles
x: to Minerva OH
y: to Coshocton & Columbus OH
z: to Brewster & Bellevue OH
1: Adah
2: Middle Run Jct
3: Gates
4: Edenborn
5: Old Home Works
6: Lardin
7: Moser Run Jct
8: Leckrone
9: Parshall Bch Jct
10: Ache Jct
Pittsburgh
McKeesport
Clairton
Monessen
Brownsville
Connellsville
Scottdale
Youngwood
Greensburg
Latrobe
Uniontown
Washington
Waynesburg
Morgantown
Wheeling
Steubenville
Weirton
Ohio Pyle
Confluence
Ligonier
Blairsville
Smithfield
Point Marion
Stewarton
Pennsylvania
West Virginia
Maryland
Ohio
PA-3 p49
PA-6 p52
PA-7 p53
PA-8 p54
PA-9 p55
PA-14 p60
p9 MD-2
to Cleveland OH
to Adena OH
to Columbus OH
to Zanesville OH
to Brewster & Bellevue OH
to Huntington WV
to Clarksburg & Grafton WV
to Fairmont & Grafton WV
to Rowlesburg WV
©SPP 1998

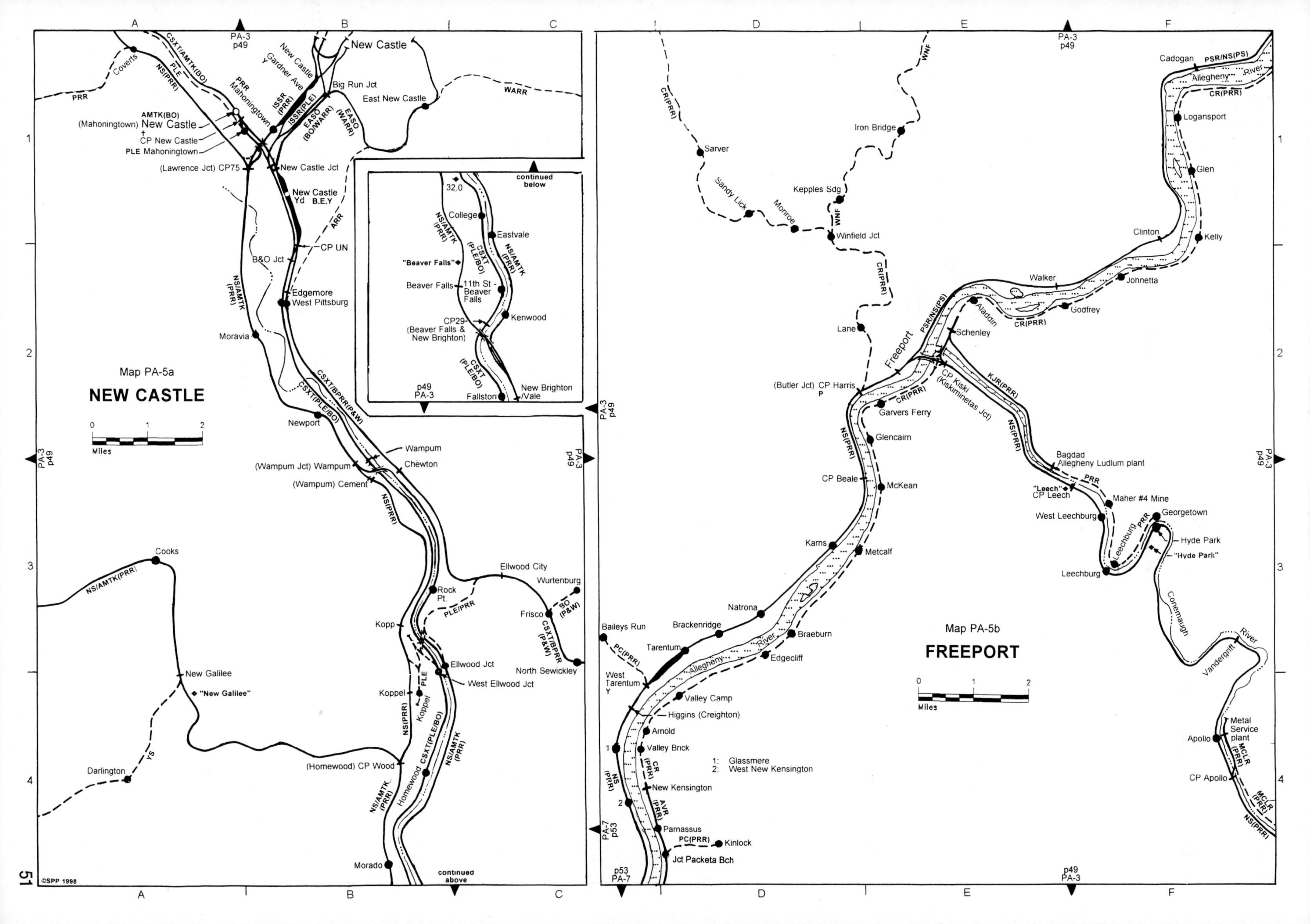

Map PA-5a
NEW CASTLE
Map PA-5b
FREEPORT
0 1 2
Miles
New Castle
New Castle Gardner Ave Y
Big Run Jct
East New Castle
WARR
PRR
Coverts
CSXT/AMTK(BO)
PLE
NS(PRR)
PRR Mahoningtown
ISSR (PRR)
ISSR(PLE)
EASO (BO/WARR)
EASO (WARR)
AMTK(BO)
(Mahoningtown) New Castle
CP New Castle
PLE Mahoningtown
(Lawrence Jct) CP75
New Castle Jct
New Castle Yd B.E.Y
ARR
CP UN
B&O Jct
Edgemore
West Pittsburg
NS/AMTK (PRR)
Moravia
32.0
College
Eastvale
NS/AMTK (PRR)
CSXT (PLE/BO)
"Beaver Falls"
Beaver Falls
11th St - Beaver Falls
Kenwood
CP29
(Beaver Falls & New Brighton)
Fallston
New Brighton /Vale
continued below
CSXT/BPRR(P&W)
CSXT(PLE/BO)
Newport
Wampum
Chewton
(Wampum Jct) Wampum
(Wampum) Cement
Cooks
NS/AMTK(PRR)
Ellwood City
Wurtenburg
Rock Pt.
PLE/PRR
Frisco
BO (P&W)
CSXT/BPRR (P&W)
Kopp
Ellwood Jct
West Ellwood Jct
North Sewickley
New Galilee
"New Galilee"
Koppel
Koppel
YS
Darlington
(Homewood) CP Wood
Homewood CSXT(PLE/BO)
Morado
continued above
©SPP 1998
PA-3 p49
PA-7 p53
CR(PRR)
Sarver
Sandy Lick
Monroe
Kepples Sdg
WNF
Winfield Jct
Iron Bridge
Lane
(Butler Jct) CP Harris P
Freeport
PSR/NS(PS)
Aladdin
Schenley
CP Kiski (Kiskiminetas Jct)
KJR(PRR)
Garvers Ferry
Glencairn
CP Beale
McKean
Karns
Metcalf
Natrona
Brackenridge
Braeburn
Edgecliff
Allegheny River
Baileys Run
PC(PRR)
Tarentum
West Tarentum Y
Valley Camp
Higgins (Creighton)
Arnold
Valley Brick
1: Glassmere
2: West New Kensington
New Kensington
AVR (PRR)
Parnassus
Kinlock
Jct Packeta Bch
Cadogan
Logansport
Glen
Clinton
Kelly
Walker
Johnetta
Godfrey
Bagdad
Allegheny Ludlum plant
"Leech" CP Leech
Maher #4 Mine
West Leechburg
Georgetown
Leechburg
Hyde Park
"Hyde Park"
Conemaugh
Vandergrift
Metal Service plant
Apollo
MCLR (PRR)
CP Apollo
NS(PRR)
A B C D E F
1 2 3 4

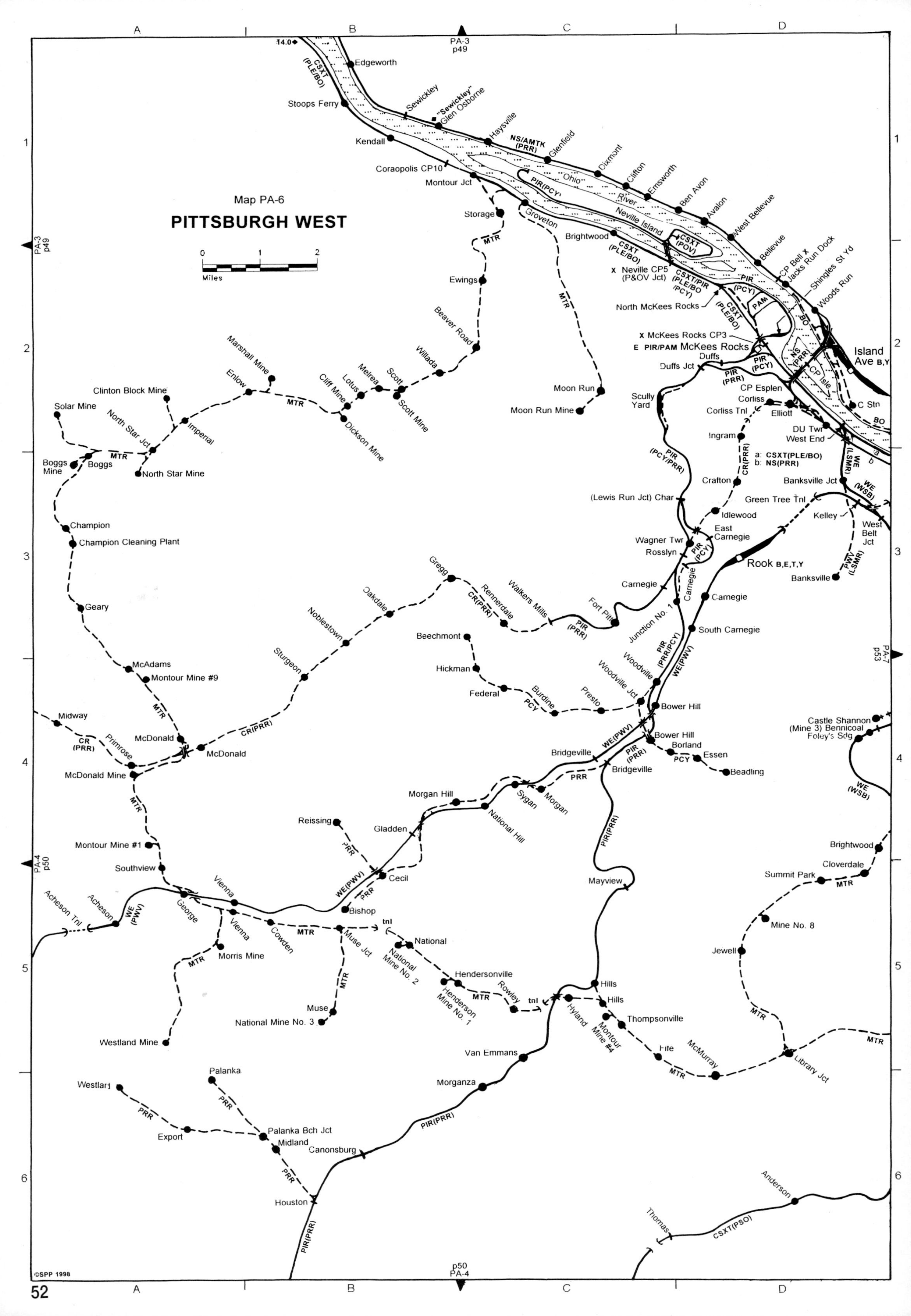
Map PA-6
PITTSBURGH WEST
0 1 2
Miles
A B C D
1 2 3 4 5 6
PA-3 p49
PA-4 p50
PA-7 p53
14.0
CSXT (PLE/BO)
Edgeworth
Stoops Ferry
Sewickley
"Sewickley" Glen Osborne
Haysville
Kendall
NS/AMTK (PRR)
Glenfield
Dixmont
Clifton
Emsworth
Ben Avon
Avalon
West Bellevue
Bellevue
Coraopolis CP10
Montour Jct
Ohio River
Neville Island
PIR(PCY)
Storage
Groveton
Brightwood
CSXT (PLE/BO)
CSXT (POV)
X Neville CP5 (P&OV Jct)
CSXT/PIR (PLE/BO /PCY)
PIR (PCY)
PAM
CP Bell X
Jacks Run Dock
Shingles St Yd
Woods Run
North McKees Rocks
CSXT (PLE/BO)
BO
X McKees Rocks CP3
E PIR/PAM McKees Rocks
Duffs
Duffs Jct
PIR (PCY)
PIR (PRR)
NS (PRR)
Island Ave B,Y
CP Isle
C Stn
BO
CP Esplen
Corliss
Corliss Tnl
Elliott
Scully Yard
Ingram
DU Twr
West End
a: CSXT(PLE/BO)
b: NS(PRR)
MTR
Ewings
Beaver Road
Willada
Scott
Metrea
Lotus
Cliff Mine
Scott Mine
Dickson Mine
Marshall Mine
Enlow
MTR
Clinton Block Mine
Imperial
North Star Jct
Solar Mine
MTR
Boggs Mine
Boggs
North Star Mine
Moon Run
Moon Run Mine
PIR (PCY/PRR)
CR(PRR)
Crafton
Banksville Jct
WE (LSMR)
WE (WSB)
Green Tree Tnl
(Lewis Run Jct) Char
Idlewood
Kelley
West Belt Jct
East Carnegie
Wagner Twr
Rosslyn
PIR (PCY)
Rook B,E,T,Y
Banksville
PWV (LSMR)
Champion
Champion Cleaning Plant
Geary
Gregg
Rennerdale
CR(PRR)
Walkers Mills
Oakdale
Noblestown
Carnegie
Fort Pitt
PIR (PRR)
Carnegie
Junction No. 1
Carnegie
South Carnegie
Beechmont
Hickman
Federal
Burdine
PCY
Presto
Woodville Jct
Woodville
PIR (PRR/PCY)
WE(PWV)
Sturgeon
McAdams
Montour Mine #9
MTR
Midway
CR (PRR)
Primrose
McDonald
McDonald
CR(PRR)
McDonald Mine
Bower Hill
Bower Hill
Borland
Essen
PCY
Beadling
Bridgeville
WE(PWV)
PIR (PRR)
Bridgeville
PRR
Castle Shannon
(Mine 3) Bennicoal
Foley's Sdg
WE (WSB)
Morgan Hill
Sygan
Morgan
National Hill
MTR
Reissing
PRR
Gladden
PIR(PRR)
Montour Mine #1
Southview
Cecil
WE(PWV)
PRR
Mayview
Brightwood
Cloverdale
Summit Park
MTR
Acheson Tnl
Acheson
WE (PWV)
George
Vienna
Vienna
Cowden
MTR
Bishop
tnl
Muse Jct
National
National Mine No. 2
Mine No. 8
Morris Mine
MTR
MTR
Hendersonville
Henderson Mine No. 1
MTR
Rowley
tnl
Hills
Hills
Jewell
Muse
National Mine No. 3
Hyland
Montour Mine #4
Thompsonville
MTR
Westland Mine
Van Emmans
Fife
McMurray
MTR
Library Jct
MTR
Palanka
Westland
PRR
PRR
Morganza
Export
Palanka Bch Jct
Midland
PIR(PRR)
Canonsburg
PRR
Houston
Anderson
Thomas
CSXT(PSO)
PIR(PRR)
©SPP 1998
p50 PA-4

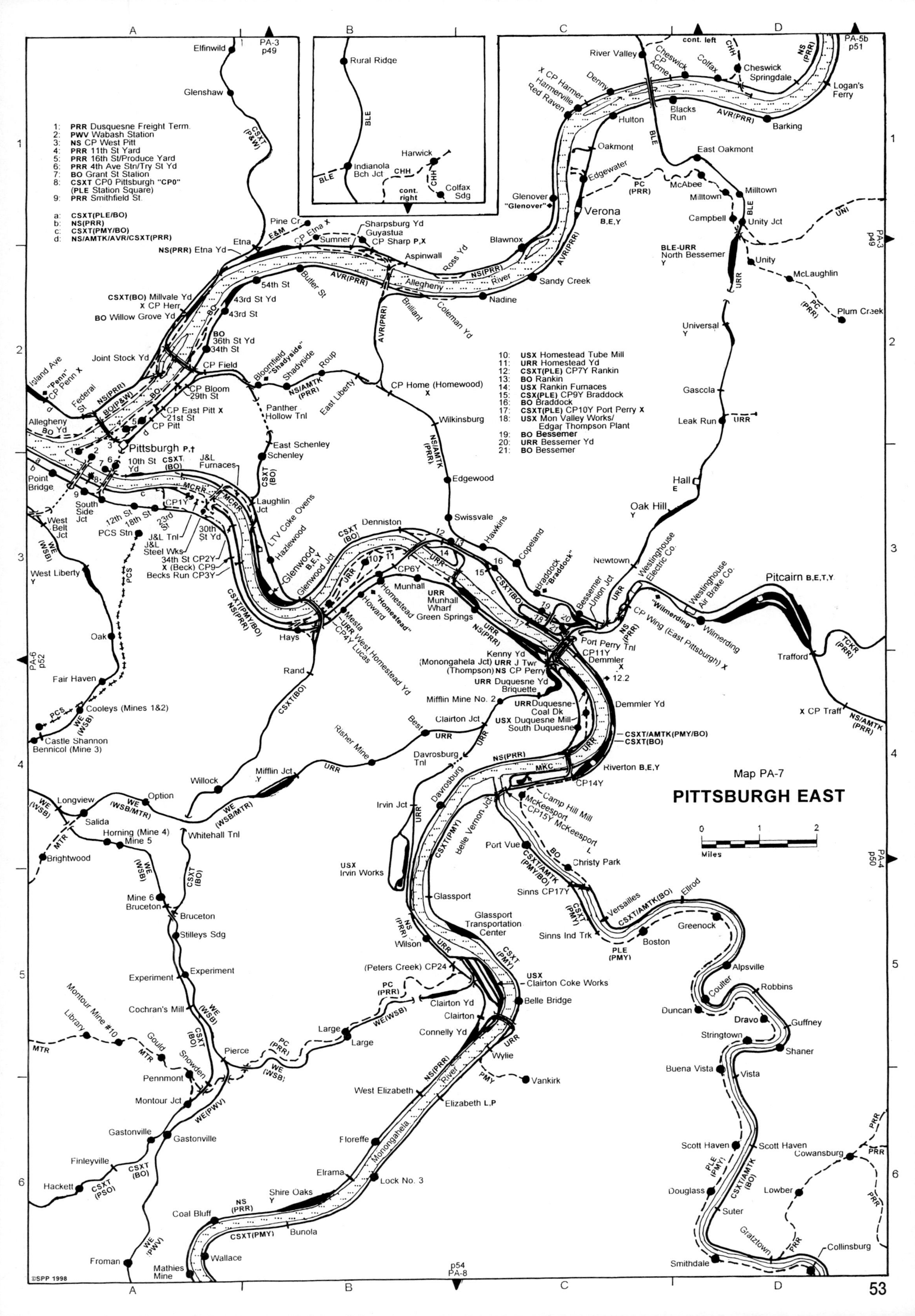
Map PA-7
PITTSBURGH EAST
1: PRR Dusquesne Freight Term.
2: PWV Wabash Station
3: NS CP West Pitt
4: PRR 11th St Yard
5: PRR 16th St/Produce Yard
6: PRR 4th Ave Stn/Try St Yd
7: BO Grant St Station
8: CSXT CP0 Pittsburgh "CP0" (PLE Station Square)
9: PRR Smithfield St.
a: CSXT(PLE/BO)
b: NS(PRR)
c: CSXT(PMY/BO)
d: NS/AMTK/AVR/CSXT(PRR)
10: USX Homestead Tube Mill
11: URR Homestead Yd
12: CSXT(PLE) CP7Y Rankin
13: BO Rankin
14: USX Rankin Furnaces
15: CSX(PLE) CP9Y Braddock
16: BO Braddock
17: CSXT(PLE) CP10Y Port Perry X
18: USX Mon Valley Works/ Edgar Thompson Plant
19: BO Bessemer
20: URR Bessemer Yd
21: BO Bessemer
0 1 2
Miles
PA-3 p49
PA-5b p51
PA-3 p49
PA-6 p52
PA-4 p50
p54 PA-8
cont. left
cont. right
Rural Ridge
BLE
Harwick
CHH
Indianola Bch Jct
Colfax Sdg
Elfinwild
Glenshaw
CSXT (P&W)
Pine Cr.
E&M
Etna
NS(PRR) Etna Yd
CP Etna X
Sharpsburg Yd
Guyastua
Sumner
CP Sharp P,X
Aspinwall
AVR(PRR)
Allegheny River
Brilliant
Coleman Yd
Butler St
54th St
43rd St Yd
43rd St
BO 36th St Yd
34th St
CSXT(BO) Millvale Yd
X CP Herr
BO Willow Grove Yd
Joint Stock Yd
CP Field
CP Bloom
29th St
CP East Pitt X
21st St
CP Pitt
Island Ave
"Penn" CP Penn X
Federal St
NS(PRR)
BO(P&W)
Allegheny BO Yd
Pittsburgh P,T
10th St Yd
CSXT (BO)
J&L Furnaces
Point Bridge
South Side Jct
West Belt Jct
WE (WSB)
12th St
18th St
23rd St
CP1Y
MCRR
J&L Tnl
J&L Steel Wks
30th St Yd
34th St CP2Y
X (Beck) CP9
Becks Run CP3Y
PCS Stn
PCS
West Liberty Y
Oak
Fair Haven
Cooleys (Mines 1&2)
Castle Shannon
Bennicol (Mine 3)
Bloomfield
"Shadyside"
Shadyside
Roup
NS/AMTK (PRR)
East Liberty
Panther Hollow Tnl
East Schenley
Schenley
Laughlin Jct
LTV Coke Ovens
Hazlewood
Glenwood B,E,Y
Glenwood Jct
CSXT(PMY/BO) NS(PRR)
Hays
CP Home (Homewood) X
Wilkinsburg
Edgewood
Swissvale
Hawkins
Copeland
Denniston
CP6Y
Munhall
URR Munhall Wharf
Green Springs
"Homestead"
Howard
Mesta
URR CP4Y Lucas
West Homestead Yd
Rand
CSXT(BO)
Braddock "Braddock"
Bessemer Union Jct
Port Perry Tnl
CP11Y
Demmler X
12.2
Kenny Yd
(Monongahela Jct) URR J Twr
(Thompson) NS CP Perry
URR Duquesne Yd
Briquette
Mifflin Mine No. 2
URR Duquesne-Coal Dk
USX Duquesne Mill
South Duquesne
Demmler Yd
CSXT/AMTK(PMY/BO)
CSXT(BO)
Clairton Jct
Best
Risher Mine
Davrosburg Tnl
Davrosburg
Riverton B,E,Y
CP14Y
MKC
Camp Hill Mill
McKeesport
CP15Y McKeesport L
Belle Vernon Jct
Irvin Jct
USX Irvin Works
Port Vue
CSXT/AMTK (PMY/BO)
Christy Park
Sinns CP17Y
Versailles
CSXT/AMTK(BO)
Ellrod
Greenock
Sinns Ind Trk
Boston
PLE (PMY)
Glassport
Glassport Transportation Center
Wilson
(Peters Creek) CP24
USX Clairton Coke Works
Belle Bridge
Clairton Yd
Clairton
Connelly Yd
Wylie
Vankirk
PMY
West Elizabeth
Elizabeth L,P
Monongahela River
Floreffe
Elrama
Lock No. 3
Shire Oaks Y
Coal Bluff
Bunola
CSXT(PMY)
Wallace
Mathies Mine
Willock
Mifflin Jct Y
Longview
Salida
Option
WE (WSB/MTR)
Whitehall Tnl
MTR
Horning (Mine 4)
Mine 5
Brightwood
Mine 6
Bruceton
Stilleys Sdg
Experiment
Cochran's Mill
Montour Mine #10
Library
Gould
Pierce
PC (PRR)
WE(WSB)
Large
Pennmont
Snowden
Montour Jct
WE(PWV)
Gastonville
Finleyville
Hackett
CSXT (PSO)
Froman
River Valley
Cheswick CP Acme
Colfax
Cheswick
Springdale
Logan's Ferry
X CP Harmer
Harmerville
Red Raven
Denny
Hulton
Blacks Run
AVR(PRR)
Barking
Oakmont
Edgewater
East Oakmont
PC (PRR)
McAbee
Milltown
Glenover
"Glenover"
Verona B,E,Y
Campbell
Unity Jct
UNI
Blawnox
Ross Yd
Sandy Creek
Nadine
BLE-URR North Bessemer Y
Unity
McLaughlin
Plum Creek
Universal Y
Gascola
Leak Run
URR
Hall E
Oak Hill Y
Newtown
Westinghouse Electric Co.
Westinghouse Air Brake Co.
Pitcairn B,E,T,Y.
"Wilmerding"
Wilmerding
CP Wing (East Pittsburgh) X
Trafford
TCKR (PRR)
X CP Traff
NS/AMTK (PRR)
Alpsville
Coulter
Robbins
Duncan
Dravo
Guffney
Stringtown
Shaner
Buena Vista
Vista
Scott Haven
Cowansburg
PRR
Douglass
Lowber
Suter
Gratztown
FRR
Collinsburg
Smithdale
©SPP 1998

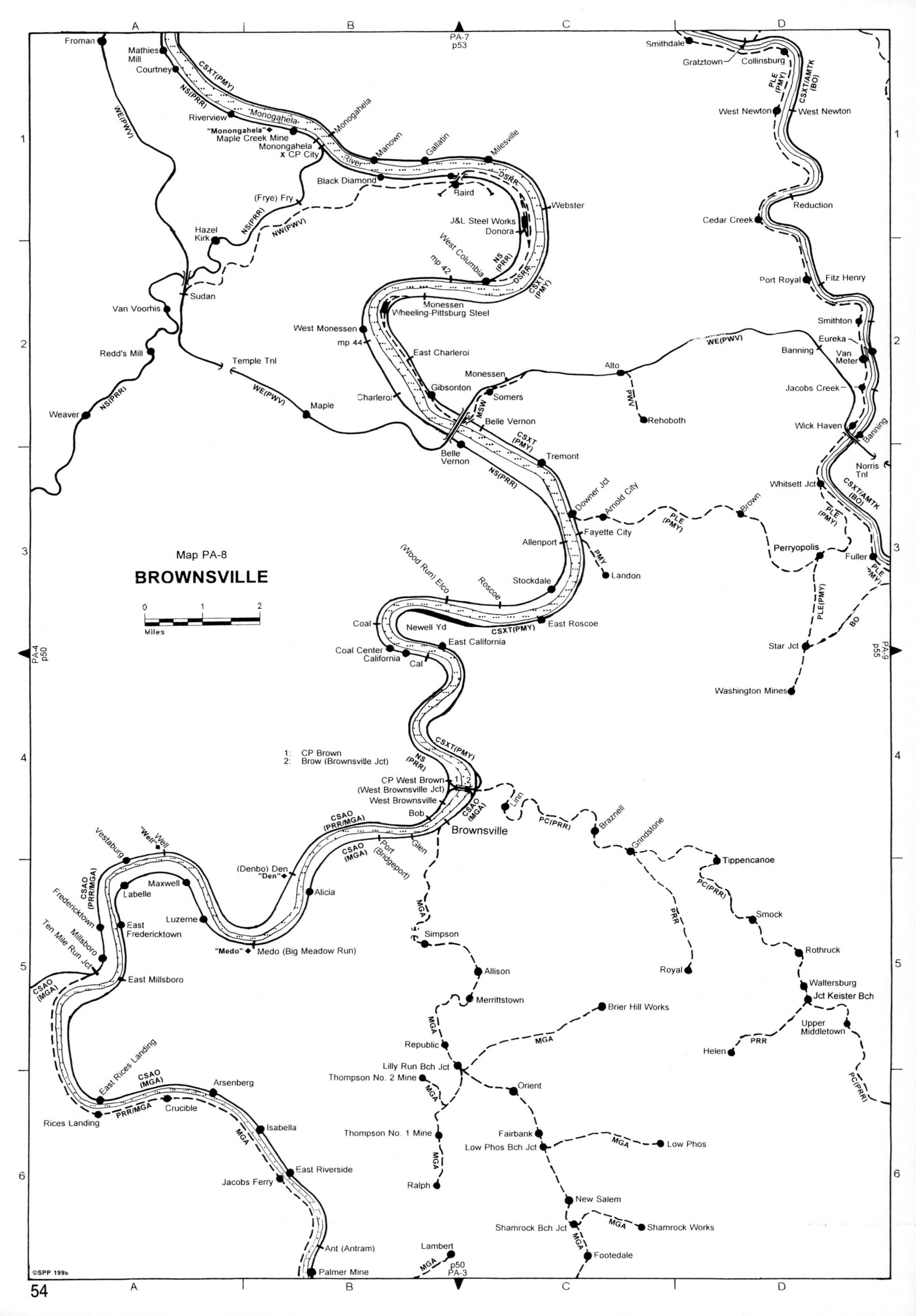

Map PA-8
BROWNSVILLE
0
1
2
Miles
PA-7
p53
PA-4
p50
PA-9
p55
p50
PA-3
Froman
Mathies Mill
Courtney
CSXT(PMY)
NS(PRR)
Riverview
Monogahela
River
Monogahela
"Monongahela"
Maple Creek Mine
Monongahela
X CP City
Manown
Gallatin
Milesville
Black Diamond
Baird
DSRR
Webster
J&L Steel Works
Donora
West Columbia
mp 42
NS (PRR)
CSXT (PMY)
WE(PWV)
(Frye) Fry
NS(PRR)
NW(PWV)
Hazel Kirk
Sudan
Van Voorhis
Monessen
Wheeling-Pittsburg Steel
West Monessen
mp 44
East Charleroi
Redd's Mill
Temple Tnl
WE(PWV)
Maple
Weaver
NS(PRR)
Charleroi
Gibsonton
Monessen
Somers
MSW
Belle Vernon
Belle Vernon
CSXT (PMY)
Tremont
NS(PRR)
Alto
WE(PWV)
PWV
Rehoboth
Smithdale
Gratztown
Collinsburg
PLE (PMY)
CSXT/AMTK (BO)
West Newton
West Newton
Reduction
Cedar Creek
Port Royal
Fitz Henry
Smithton
Eureka
Banning
Van Meter
Jacobs Creek
Wick Haven
Banning
Norris Tnl
Whitsett Jct
CSXT/AMTK (BO)
PLE (PMY)
Downer Jct
Arnold City
PLE (PMY)
Brown
Fayette City
Allenport
PMY
Landon
Perryopolis
Fuller
PLE (PMY)
(Wood Run) Elco
Roscoe
Stockdale
PLE(PMY)
BO
Coal
Newell Yd
CSXT(PMY)
East Roscoe
East California
Coal Center
California
Cal
Star Jct
Washington Mines
CSXT(PMY)
NS (PRR)
1: CP Brown
2: Brow (Brownsville Jct)
CP West Brown
(West Brownsville Jct)
West Brownsville
Bob
CSAO (MGA)
Linn
PC(PRR)
Braznell
Brownsville
Grindstone
Tippencanoe
CSAO (PRR/MGA)
CSAO (MGA)
Port (Bridgeport)
Glen
Vestaburg
"Well" Well
(Denbo) Den
"Den"
Maxwell
Alicia
CSAO (PRR/MGA)
Labelle
Fredericktown
East Fredericktown
Luzerne
MGA
PRR
PC(PRR)
Smock
Simpson
Millsboro
Ten Mile Run Jct
"Medo"
Medo (Big Meadow Run)
Rothruck
Royal
Allison
East Millsboro
CSAO (MGA)
Waltersburg
Jct Keister Bch
Merrittstown
Brier Hill Works
MGA
Upper Middletown
Republic
MGA
PRR
Helen
East Rices Landing
Lilly Run Bch Jct
PC(PRR)
CSAO (MGA)
Arsenberg
Thompson No. 2 Mine
MGA
Orient
Rices Landing
PRR/MGA
Crucible
Isabella
MGA
Thompson No. 1 Mine
Fairbank
Low Phos Bch Jct
MGA
Low Phos
East Riverside
Jacobs Ferry
MGA
Ralph
New Salem
Shamrock Bch Jct
MGA
Shamrock Works
MGA
Ant (Antram)
Lambert
Footedale
MGA
Palmer Mine
©SPP 1996
A
B
C
D
1
2
3
4
5
6

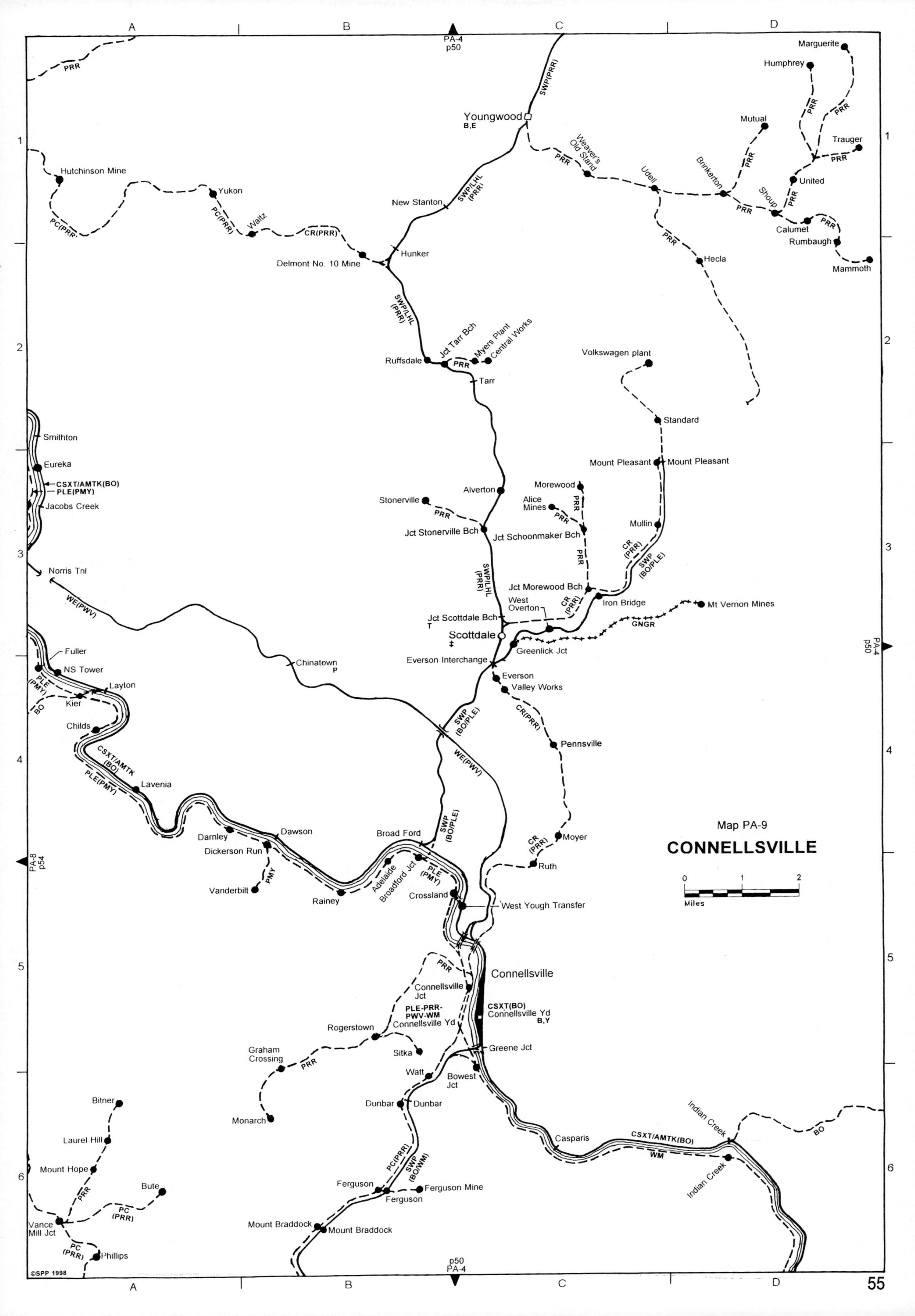
Map PA-9
CONNELLSVILLE
Youngwood
B,E
New Stanton
Hunker
Delmont No. 10 Mine
Ruffsdale
Jct Tarr Bch
Myers Plant
Central Works
Tarr
Hutchinson Mine
Yukon
Waltz
Weaver's Old Stand
Udell
Brinkerton
Mutual
Marguerite
Humphrey
Trauger
United
Shoup
Calumet
Rumbaugh
Mammoth
Hecla
Volkswagen plant
Standard
Mount Pleasant
Mount Pleasant
Mullin
Morewood
Alice Mines
Alverton
Stonerville
Jct Stonerville Bch
Jct Schoonmaker Bch
Jct Morewood Bch
West Overton
Iron Bridge
Mt Vernon Mines
Jct Scottdale Bch
Scottdale
Greenlick Jct
Everson Interchange
Everson
Valley Works
Pennsville
Moyer
Ruth
Smithton
Eureka
Jacobs Creek
Norris Tnl
Fuller
NS Tower
Layton
Kier
Childs
Lavenia
Chinatown
Darnley
Dawson
Dickerson Run
Vanderbilt
Rainey
Adelaide
Broadford Jct
Broad Ford
Crossland
West Yough Transfer
Connellsville
Connellsville Jct
PLE-PRR-PWV-WM Connellsville Yd
CSXT(BO) Connellsville Yd
B,Y
Greene Jct
Rogerstown
Sitka
Graham Crossing
Monarch
Watt
Bowest Jct
Dunbar
Dunbar
Casparis
Indian Creek
Indian Creek
Ferguson
Ferguson
Ferguson Mine
Mount Braddock
Mount Braddock
Bitner
Laurel Hill
Mount Hope
Bute
Vance Mill Jct
Phillips
CSXT/AMTK(BO)
PLE(PMY)
WE(PWV)
SWP(PRR)
SWP/LHL (PRR)
SWP (BO/PLE)
SWP (BO/WM)
PC(PRR)
CR(PRR)
PRR
GNGR
PMY
WM
BO
0 1 2
Miles
PA-4 p50
PA-8 p54
©SPP 1998

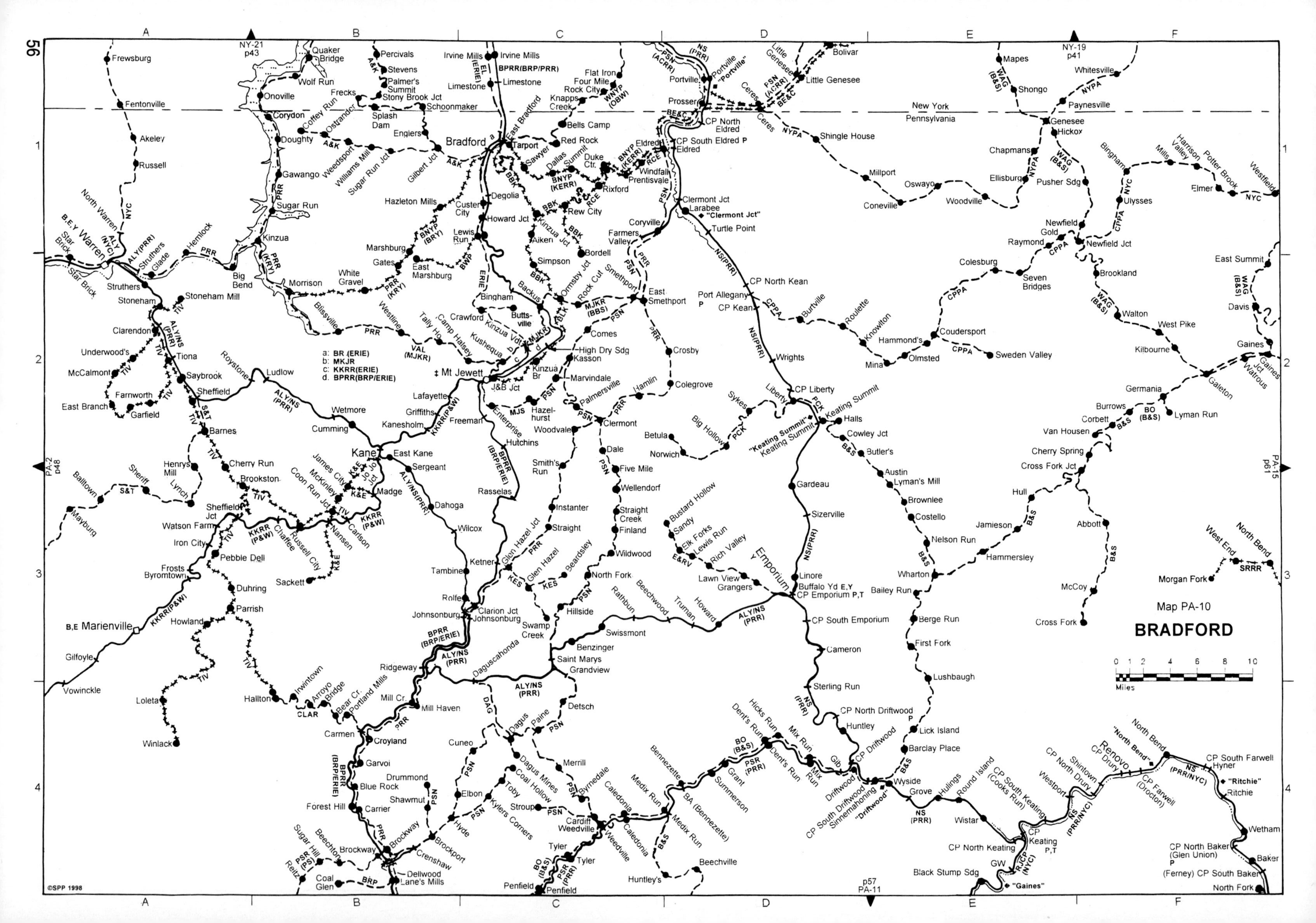
Map PA-10
BRADFORD
0 1 2 4 6 8 10
Miles
NY-21
p43
NY-19
p41
PA-2
p48
PA-15
p61
p57
PA-11
New York
Pennsylvania
a: BR (ERIE)
b: MKJR
c: KKRR(ERIE)
d: BPRR(BRP/ERIE)
Bradford
Emporium
Kane
Mt Jewett
Warren
Marienville
Renovo
Ridgeway
Johnsonburg
Saint Marys
Galeton
Coudersport
Port Allegany
East Smethport
Eldred
Portville
Genesee
Westfield
Driftwood
Keating Summit
Austin
Sheffield
Brockway
Penfield
Bennezette
Weedville
©SPP 1998

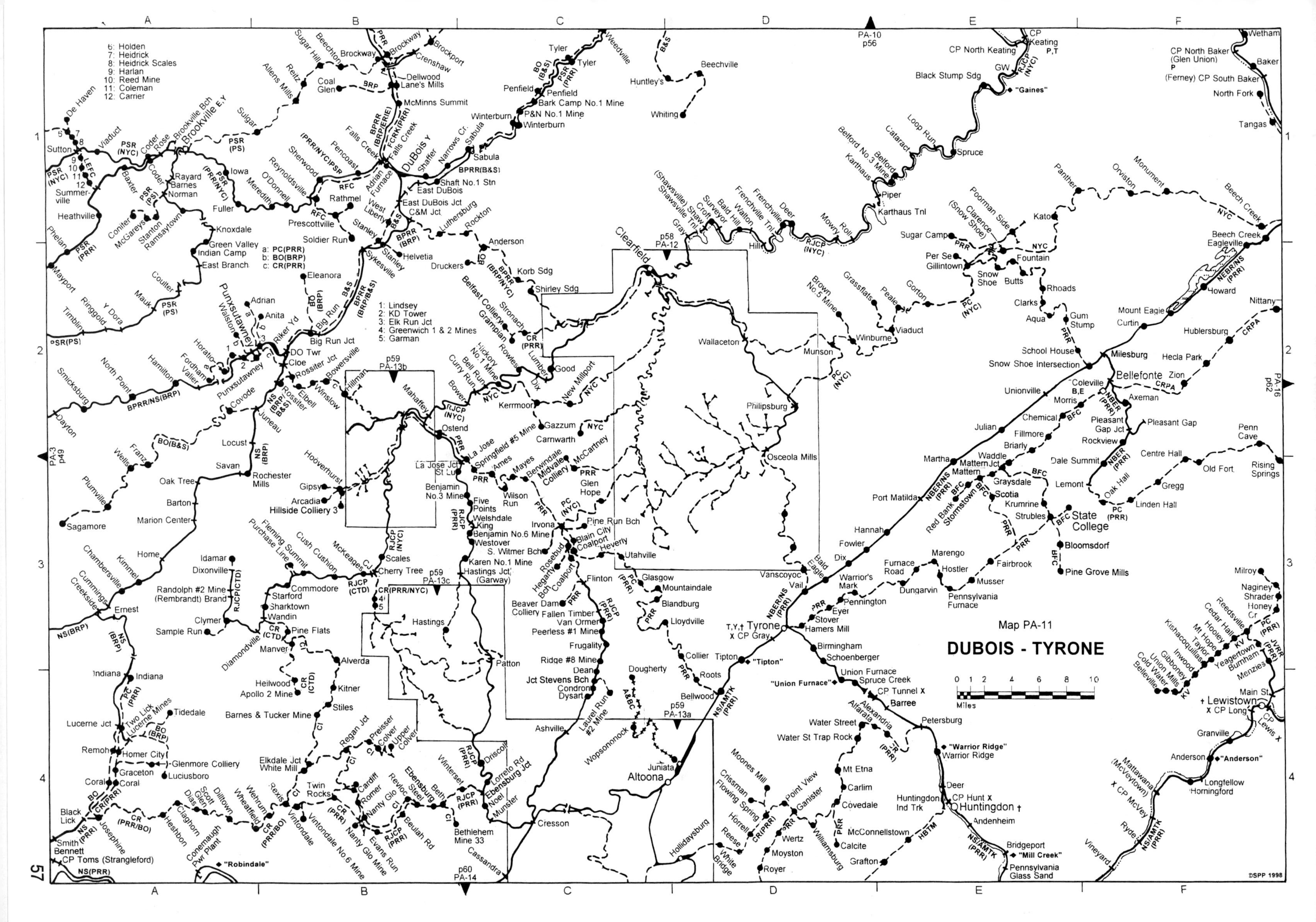
Map PA-11
DUBOIS - TYRONE
Miles
0 1 2 4 6 8 10
©SPP 1998
PA-10 p56
PA-16 p62
PA-12 p58
PA-13a p59
PA-13b p59
PA-13c p59
PA-14 p60
PA-3 p49
Clearfield
DuBois
Punxsutawney
Brookville
Tyrone
Altoona
Huntingdon
Lewistown
State College
Bellefonte
Philipsburg
Indiana
Ebensburg
Hollidaysburg
Juniata
6: Holden
7: Heidrick
8: Heidrick Scales
9: Harlan
10: Reed Mine
11: Coleman
12: Carrier
a: PC(PRR)
b: BO(BRP)
c: CR(PRR)
1: Lindsey
2: KD Tower
3: Elk Run Jct
4: Greenwich 1 & 2 Mines
5: Garman

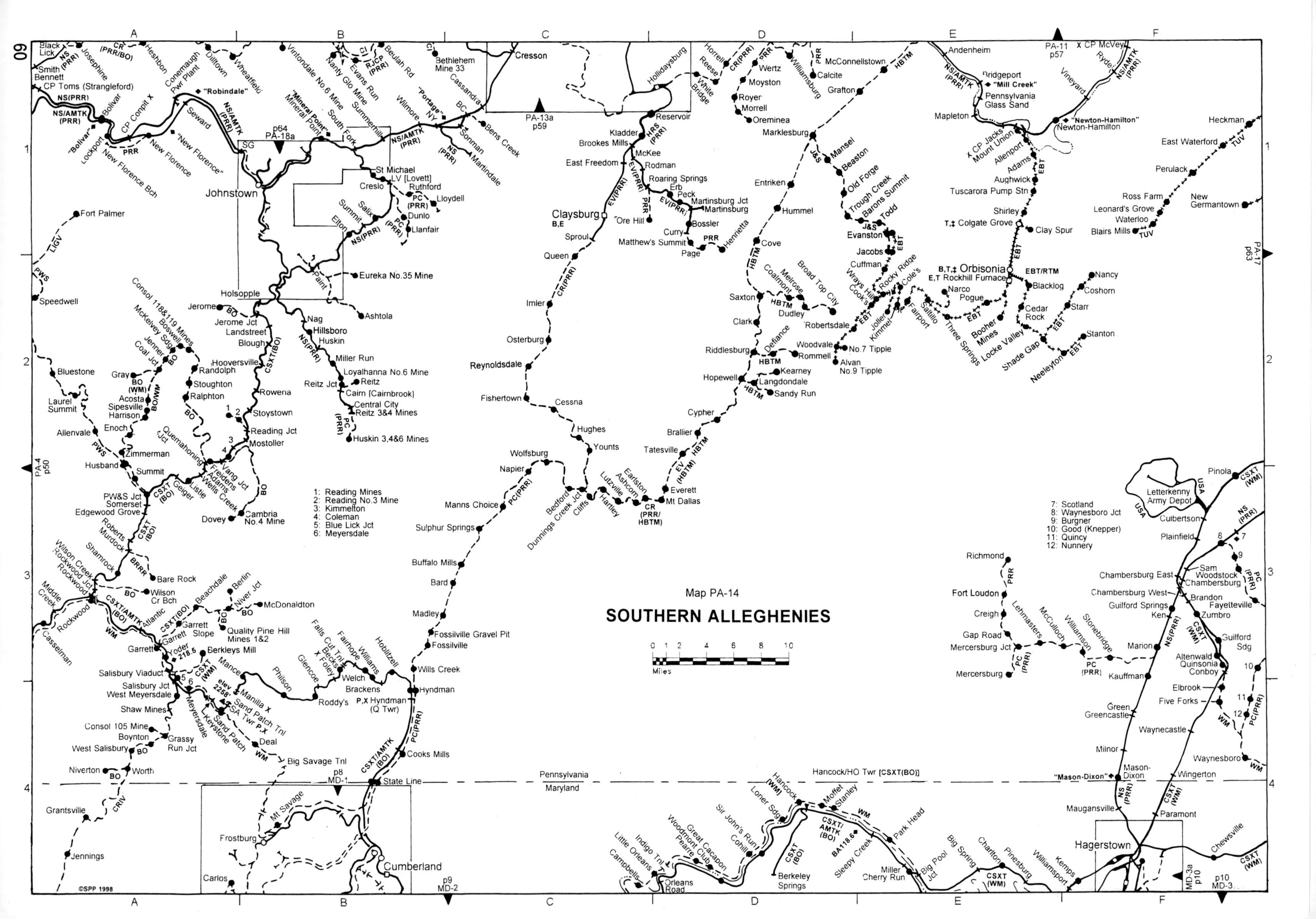
Map PA-14
SOUTHERN ALLEGHENIES
0 1 2 4 6 8 10
Miles
A
B
C
D
E
F
1
2
3
4
PA-11 p57
PA-17 p63
PA-13a p59
PA-18a p64
PA-4 p50
p8 MD-1
p9 MD-2
p10 MD-3
MD-3a p10
Pennsylvania
Maryland
Hancock/HO Twr [CSXT(BO)]
Johnstown
Cresson
Claysburg
B,E
Orbisonia
Hagerstown
Cumberland
Letterkenny Army Depot
USA
Frostburg
Mt Savage
Carlos
Jennings
Grantsville
Niverton
Worth
West Salisbury
Boynton
Consol 105 Mine
Grassy Run Jct
Shaw Mines
Salisbury Viaduct
Salisbury Jct
West Meyersdale
Meyersdale
Keystone
Sand Patch
Sand Patch Tnl
Deal
Big Savage Tnl
State Line
Cooks Mills
Hyndman
P,X Hyndman (Q Twr)
Wills Creek
Fossilville
Fossilville Gravel Pit
Madley
Bard
Buffalo Mills
Sulphur Springs
Manns Choice
Napier
Wolfsburg
Bedford
Dunnings Creek Jct
Cliffs
Hartley
Lutzville
Ashcom
Earlston
Mt Dallas
Everett
Tatesville
Brallier
Cypher
Hopewell
Langdondale
Sandy Run
Kearney
Riddlesburg
Rommell
Woodvale
No.7 Tipple
Alvan
No.9 Tipple
Robertsdale
Dudley
Coalmont
Melrose
Broad Top City
Saxton
Clark
Cove
Hummel
Entriken
Marklesburg
Grafton
Calcite
McConnellstown
Williamsburg
Wertz
Moyston
Royer
Morrell
Oreminea
Horrell
Reese
White Bridge
Hollidaysburg
Reservoir
Kladder
Brookes Mills
East Freedom
McKee
Rodman
Roaring Springs
Erb
Peck
Martinsburg Jct
Martinsburg
Bossler
Curry
Matthew's Summit
Page
Henrietta
Ore Hill
Sproul
Queen
Imler
Osterburg
Reynoldsdale
Fishertown
Cessna
Hughes
Younts
Mansel
Beaston
Old Forge
Trough Creek
Barons Summit
Todd
Evanston
Jacobs
Cuffman
Wrays Hill
Cook's
Rocky Ridge
Cole's
Joller
Kimmel
Fairport
Saltillo
Three Springs
Narco
Pogue
Booher Mines
Locke Valley
Shade Gap
Neeleyton
Cedar Rock
Blacklog
Starr
Stanton
Nancy
Coshom
B,T,‡ Orbisonia
E,T Rockhill Furnace
Clay Spur
T,‡ Colgate Grove
Shirley
Tuscarora Pump Stn
Aughwick
Adams
Allenport
Mount Union
CP Jacks
Mapleton
Bridgeport
"Mill Creek"
Pennsylvania Glass Sand
Andenheim
"Newton-Hamilton"
Newton-Hamilton
Vineyard
Ryde
CP McVey
Heckman
East Waterford
Perulack
Ross Farm
Leonard's Grove
Waterloo
Blairs Mills
New Germantown
Pinola
Culbertson
Plainfield
Sam Woodstock
Chambersburg
Chambersburg East
Chambersburg West
Guilford Springs
Ken
Brandon
Fayetteville
Zumbro
Guilford Sdg
Altenwald
Quinsonia
Conboy
Elbrook
Five Forks
Waynecastle
Waynesboro
Wingerton
Marion
Kauffman
Green
Greencastle
Milnor
Mason-Dixon
"Mason-Dixon"
Maugansville
Paramont
Chewsville
Kemps
Williamsport
Pinesburg
Charlton
Big Spring
Big Pool Jct
Miller
Cherry Run
Sleepy Creek
Park Head
BA118.6
Stanley
Moffet
Hancock
Loner Sdg
Sir John's Run
Cohill
Great Cacapon
Woodmont Club
Pearre
Indigo Tnl
Little Orleans
Campbells
Orleans Road
Berkeley Springs
Richmond
Fort Loudon
Creigh
Gap Road
Mercersburg Jct
Mercersburg
Lehmasters
McCulloch
Williamson
Stonebridge
7: Scotland
8: Waynesboro Jct
9: Burgner
10: Good (Knepper)
11: Quincy
12: Nunnery
1: Reading Mines
2: Reading No.3 Mine
3: Kimmelton
4: Coleman
5: Blue Lick Jct
6: Meyersdale
Black Lick
Smith
Bennett
CP Toms (Strangleford)
Josephine
Heshbon
Conemaugh Pwr Plant
Dilltown
Wheatfield
"Robindale"
Bolivar
"Bolivar"
Lockport
CP Conpit X
Seward
New Florence
"New Florence"
New Florence Bch
Fort Palmer
Speedwell
Vintondale No.6 Mine
Nanty Glo Mine
Evans Run
Beulah Rd
Bethlehem Mine 33
Cassandra
Bens Creek
Sonman
Martindale
"Portage" NY
Wilmore
Summerhill
South Fork
"Mineral Point"
Mineral Point
St Michael
LV [Lovett]
Rutfford
Creslo
Lloydell
Dunlo
Llanfair
Salix
Summit
Elton
Paint
Eureka No.35 Mine
Ashtola
Holsopple
Jerome
Jerome Jct
Landstreet
Blough
Nag
Hillsboro
Huskin
Miller Run
Loyalhanna No.6 Mine
Reitz
Reitz Jct
Cairn [Cairnbrook]
Central City
Reitz 3&4 Mines
Huskin 3,4&6 Mines
Hooversville
Randolph
Stoughton
Ralphton
Rowena
Stoystown
Reading Jct
Mostoller
Consol 118&119 Mines
Boswell
McKelvey Sdg
Jenner
Coal Jct
Gray
Acosta
Sipesville
Harrison
Bluestone
Laurel Summit
Allenvale
Enoch
Zimmerman
Husband
Quemahoning Jct
Vang Jct
Friedens
Adams
Wells Creek
Listie
Geiger
Cambria No.4 Mine
Dovey
PW&S Jct
Somerset
Edgewood Grove
Roberts
Murdock
Shamrock
Bare Rock
Wilson Cr Bch
Wilson Creek
Rockwood Jct
Rockwood
Middle Creek
Casselman
Beachdale
Berlin
Niver Jct
McDonaldton
Garrett Slope
Quality Pine Hill Mines 1&2
Atlantic
Garrett
Yoder 218.5
Berkleys Mill
Mance
elev 2258'
Manilla X
SA Twr P,X
Philson
Glencoe
Roddy's
Falls Cut Tnl
Becks
X Foley
Welch
Brackens
Fairhope
Williams
Hobitzell
©SPP 1998

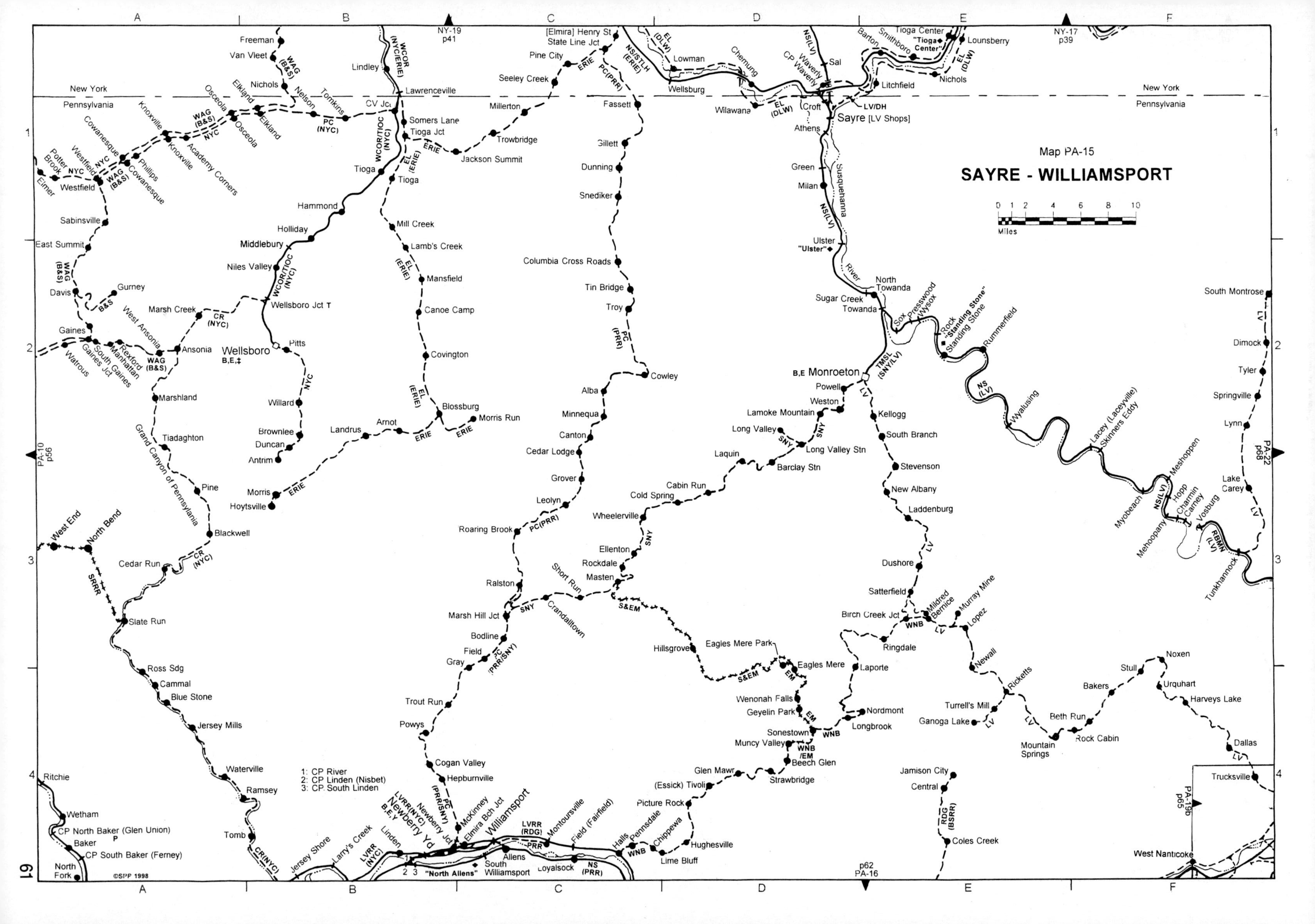

Map PA-15
SAYRE - WILLIAMSPORT
0 1 2 4 6 8 10
Miles
New York
Pennsylvania
NY-19
p41
NY-17
p39
PA-22
p68
PA-19b
p65
PA-16
p62
PA-10
p56
Freeman
Van Vleet
WAG (B&S)
Nichols
Nelson
Tomkins
Lindley
WCOR (NYC/ERIE)
Lawrenceville
CV Jct
PC (NYC)
Osceola
Elkland
Elkland
Osceola
WAG (B&S)
NYC
Knoxville
Knoxville
Academy Corners
Cowanesque
Cowanesque
Phillips
Westfield
Westfield
NYC
WAG (B&S)
Potter Brook
Elmer
Sabinsville
East Summit
WAG (B&S)
Davis
Gurney
B&S
Gaines
Watrous
Gaines Jct
South Gaines
Manhattan
Rexford
West Ansonia
WAG (B&S)
Ansonia
Marsh Creek
CR (NYC)
Wellsboro Jct T
Wellsboro
B,E,‡
Pitts
NYC
Willard
Brownlee
Duncan
Antrim
Marshland
Tiadaghton
Grand Canyon of Pennsylvania
Pine
Blackwell
CR (NYC)
Cedar Run
West End
North Bend
SRRR
Slate Run
Ross Sdg
Cammal
Blue Stone
Jersey Mills
Waterville
Ramsey
Tomb
CR(NYC)
Ritchie
Wetham
CP North Baker (Glen Union)
P
Baker
CP South Baker (Ferney)
North Fork
©SPP 1998
Somers Lane
Tioga Jct
ERIE
EL (ERIE)
WCOR/TIOC (NYC)
Tioga
Tioga
Hammond
Holliday
Middlebury
Niles Valley
WCOR/TIOC (NYC)
Mill Creek
Lamb's Creek
EL (ERIE)
Mansfield
Canoe Camp
Covington
EL (ERIE)
Blossburg
Morris Run
ERIE
ERIE
Arnot
Landrus
ERIE
Morris
Hoytsville
Jackson Summit
Trowbridge
Millerton
Seeley Creek
Pine City
[Elmira] Henry St
State Line Jct
ERIE
PC(PRR)
NS/STLH (ERIE)
Fassett
Gillett
Dunning
Snediker
Columbia Cross Roads
Tin Bridge
Troy
PC (PRR)
Cowley
Alba
Minnequa
Canton
Cedar Lodge
Grover
Leolyn
Roaring Brook
PC(PRR)
Ralston
Marsh Hill Jct
SNY
Crandalltown
Short Run
Bodine
Field
Gray
PC (PRR/SNY)
Trout Run
Powys
Cogan Valley
Hepburnville
PC (PRR/SNY)
1: CP River
2: CP Linden (Nisbet)
3: CP South Linden
Jersey Shore
Larry's Creek
LVRR (NYC)
Linden
LVRR (NYC)
Newberry Yd
B.E,Y
Newberry Jct
McKinney
Elmira Bch Jct
Williamsport
"North Allens"
South Williamsport
Allens
LVRR (RDG)
PRR
Montoursville
Field (Fairfield)
Loyalsock
NS (PRR)
EL (DLW)
Lowman
Wellsburg
Chemung
Wilawana
EL (DLW)
NS(LV)
Sal
Waverly
CP Waverly
Croft
Athens
LV/DH
Sayre [LV Shops]
Barton
Smithboro
Tioga Center
"Tioga Center"
Lounsberry
EL (DLW)
Nichols
Litchfield
Green
Milan
Susquehanna
NS(LV)
Ulster
"Ulster"
River
North Towanda
Sugar Creek
Towanda
Sox
Presswood
Wysox
Rock
"Standing Stone"
Standing Stone
Rummerfield
B,E Monroeton
TMSL (SNY/LV)
LV
Powell
Weston
Lamoke Mountain
Long Valley
SNY
SNY
Long Valley Stn
Laquin
Barclay Stn
Cabin Run
Cold Spring
Wheelerville
SNY
Ellenton
Rockdale
Masten
S&EM
Hillsgrove
Eagles Mere Park
Eagles Mere
EM
S&EM
Wenonah Falls
Geyelin Park
EM
Sonestown
WNB
Muncy Valley
WNB /EM
Beech Glen
Strawbridge
Glen Mawr
(Essick) Tivoli
Picture Rock
Halls
Pennsdale
WNB
Chippewa
Hughesville
Lime Bluff
Kellogg
South Branch
Stevenson
New Albany
Laddenburg
LV
Dushore
Satterfield
Birch Creek Jct
WNB
Mildred
Bernice
Murray Mine
Lopez
LV
Ringdale
Laporte
Nordmont
Longbrook
Newall
Ricketts
Turrell's Mill
Ganoga Lake
LV
LV
Beth Run
Mountain Springs
Rock Cabin
Bakers
Stull
Noxen
Urquhart
Harveys Lake
Dallas
LV
Trucksville
West Nanticoke
Jamison City
Central
RDG (BSRR)
Coles Creek
NS (LV)
Wyalusing
Lacey (Laceyville)
Skinners Eddy
Myobeach
Meshoppen
NS(LV)
Hopp
Charmin
Carney
Vosburg
Mehoopany
RBMN (LV)
Tunkhannock
South Montrose
LV
Dimock
Tyler
Springville
Lynn
Lake Carey
LV

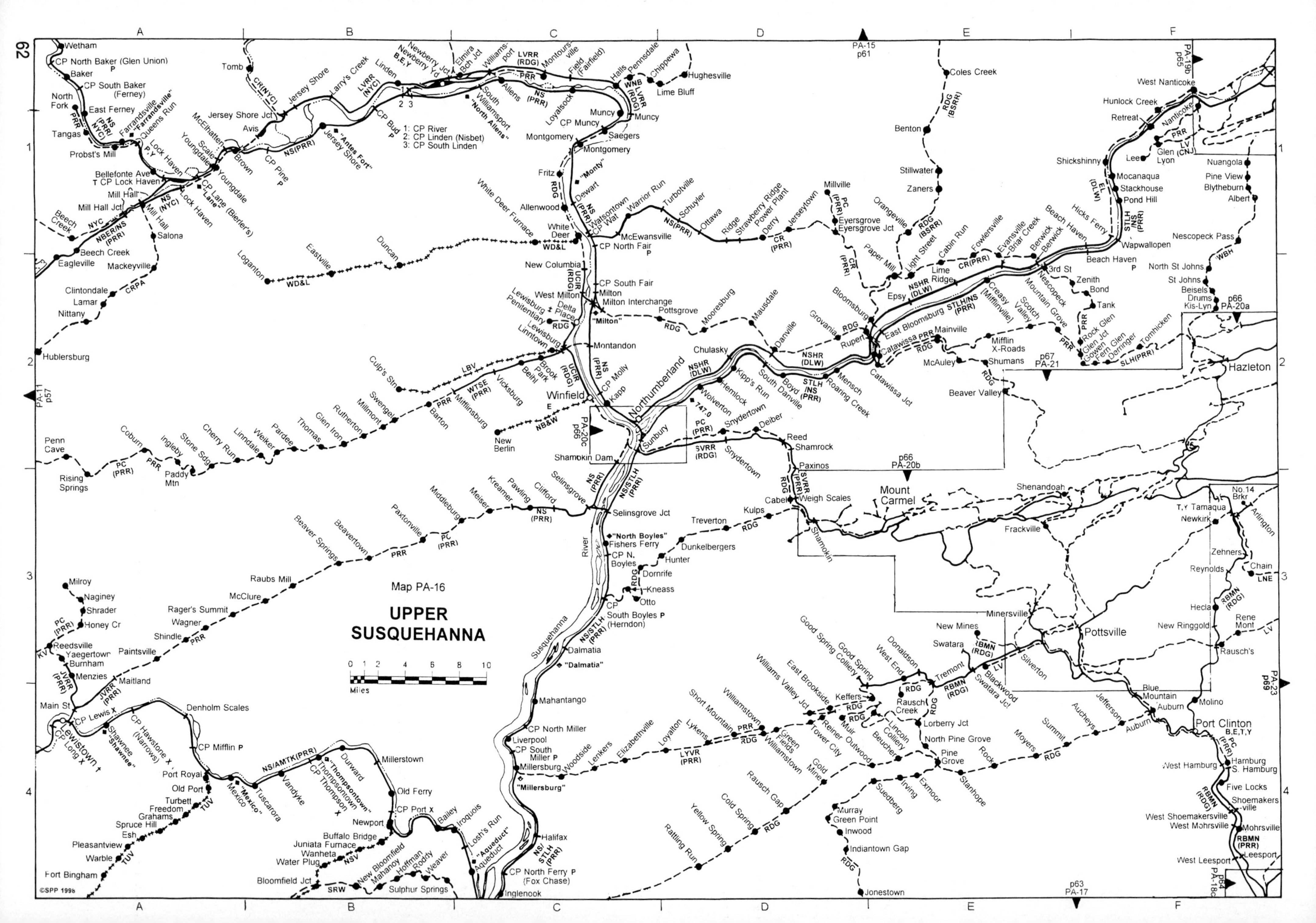
Map PA-16
UPPER SUSQUEHANNA
Miles
0 1 2 4 6 8 10
1: CP River
2: CP Linden (Nisbet)
3: CP South Linden
Northumberland
Sunbury
Winfield
Hazleton
Mount Carmel
Pottsville
Port Clinton
Susquehanna
River
PA-15 p61
PA-19b p65
PA-11 p57
PA-20a p66
PA-21 p67
PA-20b p66
PA-20c p66
PA-23 p69
PA-17 p63
PA-18c p64
©SPP 1996

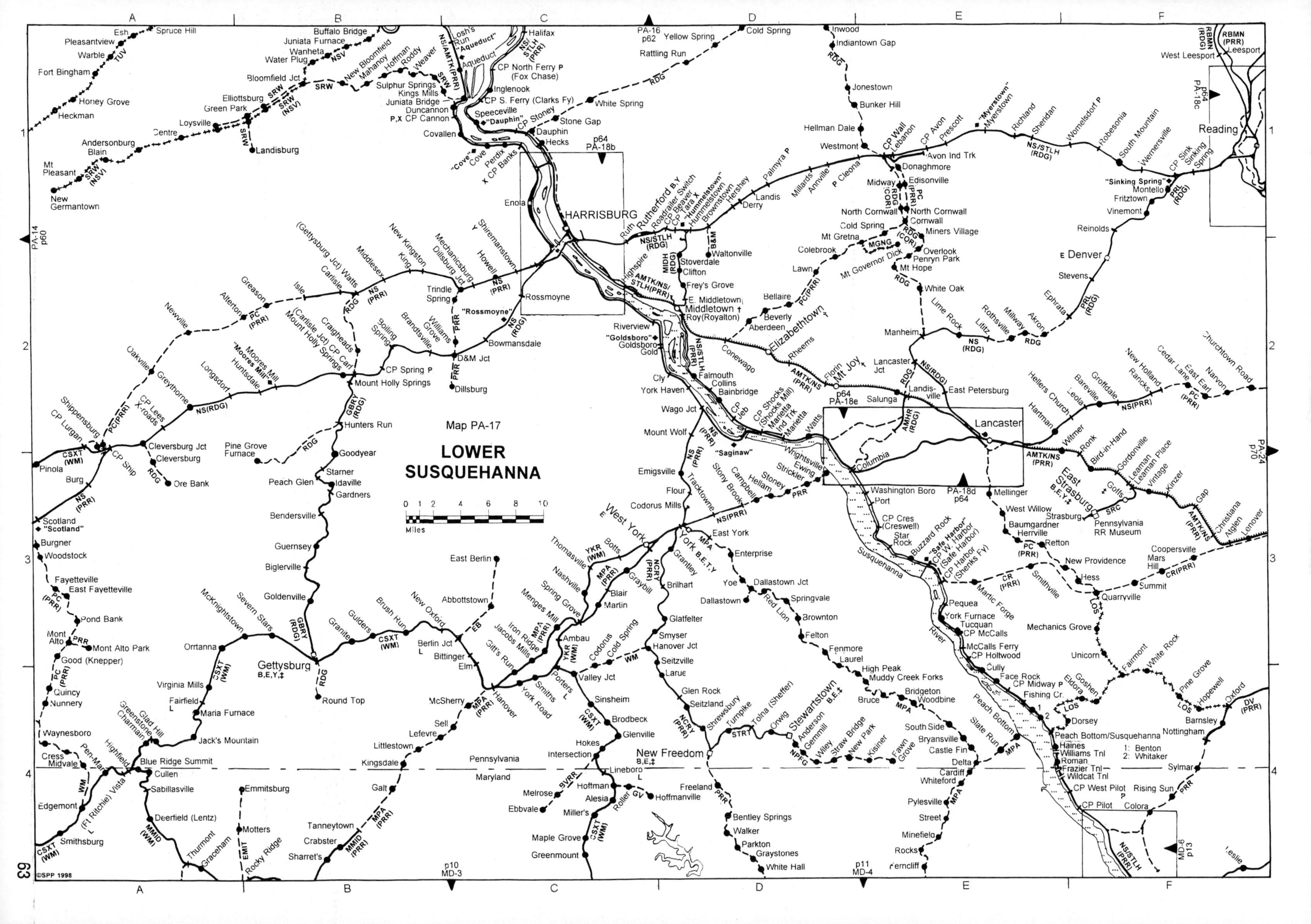
Map PA-17
LOWER SUSQUEHANNA
0 1 2 4 6 8 10
Miles
HARRISBURG
Lancaster
Reading
York
West York
Gettysburg
East Strasburg
Elizabethtown
Mt Joy
Middletown
Denver
Lebanon
New Freedom
Stewartstown
Hanover
Shippensburg
Carlisle
Mechanicsburg
Dillsburg
Columbia
Wrightsville
Susquehanna River
Pennsylvania
Maryland
PA-24 p70
PA-18c p64
PA-18d p64
PA-18e p64
PA-18b p64
PA-16 p62
PA-14 p60
MD-6 p13
MD-4 p11
MD-3 p10
NS/AMTK(PRR)
AMTK/NS (PRR)
NS/STLH (RDG)
NS/STLH (PRR)
CSXT (WM)
NS (PRR)
GBRY (RDG)
MPA
NCRY (PRR)
YKR
SRW
©SPP 1998

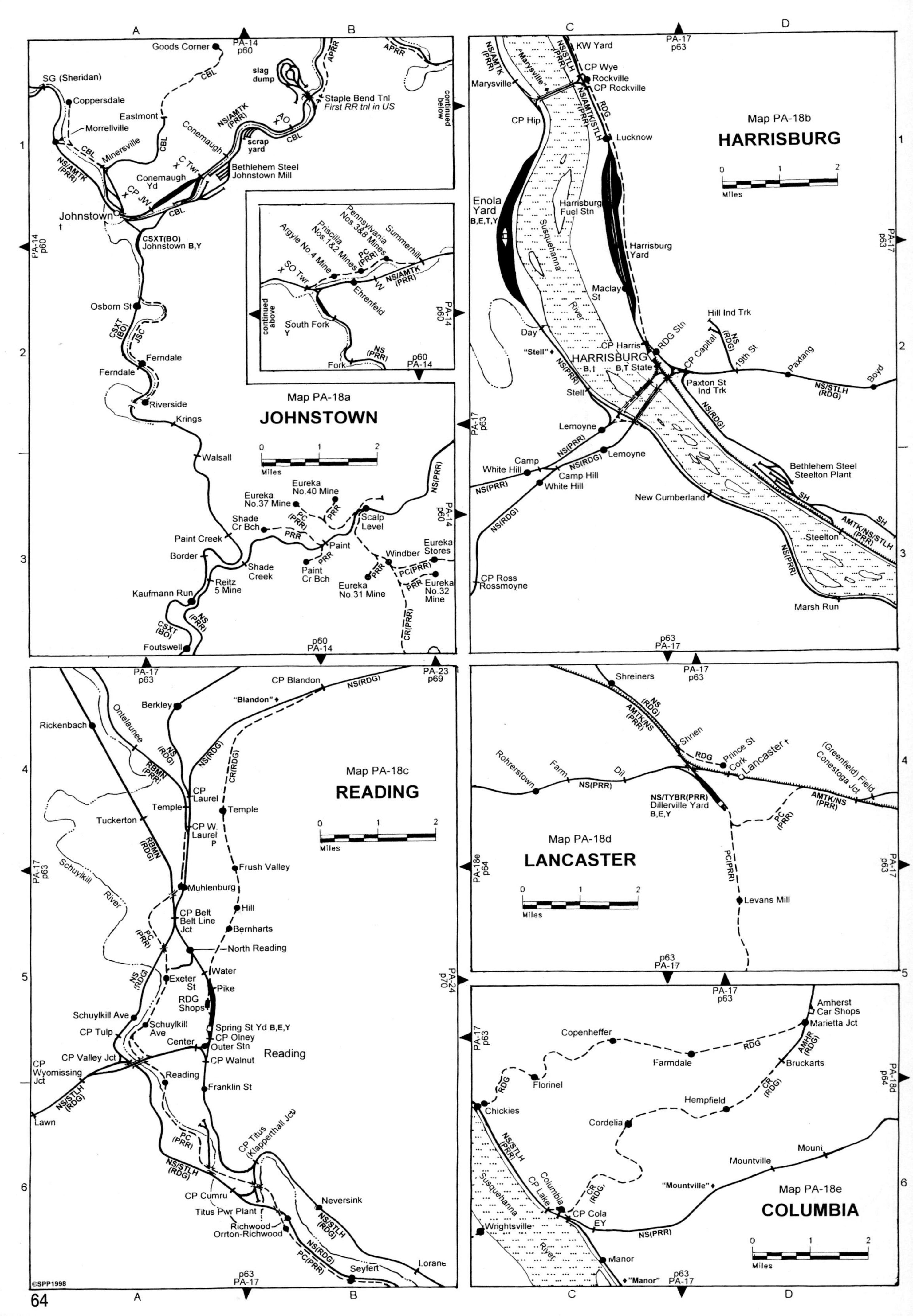
Map PA-18a
JOHNSTOWN
Goods Corner
SG (Sheridan)
Coppersdale
Morrellville
Eastmont
Minersville
Conemaugh
Conemaugh Yd
C Twr
CP JW
Johnstown
CSXT(BO) Johnstown B,Y
Bethlehem Steel Johnstown Mill
scrap yard
slag dump
Staple Bend Tnl
First RR tnl in US
NS/AMTK (PRR)
CBL
APRR
AO
continued below
Osborn St
CSXT (BO)
JSC
Ferndale
Riverside
Krings
Walsall
Paint Creek
Border
Kaufmann Run
Reitz 5 Mine
Shade Creek
Shade Cr Bch
Eureka No.37 Mine
Eureka No.40 Mine
Scalp Level
Paint
Paint Cr Bch
Windber
Eureka Stores
Eureka No.31 Mine
Eureka No.32 Mine
PC(PRR)
PRR
CR(PRR)
Foutswell
Pennsylvania Nos 3&8 Mines
Priscilla Nos 1&2 Mines
Argyle No.4 Mine
Summerhill
SO Twr
Ehrenfeld
South Fork Y
Fork
continued above
Map PA-18b
HARRISBURG
KW Yard
CP Wye
Rockville
CP Rockville
Marysville
"Marysville"
CP Hip
Lucknow
Enola Yard B,E,T,Y
Harrisburg Fuel Stn
Susquehanna River
Harrisburg Yard
Maclay St
Day
"Stell"
CP Harris
RDG Stn
HARRISBURG B,† B,T State
CP Capital
Hill Ind Trk
19th St
Paxtang
Boyd
Paxton St Ind Trk
Stell
Lemoyne
Camp
White Hill
Camp Hill
New Cumberland
Bethlehem Steel Steelton Plant
Steelton
Marsh Run
CP Ross Rossmoyne
NS(PRR)
NS(RDG)
NS/STLH (RDG)
AMTK/NS/STLH (PRR)
SH
Map PA-18c
READING
CP Blandon
"Blandon"
Berkley
Rickenbach
Ontelaunee
RBMN (PRR)
RBMN (RDG)
CP Laurel
Temple
CP W Laurel P
Tuckerton
Frush Valley
Schuylkill River
Muhlenburg
CP Belt Belt Line Jct
Hill
Bernharts
North Reading
Water
Exeter St
Pike
RDG Shops
Schuylkill Ave
CP Tulp
Spring St Yd B,E,Y
CP Olney
Outer Stn
Center
CP Walnut
Reading
CP Valley Jct
CP Wyomissing Jct
Lawn
Franklin St
CP Titus (Klapperthall Jct)
CP Cumru
Titus Pwr Plant
Richwood
Orrton-Richwood
Neversink
Seyfert
Lorane
CR(RDG)
PC (PRR)
NS/STLH (RDG)
PC(PRR)
Map PA-18d
LANCASTER
Shreiners
Shren
RDG
Prince St
Cork
Lancaster
(Greenfield) Field
Conestoga Jct
Rohrerstown
Farm
Dil
NS(PRR)
NS/TYBR(PRR) Dillerville Yard B,E,Y
AMTK/NS (PRR)
PC (PRR)
PC(PRR)
Levans Mill
Map PA-18e
COLUMBIA
Amherst Car Shops
Marietta Jct
Copenheffer
Farmdale
Bruckarts
AMHR (RDG)
CR (RDG)
Florinel
Chickies
Hempfield
Cordelia
Mountville
Mount
"Mountville"
NS/STLH (PRR)
Susquehanna River
Columbia
CP Lake
CP Cola
EY
Wrightsville
Manor
"Manor"
NS(PRR)
Miles
©SPP1998

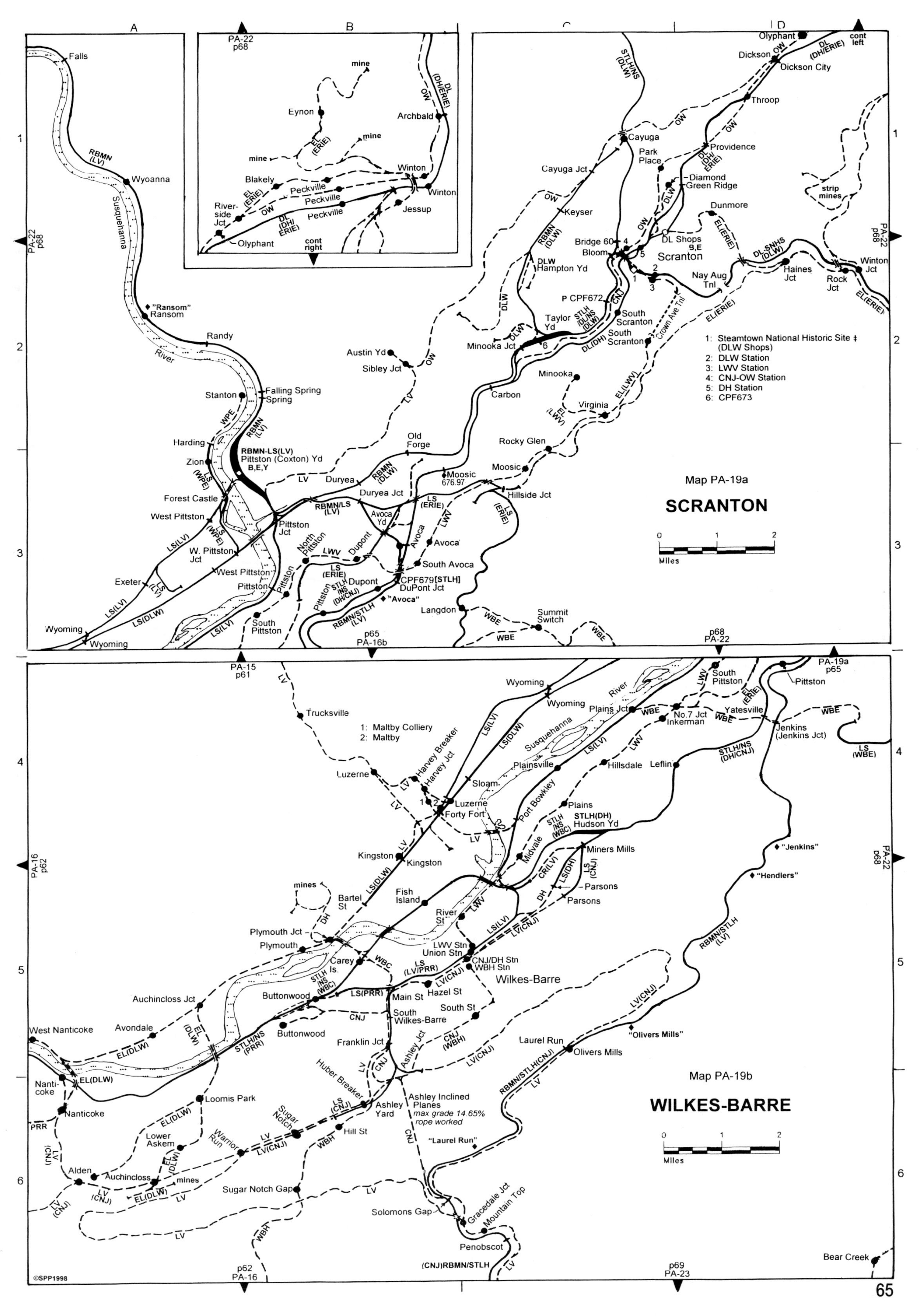
Map PA-19a
SCRANTON
1: Steamtown National Historic Site ‡ (DLW Shops)
2: DLW Station
3: LWV Station
4: CNJ-OW Station
5: DH Station
6: CPF673
Miles
Map PA-19b
WILKES-BARRE
1: Maltby Colliery
2: Maltby
Ashley Inclined Planes
max grade 14.65%
rope worked
Scranton
Wilkes-Barre
Pittston (Coxton) Yd
Taylor Yd
Hudson Yd
Susquehanna River
©SPP1998

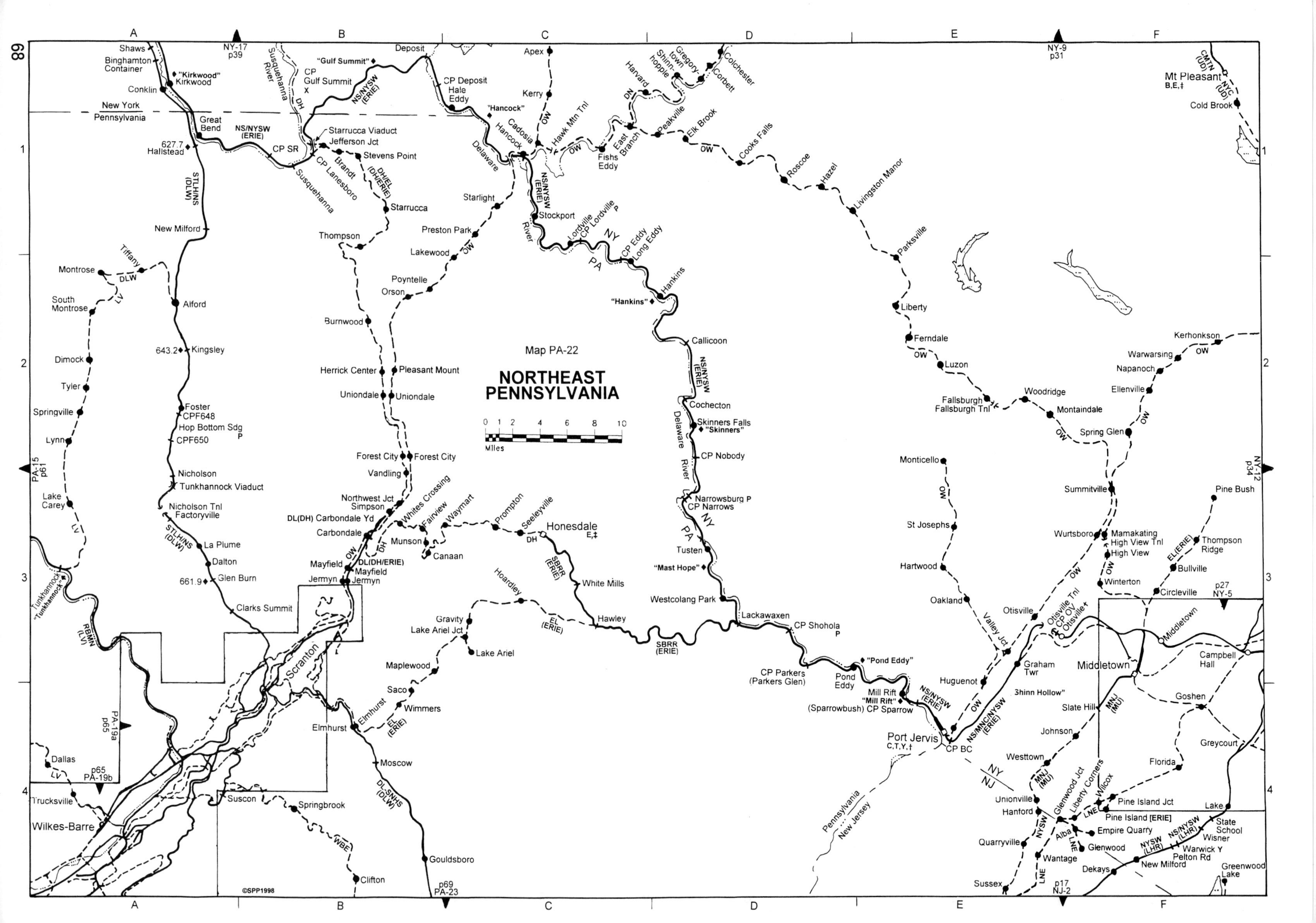

Map PA-22
NORTHEAST PENNSYLVANIA
0 1 2 4 6 8 10
Miles
A
B
C
D
E
F
1
2
3
4
NY-17
p39
NY-9
p31
NY-12
p34
p27
NY-5
p17
NJ-2
p69
PA-23
PA-15
p61
PA-19a
p65
p65
PA-19b
New York
Pennsylvania
NY
PA
NY
NJ
Pennsylvania
New Jersey
Shaws
Binghamton Container
"Kirkwood"
Kirkwood
Conklin
Great Bend
627.7
Hallstead
NS/NYSW (ERIE)
CP SR
STLH/NS (DLW)
New Milford
Susquehanna River
DH
CP Gulf Summit
"Gulf Summit"
Deposit
NS/NYSW (ERIE)
Starrucca Viaduct
Jefferson Jct
Stevens Point
Brandt
CP Lanesboro
Susquehanna
DH/EL (DH/ERIE)
Starrucca
Thompson
CP Deposit
Hale Eddy
"Hancock"
Apex
Kerry
OW
Hancock
Cadosia
Hawk Mtn Tnl
Delaware
Starlight
Preston Park
Lakewood
Poyntelle
Orson
Burnwood
Herrick Center
Pleasant Mount
Uniondale
Uniondale
Forest City
Forest City
Vandling
Northwest Jct
Simpson
DL(DH) Carbondale Yd
Carbondale
Whites Crossing
Fairview
Waymart
Munson
Canaan
Mayfield
Mayfield
DL(DH/ERIE)
Jermyn
Jermyn
Montrose
Tiffany
DLW
South Montrose
LV
Alford
643.2
Kingsley
Dimock
Tyler
Springville
Lynn
Foster
CPF648
Hop Bottom Sdg
P
CPF650
Nicholson
Tunkhannock Viaduct
Nicholson Tnl
Factoryville
STLH/NS (DLW)
La Plume
Dalton
661.9
Glen Burn
Clarks Summit
Lake Carey
Tunkhannock
"Tunkhannock"
RBMN (LV)
Scranton
Dallas
Trucksville
Wilkes-Barre
Suscon
Springbrook
WBE
Clifton
Elmhurst
Elmhurst
EL (ERIE)
Wimmers
Saco
Maplewood
Gravity
Lake Ariel Jct
Lake Ariel
Moscow
DL-SNHS (DLW)
Gouldsboro
©SPP1998
Hoardley
EL (ERIE)
Hawley
SBRR (ERIE)
White Mills
Honesdale
E,‡
Seelyville
Prompton
Fishs Eddy
East Branch
Peakville
Harvard
DN
Gregory-town
Shinn-hopple
Corbett
Colchester
Elk Brook
Cooks Falls
Roscoe
Hazel
Livingston Manor
Parksville
Liberty
Ferndale
Luzon
Fallsburgh
Fallsburgh Tnl
Woodridge
Montaindale
Spring Glen
Stockport
River
Lordville
CP Lordville
CP Eddy
Long Eddy
Hankins
"Hankins"
Callicoon
NS/NYSW (ERIE)
Cochecton
Skinners Falls
"Skinners"
Delaware River
CP Nobody
Narrowsburg P
CP Narrows
Tusten
"Mast Hope"
Westcolang Park
Lackawaxen
CP Shohola
P
"Pond Eddy"
Pond Eddy
CP Parkers
(Parkers Glen)
Mill Rift
"Mill Rift"
(Sparrowbush) CP Sparrow
NS/NYSW (ERIE)
Port Jervis
C,T,Y,†
CP BC
NS/MNC/NYSW (ERIE)
Monticello
St Josephs
Hartwood
Oakland
Valley Jct
Huguenot
Otisville
Otisville Tnl
CP OV
Otisville†
Graham Twr
"Shinn Hollow"
Slate Hill
MNJ (MU)
Middletown
Middletown
Campbell Hall
Goshen
Greycourt
Florida
Johnson
Westtown
Unionville
Hanford
Quarryville
Sussex
Glenwood Jct
Liberty Corners
Wilcox
Pine Island Jct
Pine Island [ERIE]
Empire Quarry
Alba
LNE
Glenwood
Wantage
Dekays
New Milford
NYSW (LHR)
NS/NYSW (LHR)
Warwick Y
Pelton Rd
Wisner
State School
Lake
Greenwood Lake
Summitville
Wurtsboro
Mamakating
High View Tnl
High View
Winterton
Circleville
Bullville
EL(ERIE)
Thompson Ridge
Pine Bush
Kerhonkson
Warwarsing
Napanoch
Ellenville
Mt Pleasant
B,E,‡
CMTN (UD)
NYC (UD)
Cold Brook

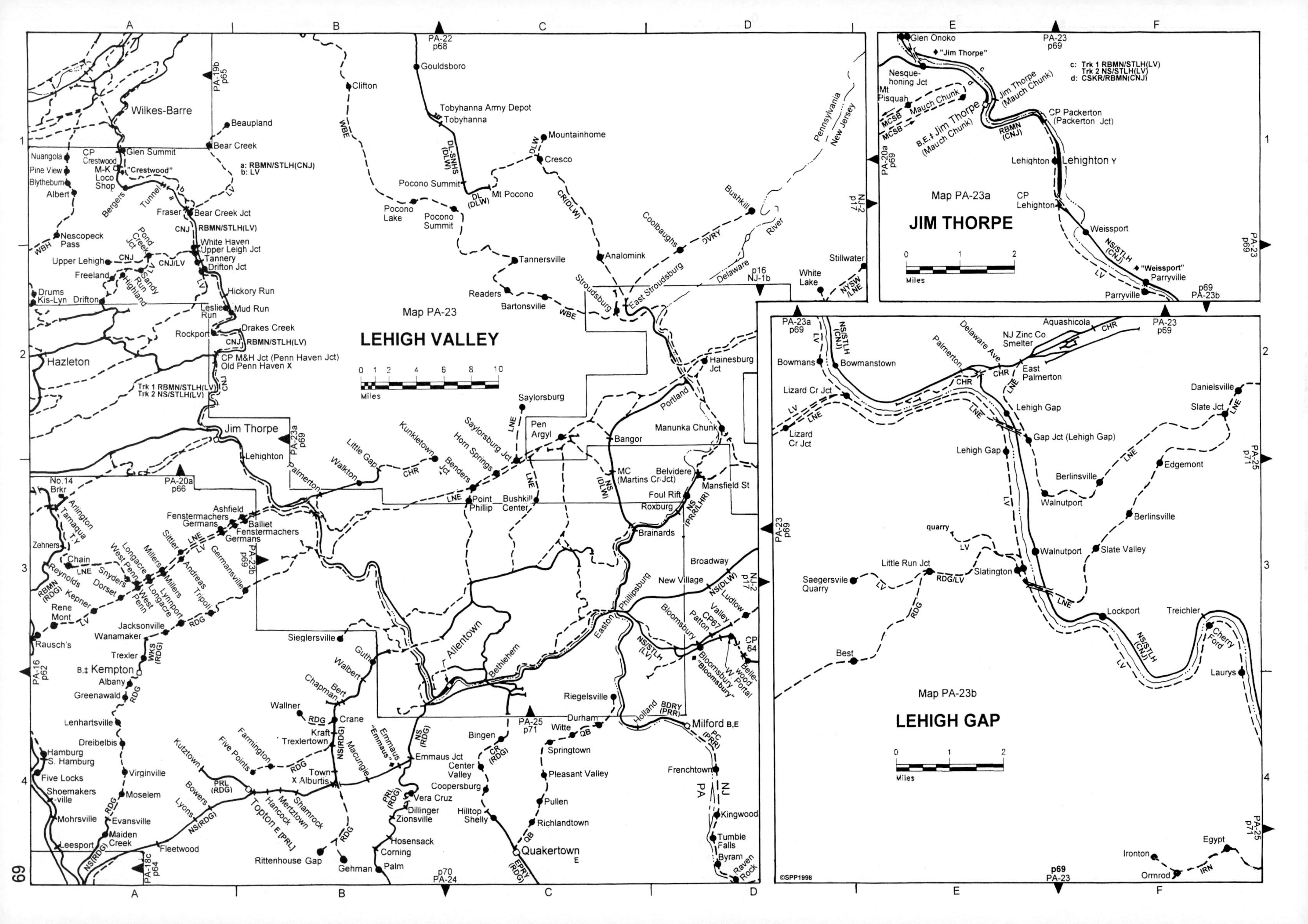
Map PA-23
LEHIGH VALLEY
Miles
Map PA-23a
JIM THORPE
c: Trk 1 RBMN/STLH(LV) Trk 2 NS/STLH(LV)
d: CSKR/RBMN(CNJ)
Map PA-23b
LEHIGH GAP
a: RBMN/STLH(CNJ)
b: LV
Trk 1 RBMN/STLH(LV)
Trk 2 NS/STLH(LV)
Wilkes-Barre
Hazleton
Jim Thorpe
Allentown
Bethlehem
Easton
Phillipsburg
Stroudsburg
East Stroudsburg
Quakertown
Kempton
Topton
Pennsylvania
New Jersey
Delaware River
©SPP1998

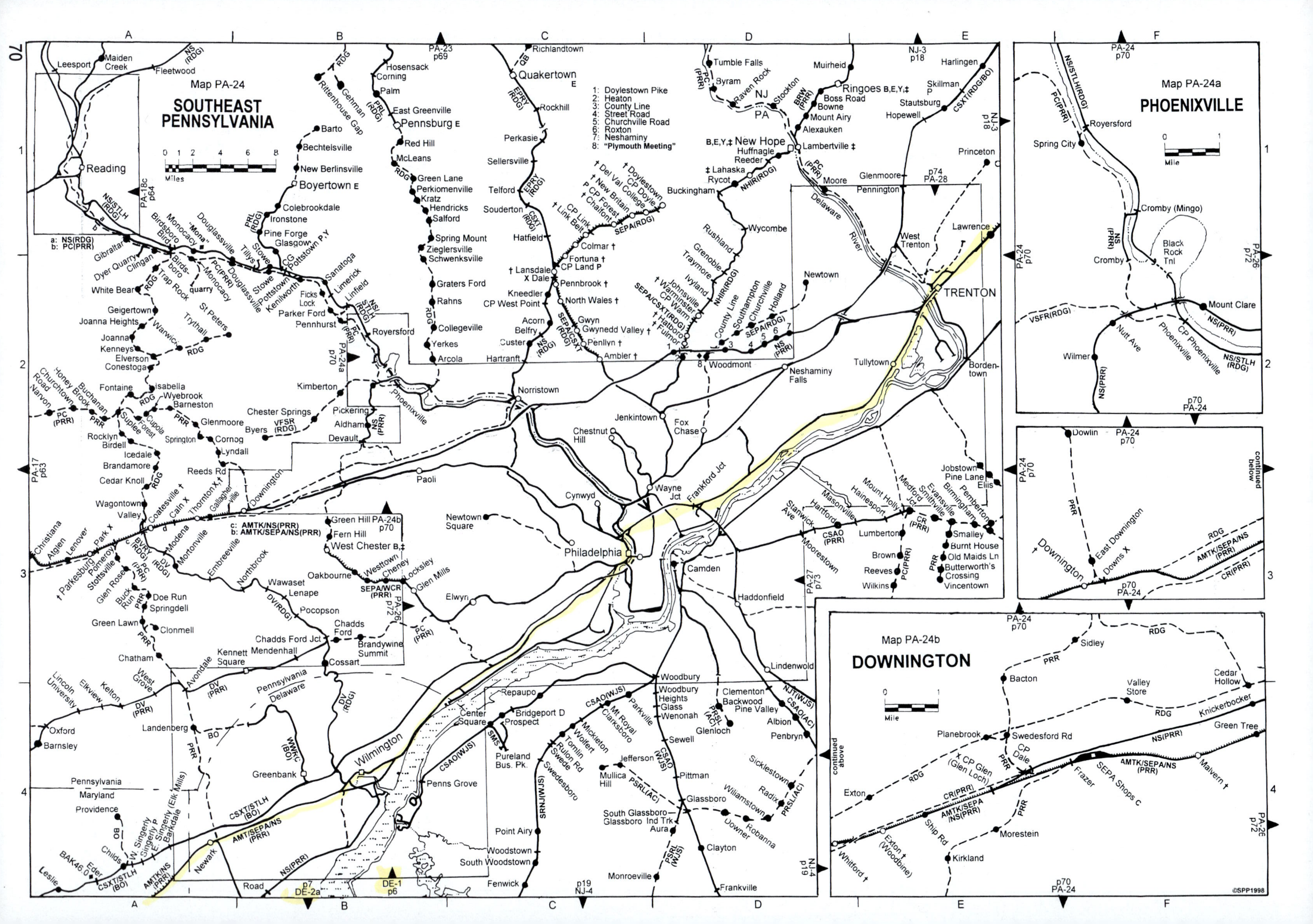
Map PA-24
SOUTHEAST PENNSYLVANIA
Miles
1: Doylestown Pike
2: Heaton
3: County Line
4: Street Road
5: Churchville Road
6: Roxton
7: Neshaminy
8: "Plymouth Meeting"
a: NS(RDG)
b: PC(PRR)
c: AMTK/NS(PRR)
b: AMTK/SEPA/NS(PRR)
Map PA-24a
PHOENIXVILLE
Mile
Map PA-24b
DOWNINGTON
Mile
continued below
continued above
Reading
Philadelphia
TRENTON
Camden
Wilmington
Norristown
Phoenixville
Downington
West Chester
Coatesville
Pottstown
Quakertown
Pennsburg
Boyertown
Lansdale
Doylestown
New Hope
Lambertville
Delaware River
Newark
Glassboro
Woodbury
Paoli
Malvern
Exton
Frazer
Royersford
Spring City
Mount Clare
Black Rock Tnl
CP Phoenixville
Nutt Ave
Wilmer
Cromby
Cromby (Mingo)
Pennsylvania
Delaware
Maryland
NJ
PA
NS/STLH(RDG)
PC(PRR)
NS(PRR)
AMTK/SEPA/NS (PRR)
SEPA/CSXT (RDG)
PA-26 p72
PA-24 p70
NJ-3 p18
NJ-4 p19
PA-23 p69
PA-17 p63
PA-18c p64
DE-1 p6
DE-2a p7
PA-27 p73
PA-28 p74
©SPP1998

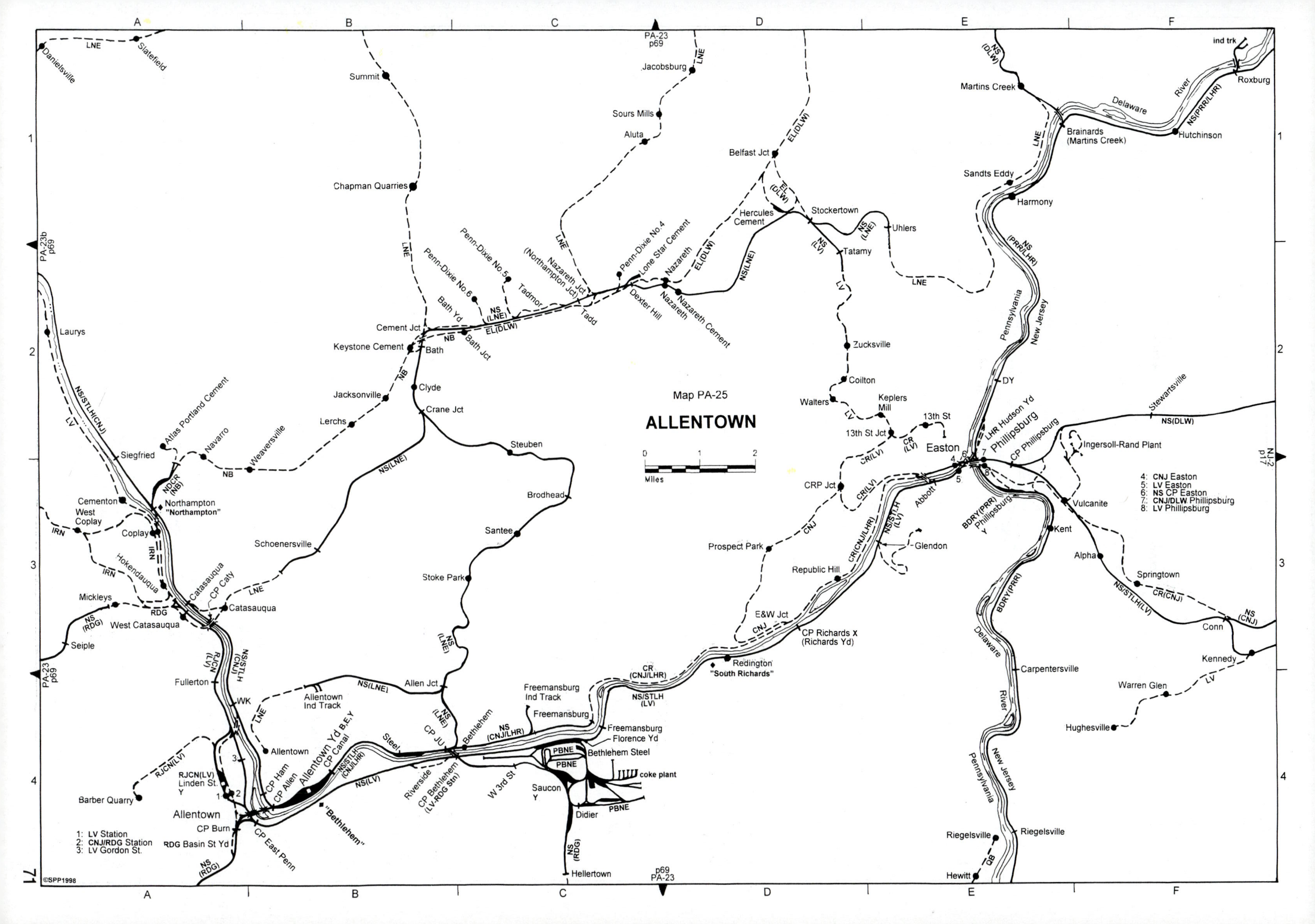
Map PA-25
ALLENTOWN
0 1 2
Miles
PA-23
p69
PA-23b
p69
NJ-2
p17
Danielsville
LNE
Slatefield
Summit
Jacobsburg
LNE
Sours Mills
Aluta
Belfast Jct
EL(DLW)
Chapman Quarries
LNE
EL
(DLW)
Hercules
Cement
Stockertown
NS
(LNE)
Uhlers
NS
(LV)
Tatamy
LNE
Penn-Dixie No.4
Lone Star Cement
Nazareth
EL(DLW)
NS(LNE)
Penn-Dixie No.5
Penn-Dixie No.6
Nazareth Jct
(Northampton Jct)
Tadmor
Tadd
Dexter Hill
Nazareth
Nazareth Cement
Bath Yd
NS
(LNE)
EL(DLW)
Cement Jct
NB
Bath Jct
Keystone Cement
Bath
LV
Zucksville
Coilton
Walters
Keplers
Mill
13th St
13th St Jct
CR
(LV)
Easton
CR(LV)
CRP Jct
Laurys
NS/STLH(CNJ)
LV
Jacksonville
NB
Clyde
Crane Jct
Lerchs
Atlas Portland Cement
Navarro
Weaversville
NB
Siegfried
NS(LNE)
Steuben
Brodhead
NDCR
(NB)
Cementon
Northampton
"Northampton"
West
Coplay
IRN
Coplay
IRN
Hokendauqua
IRN
Schoenersville
Santee
Catasauqua
CP Caty
LNE
Catasauqua
Mickleys
RDG
NS
(RDG)
West Catasauqua
Seiple
Stoke Park
NS
(LNE)
RJCN
(LV)
NS/STLH
(CNJ)
Fullerton
Allen Jct
NS(LNE)
Allentown
Ind Track
WK
LNE
Allentown
NS
(LNE)
CP JU
Bethlehem
NS
(CNJ/LHR)
Freemansburg
Ind Track
Freemansburg
Freemansburg
Florence Yd
Bethlehem Steel
PBNE
PBNE
coke plant
Steel
Allentown Yd B,E,Y
CP Canal
NS/STLH
(CNJ/LHR)
CP Ham
CP Allen
NS(LV)
Riverside
CP Bethlehem
(LV-RDG Stn)
W 3rd St
Saucon
Y
Didier
PBNE
"Bethlehem"
RJCN(LV)
RJCN(LV)
Linden St.
Y
Barber Quarry
Allentown
CP Burn
RDG Basin St Yd
CP East Penn
NS
(RDG)
1: LV Station
2: CNJ/RDG Station
3: LV Gordon St.
NS
(RDG)
Hellertown
Prospect Park
CNJ
CR(CNJ/LHR)
NS/STLH
(LV)
Abbott
Glendon
Republic Hill
E&W Jct
CNJ
CP Richards X
(Richards Yd)
CR
(CNJ/LHR)
NS/STLH
(LV)
Redington
"South Richards"
NS
(DLW)
Martins Creek
Delaware
River
NS(PRR/LHR)
Roxburg
ind trk
Brainards
(Martins Creek)
Hutchinson
LNE
Sandts Eddy
Harmony
NS
(PRR/LHR)
Pennsylvania
New Jersey
DY
LHR Hudson Yd
Phillipsburg
CP Phillipsburg
Stewartsville
NS(DLW)
Ingersoll-Rand Plant
4: CNJ Easton
5: LV Easton
6: NS CP Easton
7: CNJ/DLW Phillipsburg
8: LV Phillipsburg
BDRY(PRR)
Phillipsburg
Y
Vulcanite
Kent
Alpha
Springtown
CR(CNJ)
NS/STLH(LV)
NS
(CNJ)
Conn
BDRY(PRR)
Delaware
River
Carpentersville
Kennedy
LV
Warren Glen
Hughesville
Pennsylvania
New Jersey
Riegelsville
Riegelsville
QB
Hewitt
©SPP1998
A
B
C
D
E
F
1
2
3
4

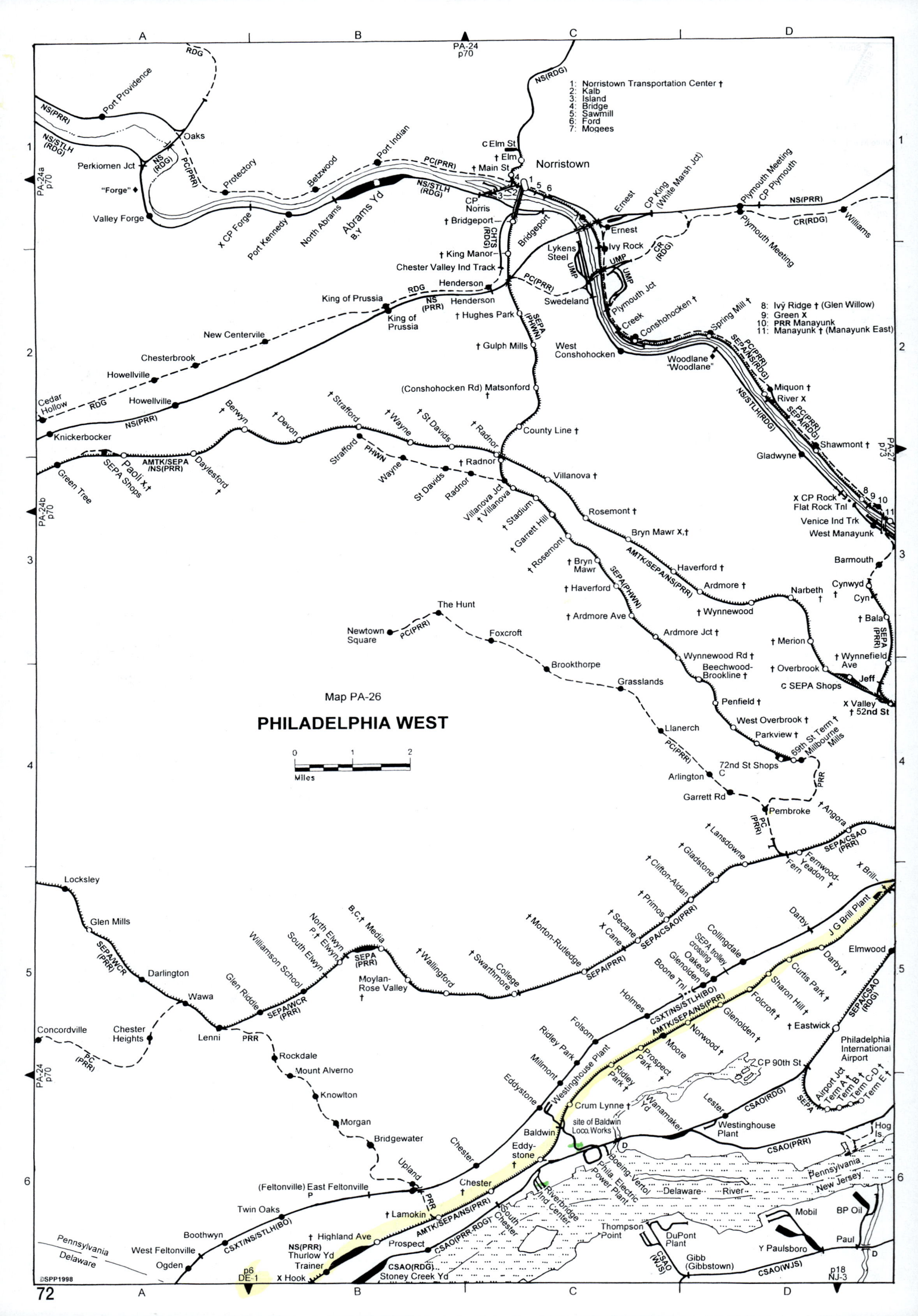
Map PA-26
PHILADELPHIA WEST
0 1 2
Miles
PA-24
p70
1: Norristown Transportation Center †
2: Kalb
3: Island
4: Bridge
5: Sawmill
6: Ford
7: Mogees
8: Ivy Ridge † (Glen Willow)
9: Green X
10: PRR Manayunk
11: Manayunk † (Manayunk East)
Norristown
NS(RDG)
c Elm St
† Elm
† Main St
CP Norris
† Bridgeport
Bridgeport
CHTS (RDG)
† King Manor
Chester Valley Ind Track †
Henderson
Henderson
PC(PRR)
RDG
NS (PRR)
King of Prussia
King of Prussia
New Centervile
Chesterbrook
Howellville
Howellville
Cedar Hollow
RDG
NS(PRR)
Knickerbocker
Green Tree
Paoli X,†
SEPA Shops
AMTK/SEPA /NS(PRR)
Daylesford †
† Berwyn
† Devon
† Strafford
Strafford
PHWN
† Wayne
Wayne
† St Davids
St Davids
† Radnor
† Radnor
Radnor
Villanova Jct
† Villanova
† Stadium
† Garrett Hill
† Rosemont
† Bryn Mawr
† Haverford
† Ardmore Ave
SEPA(PHWN)
Villanova †
Rosemont †
Bryn Mawr X,†
AMTK/SEPA/NS(PRR)
Haverford †
Ardmore †
† Wynnewood
Narbeth †
Ardmore Jct †
Wynnewood Rd †
Beechwood-Brookline †
Penfield †
West Overbrook †
Parkview †
69th St Term †
Millbourne Mills
72nd St Shops C
County Line †
(Conshohocken Rd) Matsonford †
† Gulph Mills
† Hughes Park
SEPA (PHWN)
Port Providence
NS(PRR)
NS/STLH (RDG)
RDG
Oaks
Perkiomen Jct
NS (RDG)
PC(PRR)
"Forge" ◆
Valley Forge
Protectory
X CP Forge
Port Kennedy
Betzwood
North Abrams
Abrams Yd B,Y
Port Indian
PC(PRR)
NS/STLH (RDG)
Ernest
Ernest
CP King (White Marsh Jct)
Plymouth Meeting
CP Plymouth
Plymouth Meeting
NS(PRR)
CR(RDG)
Williams
CR (RDG)
Ivy Rock
Lykens Steel
UMP
UMP
UMP
Swedeland
Plymouth Jct
Creek
Conshohocken †
Spring Mill †
West Conshohocken
Woodlane ◆ "Woodlane"
PC(PRR) SEPA/NS(RDG)
NS/STLH(RDG)
Miquon †
River X
PC(PRR) SEPA(RDG)
Shawmont †
Gladwyne
PA-27 p73
X CP Rock
Flat Rock Tnl
Venice Ind Trk
West Manayunk
Barmouth
Cynwyd †
Cyn †
† Bala
SEPA (PRR)
† Merion
† Wynnefield Ave
† Overbrook
Jeff
c SEPA Shops
X Valley
† 52nd St
The Hunt
Newtown Square
PC(PRR)
Foxcroft
Brookthorpe
Grasslands
Llanerch
PC(PRR)
Arlington C
Garrett Rd
PRR
Pembroke
PC (PRR)
† Angora
SEPA/CSAO (PRR)
† Lansdowne
† Gladstone
Fernwood-Yeadon †
Fern
X Brill
J G Brill Plant
Darby
Darby †
Elmwood
† Clifton-Aldan
† Primos
† Secane
X Cane
SEPA/CSAO(PRR)
† Morton-Rutledge
SEPA(PRR)
† Swarthmore
College
† Wallingford
Moylan-Rose Valley †
B,C,† Media
SEPA (PRR)
North Elwyn
P,† Elwyn
South Elwyn
Williamson School
Glen Riddle
SEPA/WCR (PRR)
Locksley
Glen Mills
SEPA/WCR (PRR)
Darlington
Wawa
Lenni
PRR
Concordville
Chester Heights
PC (PRR)
PA-24 p70
Rockdale
Mount Alverno
Knowlton
Morgan
Bridgewater
Upland
PRR
Collingdale
SEPA trolley crossing
Oakeola
Glenolden
Boone Tnl
CSXT/NS/STLH(BO)
Holmes
AMTK/SEPA/NS(PRR)
Glenolden †
Folcroft †
Sharon Hill †
Curtis Park †
† Eastwick
SEPA/CSAO (RDG)
Philadelphia International Airport
Airport Jct
Term A †
Term B †
Term C-D †
Term E †
SEPA
Folsom
Ridley Park
Westinghouse Plant
Ridley Park †
Prospect Park †
Moore
Norwood †
Milmont
Eddystone
Crum Lynne †
Wanamaker Yd
CP 90th St
Lester
CSAO(RDG)
Westinghouse Plant
Hog Is.
CSAO(PRR)
site of Baldwin Loco. Works
Baldwin
Eddystone †
Chester
Chester †
Boeing-Vertol
Phila. Electric Power Plant
Riverbridge Ind Center
South Chester
Thompson Point
DuPont Plant
CSAO (WJS)
Gibb (Gibbstown)
CSAO(WJS)
Pennsylvania
New Jersey
Delaware River
Mobil
BP Oil
Paul
Y Paulsboro
p18 NJ-3
D
(Feltonville) East Feltonville P
Twin Oaks
Boothwyn
CSXT/NS/STLH(BO)
West Feltonville
Ogden
† Lamokin
AMTK/SEPA/NS(PRR)
† Highland Ave
Prospect
NS(PRR) Thurlow Yd Trainer
CSAO(PRR-RDG)
CSAO(RDG)
Stoney Creek Yd
X Hook
p6 DE-1
Pennsylvania
Delaware
PA-24a p70
PA-24b p70
©SPP1998
A B C D
1 2 3 4 5 6

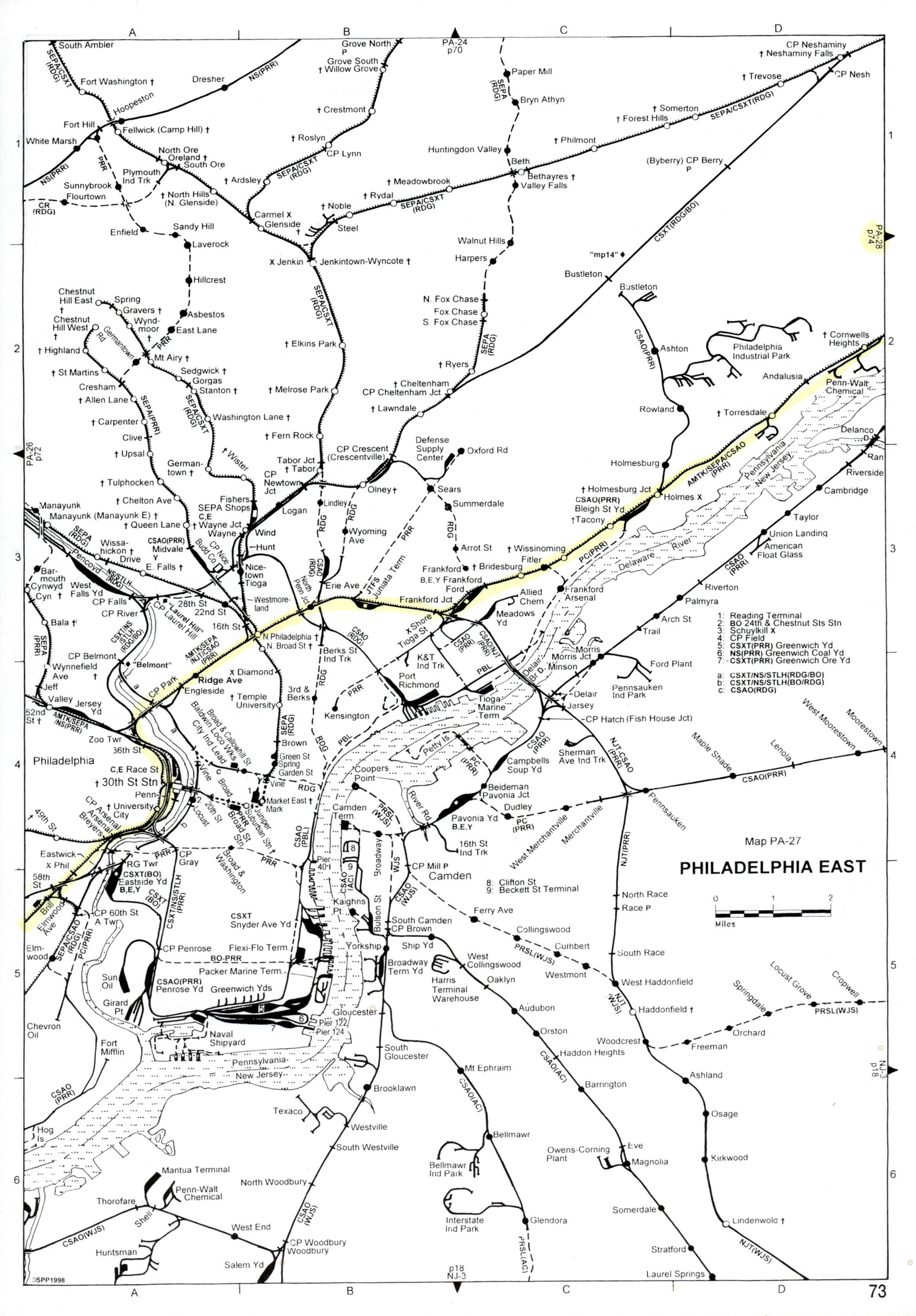

Map PA-27
PHILADELPHIA EAST
A
B
C
D
1
2
3
4
5
6
PA-24
p70
PA-28
p74
PA-26
p72
NJ-3
p18
p18
NJ-3
South Ambler
SEPA/CSXT (RDG)
Fort Washington †
Dresher
NS(PRR)
Hoopeston
Fort Hill
Fellwick (Camp Hill) †
White Marsh
NS(PRR)
PRR
North Ore
Oreland †
South Ore
Plymouth Ind Trk
Sunnybrook
Flourtown
CR (RDG)
† North Hills (N. Glenside)
Enfield
Sandy Hill
Laverock
Hillcrest
Asbestos
East Lane
Grove North P
Grove South
† Willow Grove
† Crestmont
† Roslyn
CP Lynn
† Ardsley
SEPA/CSXT (RDG)
Carmel X
Glenside
† Noble
Steel
X Jenkin
Jenkintown-Wyncote †
† Meadowbrook
† Rydal
SEPA/CSXT (RDG)
Paper Mill
SEPA (RDG)
Bryn Athyn
Huntingdon Valley
Beth
Bethayres †
Valley Falls
Walnut Hills
Harpers
CP Neshaminy
† Neshaminy Falls
CP Nesh
† Trevose
† Somerton
† Forest Hills
SEPA/CSXT(RDG)
† Philmont
(Byberry) CP Berry P
CSXT(RDG/BO)
"mp14"
Bustleton
Bustleton
CSAO(PRR)
Ashton
Philadelphia Industrial Park
† Cornwells Heights
Andalusia
Penn-Walt Chemical
Rowland
† Torresdale
Delanco
Holmesburg
AMTK/SEPA/CSAO (PRR)
Pennsylvania
New Jersey
Riverside
Cambridge
† Holmesburg Jct
CSAO(PRR) Bleigh St Yd
Holmes X
†Tacony
Taylor
Union Landing
American Float Glass
Chestnut Hill East †
Spring
Gravers †
Wyndmoor †
Chestnut Hill West †
Germantown Rd
PRR
† Highland
Mt Airy †
Sedgwick †
Gorgas
Stanton †
† St Martins
Cresham
† Allen Lane
SEPA(PRR)
SEPA/CSXT (RDG)
Washington Lane †
† Carpenter
Clive
† Upsal
† Wister
Germantown †
† Tulpehocken
† Chelton Ave
Fishers
SEPA Shops C,E
Manayunk
Manayunk (Manayunk E) †
† Queen Lane
† Wayne Jct
Wayne
SEPA (RDG)
Wissahickon †
Drive
CSAO(PRR) Midvale Y
E. Falls †
Budd Co.
CP Nice
Wind
Hunt
Nicetown Tioga
Bar-mouth
Cynwyd Cyn †
West Falls Yd
Pencoyd
NS/STLH (RDG)
CP Falls
CP River
Bala †
SEPA (PRR)
CP Belmont
Wynnefield Ave †
Jeff
Valley
52nd St †
"Belmont"
CP "Laurel Hill" CP Laurel Hill
CSXT/NS/STLH (RDG/BO)
28th St
22nd St
16th St
Westmoreland
AMTK/SEPA /NJT/CSAO (PRR)
N.Philadelphia †
N. Broad St †
X Diamond
Ridge Ave
Engleside
CP Park
a
Jersey Yd
AMTK/SEPA /NS(PRR)
Zoo Twr
36th St
Philadelphia
C,E Race St
† 30th St Stn
Penn
CP Arsenal
Arsenal
Breyers
† University City
49th St
Eastwick
X Phil
58th St
Brill
Elmwood Ave
CP 60th St
A Twr
Elm-wood
SEPA/CSAO (RDG)
PC(PRR)
RG Twr
CSXT(BO) Eastside Yd B,E,Y
CSXT (BO)
CSXT/NS/STLH (PRR)
CP Gray
PRR
Broad & Washington
PRR
CSXT Snyder Ave Yd
CP Penrose
Flexi-Flo Term.
BO-PRR
Packer Marine Term.
Sun Oil
CSAO(PRR) Penrose Yd
Greenwich Yds
Girard Pt.
Chevron Oil
Naval Shipyard
Fort Mifflin
Pennsylvania
New Jersey
CSAO (PRR)
Hog Is.
Pier 122
Pier 124
Gloucester
Broad & Callowhill St
Baldwin Loco Wks
City Ind Lead
Vine
Broad
20th St
Locust
PRR
Broad St Stn
Juniper
Suburban Stn
Temple University
† Temple University
3rd & Berks
Brown
Green St
Spring Garden St
Vine
RDG
Market East †
Mark
Camden Term.
Pier 40
CSAO (PBL)
Broadway
Kaighns Pt.
CSAO (AC)
Bulson St
WJS
CSAO (WJS)
South Camden
CP Brown
Yorkship
Ship Yd
Broadway Term Yd
8
9
CP Mill P
Camden
Coopers Point
PRSL (WJS)
River Rd
Petty Is.
PC (PRR)
PBL
Tabor Jct
† Tabor
CP Newtown Jct
Logan
Lindley
RDG
Wyoming Ave
RDG
CSAO (RDG)
North Penn Jct
Erie Ave
JTFS
Juniata Term.
PRR
Frankford Jct
CP Crescent (Crescentville)
Olney †
Defense Supply Center
Oxford Rd
Sears
Summerdale
RDG
Arrot St
† Wissinoming
Fitler
† Bridesburg
Frankford
B,E,Y Frankford Ford
PC(PRR)
Allied Chem.
Frankford Arsenal
Meadows Yd
X Shore
Tioga St
CSAO (PRR)
CSAO/NJT (PRR)
CSAO (RDG)
Berks St Ind Trk
K&T Ind Trk
Port Richmond
PBL
Tioga Marine Term
Kensington
PRR
Delair Br.
Morris
Morris Jct
D. Minson
Delair
Jersey
CP Hatch (Fish House Jct)
Delaware River
† Elkins Park
† Melrose Park
† Fern Rock
† Cheltenham
CP Cheltenham Jct
† Lawndale
† Ryers
N. Fox Chase
Fox Chase
S. Fox Chase
SEPA (RDG)
CSAO (PRR)
Riverton
Palmyra
Arch St
Trail
Ford Plant
Pennsauken Ind Park
1: Reading Terminal
2: BO 24th & Chestnut Sts Stn
3: Schuylkill X
4: CP Field
5: CSXT(PRR) Greenwich Yd
6: NS(PRR) Greenwich Coal Yd
7: CSXT(PRR) Greenwich Ore Yd
a: CSXT/NS/STLH(RDG/BO)
b: CSXT/NS/STLH(BO/RDG)
c: CSAO(RDG)
West Moorestown
Moorestown
Maple Shade
Lenola
CSAO(PRR)
Sherman Ave Ind Trk
NJT-CSAO (PRR)
Campbells Soup Yd
CSAO (PRR)
Beideman
Pavonia Jct
Dudley
PC (PRR)
Pavonia Yd B,E,Y
16th St Ind Trk
West Merchantville
Merchantville
Pennsauken
NJT(PRR)
8: Clifton St
9: Beckett St Terminal
0 1 2 Miles
North Race
Race P
Ferry Ave
Collingswood
Cuthbert
PRSL(WJS)
Westmont
South Race
West Collingswood
Oaklyn
Harris Terminal Warehouse
West Haddonfield
NJT (WJS)
Haddonfield †
Springdale
Locust Grove
Cropwell
PRSL(WJS)
Orchard
Freeman
Woodcrest
Audubon
Orston
Haddon Heights
CSAO(AC)
South Gloucester
Mt Ephraim
CSAO(AC)
Barrington
Ashland
Brooklawn
Texaco
Westville
South Westville
Bellmawr
Bellmawr Ind Park
Owens-Corning Plant
Eve
Magnolia
Osage
Kirkwood
North Woodbury
CSAO (WJS)
Mantua Terminal
Penn-Walt Chemical
Thorofare
Shell
West End
CSAO(WJS)
CP Woodbury
Woodbury
Huntsman
Salem Yd
Interstate Ind Park
Glendora
PRSL(AC)
Somerdale
Lindenwold †
NJT(WJS)
Stratford
Laurel Springs
©SPP1998

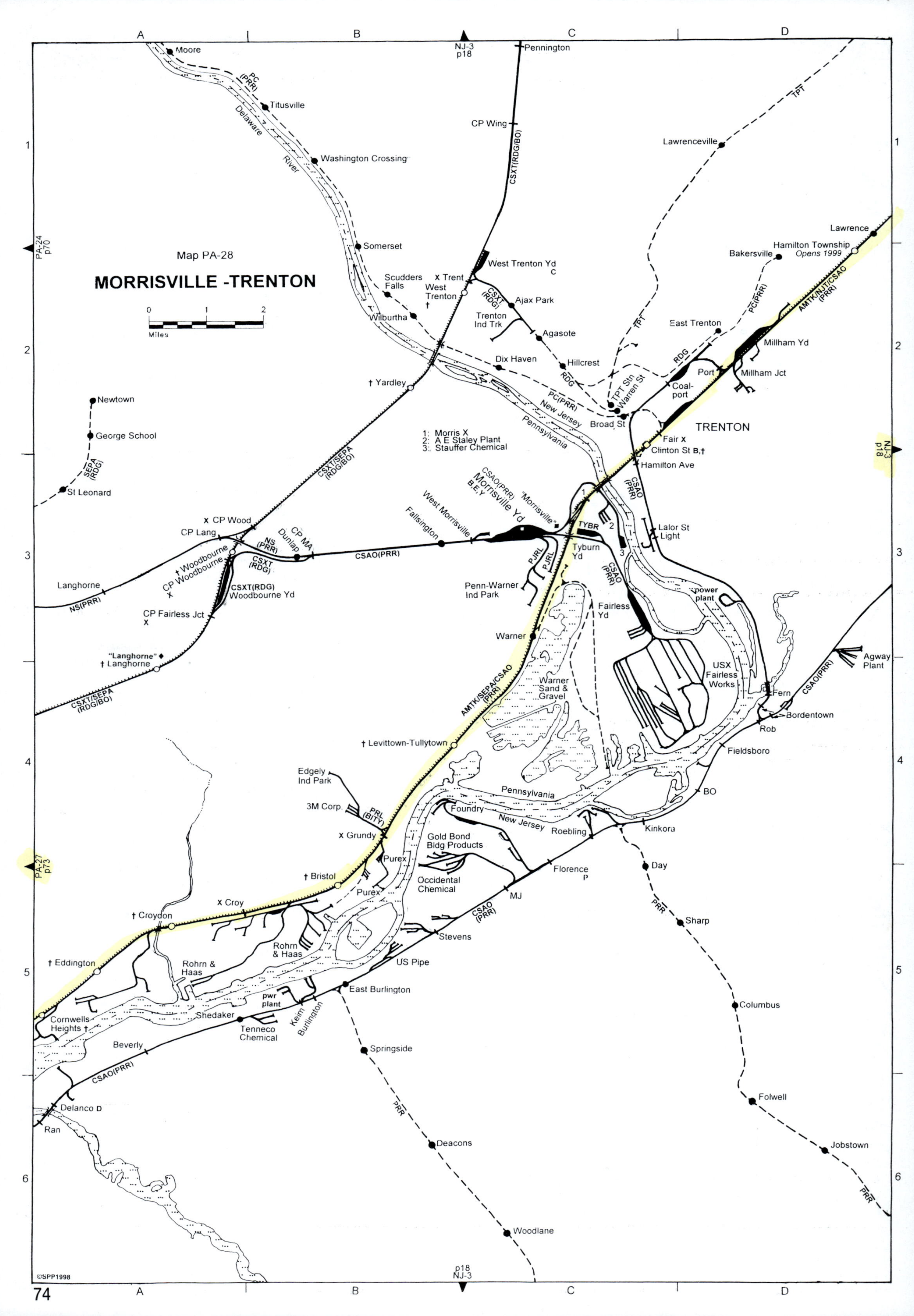
Map PA-28
MORRISVILLE -TRENTON
Miles
Moore
Titusville
Delaware River
Washington Crossing
Pennington
CP Wing
CSXT(RDG/BO)
Somerset
Scudders Falls
X Trent
West Trenton
West Trenton Yd
Ajax Park
Trenton Ind Trk
Agasote
Wilburtha
Dix Haven
Hillcrest
Yardley
Newtown
George School
St Leonard
Lawrenceville
TPT
Lawrence
Hamilton Township
Opens 1999
Bakersville
AMTK/NJT/CSAO (PRR)
PC(PRR)
East Trenton
Millham Yd
Millham Jct
RDG
Port
Coal-port
TPT Stn
Warren St
Broad St
TRENTON
Fair X
Clinton St B,†
Hamilton Ave
1: Morris X
2: A E Staley Plant
3: Stauffer Chemical
New Jersey
Pennsylvania
CSXT/SEPA (RDG/BO)
CSAO(PRR)
Morrisville Yd
B.E.Y
"Morrisville"
West Morrisville
Fallsington
X CP Wood
CP Lang
CP MA
Dunlap
NS (PRR)
CSXT (RDG)
TYBR
Tyburn Yd
Lalor St
Light
Woodbourne
CP Woodbourne
CSXT(RDG)
Woodbourne Yd
Langhorne
NS(PRR)
PJRL
Penn-Warner Ind Park
Fairless Yd
power plant
CP Fairless Jct
Warner
"Langhorne"
† Langhorne
Warner Sand & Gravel
USX Fairless Works
Agway Plant
Fern
Bordentown
Rob
CSXT/SEPA (RDG/BO)
AMTK/SEPA/CSAO (PRR)
Levittown-Tullytown
Fieldsboro
Edgely Ind Park
3M Corp.
PRL (BITY)
BO
Foundry
Roebling
Kinkora
X Grundy
Gold Bond Bldg Products
Purex
Day
Bristol
Occidental Chemical
Florence
MJ
X Croy
Croydon
CSAO (PRR)
PRR
Sharp
Stevens
Rohrn & Haas
Eddington
US Pipe
East Burlington
pwr plant
Columbus
Cornwells Heights †
Shedaker
Tenneco Chemical
Keim
Burlington
Beverly
Springside
CSAO(PRR)
Folwell
Delanco D
Ran
Deacons
Jobstown
Woodlane
NJ-3 p18
PA-24 p70
PA-27 p73
©SPP1998

APPENDIX

RAILROAD REPORTING & IDENTIFICATION MARKS

Wherever possible the marks used in this Atlas to identify railroads are based on the system of Reporting Marks issued by the Association of American Railroads (AAR), exceptions are for long deceased companies or industrial, lumber and tourist operators not covered by the AAR system.

MARK	COMPANY TITLE	*REMARKS*
A&BC	Altoona & Beech Creek Railroad	*3' gauge*
A&ER	Annapolis & Elk Ridge Railroad	*later WBA*
A&K	Alleghany and Kinzua Railroad	
A&SL	Adirondack & St Lawrence Railroad	
AC	Atlantic City Railroad	*RDG subsidiary, later PRSL*
ACJY	Ashtabula Carson & Jefferson Railroad	
ACRR	Allegany Central Railroad	*3' gauge, later CNYW*
ALBY	Albany Port Railroad	*CSXT-STLH(DH-NYC) joint*
ALCo	American Locomotive Company	
ALQS	Aliquippa and Southern Railroad	*LTV Steel subsidiary*
ALY	Allegheny & Eastern Railroad	*GWI subsidiary*
AMHR	Landisville Railroad	
AMTK	National Railroad Passenger Corporation - "Amtrak"	
APRR	Allegheny Portage Railroad	
ARA	Arcade and Attica Railroad	
ARDC	Adirondack Railway	
ASR	Adirondack Scenic Railroad	*tourist operation*
ASRY	Ashland Railway	
AVR	Allegheny Valley Railroad	
B&M	Brownstone & Middletown Railroad	
B&S	Buffalo & Susquehanna Railroad	*later BO*
BA	Boston & Albany Railroad	*NYC subsidiary, later PC*
BASL	Baltimore & Annapolis Short Line Railroad	*later WBA*
BBK	Bradford Bordell and Kinzua Railway	*3' gauge*
BBS	Bradford Bordell & Smethport Railroad	*3' gauge, BBK subs., later MJKR*
BC&A	Baltimore Chesapeake & Atlantic Railroad	*later BE*
BCK	Buffalo Creek Railroad	*ERIE-LV joint, later CR*
BDRV	Belvidere & Delaware River Railway	*BRW affiliate*
BE	Baltimore and Eastern Railroad	*PRR subsidiary*
BE&C	Bradford Eldred & Cuba Railroad	*3' gauge*
BEDT	Brooklyn Eastern District Terminal Railroad	*later NYCH*
BFC	Bellefonte Central Railroad	
BH	Bath and Hammondsport Railroad	*later CGNE*
BITY	Bristol Industrial Terminal Railway	*later PRL*
BKRR	Batten Kill Railroad	
BLA	Baltimore and Annapolis Railroad	*later MMTA/CTN*
BLE	Bessemer and Lake Erie Railroad	*Transtar subsidiary*
BLK	Big Level & Kinzua Railroad	*3' gauge, later BO*
BM	Boston and Maine Railroad	*later ST*
BMRR	Bombay & Moira Railroad	
BNYP	Buffalo New York & Philadelphia Railroad	*PRR subsidiary*
BO	Baltimore & Ohio Railroad	*later CSXT*
BPRR	Buffalo & Pittsburgh Railroad	*GWI subsidiary*
BR	Bradford Industrial Rail	*GWI subsidiary*
BRP	Buffalo Rochester & Pittsburgh Railway	*later BO*
BRR	Barnegat Railroad	*TUCK subsidiary*
BRRR	Bare Rock Railroad	
BRW	Black River & Western Corp.	
BRY	Bradford Railway	*3' gauge, later BNYP*
BSOR	Buffalo Southern Railroad	
BSRR	Bloomsburg & Sullivan Railroad	*later RDG*
BST	Bayshore Terminal Railway	*ME subsidiary*
BT	Bush Terminal Railroad	*later NYCH*
BV	Beaver Valley Railroad	

MARK	COMPANY TITLE	*REMARKS*
BVRR	Bachman Valley Railroad	
BVRY	Brandywine Valley Railroad	*Lukens Steel subsidiary*
BWP	Bradford & Western Pennsylvania Railroad	*3' gauge*
C&C	Carthage & Copenhagen Railroad	
C&T	Catskill & Tannersville Railroad	*3' gauge*
CACV	Cooperstown & Charlotte Valley Railway	
CAIRO	Cairo Railroad	*3' gauge*
CB	Cheaspeake Beach Railroad	*part later EW*
CBL	Conemaugh & Black Lick Railroad	*Bethlehem Steel subsidiary*
CBR	Clove Branch Railroad	
CGNE	Champagne Railroad	*later LAL*
CHAT	Chateaugay Railroad	*3' gauge, later DH*
CHH	Cheswick & Harmer Railroad	
CHR	Chesnut Ridge Railway	
CHRR	Chesapeake Railroad	*tourist operation*
CHTS	Chester Valley Railroad	*affiliated with EPRY*
CI	Cambria and Indiana Railroad	
CICR	Clifton Iron Companyís Railroad	
CKMR	Catskill Mountain Railway	*3' gauge*
CLAR	Clarion River Railway	
CLP	The Clarendon and Pittsford Railroad	*VTR subsidiary*
CLR	Cranberry Lake Railroad	
CLRT	Baltimore Central Light Rail Line	*electric 750V dc o/h, MDTA owned*
CMSL	Cape May Seashore Lines	*tourist operation*
CMTN	Catskill Mountain Railroad	*tourist operation*
CN	Canadian National Railways	
CNJ	The Central Railroad Company of New Jersey	*later CR*
CNoR	Canadian Northern Railway	*later CN*
CNYK	Central New York Railroad	
CNYS	Central New York Southern Railroad	
CNYW	Central New York & Western Railroad	*later PSN*
CO	Chesapeake and Ohio Railway	*later CSXT*
COR	Cornwall Railroad	*Bethlehem Steel subsidiary, later RDG*
CP	Canadian Pacific Railway	
CPA	Cumberland and Pennsylvania Railroad	*later WM*
CPIC	Crown Point Iron Company's Railroad	*3' gauge*
CPPA	Coudersport and Port Allegany Railroad	
CR	Consolidated Railroad Corporation - "Conrail"	*later CSXT and NS*
CRIV	Castleman River Railroad	
CRPA	Central Railroad Company of Pennsylvania	
CSAO	Conrail Shared Assets Operation	*CSXT-NS joint operation, see note 1*
CSKR	Carbon & Schuykill Railroad	
CSXT	CSX Transportation	
CTD	Cherry Tree and Dixonville Railroad	*NYC-PRR joint, later PC*
CTN	Canton Railroad	
CUMB	Cumberland Mining Railroad	*Cyprus Northshore Mining (USX)*
CUOH	The Columbus & Ohio River Railroad	*Ohio Central affiliate*
CURB	Curtis Bay Railroad	
CV	Central Vermont Railway	*CN subsidiary, later NECR*
CVAL	Central Valley Railroad	*3' gauge*

MARK	COMPANY TITLE	*REMARKS*
D&N	Dexter and Northern Railroad	*later NYC*
D&S	Dillonvale & Smithfield Railway	
DAG	Daguscahonda Railroad	
DH	The Delaware and Hudson Railroad	*later STLH*
DL	Delaware-Lackawanna Railroad	*GVT subsidiary*
DLC	Duquesne Light Co.	*operated by CSXT*
DLW	The Delaware Lackawanna & Western Railroad	*later EL*
DLWR	Depew Lancaster & Western Railroad	*GVT subsidiary*
DMM	Dansville and Mount Morris Railroad	*GWI subsidiary*
DN	Delaware & Northern Railroad	
DRHY	Durham Transport	
DSRR	Donora Southern Railroad	
DTRR	Danbury Terminal Railroad	*affiliated with HRRC*
DURR	Delaware & Ulster Rail Ride	*tourist operation*
DV	Delaware Valley Railway	*present company, RailAmerica sub.*
DVRY	Delaware Valley Railway	*former shortline*
E&M	Etna & Montrose Railroad	
E&RV	Emporium and Rich Valley Railroad	
EASO	EASX Railroad	*operated by ISSR*
EB	East Berlin Railway	
EBT	East Broad Top Railroad & Coal Co.	*3' gauge*
EEC	East Erie Commercial Railroad	*General Electric subsidiary*
EJR	East Jersey Railroad & Terminal	
EL	Erie Lackawanna Railway	*later CR*
EM	Eagles Mere Railroad	*3' gauge*
EMHR	East Mahanoy & Hazleton Railroad	*RBMN subsidiary*
EMIT	Emmitsburg Railroad	
ENYU	East New York Utilities-Albany Southern	*electric*
EPRY	East Penn Railway	*affiliated with CHTS*
ERIE	Erie Railroad	*later EL*
ESHR	Eastern Shore Railroad	
EV	Everett Railroad	
EW	East Washington Railway	
FCRK	Falls Creek Railroad	
FGLK	Finger Lakes Railway	
FJG	Fonda Johnsown & Gloversville Railroad	
FRR	Falls Road Railroad	*GVT subsidiary*
G&ER	Glendale & East River Railroad	*3' gauge*
G&W	Glenfield & Western Railroad	
GBRY	Gettysburg Railway	*RailAmerica subsidiary*
GCC	Georges Creek & Cumberland Railroad	*later WM*
GJ	Greenwich & Johnsonville Railway	*DH subsidiary, part later BKRR*
GNGR	Greenlick Narrow Gauge Railroad	*3' gauge*
GMLG	General Motors Locomotive Group	
GNWR	Genesee and Wyoming Railroad	*GWI subsidiary*
GR	Grasse River Railroad	
GT	Grand Trunk Railway	*later CN*
GV	Gunpowder Valley Railroad	
GVT	Genesee Valley Transportation Co.	
GWI	Genesee and Wyoming Industries	
H&F	Hagerstown & Frederick Railroad	*electric, later POTED*
H&M	Hudson & Manhattan Railroad	*PRR subsidiary, later PATH*
HBTM	The Huntingdon and Broad Top Mountain Railroad & Coal Co.	
HOC	Hanna Ore Company Railroad	
HR	Hannawa Railroad	
HRRC	Housatonic Railroad	
HRS	Holidaysburg & Roaring Spring Railroad	*operated by EV*
HSR	Hoboken Shore Railroad	
HT	Harlem Transfer Co.	*DLW subsidiary*
HV	Hickory Valley Railroad	
HVR	Hudson Valley Railroad	*electric*

MARK	COMPANY TITLE	*REMARKS*
INT	International Railway	*electric, ERIE subsidiary*
IRN	The Ironton Railroad	*LV-RDG joint, later CR*
ISSR	ISS Rail	*affiliated with KJR*
J&S	Juniata & Southern Railroad	
JCLE	Jamestown Chautauqua & Lake Erie Railroad	*electric, later JWNW*
JR	Jerseyfield Railroad	
JSC	Johnstown & Stony Creek Railroad	
JSCR	The Jay Street Connecting Railroad	
JTFS	Juniata Terminal Co.	
JVRR	Juniata Valley Railroad	
JWNW	Jamestown Westfield & Northwestern Railroad	
K&E	Kane & Elk Railroad	*3' gauge*
K&P	Kanona & Prattsburgh Railway	*later PRAT*
KACL	Keeseville Ausable Chasm & Lake Champlain Railroad	
KCDX	Eastman Kodak Co.	
KERR	Kendall & Eldred Railroad	*3' gauge, later BNYP*
KES	Kether Elbon and Shawmut Railroad	
KH	Kinderkook and Hudson Railway	*later ENYU*
KJR	Kiski Junction Railroad	
KKRR	Knox & Kane Railroad	
KRR	Kaaterskill Railroad	*3' gauge, later UD*
KRY	Kinzua Railway	*3' gauge, later BNYP*
KV	Kishacoquillas Valley Railroad	
L&Y	Lewiston & Youngstown Railway	
LAL	Livonia Avon & Lakeville Railroad	
LBCV	Little Beaver Creek Valley Railroad	
LBR	Lowville & Beaver River Ralroad	*GVT subsidiary*
LBV	Lewisburg & Buffalo Valley Railroad	*3' gauge*
LCM	Lake Champlain and Moriah Railroad	
LEAW	Lake Erie Alliance & Western Railroad	*3' gauge, later NYC*
LEFC	Lake Erie Franklin & Clarion Railroad	
LHL	Laurel Highlands Railroad	*tourist operation*
LHR	The Lehigh and Hudson River Railway	*later CR*
LIGV	Ligonier Valley Railroad	
LIRR	Long Island Rail Road	*PRR later NYMTA subsidiary*
LNE	Lehigh and New England Railroad	
LOS	Lancaster Oxford & Southern Railroad	*3' gauge*
LS	Luzerne & Susquehanna Railway	
LSMR	Little Saw Mill Run Railroad	*later PWV*
LSMS	Lake Shore & Michigan Southern	*later NYC*
LV	Lehigh Valley Railroad	*later CR*
LVRR UCIR	Lycoming Valley Railroad	*affiliated with NSHR SVRR*
LWV	Lackawanna & Wyoming Valley Railroad	*electric, later DLW*
LYVR	Lykens Valley Railroad	
M&DC	Maryland & Delaware Coast Railroad	*later BE*
M&S	Middleburg & Schoharie Railroad	
MARC	Maryland Dept. of Transportation	
MC	Michigan Central Railway	*NYC subsidiary, later NYC*
MCLR	McLaughlin Line Railroad	
MCRR	Monongahela Connecting Railroad	*LTV Steel subsidiary*
MCSB	Mauch Chunk Switchback Railway	*cable & gravity tourist line*
MDDE	Maryland & Delaware Railroad	
MDLR	Midland Terminal Co.	*LTV Steel subsidiary*
MDTA	Maryland Transit Authority	*electric, 750V dc 3rd rail*
ME	Morristown & Erie Railway	
MGA	Monongahela Railway	*BO-PLE-PRR joint, later CR*
MGNG	Mount Gretna Narrow Gauge Railroad	*2' gauge*
MHM	Mount Hope Mineral Railroad	*CNJ subsidiary*
MHWA	Mohawk Adirondack & Northern Railroad	*GVT subsidiary*
MIDH	Middletown & Hummelstown Railroad	
MJKR	Mount Jewett Kinzua and Riterville Railroad	*later BO*

MARK	COMPANY TITLE	*REMARKS*
MJS	Mount Jewett and Smethport Railroad	
MKC	McKeesport Connecting Railroad	*Transtar subsidiary*
MMID	Maryland Midland Railway	
MNC	Metro-North Railroad	*NYMTA subsidiary*
MNJ	Middletown and New Jersey Railway	
MOL	Marcellus & Otisco Lakes Railroad	
MPA	Maryland & Pennsylvania Railroad	*affliated with PRL and YKR*
MSL	Mahoning State Line Rairoad	*PLE subsidiary*
MSTR	Massena Terminal Railroad	
MSW	Monessen-Southwestern Railway	*Wheeling-Pittsburgh Steel*
MTR	Montour Railroad	*PLE-PRR joint subsidiary*
MU	Middletown & Unionville Railroad	*later MNJ*
NB	Northampton and Bath Railroad	
NB&W	New Berlin & Winfield Railroad	*3' gauge*
NBER	Nittany & Bald Eagle Railroad	
NC&F	New Castle & Frenchtown Railroad	*later PRR*
NCRY	Northern Central Railway	*tourist operation*
ND	National Docks Railroad	*LV subsidiary, later CR*
NDCR	Northampton Switching Co.	
NECR	New England Central Railroad	*RailTex subsidiary*
NFN	Newton Falls & Northern Railroad	
NH	New York New Haven and Hartford Railroad	*later PC*
NIAJ	Niagara Junction Railroad	*ERIE-LV-NYC joint, later CR*
NJ	Napierville Junction Railway	*DH subsidiary, later STLH*
NJNY	The New Jersey and New York Railroad	*ERIE subsidiary, later EL*
NJT	New Jersey Transit	
NKP	New York Chicago & St Louis Railroad - "Nickel Plate"	*later NW*
NLI	National Lead Industries	*operated by DH*
NNJ	Northern Railroad of New Jersey	*ERIE subsidiary, later EL*
NPFG	New Park & Fawn Grove Railroad	
NS	Norfolk Southern Corporation	
NSCT	Niagara St Catharines & Toronto Railway	*electric, CN subsidiary*
NSHR	North Shore Railroad	*affiliated with LVRR SVRR UCIR*
NSL	Norwood & St. Lawrence Railroad	*later SLAW*
NSV	Newport & Shermans Valley Railroad	*3' gauge*
NW	Norfolk & Western Railway	*later NS*
NYA	New York & Atlantic Railway	*Anacosta & Pacific subsidiary*
NYC	New York Central System	*later PC*
NYCH	New York Cross Harbor Railroad Terminal Corp.	*later NYRR*
NYCR	New York Connecting Railroad	*LIRR-NH-PRR joint, later AMTK-PC*
NYCT	New York City Transit Authority	*NYMTA subsidiary*
NYD	New York Dock Railway	*later NYCH*
NYG	New York & Greenwood Lake Railway	*ERIE subsidiary, later EL*
NYGL	New York & Greenwood Lake Railroad	*present company*
NYLB	The New York and Long Branch Railroad	*CNJ-PRR joint subsidiary, later CR*
NYLE	New York & Lake Erie Railroad	*affiliated with SLRR*
NYMTA	New York Metropolitan Transportation Authority	
NYPA	New York & Pennsylvania Railway	
NYRR	New York Regional Rail Corp.	
NYSW	New York Susquehanna and Western Railroad	
NYSX	New York State Electric & Gas Corp.	
NYWB	New York Westchester & Boston Railway	*electric, NH subsidiary*
O&H	Otsego & Herkimer Railroad	*electric, later SONY*
OBW	Olean Bradford & Warren Railway	*3' gauge, later BNYP*
OCTL	Oil Creek & Titusville Lines	*NYLE affiliate*
OE	Otis Elevating Railway	*3' gauge funicular*
OHIC	Ohio-Rail Corporation	

MARK	COMPANY TITLE	*REMARKS*
OHPA	Ohio & Pennsylvania Railroad	*Ohio Central affiliate*
OHRY	Owego & Harford Railway	
OMID	Ontario Midland Railroad	
ONCT	Ontario Central Railroad	
ONER	Ontario Eastern Railroad	
OR&W	Ohio River & Western Railway	*3' gauge, later PRR*
OW	New York Ontario and Western Railway	
P&S	Pittsburgh & Susquehanna Railroad	
P&W	Pittsburgh & Western Railroad	*3' gauge, later BO*
PAM	Pittsburgh Allegheny & McKees Rocks Railroad	
PATH	Port Authority Trans-Hudson	
PAUT	Pennsylvania & Atlantic Railroad	*PRR subsidiary, later UTC*
PBH	Philadelphia & Beach Haven Railroad	*TUCK subsidiary*
PBL	Philadelphia Belt Line Railroad	
PBNE	Philadelphia Bethlehem & New England Railroad	*Bethlehem Steel subsidiary*
PBR	Patapsco & Back Rivers Railroad	*Bethlehem Steel subsidiary*
PC	Penn Central Transportation	*later CR*
PCK	Potato Creek Railroad	
PCS	Pittsburgh and Castle Shannon Railroad	*3' 4" gauge, see note 2*
PCY	Pittsburgh Chartiers & Youghiogheny Railway	*PLE-PRR joint, later CR*
PHWN	Philadelphia & Western Railroad	*3rd rail electric, later SEPA*
PIR	Pittsburgh Industrial Railroad	*RailTex subsidiary*
PJR	Port Jersey Railroad	
PJRL	Penn-Jersey Rail Lines	*affiliated with SMS*
PLE	Pittsburgh & Lake Erie Railroad	*PC(NYC) subsidiary, later CSXT*
PM	Pere Marquette Railway	*later CO*
PMY	Pittsburgh McKeesport & Youghiogheny Railroad	*NYC-PLE subsidiary, later PLE*
POTED	The Potomac Edison Co.	*electric*
POV	Pittsburgh and Ohio Valley Railway	*later CSXT*
PRAT	Prattsburgh Railway	
PRES	Preston Railroad	
PRL	Penn Eastern Rail Lines	*affiliated to MPA and YKR*
PRR	Pennsylvania Railroad	*later PC*
PRSL	Pennsylvania - Reading Seashore Lines	*PRR-RDG joint, later CR*
PS	The Pittsburg & Shawmut Railroad	*later PSR*
PSE	Paul Smithís Electric Railroad	*electric*
PSN	Pittsburg Shawmut & Northern Railroad	
PSO	Pittsburgh Southern Railroad	*3' gauge, later BO*
PSR	Pittsburgh & Shawmut Railroad	*GWI subsidiary*
PW	Providence and Worcester Railroad	
PWB	Philadelphia Wilmington & Baltimore Railroad	*later PRR*
PWS	Pittsburg Westmoreland & Somerset Railroad	
PWV	Pittsburgh & West Virginia Railway	*later NW*
QARR	Queen Anne Railroad	*tourist operation*
QB	Quakertown & Bethlehem Railroad	
RBMN	Reading Blue Mountain & Northern Railroad	
RDG	Reading Company	*later CR*
RFC	Reynoldsville and Falls Creek Railroad	
RFP	Richmond Fredericksburg and Potomac Railroad	*later CSXT*
RJCN	R J Corman Railroad - Allentown Lines	
RJCP	R J Corman Railroad - Pennsylvania Lines	
RRRR	Raritan River Railroad	*later CR*
RSR	Rochester & Southern Railroad	*GWI subsidiary*
RTM	Rockhill Trolley Museum	*electric, tourist operation*

MARK	COMPANY TITLE	*REMARKS*
RUT	Rutland Railway	
RV	Rahway Valley Railroad	
RVY	Rockaway Valley Railroad	
RWO	Rome Watertown & Ogdensburg Railroad	*later NYC*
S&B	Syracuse & Baldwinsville Railroad	*DLW subsidiary*
S&EM	Susquehanna & Eagles Mere Railroad	*3' gauge*
SBLN	Sterling Belt Line Railroad	
SCR	Somerset County Railroad	*3' gauge*
SH	Steelton & Highspire Railroad	*Bethlehem Steel subsidiary*
SLH	Sugar Loaf & Hazeton Railroad	
SLRR	St. Lawrence & Raquette River Railroad	*affilated with NYLE*
SMMLG	Saratoga Mt. McGregor & Lake George Railroad	*3' gauge, later HVR*
SMR	Sterling Mountain Railway	
SMS	SMS Switching Services	*affiliated with PJRL*
SNHS	Steamtown National Historic Site - National Parks Service	*tourist operation*
SNY	The Susquehanna& New York Railroad	
SOM	Somerset Railroad	*owned by NYSX, operated by CSXT*
SONY	Southern New York Railway	
SOU	Southern Railway	*later NS*
SRC	Strasburg Rail Road	
SRNJ	Southern Railroad Co. of New Jersey	
SRRR	Slate Run Railroad	*3' gauge*
SRW	Susquehanna River & Western Railroad	*standard and 3' gauge*
SSL	Skaneateles Short Line Railroad	
ST	Guilford Rail System - Springfield Terminal	
STLH	St. Lawrence & Hudson Railway	*CP subsidiary*
STRT	Stewartstown Railroad	*tourist operation*
SVR	Schoharie Valley Railroad	
SVRR	Shamokin Valley Railroad	*affiliated with LVRR NSHR UCIR*
SWP	Southwestern Pennsylvania Railroad	
TCKR	Turtle Creek Industrial Railroad	
TIOC	Tioga Central Railroad	*tourist operation*
TIOS	Tioga Scenic Railroad	*tourist operation*
TIRL	Tonawanda Island Railroad	
TIRY	Ther Thousand Islands Railway	*later CN*
TIV	Tionesta Valley Railroad	*3' gauge*
TM&P	Twin Mountain & Potomac Railroad	*3' gauge*
TMSL	Towand-Monroeton Shippers Lifeline	
TNY	Trolley Museum of New York	*tourist operation*
TPT	Trenton-Princeton Traction Co.	*electric, RDG subsidiary*
TUCK	Tuckerton Railroad	
TURR	The Troy Union Railroad	*BM-DH-NYC joint*
TUV	Tuscarora Valley Railroad	*3' gauge*
TVC	Tonawanda Valley & Cuba Railroad	*later ARA*
TYBR	Tyburn Railroad	
UCIR	Union County Industrial Railroad	*affiliated with LVRR NSHR SVRR*
UD	Ulster & Delaware Railroad	*later NYC*
UMP	Upper Merion & Plymouth Railroad	*Lykens Steel subsidiary*
UNF	Ursina & North Fork Railway	
UNI	Unity Railways	
URR	Union Railroad	*Transtar subsidiary*
USA	United States Army	
USG	United States Government	
USMC	United States Marine Corps.	
USN	United States Navy	
USX	United States Steel Corp.	
UTC	Union Transportation Co.	*later CR*
UV	Unadilla Valley Railway	

MARK	COMPANY TITLE	*REMARKS*
VAL	Valley Railroad	
VFSR	Valley Forge Scenic Railroad	
VIA	VIA Rail Canada	
VRE	Northern Virginia Transportation Commission - "Virginia Railway Express"	
VTR	Vermont Railway	
WAB	Wabash Railway	*later NW*
WAG	Wellsville Addison & Galeton Railroad	
WARR	Western Allegheny Railroad	*later BLE*
WAW	Waynesburg and Washington Railroad 3' gauge	*later PRR*
WBA	Washington Baltimore & Annapolis Electric Railroad electric	*part later BLA*
WBC	Wilkes-Barre Connecting Railroad	*DH subsidiary*
WBE	Wilkes-Barre & Eastern Railroad	*NYSW subsidiary*
WBH	Wilkes-Barre & Hazleton Railway	*electric*
WBPL	Washington Brandywine & Point Lookout Railroad	
WCOR	Wellsboro & Corning Railroad	
WCR	West Chester Railroad	*tourist operation*
WD&L	White Deer & Loganton Railway	*3' gauge*
WDB	Wildwood and Delaware Bay Short Line Railroad	
WE	The Wheeling & Lake Erie Railway	*present company*
WHN	Wharton & Northern Railroad	*CNJ subsidiary*
WJS	West Jersey and Seashore Railroad	*PRR subsidiary, later PRSL*
WKS	Wanamaker Kempton & Souther Inc.	*tourist operation*
WLE	Wheeling & Lake Erie Railway	*later NKP*
WM	Western Maryland Railway	*later CSXT*
WMS	Western Maryland Scenic Railroad	*tourist operation*
WNB	Williamsport & North Branch Railroad	
WNF	The Winfield Railroad	
WNYP	Western New York & Pennsylvania Traction	*electric*
WOD	Washington & Old Dominion Railroad	*later CO*
WPE	West Pittson-Exeter Railroad	*later LV*
WS	West Shore Railroad	*NYC subsidiary, later PC*
WSB	West Side Belt Railroad	*WLE subsidiary, later PWV*
WSO	Walkersville Southern Railroad	*tourist operation*
WT	The Washington Terminal Co.	*BO-PRR joint, later AMTK*
WTSE	West Shore Railroad	*operated by UCIR*
WVRR	Wallkill Valley Railroad	
WW	Winchester & Western Railroad	
WWRC	Wilmington & Western Railway	
YKR	Yorkrail Inc.	*affiliated with MPA and PRL*
YOR	Youngstown & Ohio River Railroad	
YS	Youngstown & Southern Railway	*MTR subsidiary, later OHPA*

NOTE:

1: *Following the takeover of Conrail by CSXT and NS, certain lines are jointly operated by the two owners under the Conrail name. The unofficial mark CSAO is used to identify these lines separately from the old Conrail.*

2: *PCS later became part of the Pittsburgh Railways 5' 2" gauge streetcar system, route 47.*

MAINLINE ELECTRIFICATION SYSTEMS:

AMTK	ex-NH and PRR lines: 11.5kV 60Hz ac overhead. ex-NYC lines: 680V dc third rail (bottom contact).
DLW	3000V dc overhead, changed to 25kV 60Hz ac overhead by NJT.
LIRR	750V dc third rail (top contact).
NH	11kV 25Hz ac overhead.
NJT	25kV 60Hz ac overhead (ex-DLW lines)
NYC	680V dc third rail (bottom contact)
PRR	11kV 25Hz ac overhead..
RDG	11kV 25Hz ac overhead.

INDEX

Each page of this volume is divided into a 6 x 4 grid of squares lettered from West to East and numbered from North to South. This index places all locations into one of these squares.

The entry for each location comprises Place Name, State Code and Map Reference. The map reference for any location in the index is made up of a combination of a page number and grid square (e.g. 29B4 places a location on page 29, column B, row 4).

All names shown on the maps appear in the index with the following exceptions; milepost locations (MP), numbered control points (CP), numbered tunnels and workshops and engine facilities where they are located adjacent to the town/city/station/yard of the same name.

In crowded urban areas some locations sharing the same name are differentiated by the initials of either the current or former owner.

Entries whose names begin with a number will be found at the beginning of the index. In the case of names such as St Andrews, these will be found under 'St' rather than the full spelling of 'Saint'.

Conventional two letter codes are used to identify the various States and Canadian Provinces

Richard Cossey

Place	State	Page	Grid
3M Corporation [Edgerly]	PA	74	B4
3rd & Berks Streets [Philadelphia]	PA	73	B4
3rd Street [Nescopeck]	PA	62	E2
4H Fairgrounds [Cape May Court House]	NJ	19	C4
4th Avenue [Newark]	NJ	22	A4
4th Avenue Station [Pittsburgh]	PA	53	A3
4th Street [Ocean City]	NJ	19	D3
5th Avenue [Pelham]	NY	25	D4
5th Street [Elmira]	NY	41	F3
5th Street [Hoboken]	NJ	22	C5
5th Street Yard [Queens]	NY	23	B3
7th Street Station [Washington]	DC	14	C5
9th Street [Manhattan]	NY	23	A3
10th Street [Ocean City]	NJ	19	D3
10th Street Yard [Pittsburgh]	PA	53	A3
11th Street [Hoboken]	NJ	22	C4
11th Street - Beaver Falls	PA	51	C2
11th Street Yard [Pittsburgh]	PA	53	A2
12th Street [Pittsburgh]	PA	53	A3
12th Street [Pottsville]	PA	67	B5
13th Street [Easton]	PA	71	E2
13th Street Junction [Easton]	PA	71	E2
14th Street [Manhattan]	NY	23	A3
14th Street [Ocean City]	NJ	19	D3
15th Street [Hoboken]	NJ	22	C4
16th Street [Philadelphia]	PA	73	B3
16th Street [Pittsburgh]	PA	53	A2
16th Street Industrial Track [Camden]	NJ	73	B4
18th Street [Pittsburgh]	PA	53	A3
19th Street [Harrisburg]	PA	64	D2
19th Street [Manhattan]	NY	23	A3
20th Street [Philadelphia]	PA	73	A4
21st Street [Pittsburgh]	PA	53	A2
22nd Street [Philadelphia]	PA	73	A3
23rd Street [Manhattan]	NY	23	A3
23rd Street [Pittsburgh]	PA	53	A3
24th Street [Ocean City]	NJ	19	D3
24th & Chestnut Streets Station [Philadelphia]	PA	73	A4
26th Street [Manhattan]	NY	23	B3
27th Street [Manhattan]	NY	23	A3
28th Street [Brooklyn]	NY	23	A4
28th Street [Manhattan]	NY	23	A3
28th Street [Philadelphia]	PA	73	A3
29th Street [Altoona]	PA	59	D2
29th Street [Manhattan]	NY	23	A3
29th Street [Pittsburgh]	PA	53	A2
30th Street Post Office [Manhattan]	NY	23	A3
30th Street Station [Philadelphia]	PA	73	A4
30th Street Yard [Manhattan]	NY	23	A3
30th Street Yard [Pittsburgh]	PA	53	A3
33rd Street [Manhattan]	NY	23	A3
34th Street [Ocean City]	NJ	19	D3
34th Street [Pittsburgh North Side]	PA	53	A2
34th Street [Pittsburgh South Side]	PA	53	A3
36th Street [Philadelphia]	PA	73	A4
36th Street Yard [Pittsburgh]	PA	53	A2
37th Street [Manhattan]	NY	23	A2
39th Street [Brooklyn]	NY	23	A4
43rd Street [Pittsburgh]	PA	53	A2
43rd Street [Pittsburgh]	PA	53	A2
49th Street [Philadelphia]	PA	73	A4
50th Street [Brooklyn]	NY	23	A5
51st Street [Ocean City]	NJ	19	D3
52nd Street [Philadelphia]	PA	72	D4
54th Street [Pittsburgh]	PA	53	A2
58th Street [Philadelphia]	PA	73	A5
60th Street [Philadelphia]	PA	73	A5
60th Street Yard [Manhattan]	NY	23	A2
63rd Street [Brooklyn]	NY	23	A5
69th Street Terminal [Philadelphia]	PA	72	D4
72nd Street Shops [Philadelphia]	PA	72	D4
90th Street [Philadelphia]	PA	72	D5
125th Street [Manhattan]	NY	23	B2
130th Street [Manhattan]	NY	23	B1
133rd Street [Bronx]	NY	23	B2
138th Street [Bronx]	NY	23	B1
149th Street [Bronx]	NY	23	B1
152nd Street [Manhattan]	NY	23	B1
155th Street [Manhattan]	NY	23	B1
183rd Street [Tremont]	NY	23	C1
A			
A Avenue [Bayonne]	NJ	22	B6
A Tower [Philadelphia]	PA	73	A5
A H Smith Memorial Bridge	NY	33	C1
A&P [Hempstead]	NY	24	C4
Abbot	PA	56	F3
Abbott	PA	71	E3
Abbott Road [Lackawanna]	NY	46	C6
Abbott Road Yard [Buffalo]	NY	46	B5
Abbottstown	PA	63	C3
Aberdeen	MD	11	C2
Aberdeen	MD	13	C2
Aberdeen	PA	63	D2
Aberdeen Military Proving Ground	MD	13	D3
Abnaki	VT	28	F2
Abrams Yard [Norristown]	PA	72	B1
Absecon	NJ	19	D2
Absecon Road	NJ	19	D2
Academy Corners	PA	61	A1
Accord	NY	31	C4
Ache Junction	PA	50	D3
Acheson	PA	52	A5
Acheson Tunnel	PA	52	A5
Ackerson	NJ	16	C2
Acme [Cheswick]	PA	53	C1
Acorn	PA	70	C2
Acosta	PA	60	A2
Adah	PA	50	D3
Adams	NJ	18	D1
Adams	NY	37	C2
Adams [CSXT(BO)]	PA	60	A3
Adams [EBT]	PA	60	E1
Adams Basin	NY	40	B2
Adams Center	NY	37	C2
Adams Crossing	NY	31	F1
Adams Street [Troy]	NY	32	F2
Adamsburg	PA	50	E1
Adamsdale	PA	67	C6
Adamstown	MD	10	B2
Adamsville	DE	7	D2
Adamsville	PA	48	B3
Addison	NY	41	D3
Addison Junction	NY	29	B4
Adelaide	PA	55	B5
ADM Mill [Elizabethport]	NJ	22	A6
ADM Mill [Hudson]	NY	33	C6
Adrian	NY	41	C2
Adrian	PA	57	A2
Adrian Furnace	PA	57	B1
Adriance	NY	34	F1
A E Staley Plant [Morrisville]	PA	74	C3
AF Interlocking [Alexandria]	VA	14	B6
Afton	NY	39	E2
Agasote	NJ	74	C2
Agway Plant [Bordentown]	NJ	74	D4
Agway Station [Middletown]	NY	27	A2
AH [Calverton]	NY	35	A5
Aireys	MD	11	C6
Aiken	PA	56	C1
Aikin	MD	11	C1
Airport Junction [Philadelphia]	PA	72	D6
Ajax Park	NJ	74	C2
AK [Dunkirk]	NY	43	C1
AK Bridge [Arthur Kill]	NY	20	E1
Akeley	PA	56	A1
Akron	NY	42	F2
Akron	PA	63	E2
Akron Junction	NY	42	F2
Alabama	NY	42	F2
Aladdin	PA	51	E2
Alaska	PA	66	B5
Alba	NY	34	C3
Alba	PA	61	C2
Albany	NY	30	E4
Albany	NY	32	E4
Albany	PA	69	A4
Albany-Rensselaer (Rensselaer)	NY	32	E4
Albert	PA	62	F1
Alberton	MD	10	D2
Albertson	NY	24	B3
Albion	NJ	18	B4
Albion	NY	40	A1
Albion	PA	48	B1
Alburg	NY	28	B2
Alburgh	VT	28	F1
Alburtis	PA	69	B4
ALCo Locomotive Works [Schenectady]	NY	32	B2
Alcoa Plant [Massena]	NY	28	A1
Alden	NY	42	F3
Alden	PA	65	A6
Aldene	NJ	21	D6
Alder Creek	NY	37	E4
Aldham	PA	70	B2
Aldrich	NY	37	F1
Aldridge	WV	9	F3
Alesia	MD	10	D1
Alexander	NY	40	A3
Alexandria	PA	57	E4
Alexandria	VA	14	B6
Alexandria Junction [Hyattsville]	MD	14	D3
Alexandria Union Station	VA	14	B6
Alexauken	NJ	18	C2
Alfarata	PA	57	D4
Alfold	PA	68	A2
Alfred	NY	41	C2
Alicia	PA	54	B5
Aliquippa	PA	49	C3
Allaire	NJ	18	E3
Allaire State Park	NJ	18	E3
Allamuchy	NJ	17	C3
Allegany	MD	8	B1
Alleghany	NY	43	F3
Allegheny Ludlum Plant [Bagdad]	PA	51	E3
Allegheny Tunnel [Gallitzin]	PA	59	B2
Allegheny Yard [Pittsburgh]	PA	53	A2
Allegrippus	PA	59	B2
Allendale	NJ	17	E2
Allenhurst	NJ	18	F2
Allenport [EBT]	PA	60	E1
Allenport [NS(PRR)]	PA	54	C3
Allen [Allentown]	PA	71	B4
Allen Junction	PA	71	B4
Allen Lane	PA	73	A2
Allens	NJ	18	D2
Allens	PA	61	C4
Allens Mills	PA	57	B1
Allentown	NY	41	B3
Allentown	PA	17	A4
Allentown	PA	71	A4
Allentown Industrial track	PA	71	B4
Allentown Yard	PA	71	B4
Allenvale	PA	60	A2
Allenwood	NJ	18	F3
Allenwood	PA	62	C1
Alley (Pine Grove)	DE	7	E1
Allied Chemical [Frankford]	PA	73	C3
Allied Chemical [Solvay]	NY	36	A1
Allied Junction	NJ	22	B5
Allison [MGA]	PA	54	C5
Allison [RDG]	PA	67	A6
Allison Park	PA	49	D4
Alloway	NJ	19	A1
Alloway Junction	NJ	19	A1
Allwood	NJ	22	A3
Allworth	PA	50	F1
Ally [Alleghany]	NY	43	F3
Almond	NY	41	C2
Aloquin	NY	40	E3
Alpha	NJ	71	F3
Alphano	NJ	17	C3
Alpine	NY	41	F2
Alpsville	PA	53	D5
Alsen	NY	31	D3
Altamont	MD	9	A2
Altamont	NY	30	D4
Altenwald	PA	60	F3
Althom	PA	48	F2
Alterton	PA	63	B2
Altmar	NY	37	C4
Alto [NW(PWV)]	PA	54	C2
Alto Tower [Altoona]	PA	59	D2
Alton	NY	40	E2
Altona	NY	28	E1
Altoona	PA	57	C4
Altoona	PA	59	D2
Alum	PA	49	F4
Alum Rock	PA	49	E1
Aluta	PA	71	C1
Alvan No.9 Tipple	PA	60	D2
Alverda	PA	57	B3
Alverson	NY	37	C2
Alverton	PA	55	C3
Amagansett	NY	35	C5
Amasa	PA	47	D1
Amatol Junction	NJ	19	D1
Amawalk	NY	34	F3
Ambau	PA	63	C3
Ambler	PA	70	C2
Amboy	NY	38	B2
Ambridge	PA	49	C4
Ambulco	NY	41	B1
Amcelle	MD	8	C3
Amenia	NY	31	E4
Amerail Shops [Hornell]	NY	41	C2
American Docks [St. George]	NY	20	F1
American Float Gass Plant [Riverton]	NJ	73	D3
American Legion (Horseshoe)	NY	29	B1
Ames	PA	57	C3
Ames Street Junction [Rochester]	NY	44	C3
Amesville Junction	PA	58	B5
Amherst Car Shops	PA	64	D5
Amityville	NY	35	C3
Ammendale	MD	10	D4
Amos Siding	NY	37	F4
Amott	NY	35	C2
Ampere	NJ	22	A4
Amsbry	PA	59	A1
Amsterdam	NY	30	C3
Anacostia	DC	14	C5
Anacostia Junction	DC	14	C5
Analomink	PA	69	C2
Anchor (Blue Anchor)	NJ	19	C1
Ancora	NJ	19	C1
Ancram	NY	31	E3
Ancram Lead Mines	NY	31	E3
Andalusia	PA	73	D2
Andenheim	PA	57	E4
Anderson [BO(BRP)]	PA	57	C2
Anderson [BO(PSO)]	PA	52	D6
Anderson [NPFG]	PA	63	D4
Anderson [NS(PRR)]	PA	57	F4
Anderson Mine	PA	58	B5
Anderson Road	PA	49	C4
Andersonburg	PA	63	A1
Andes	NY	31	A2
Andes Junction	NY	31	A3
Andover	NJ	17	C3
Andover	NY	41	B3
Andover	OH	48	B3
Andover Junction	NJ	17	C3
Andreas	PA	69	A3
Andrews Avenue [Wildwood]	NJ	19	C4
Andrico	PA	50	F1
Angelica	NY	41	B2
Anglesea	NJ	19	C4
Angola	NY	42	D4
Angora	PA	72	D4
Angus	NY	40	E4
Anita	PA	57	B2
Annadale	NY	20	E2
Annandale	NJ	17	C4
Annandale	PA	49	D1
Annapolis	MD	11	B4
Annsville Creek	NY	26	B2
Annville	PA	63	D1
Anson Crossing	NY	31	E4
Anson Tunnel	NY	34	B3
Ansonia	PA	61	A2
Ant (Antram)	PA	54	B6
Antes Fort [defect detector]	PA	62	B1
Anthracite Bag Plant [Arters]	PA	66	B6
Antietam	MD	10	A2
Antis [Altoona]	PA	59	D1
Antram	PA	54	B6
Antrim	PA	61	B3
Antwerp	NY	36	D4
AO Interlocking [Conemaugh]	PA	64	B1
Apex	NY	39	E3
Apollo	PA	51	F4
Apollo 2 Mine	PA	57	B4
Appalachian Trail	NY	34	F1
Appalachin	NY	39	B3
Appleton	NY	42	E1
Apulia	NY	38	C3
Aqua	PA	57	E2
Aquashicola	PA	69	F2
Aquebogue	NY	35	B5
Aqueduct	NY	32	C2
Aqueduct	PA	62	C4
Aqueduct North Conduit Avenue Ramblers)	NY	23	D4
Aqueduct Racetrack	NY	23	D4
AR Tower [Gallitzin]	PA	59	B2
Arbutus	MD	12	A3
Arcade	NY	43	F1
Arcade Center	NY	43	F1
Arcade Junction	NY	43	F1
Arcadia	MD	10	D1
Arcadia	PA	57	B3
Arch	NJ	17	C4
Arch Street [Palmyra]	NJ	73	C3
Archbald	PA	65	B1
Archdale	NY	30	F2
Arcola	PA	70	B2
Arden	DE	6	E1
Arden	MD	15	B2
Arden	NY	34	D3
Arden	PA	50	C2
Ardmore	MD	10	D4
Ardmore	PA	72	D3
Ardmore Avenue [Ardmore]	PA	72	C3
Ardmore Junction	PA	72	C3
Ardsley	PA	73	B1
Ardsley (Ardsley-on-Hudson)	NY	25	C1
Ardsley [Putnam Division]	NY	25	C2
Ardsley-on-Hudson	NY	25	C1

Location	State	Map	Grid
Arena	NY	31	A3
Argentine	PA	49	D1
Argyle No.4 Mine	PA	64	B2
Aristes (Montana)	PA	66	D4
Ark (Clarksville)	PA	50	C3
Arkport	NY	41	C2
Arkville	NY	31	B3
Arlington	MD	12	B1
Arlington	NJ	22	B4
Arlington	NY	20	E1
Arlington [PC(PRR)]	PA	72	D4
Arlington [RBMN(LNE)]	PA	62	F3
Arlington Avenue [Jersey City]	NJ	22	C5
Arlington Siding (Briggs)	NY	34	E1
Armory Square [Syracuse]	NY	36	A1
Armstrong	DE	7	A2
Arnold	MD	11	B4
Arnold	PA	51	C4
Arnold City	PA	54	C3
Arnot	PA	61	B2
Arona	PA	50	E1
Arrochar	NY	20	F1
Arrot Street [Philadelphia]	PA	73	C3
Arrow (Arrowhead)	NY	38	B1
Arrowhead	NY	38	B1
Arroyo	PA	56	B4
Arroyo	WV	49	A4
Arsenal [Philadelphia]	PA	73	A4
Arsenberg	PA	54	A6
Arters	PA	66	B6
Arthur Kill Bridge	NY	20	E1
Arthurs	PA	48	F4
Arthursburgh	NY	34	F1
Arundel	MD	11	A4
Arverne	NY	23	D6
Asbestos	MD	10	D2
Asbestos	PA	73	A2
Asbury	NY	39	A1
Asbury Park	NJ	18	F2
Ash Brook	NJ	20	C1
Ashburn	VA	10	B4
Ashby	VA	9	E4
Ashcom	PA	60	C3
Ashfield	PA	69	B3
Ashford	NY	43	E2
Ashland	DE	6	C1
Ashland [Baltimore County]	MD	11	A2
Ashland [Queen Anne County]	MD	11	C4
Ashland	NJ	73	D6
Ashland	PA	66	D5
Ashley Falls	MA	31	F3
Ashley Inclined Planes	PA	65	B6
Ashley Junction	PA	65	B6
Ashley Yard	PA	65	B6
Ashmore	PA	66	B1
Ashokan	NY	31	C3
Ashtabula	OH	48	A1
Ashtabula Harbor	OH	48	A1
Ashtabula Siding	OH	48	A2
Ashtola	PA	60	B2
Ashton	PA	73	C2
Ashville	NY	43	C3
Ashville	PA	59	B1
Ashwood	NY	40	A1
Aspinwall	PA	53	B2
Astral	PA	48	D4
Atchison	PA	50	D4
Atco	NJ	18	C4
Atglen	PA	63	F3
Athenia	NJ	22	A2
Athens	ON	36	C2
Athens	PA	61	D1
Athol Springs	NY	46	B6
Atlanta	NY	41	D1
Atlantic [CSXT(BO)]	PA	60	A3
Atlantic [EL(ERIE)]	PA	48	B3
Atlantic [Atlantic City]	NJ	19	F4
Atlantic [Tottenville]	NY	20	D3
Atlantic Avenue [Atlantic City]	NJ	19	F4
Atlantic Avenue Tunnel	NY	23	C4
Atlantic City	NJ	19	E2
Atlantic City	NJ	19	F4
Atlantic City Electric Power Plant [Deepwater]	NJ	6	E3
Atlantic Highlands	NJ	18	F1
Atlantic Terminal [Brooklyn]	NY	23	A4
Atlas	PA	66	C5
Atlas Colliery	PA	66	B5
Atlas Point	DE	6	D3
Atlas Portland Cement [Northampton]	PA	71	B2
Atlas Quarry	NJ	16	D1
Atlasburg	PA	50	B1
Atsion	NJ	18	C4
Attica	NY	40	A3
Attlebury	NY	31	E4
Atwaters	NY	40	F4
Auburn	NY	38	A3
Auburn	PA	62	F4
Auburn Junction [Ithaca]	NY	39	A1
Auburndale	NY	23	D2
Aucheys	PA	62	F4
Auchincloss	PA	65	A6
Auchincloss Junction	PA	65	A5
Audenried	PA	66	A2
Audubon	NJ	73	C5
Aughwick	PA	60	E1
Augusta	MD	10	A2
Augusta	NJ	16	B1
Aultman	PA	49	F4
Aultrey Park	MD	10	C4
Aultsville	ON	36	F1
Aura	NJ	19	B1
Auriesville	NY	30	C3
Aurora	NY	40	F4
Ausable Chasm	NY	28	F3
Ausable Forks	NY	28	E3
Austin	PA	56	E3
Austin Yard [Scranton]	PA	65	B2
Austinburg	OH	48	A2
AutoTrain Terminal [Lorton]	VA	10	C5
Avalon	NJ	19	D4
Avalon	PA	52	D1
Avella	PA	50	B1
Avenel	NJ	20	C2
Avenue Interlocking [Washington]	DC	14	C4
Avis	PA	62	B1
Avoca	NY	41	D2
Avoca	PA	65	B3
Avoca Yard	PA	65	B3
Avon	NY	40	C3
Avon	PA	63	E1
Avon Industrial Track	PA	63	E1
Avondale [DV(PRR)]	PA	6	A1
Avondale [EL(DLW)]	PA	65	A5
Avonmore	PA	49	E4
Axeman	PA	57	F2

B

Location	State	Map	Grid
B&O Junction [NYC Clearfield]	PA	58	A1
B&O Junction [PLE New Castle]	PA	51	B2
B&O Museum [Baltimore]	MD	12	B2
B&P Junction [Baltimore]	MD	12	B2
B&P Tunnels [Baltimore]	MD	12	B2
B&W Junction [Curwensville]	PA	58	C1
BA (Bennezette)	PA	56	D4
Babbit	NJ	22	C3
Babcock Street Yard [Buffalo]	NY	46	B5
Babylon	NY	35	C3
Babylon Yard	NY	35	C3
Back River Junction	MD	12	D2
Backus	NY	37	E1
Backus	PA	56	C2
Bacon	MD	11	D1
Bacon Hill	MD	11	D1
Bacons	DE	7	E4
Bacons Neck	NJ	19	A2
Bacton	PA	70	E3
Baden	PA	49	C3
Bagdad	PA	51	E3
Baggaley	PA	50	F2
Bail	PA	50	B3
Bailey	NY	44	B4
Bailey	PA	62	B4
Bailey Avenue [Buffalo]	NY	46	B4
Bailey Mine	PA	50	B3
Bailey Run	PA	56	E3
Baileys	MD	12	B3
Baileys Run	PA	51	C3
Bainbridge	NY	39	E2
Bainbridge	PA	63	D2
Bainbridge Power Plant	NY	39	E2
Baird	PA	54	B1
Bairdford	PA	49	D3
Bairdís Farm	NY	34	C3
Baker	NJ	21	A4
Baker [Corning]	NY	41	E3
Baker [PRR]	PA	56	F4
Baker [PRR(WAW)]	PA	50	C2
Baker Mine	PA	59	B2
Baker Street Yard [Corning]	NY	41	E3
Bakerlite	NJ	20	F4
Bakers	PA	61	F4
Bakerstown	PA	49	D3
Bakersville [PC(PRR)]	NJ	74	D2
Bakersville [WJS]	NJ	19	D2
Bakerton	PA	59	C5
Bakerton	WV	10	A2
Bala	PA	72	D3
Bald Eagle	PA	57	D3
Bald Hill	PA	57	D1
Baldwin	MD	11	B2
Baldwin	NY	24	C5
Baldwin	PA	72	C6
Baldwin Locomotive Works [Eddystone]	PA	72	C6
Baldwin Locomotive Works [Philadelphia]	PA	73	A4
Baldwin Place	NY	34	F2
Baldwinsville	NY	38	B2
Balesville	NJ	16	A2
Balliet	PA	69	B3
Ballston Industrial Track	NY	30	D2
Ballston Lake	NY	32	C1
Ballston Spa	NY	30	D2
Balltown	PA	48	F3
Balmat	NY	36	E4
Baltic Terminal [Brooklyn]	NY	23	A4
Baltimore	MD	11	A2
Baltimore Highlands	MD	12	B3
Baltimore Streetcar Museum	MD	12	B2
Baltusrol	NJ	21	C5
Bangall	NY	31	E4
Bangor	NY	28	C1
Bangor	PA	16	A6
Bangor	PA	69	C2
Bangor Junction	PA	16	A6
Banian Branch	PA	58	A5
Banian Junction	PA	58	A5
Bank [Red Bank]	NJ	18	F2
Banks [NS(PRR)]	PA	63	C1
Banks [STLH(PRR)]	PA	66	B6
Banksville	PA	52	D3
Banksville Junction	PA	52	D3
Banner Mine	WV	9	A2
Banning	PA	54	D2
Barb (Barber)	NJ	20	D2
Barber	NJ	20	D2
Barber Quarry	PA	71	A4
Barclay	MD	11	D3
Barclay Place	PA	56	E4
Barclay Station	PA	61	D3
Barcroft	VA	14	A5
Bard	PA	60	C3
Bardane	WV	9	F2
Bardonia	NY	26	A6
Bare Hills	MD	12	B1
Bare Rock	PA	60	A3
Bareville	PA	63	F2
Bark Camp No.1 Mine	PA	57	C1
Barkdale	MD	11	D1
Barker	NY	42	E1
Barking	PA	53	D1
Barmouth	PA	72	D3
Barnard	NJ	19	C1
Barnard	NY	44	B2
Barnard	VA	10	C5
Barnegat	NJ	19	E1
Barnegat City	NJ	19	F1
Barnegat Park	NJ	18	E4
Barnegat Pier	NJ	18	E4
Barnersville	NY	30	B4
Barnes	NY	41	E1
Barnes [PSR(PS)]	PA	57	A1
Barnes [S&T TIV]	PA	56	A2
Barnes & Tucker Mine	PA	57	B4
Barnesboro	PA	59	B4
Barneston	PA	70	A2
Barnesville	MD	10	B3
Barnesville	PA	67	D3
Barneveld	NY	38	F1
Barney Street [Baltimore]	MD	12	B3
Barnsley	PA	63	F4
Barnum	WV	8	C6
Barons Summit	PA	60	E1
Barree	PA	57	E4
Barrelville	MD	8	C1
Barrett	PA	58	B1
Barrington	NJ	73	C6
Barry Junction	PA	67	B3
Barrytown	NY	31	D3
Bartel Street [Kingston]	PA	65	B5
Bartholow	MD	10	C2
Bartlett	NY	38	E2
Bartley	NJ	17	C3
Bartley	PA	49	D3
Barto	PA	70	B1
Barton	MD	8	D5
Barton	NY	39	A3
Barton [NS(BRP)]	PA	57	A3
Barton [PRR]	PA	62	B2
Bartonsville	PA	69	C2
Bartonville	VA	9	E3
Basin Street Yard [Allentown]	PA	71	A4
Basket	MD	15	C2
Basking Ridge	NJ	17	D4
Bass	PA	59	B4
Batavia	NY	40	A3
Batavia	NY	45	A1
Batavia [defect detector]	NY	40	A3
Batavia Yard	NY	45	A1
Bath	NJ	18	F2
Bath	NY	41	D2
Bath	PA	71	B2
Bath Junction	NY	23	A5
Bath Junction	PA	71	C2
Bath Yard	PA	71	C2
Battenville	NY	30	F2
Baum	PA	48	E3
Baumgardner	PA	63	E3
Baxter	PA	57	A1
Bay [Bay Side]	MD	12	C2
Bay [Bayside]	NY	24	A3
Bay Head Junction	NJ	18	F3
Bay Pond	NY	28	C3
Bay Ridge [Brooklyn]	NY	23	A5
Bay Shore	NY	35	C3
Bay Side	NJ	19	A2
Bay Terrace	NY	20	E2
Bay View	MD	12	C2
Bay View	NY	46	B6
Bay View	VA	15	A6
Bay View [defect detector]	NY	42	D4
Bay View Yard [Baltimore]	MD	12	D2
Bayard	WV	9	A3
Baychester	NY	23	D1
Baychester Avenue [Bronx]	NY	25	D4
Bayport	NY	35	D3
Bayside	NY	24	A3
Bayonne Terminal	NJ	22	B6
Bayonne Yard	NJ	22	B6
Bayway	NJ	20	D1
Bazetta [defect detector]	OH	48	A4
BC [Bens Creek]	PA	60	C1
BC Junction [Buffalo]	NY	46	B5
Beadling	PA	52	D4
Beach [Atlantic City]	NJ	19	F4
Beach 25 Street Wavecrest	NY	24	A6
Beach 36 Street Edgemere	NY	24	A6
Beach 44 Street Frank Avenue	NY	23	D6
Beach 60 Street Straiton Avenue	NY	23	D6
Beach 67 Street (Arverne)	NY	23	D6
Beach 90 Street (Holland)	NY	23	D6
Beach 98 Street (Steeple Chase)	NY	23	D6
Beach 105 Street (Seaside)	NY	23	D6
Beach Arlington	NJ	19	F1
Beach Glen	NJ	21	A1
Beach Haven	NJ	19	E1
Beach Haven	PA	62	F1
Beach Ridge	NY	46	B1
Beachdale	PA	60	A3
Beachwood	NJ	18	E4
Beacon	NJ	18	F3
Beacon	NY	26	C1
Beacon	NY	34	E2
Beacon Colliery 2	PA	58	C4
Beale	PA	51	D3
Beam	NY	41	D1
Bear	DE	6	C4
Bear [Fulton]	NY	38	B1
Bear Creek [CLAR]	PA	56	B4
Bear Creek [LV]	PA	69	A1
Bear Creek Bridge	MD	12	D3
Bear Creek Junction	PA	69	A1
Bear Lake	PA	48	E1
Bear Shops	DE	7	A2
Bear Siding	NY	38	B1
Bear Mountain	NY	26	A2
Bear Mountain Tunnel	NY	26	B2
Bear Run Junction	PA	67	B3
Beardsley	PA	56	C3
Beaston	PA	60	D1
Beatty	PA	50	F1
Beaufort	NJ	21	C3
Beaupland	PA	69	A1
Beaver [CSXT(BO)]	PA	49	C3
Beaver [NS(RDG)]	PA	63	D1
Beaver [PRR]	PA	49	C3
Beaver Brook Colliery	PA	66	A2
Beaver Dam	MD	15	C3
Beaver Dam Colliery	PA	57	C3
Beaver Dams	NY	41	E2
Beaver Falls	NY	37	E2
Beaver Falls	PA	51	C2
Beaver Falls & New Brighton	PA	51	C2
Beaver Hill	NY	25	D1
Beaver Lake	NJ	16	D1
Beaver Meadow Colliery	PA	66	B2
Beaver River	NY	29	A2
Beaver Road	PA	52	C2
Beaver Siding	NY	43	E2
Beaver Springs	PA	62	B3
Beaver Valley	PA	67	A1
Beavertown	PA	62	B3
Bechtelsville	PA	70	B1
Beck [Becks Run]	PA	53	A3
Beckett Street Terminal [Camden]	NJ	73	B4
Becks [BO]	PA	60	A3
Becks [RDG]	PA	67	B6
Becks Run	PA	53	A3
Beckton	PA	67	B6
Bedford	NJ	18	F1
Bedford	PA	60	C3
Bedford Hills	NY	34	F3
Bee Bee Power Plant [Rochester]	NY	44	C2
Bee Hive Crossing	VT	30	F3
Beech [Clearfield]	PA	58	A1
Beech Bottom	WV	50	A2
Beech Creek	PA	57	F1
Beech Glen	PA	61	D4
Beechmont	PA	52	C3
Beechton	PA	56	B4
Beechville	PA	56	D4
Beechwood	PA	56	D3
Beechwood	WV	9	A3
Beechwood-Brookline	PA	72	D4
Beekman	NY	34	F1
Beekmantown	NY	28	F2
Beeler's Summit	MD	10	A2
Beerston	NY	39	F3
Beesley's Point Power Plant	NJ	19	D3
Beideman [Camden]	NJ	73	C4
Beihl	PA	62	C2
Beisels	PA	62	F2
Bel Air	MD	11	B1
Belair Road [Grasmere]	NY	20	F1
Belcamp	MD	13	B3
Belden Tunnel	NY	39	D2
Belfast	NY	41	A2
Belfast Colliery	PA	57	C2
Belfast Junction	PA	71	D1
Belford	PA	57	E1
Belford No.3 Mine	PA	57	E1
Belfry	PA	70	C2
Bell	DE	6	E2
Bell	MD	10	D4
Bell [Bellevue]	PA	52	D2
Bell Run	PA	57	C2
Bellaire	OH	50	A3
Bellaire	PA	63	D2
Bellamy	ON	36	D2
Belle Bridge	PA	53	C5
Belle Haven	VA	15	B5
Belle Mead	NJ	18	D1
Belle Valley	PA	47	C6
Belle Vernon [CSXT(PMY)]	PA	54	C2
Belle Vernon [PC(PRR)]	PA	54	B3
Belle Vernon Colliery	PA	58	C5
Belle Vernon Junction	PA	53	C4
Bellefonte	PA	57	F2
Bellefonte Avenue [Lock Haven]	PA	62	A1
Belleplain	NJ	19	C3
Bellerose	NY	24	A4
Belleview	NY	43	C3
Belleville	NJ	22	A4
Belleville	PA	57	F4
Belleville-Cleveland Street	NJ	22	A4
Bellevue	DE	6	E2
Bellevue	PA	52	D2
Bellewood	NJ	17	B4
Bellfield	PA	50	B1
Bellhurst	NJ	19	C1
Bellmawr	NJ	73	C6
Bellmawr Industrial Park	NJ	73	B6
Bellmore	NY	24	D5
Bellnap	PA	59	A5
Bellona	NY	40	E4

Location	State	Page	Grid
CP West Laurel [Reading]	PA	64	A4
CP West Pilot	MD	11	C1
CP West Pitt [Pittsburgh]	PA	53	A2
CP West Point	PA	70	C2
CP West Rock	MD	13	A1
CP West Summit	NJ	21	B5
CP Wing	NJ	74	C1
CP Wing [East Pittsburgh]	PA	53	C3
CP Works [Altoona]	PA	59	D1
CP Wood [Homewood]	PA	51	B4
CP Wood [Woodbourne]	PA	74	B3
CP Woodbourne	PA	74	A3
CP Woodbury	NJ	73	B6
CP Wye [Rockville]	PA	64	C1
CP Wyomissing Junction [Reading]	PA	64	A5
CP Yellow Creek	OH	49	A4
CQ [South Amboy]	NJ	20	C3
CR Tower [Harmon]	NY	26	C4
Crabster	MD	10	C1
Crabtree	PA	50	E1
Crafton	PA	52	D3
Crafts	NY	34	F2
Craigheads	PA	63	B2
Craigs	NY	45	E3
Craigsville	PA	49	E2
Craigville	NY	27	D3
Cranberry	MD	10	D1
Cranberry Creek	NY	30	C2
Cranberry Lake	NJ	17	C3
Cranberry Lake	NY	28	A4
Cranberry Junction	PA	66	A1
Cranbury	NJ	18	D2
Crandalltown	PA	61	C3
Crane	PA	69	B4
Crane Junction	PA	71	B2
Crane Power Plant	MD	12	F2
Cranesville	PA	48	B1
Cranford	NJ	21	C6
Craryville	NY	31	E2
Crawford	NY	41	A2
Craword	PA	56	C2
Crawford Junction	NY	27	A1
Crayton	PA	48	B1
Creagerstown	MD	10	B1
Cream Ridge	NJ	18	D3
Creasy [Mifflinville]	PA	62	E2
Creedmoor	NY	24	A4
Creek [Conshohocken]	PA	72	C2
Creekside	PA	57	A3
Creigh	PA	60	E3
Creighton	PA	51	E4
Crellin	MD	9	A2
Crenshaw	PA	56	B4
Cres (Creswell)	PA	63	E3
Cresap	WV	50	A3
Crescent	NY	32	E1
Crescent (Crescentville)	PA	73	B3
Crescentville	PA	73	B3
Cresco	PA	69	C1
Cresham	PA	73	A2
Creslo	PA	60	B1
Cress	PA	63	A4
Cresskill	NJ	22	D1
Cresson	PA	59	A2
Cressona	PA	67	B6
Crestmont	PA	73	B1
Crestmoor	NJ	17	C4
Crestwood	NY	25	D3
Crestwood	PA	69	A1
Creswell	PA	63	E3
Cribb	PA	50	E1
Cribbs	PA	49	F4
Crisfield	MD	15	A3
Crissman	PA	57	D4
Crittenden [ERIE]	NY	44	B4
Crittenden [NYC]	NY	42	F3
Crocketts	NY	38	A1
Croft [NC(LV)]	PA	61	D1
Croft [NYC]	PA	57	D1
Croghan	NY	37	E2
Cromby [NS(PRR)]	PA	70	F2
Cromby (Mingo) [NS(RDG)]	PA	70	F1
Cromwell/Glen Burnie	MD	12	B4
Croom	MD	11	A5
Cropwell	NJ	73	D5
Crosby	PA	56	D2
Cross Fork	PA	56	F3
Cross Fork Junction	PA	56	F3
Cross Roads	NY	38	A3
Crossland	PA	55	B5
Crossley	NJ	18	E4
Croton Falls	NY	34	F2
Croton-Harmon (Harmon)	NY	26	C4
Croton Heights	NY	26	D3
Croton Lake	NY	26	D4
Croton North (Croton-on-Hudson)	NY	26	C4
Croton-on-Hudson	NY	26	C4
Crown	MD	15	B1
Crown	PA	48	F4
Crown Avenue Tunnel [Scranton]	PA	65	C2
Crown Point	NY	29	F2
Crownsville	MD	11	A4
Croxton	NJ	22	C4
Croxton Yard	NJ	22	C4
Croy [Croydon]	PA	74	A5
Croydon	PA	74	A5
Croyland	PA	56	B4
Crozier Run Junction	PA	50	D4
CRP Junction [Easton]	PA	71	D3
Crucible	PA	54	A6
Crucible Steel [Solvay]	NY	36	A1
Crugers	NY	26	B3
Crum Lynne	PA	72	C6
Crysler (Aultsville)	ON	36	F1
Crystal City	VA	14	B5
Crystal Lake	NJ	17	E2
Crystal Lake	NY	43	F1
Crystal Run	NY	27	B1
Cuba	NY	41	A2
Cuddeback	NY	40	E3
Cuffman	PA	60	E2
Culbertson	PA	60	F3
Cullen	MD	10	B1
Cully	PA	63	E4
Culmerville	PA	49	D3
Culp's Station	PA	62	B2
Culyerville	NY	40	B4
Cumberland	MD	8	D2
Cumberland	MD	9	C1
Cumberland Mine	PA	50	C4
Cumberland Shops	MD	8	D2
Cumberland Yard	MD	8	D2
Cumbola	PA	67	C5
Cumming	PA	56	B2
Cummings	PA	57	A3
Cummings Siding	NY	29	F2
Cumminsville Foster Wheeler Plant	NY	41	C1
Cumru [Reading]	PA	64	A6
Cuneo	PA	56	C4
Cunningham	PA	49	D3
Cunningham	WV	9	C4
Cupola	PA	70	A2
Curriers	NY	42	F4
Curry	PA	60	D1
Curry Run	PA	57	C2
Curtin	PA	57	F2
Curtis	NY	41	E3
Curtis Bay	MD	12	C3
Curtis Bay GSA Depot	MD	12	C4
Curtis Bay Junction	MD	12	B3
Curtis Creek Bridge	MD	12	C4
Curtis Park	PA	72	D5
Curtis-Wright	NJ	22	B3
Curtisville	PA	49	D3
Curwensville	PA	58	D1
Cush Creek Junction	PA	59	A5
Cush Cushion	PA	57	B3
Custer	PA	70	C2
Custer City	PA	56	C1
Cutchogue	NY	35	B5
Cuthbert	NJ	73	C5
Cuyler	NY	38	C4
CV Connection [Martinsburg]	WV	9	F2
CV Junction	PA	61	B1
CV Junction [Winchester]	VA	9	E3
Cylburn	MD	12	B1
Cymbria Mine	PA	59	C5
Cyn [Cynwyd]	PA	72	D3
Cynwyd	PA	72	D3
Cypher	PA	60	D2

D

Location	State	Page	Grid
D&M Junction [Dillsburg]	PA	63	C2
D&R Junction [Dover]	NJ	17	A1
Da Costa	NJ	19	C1
Dag	DE	7	F3
Dagsboro	DE	7	F3
Dagus	PA	56	C4
Dagus Mines	PA	56	C4
Daguscahonda	PA	56	C3
Dahlgren US Naval Weapons Laboratory	VA	14	A1
Dahoga	PA	56	B3
Dale	NY	45	A4
Dale [Lansdale]	PA	70	C2
Dale [NS(CR)]	PA	70	E4
Dale [PSN]	PA	56	C2
Dale Summit	PA	57	F3
Dalecarlia Reservoir	MD	14	A4
Dallas [BNYP(KERR)]	PA	56	C1
Dallas [LV]	PA	61	F4
Dallastown	PA	63	D3
Dallastown Junction	PA	63	D3
Dalmatia	PA	62	C3
Dalton	NY	41	B1
Dalton	PA	68	A3
Dalton's	NY	36	F1
Dam [Beaver Dams]	NY	41	E2
Danforth Avenue [Jersey City]	NJ	22	B5
Dannemora	NY	28	E2
Dansville	NY	41	C1
Danville	PA	62	D2
Darby	PA	72	D5
Darent	PA	50	E3
Daretown	NJ	19	B1
Danielsville	PA	69	F2
Darien	CT	35	C1
Darien Center	NY	42	F3
Dark Water	PA	67	B4
Darkesville	WV	9	F2
Darlington [LIGV]	PA	50	F1
Darlington [SEPA(PRR)]	PA	72	A5
Darlington [YS]	PA	51	A4
Darnley	PA	55	A4
Dauphin	PA	63	C1
Dave	WV	50	D4
Davenport Center	NY	31	A1
Davis [Newark]	DE	6	A4
Davis	NJ	18	D3
Davis [CNYS]	NY	39	A1
Davis [UV(OW)]	NY	39	E1
Davis	PA	56	F2
Davis	WV	9	A3
Davistown	PA	50	F3
Davrosburg	PA	53	B4
Davrosburg Tunnel	PA	53	C4
Day	NJ	74	C5
Day	PA	64	C2
Daylesford	PA	72	A2
Dawson [BO]	MD	8	A5
Dawson [CSXT(CPA)]	MD	8	D5
Dawson	PA	55	B4
Dawson Run	PA	48	F3
Dayett Station	DE	6	B4
Daysville	NY	37	B4
Dayton	NJ	18	D2
Dayton	NY	43	D2
Dayton	PA	49	F2
DB Junction [Kearny]	NJ	22	B4
De Haven	PA	49	F1
De Ruyter	NY	38	C4
Deacons	NJ	74	B6
Deal	PA	60	B4
Dean [Erie]	PA	47	C6
Dean [PC(PRR)]	PA	57	C4
Deans	NJ	18	D1
Deansboro	NY	38	E3
Deanwood	DC	14	D4
Deep [CSAO(PRR)]	NJ	20	C4
Deep [CSAO(WJS)]	NJ	6	E3
Deep Cut	NJ	20	C4
Deepwater	NJ	6	E3
Deer [NS(PRR)]	PA	57	E4
Deer [PC(NYC)]	PA	57	D1
Deer Lick	PA	50	C3
Deer Park	MD	9	A2
Deer River	NY	37	D2
Deerfield (Lentz)	MD	10	B1
Deerfield	NJ	19	B2
Defense Supply Center [Philadelphia]	PA	73	B3
Deferiet	NY	37	D1
Defiance	PA	60	D2
Degolia	PA	56	C1
Deiber	PA	62	D2
DeKalb Junction	NY	36	E3
Dekays	NJ	17	D1
Del	DE	7	A2
Del Val College [Doylestown]	PA	70	C1
Delabole	PA	16	A5
Delair	NJ	73	C4
Delair Bridge	NJ	73	C4
Delanco	NJ	73	D2
Delavan	NY	43	F1
DeLancey	NY	31	A2
Delaneys	DE	7	A3
Delano	PA	67	C2
Delano Junction	NY	29	B4
Delano Junction	PA	67	D2
Delanson	NY	30	C3
Delaplane	VA	9	F4
Delawanna	NJ	22	B3
Delaware	NJ	16	C6
Delaware Avenue [Palmerton]	PA	69	E2
Delaware City	DE	7	A2
Delaware River Pier	DE	6	E3
Delaware Water Gap	NJ	16	B4
Delhi	NY	31	A2
Dellwood	NY	42	E3
Dellwood	PA	56	B4
Delmar	DE	7	E4
Delmar	NY	32	D4
Delmont	PA	49	E4
Delmont No.10 Mine	PA	55	B2
Delphi	NY	38	C3
Delta	PA	63	E4
Delta Place	PA	62	C2
Demarest	NJ	25	B3
Demmler	PA	53	C4
Demmler Yard	PA	53	C4
Den (Denbo)	PA	54	B5
Denbo	PA	54	B5
Denholm Scales	PA	62	A4
Denley	NY	37	E4
Dennies Hollow	NY	30	C2
Denniston	PA	53	B3
Denniston's	NY	27	F1
Dennisville	NJ	19	C3
Denny	PA	53	C1
Denton	MD	11	D4
Dent's Run	PA	56	D4
Denver	PA	63	F2
Denver	WV	50	B4
Denville	NJ	21	A2
Depew [AMTK]	NY	46	C4
Depew [NS(ERIE)]	NY	46	D4
Deposit	NY	39	E3
Depressed Track [Schenectady]	NY	32	B3
Derby	NY	42	D4
Derby Junction	PA	58	D3
Derrick	NY	28	B4
Derringer	PA	62	F2
Derry [NS(RDG)]	PA	63	D1
Derry [PRR Columbia County]	PA	62	D1
Derry [PRR Westmoreland County]	PA	50	F1
Derwood	MD	10	C3
Detour	MD	10	C1
Detsch	PA	56	C4
Devault	PA	70	B2
Devereaux	NY	43	F2
Devon	CT	35	D1
Devon	PA	72	B2
Dewart	PA	62	C1
Dewey	PA	49	E2
Dewey	OH	48	B3
DeWitt Shops [East Syracuse]	NY	36	C1
DeWitt Yard [East Syracuse]	NY	36	C1
Dewittville	NY	43	C2
Dexter	NY	37	C2
Dexter Hill	PA	71	C2
Dexter Junction	NY	37	C2
DF [Bradley Junction]	PA	59	D6
Diamond [DLW]	PA	65	C1
Diamond [Philadelphia]	PA	73	B4
Diamond [PRR]	PA	49	E2
Diamondville	PA	57	B3
Diana	NY	37	E1
Dias	PA	57	A4
Dick Siding	PA	48	D4
Dickerson	MD	10	B3
Dickerson Run	PA	55	B4
Dickey	PA	47	D4
Dickinson Center	NY	28	B2
Dickson	PA	65	D1
Dickson City	PA	65	D1
Dickson Mine	PA	52	B2
Dicksonburg	PA	48	B2
Didell	NY	34	E1
Didier	PA	71	C4
Dil [Lancaster]	PA	64	C4
Dille	OH	50	A3
Dillerville Yard [Lancaster]	PA	64	D4
Dilliner	PA	50	D4
Dillinger	PA	69	B4
Dillonvale	OH	50	A2
Dillsburg	PA	63	C2
Dillsburg Junction	PA	63	C2
Dilltown	PA	57	A4
Dimeling	PA	58	A2
Dimock	PA	61	F2
Dineharts	NY	41	D1
Dishart	PA	59	C6
Dishaw's	NY	36	F1
District Line	MD	14	D5
Divener	PA	49	D2
Divide Tower [Hicksville]	NY	24	D3
Dividing Creek	NJ	19	B3
Dix [PRR]	PA	57	D3
Dix [RJCP(NYC)]	PA	57	C2
Dix Haven	NJ	74	C2
Dixmont	PA	52	C1
Dixonville	PA	57	A3
DL&W Junction	NY	45	C2
DLW Junction [Mount Morris]	NY	40	B4
DM Junction [Dayton]	NY	43	D2
DO Tower [Punxsutawney]	PA	57	B2
Dobbs Ferry	NY	25	C2
Dock [Newark]	NJ	22	A5
Dock [Norwalk]	CT	35	C1
Dock Junction [Erie]	PA	47	C6
Dodge Park	MD	10	D4
Doe Gully	WV	9	E1
Doe Run	PA	70	A3
Dolgeville	NY	30	A2
Dollie Colliery No.1	PA	58	D4
Dolphin	NJ	19	D2
Donaghmore	PA	63	E1
Donaldson	PA	62	E3
Donaldson	WV	9	D2
Donegal	PA	58	D4
Donohoe	PA	50	F1
Donora	PA	54	C1
Dongan Hills	NY	20	F2
Doodletown Bite Trestle	NY	26	A2
Dora	PA	57	A2
Dorchester	NJ	19	C3
Doremus Avenue [Newark]	NJ	22	B5
Dormers	PA	67	B5
Dornrife	PA	62	C3
Dorothy	NJ	19	C2
Dorset	OH	48	A2
Dorset	PA	69	A3
Dorsey	MD	11	A3
Dorsey	PA	63	F4
Dotter	PA	48	E4
Dottyville	PA	48	E2
Doub	MD	10	B3
Dougherty	PA	57	C4
Doughton Junction	OH	49	B1
Doughty	NJ	19	D2
Doughty	PA	56	B1
Douglas	VA	14	A5
Douglass	NY	28	F3
Douglass	PA	53	D6
Douglassville	PA	70	A2
Douglaston	NY	24	A3
Dover	DE	7	B4
Dover	NJ	17	B2
Dover Furnace	NY	34	F1
Dover Plains	NY	34	F1
Dovey	PA	60	A3
Dowler Junction	PA	59	A5
Dowlin	PA	70	F2
Downer	NJ	19	B1
Downer Junction	PA	54	C3
Downes	MD	11	D4
Downey	NY	28	C3
Downieville	PA	49	D3
Downington	PA	70	F3
Downs	MD	12	B4
Downs [Downington]	PA	70	F3
Downsville	NY	31	A3
Doyle [Doylestown]	PA	70	D1
Doylestown	PA	70	D1
Doylestown Pike	PA	70	D2
Drake Well	PA	48	E3
Drakes Creek	PA	69	B2
Draketown Junction	PA	50	F4
Dravo	PA	53	D5
Draw [Buffalo]	NY	46	B5
Dreibelbis	PA	69	A4
Dresden [DH]	NY	29	F3
Dresden [NS(NYC)]	NY	40	E4
Dresher	PA	73	A1
Drew	NJ	21	B4
Drifton	PA	69	A2
Drifton Junction	PA	69	A2

Name	State	Page	Grid
Driftwood	PA	56	D4
Driftwood [defect detector]	PA	56	E4
Driscoll	PA	57	C4
Drive	PA	73	A3
Drocton	PA	56	F4
Druckers	PA	57	C2
Druid	MD	12	B2
Drummond	PA	56	B4
Drums	PA	62	F2
Drury	PA	56	F4
Dry Run	WV	9	C2
Dryden	NY	39	B1
Du Pont	NY	46	A3
DU Tower [Pittsburgh]	PA	52	D2
DuBois	PA	57	B1
Dudley	NJ	73	C4
Dudley	PA	60	D2
Duffields	WV	10	A2
Duffs	PA	52	D2
Duffs Junction	PA	52	D2
Duhring	PA	56	A3
Duke	NY	35	C2
Duke Center	PA	56	C1
Duley	MD	10	D5
Dumont	NJ	22	D1
Dun Loring	VA	10	C4
Dunbar	PA	55	B6
Dunbarton	NJ	18	C4
Duncan [NYC]	PA	61	B2
Duncan [PLE(PMY)]	PA	53	D5
Duncan [WD&L]	PA	62	B2
Duncannon	PA	63	C1
Duncansville	PA	59	C3
Dundale	PA	50	F1
Dundalk	MD	12	D3
Dundalk Marine Terminal	MD	12	D3
Dundee	NJ	22	B2
Dundee	NY	41	E1
Dunellen	NJ	20	A2
Dungarvin	PA	57	E3
Dunkelbergers	PA	62	D3
Dunkirk	NY	43	C1
Dunlap	PA	74	B3
Dunlo	PA	60	B1
Dunmore	PA	65	D1
Dunn	PA	50	C3
Dunnfield	NJ	16	B4
Dunning	PA	61	C1
Dunnings Creek Junction	PA	60	C3
Dunn's Eddy	PA	48	F2
Dunraven	NY	31	B3
Dunton Tower [Queens]	NY	23	D4
Dunwoodie	NY	25	C3
Dupont	DE	7	B4
Dupont	PA	65	B3
DuPont Junction	PA	65	B3
DuPont Plant [Thompson Point]	NJ	72	C6
DuPont Plants [Deepwater]	NJ	6	E3
Duquesne Coal Dock	PA	53	C4
Duquesne Freight Terminal [Pittsburgh]	PA	53	A3
Duquesne Mill	PA	53	C4
Duquesne Yard	PA	53	C4
Durant	NY	26	A5
Durgon	WV	9	B4
Durham	NJ	20	B2
Durham	PA	69	C4
Durhamville	NY	38	D2
Durward	PA	62	B4
Duryea	PA	65	B3
Duryea Junction	PA	65	B3
Dushore	PA	61	E3
Dutch Kills [Queens]	NY	23	B3
Dutchess Junction	NY	26	C1
DW Tower [Buffalo]	NY	46	B5
DY [Phillipsburg]	NJ	71	E2
Dyer Quarry	PA	70	A3
Dyke	NY	41	B3
Dykemans	NY	26	D1
Dyre Avenue [Bronx]	NY	25	D4
Dysart	PA	57	C4
E			
E-Rail [Elizabethport]	NJ	22	A6
E&W Junction [Easton]	PA	71	D3
Eagle	NY	41	A1
Eagle Bay	NY	29	A3
Eagle Bridge	NY	30	F2
Eagle Harbor	NY	40	A1
Eagle Rock	PA	48	E3
Eagles Mere	PA	61	D4
Eagles Mere Park	PA	61	D3
Eagleville	OH	48	A2
Eagleville	PA	57	F2
Eakle's Mill	MD	10	A2
Earle	NJ	18	E2
Earle Naval Depot	NJ	18	E2
Earleigh Heights	MD	11	A3
Earls	NY	40	A3
Earlston	PA	60	C3
Earlville [NYSW(DLW)]	NY	38	E4
Earlville [OW WS]	NY	38	D4
East 3rd Street [Mount Vernon]	NY	25	D4
East 6th Street [Mount Vernon]	NY	25	D4
East 22nd Street [Bayonne]	NJ	22	B6
East 33rd Street [Bayonne]	NJ	22	B6
East 45th Street [Bayonne]	NJ	22	B6
East 49th Street [Bayonne]	NJ	22	B6
East Aikin (Jackson)	MD	13	E1
East Alexander	NY	45	A2
East Altoona	PA	59	D1
East Aurora	NY	42	E4
East Avalon	MD	12	A3
East Bangor	PA	16	A6
East Bergen	NY	40	B2
East Berlin	PA	63	C3
East Bethany	NY	45	B2
East Binghamton Yard	NY	36	B3
East Bloomsburg	PA	62	E2
East Bradford	PA	56	C1
East Brady	PA	49	E2
East Brady Junction	PA	49	E2
East Branch	NY	39	F4
East Branch [PSR(PS)]	PA	57	A2
East Branch [TIV]	PA	56	A2
East Brookside	PA	62	D4
East Brown	NJ	20	C4
East Brunswick	MD	10	B3
East Brunswick	NJ	20	A4
East Buffalo Junction	NY	46	C4
East Buffalo Yard [CSXT(WS)]	NY	46	C4
East Buffalo Yard [LV]	NY	46	C4
East Buffalo Yard [STLH(ERIE)]	NY	46	B4
East Burlington	NJ	74	B5
East Buskirk	NY	30	F3
East Butler	PA	49	D2
East California	PA	54	B3
East Carnegie	PA	52	D3
East Charleroi	PA	54	B2
East Chatham	NY	31	F1
East Chester	NY	27	C3
East Claremont	NJ	22	C5
East Clarence	NY	42	E2
East Concord	NY	43	E1
East Conway	PA	49	C3
East Corning	NY	41	E3
East CT (Crayton)	PA	48	B1
East Davis	MD	10	D2
East DeKalb	NY	36	E3
East Dover	NJ	21	A2
East Downington	PA	70	F3
East DuBois	PA	57	B1
East DuBois Junction	PA	57	B1
East Earl	PA	63	F2
East Earle	NJ	18	E2
East End	NJ	20	C4
East Falls	PA	73	A3
East Fayetteville	PA	63	A3
East Feltonville (Feltonville)	PA	72	B6
East Ferney	PA	62	A1
East Ferry Street [Buffalo]	NY	46	B4
East Ferry Street [Newark]	NJ	22	B5
East Fredericktown	PA	54	A5
East Freedom	PA	60	C1
East Freehold	NJ	18	E2
East Gladstone	NJ	17	D4
East Greenbush	NY	30	E4
East Greensburg	PA	50	E1
East Greenville	PA	70	B1
East Greenwich	NY	30	F2
East Hamburg	NY	46	C6
East Hampton	NY	35	C5
East Hanover	NJ	21	C3
East Homer	NY	38	C4
East Hood	MD	10	D2
East Ithaca	NY	39	A1
East Kane	PA	56	B2
East Kodak Park	NY	44	B2
East Lane	PA	73	A2
East Liberty	PA	53	B2
East Lincoln Avenue [Mount Vernon]	NY	25	D4
East Lincoln Park	NJ	21	D1
East Liverpool	OH	49	B3
East Long Branch	NJ	18	F2
East Mahanoy Junction	PA	67	D3
East Main Street [Middletown]	NY	27	A2
East Marshburg	PA	56	B2
East Matawan	NJ	20	D4
East Meredith	NY	31	A1
East Middletown	PA	63	D2
East Millsboro	PA	54	A5
East Millstone	NJ	18	D1
East Moriches	NY	35	A6
East New Market	MD	11	D6
East New Castle	PA	51	B1
East New York	NY	23	C4
East Norwalk	CT	35	C1
East Oakmont	PA	53	D1
East Orange	NJ	22	A4
East Orwell	OH	48	A3
East Palestine	OH	49	B3
East Palmerton	PA	69	E2
East Palmyra	NY	40	E2
East Paterson	NJ	22	B2
East Pembroke	NY	40	A3
East Penn [Allentown]	PA	71	B4
East Petersburg	PA	63	E2
East Pitt [Pittsburgh]	PA	53	A2
East Pittsburgh	PA	53	C3
East Plane (Plane #4)	MD	10	C2
East Reel	MD	10	B2
East Rices Landing	PA	54	A6
East River Tunnels [Manhattan]	NY	23	A3
East Riverside	PA	54	B6
East Rochester	NY	40	D2
East Rockaway	NY	24	B5
East Roscoe	PA	54	C3
East Salamanca	NY	43	E3
East Sand	NJ	18	E3
East Sandy	PA	48	D4
East Schaghticoke	NY	30	E3
East Schenley	PA	53	B2
East Schodack	NY	30	E4
East Singerly (Elk Mills)	MD	11	D1
East Smethport	PA	56	C2
East Spotswood	NJ	18	E1
East Shortsville	NY	40	E3
East Steuben	NY	37	F4
East Steubenville	WV	50	B1
East Strasburg	PA	63	F3
East Stroudsburg	PA	16	A4
East Summit	PA	56	F2
East Sunbury	PA	66	B6
East Syracuse	NY	36	C1
East Trenton	NJ	74	D2
East Van Bibber	MD	13	B3
East View	NY	26	D6
East Walden	NY	34	D1
East Waterford	PA	60	F1
East Williamson	NY	40	E1
East Williston	NY	24	C3
East Windsor	NY	39	D3
East Worcester	NY	30	B4
East X	NY	40	E3
East York	PA	63	D3
Eastbrook	PA	49	C2
Eastmont	PA	64	A1
Easton	PA	71	E2
Easton	MD	11	C5
Easton	NY	30	F2
Eastpoint	MD	12	D2
Eastport	NY	35	A6
Eastside Yard [Philadelphia]	PA	73	A5
Eastvale	PA	51	C1
Eastville	PA	62	B2
Eastville	VA	15	A6
Eastwick [CSXT(BO)]	PA	73	A5
Eastwick [SEPA]	PA	72	D5
Eastwood	NY	36	B1
Eaton	NY	38	D3
Eatontown	NJ	18	F2
Ebbvale	MD	10	D1
Eben	NY	36	F2
Ebenezer Junction Yard	NY	46	C5
Ebenezer Yard	NY	46	C5
Ebensburg	PA	57	B4
Ebensburg Junction	PA	57	C4
Ebervale	PA	66	B1
Echo	PA	49	F2
Echota	NY	42	C4
Eckenrode Mill	PA	59	D6
Eckhart	MD	8	B2
Eckhart Junction	MD	8	C1
Eckington Yard [Washington]	DC	14	C4
Eckley	PA	66	C1
Eckley Junction	PA	66	C1
Eclipse	PA	48	D4
Economy	PA	49	C4
Eddington	PA	74	A5
Eddy [Long Eddy]	NY	39	F4
Eddystone	PA	72	C6
Eddyville	PA	49	F2
Eden	MD	15	B1
Eden Center	NY	42	D4
Eden Valley	NY	42	D4
Edenborn	PA	50	D3
Edenburg [BO(P&W)]	PA	48	E4
Edenburg [PLE]	PA	49	B2
Eder	MD	11	D1
Edgar	NJ	20	C2
Edgar Thompson Plant [Braddock]	PA	53	C3
Edge Moor	DE	6	E2
Edge Moor Yard	DE	6	E2
Edgecliff	PA	51	D3
Edgely Industrial Park	PA	74	B4
Edgemont	MD	10	B1
Edgemont	PA	69	F3
Edgemore	PA	51	B2
Edgewater	NJ	22	D3
Edgewater	PA	53	C1
Edgewater Tunnel	NJ	22	D3
Edgewood	MD	13	A4
Edgewood	NY	31	C3
Edgewood	PA	53	B3
Edgewood Arsenal	MD	13	A4
Edgewood Grove	PA	60	A3
Edgeworth	PA	52	B1
Edin [Edinburg]	PA	49	B2
Edinburg	PA	49	B2
Edison [CNJ]	NJ	16	D2
Edison [NJT(PRR)]	NJ	20	B3
Edison Yard	NJ	20	B3
Edisonville	PA	63	E1
Edmeston	NY	38	E4
Edmunson	MD	12	B2
Edsall	VA	10	C5
Edwards	NY	36	E4
Edwards Park	NY	31	F2
Egg Harbor	NJ	19	D2
Egypt	PA	69	F4
Ehrenfeld	PA	64	B2
Eidenau	PA	49	C3
Eighteen Colliery	PA	58	A4
Eighty Four	PA	50	C2
Eisaman	PA	50	E1
Elba	NY	40	A2
Elbell	PA	57	B2
Elberon	NJ	18	F2
Elberta	NY	42	D1
Elbon	PA	56	B4
Elbrook	PA	60	F4
Elco [Wood Run]	PA	54	B3
Eldo (Eldorado)	PA	59	C2
Eldora	PA	63	F4
Eldorado	PA	59	C2
Eldred	PA	56	D1
Eleanora	PA	57	B2
Electra	PA	49	F1
Elfinwild	PA	53	A1
Elgin	PA	48	E1
Eliber Spring	WV	9	C3
Elizabeth	NJ	21	D6
Elizabeth	PA	53	B6
Elizabeth Colliery 2	PA	58	B6
Elizabethport	NJ	22	A6
Elizabethtown	PA	63	D2
Elizabethville	PA	62	C4
Elizaville	NY	31	E3
Elk Brook	NY	39	F4
Elk City	PA	48	E4
Elk Forks	PA	56	D3
Elk Mills	MD	11	D1
Elk Run Industrial Track	WV	9	A3
Elk Run Junction	PA	57	B2
Elkdale	NY	43	E2
Elkdale Junction	PA	57	B4
Elkins Park	PA	73	B2
Elkland	PA	61	B1
Elkridge	MD	12	A4
Elkton	MD	11	D1
Elkton	OH	49	A3
Elkview	PA	70	A4
Ellendale	DE	7	E2
Ellensburg	NY	28	E1
Ellenton	PA	61	C3
Ellenville	NY	34	C1
Ellerslie	MD	8	D1
Ellicott City	MD	10	D3
Ellicottville	NY	43	E2
Elliot Mine	PA	58	D4
Elliott	PA	52	D2
Elliottsburg	PA	63	B1
Ellis	NJ	18	C3
Ellisburg	PA	56	E1
Ellrod	PA	53	D5
Ellsworth	PA	50	D2
Ellwood	MD	11	D5
Ellwood City	PA	51	C3
Ellwood Junction	PA	51	B3
Elm	NJ	19	C1
Elm [CSXT(WM)]	PA	63	C3
Elm [Norristown]	PA	72	C1
Elm Grove	WV	50	A2
Elm Park	NY	20	E1
Elm Street [Norristown]	PA	72	C1
Elma	NY	42	E3
Elmer	NJ	19	B1
Elmer	PA	56	F1
Elmgrove	NY	44	A2
Elmhurst	NY	23	C3
Elmhurst	PA	68	B4
Elmira	NY	41	F3
Elmira Branch Junction [Williamsport]	PA	61	C4
Elmira Heights	NY	41	F3
Elmo	PA	48	E4
Elmora [Elizabeth]	NJ	21	D6
Elmora Avenue [Elizabeth]	NJ	21	D6
Elmsford	NY	25	D1
Elmwood	PA	72	D5
Elmwood Avenue [Buffalo]	NY	46	A3
Elmwood Avenue [Philadelphia]	PA	73	A5
Elmwood Park (East Paterson)	NJ	22	B2
Elmwood Road	NJ	18	C4
Elnora	NY	30	E3
Elrama	PA	53	B6
Elsmere	NY	32	D4
Elsmere Junction	DE	6	D2
Eltingville	NY	20	E2
Elton	NY	43	F1
Elton	PA	60	B1
Elrico	PA	49	E4
Elvaton	MD	11	A3
Elverson	PA	70	A2
Elwood	NJ	19	D1
Elwyn	PA	72	B5
Embreeville	PA	70	A3
Ementon	PA	48	E4
Emerson	NJ	25	A2
Emeryville	NY	36	E4
Emigsville	PA	63	D3
Emlenton	PA	49	E1
Emmaus	PA	69	B4
Emmaus Junction	PA	69	B4
Emmitsburg	MD	10	C1
Emmitsburg Junction	MD	10	C1
Emmons [DH]	NY	39	F1
Emmons [NYC(RWO)]	NY	38	B1
Emory Grove	MD	10	D2
Empire [Manhattan]	NY	23	A3
Empire	OH	49	A4
Empire Quarry	NY	34	C3
Emporium	PA	56	D3
Emsworth	PA	52	C1
Endeavor	PA	48	F3
Endicott	NY	39	C3
Enfield	PA	73	A1
Engle	WV	10	A2
Englers	PA	56	B1
Engleside [Philadelphia]	PA	71	A4
Englewood	NJ	22	D2
English Consol	MD	12	B3
Englishtown	NJ	18	E2
Enlow	PA	52	B2
Ennerdale	NY	40	E3
Enoch	PA	60	A2
Enola Yard	PA	64	C1
Enon	PA	49	B2
Ensenore	NY	38	A3
Enterprise [MJS]	PA	56	C2
Enterprise [MPA]	PA	63	D3
Entriken	PA	60	D1
Ephrata	PA	63	F2
Epsy	PA	62	E2
Erb	PA	60	D1
Erie	PA	47	C6

Name	State	Page	Grid
Erie 2 [North Tonawanda]	NY	46	A2
Erie 3 [Tonawanda]	NY	46	B2
Erie Avenue [Philadelphia]	PA	73	B3
Erie Street [Buffalo]	NY	46	A4
Erieville	NY	38	D3
Erin	NY	39	A3
Ernest [NS(BRP)]	PA	57	A3
Ernest [NS(RDG)]	PA	72	C1
Ernest [PC(PRR)]	PA	72	C1
Ernston	NJ	20	C4
Erskine	NJ	17	E2
Erwins	NY	41	E3
Esh	PA	62	A4
Esopus	NY	31	D4
Esperance	NY	30	C3
Esplen	PA	52	D2
Espyville	PA	48	B3
Essay [South Amboy]	NJ	20	C3
Essen	PA	52	D4
Essex	NY	28	F4
Essex Fells	NJ	21	D3
Essick	PA	61	D4
Esso [Elizabethport]	NJ	22	A6
Esty	NY	39	A1
Etna	NY	39	B1
Etna	PA	53	B2
Etna Yard	PA	53	B2
Euclid	PA	49	D2
Eureka	OH	49	A2
Eureka	PA	55	A3
Eureka Colliery	PA	58	B6
Eureka No.31 Mine	PA	64	B3
Eureka No.32 Mine	PA	64	B3
Eureka No.35 Mine	PA	60	B2
Eureka No.37 Mine	PA	64	B3
Eureka No.40 Mine	PA	64	B3
Eureka Stores	PA	64	B3
Evans City	PA	49	C3
Evans Mills	NY	37	D1
Evans Run	PA	57	B4
Evanston [EBT J&S]	PA	60	E1
Evanston [PRR]	PA	50	E1
Evansville [CR(PRR)]	PA	62	E2
Evansville [NS(RDG)]	PA	69	A4
Eve	NJ	73	C6
Eve	PA	50	C3
Everett	PA	60	D3
Evergreen	MD	12	B1
Evergreen	NY	23	C4
Everson	PA	55	C4
Everson Interchange	PA	55	C4
Ewansville	NJ	18	C3
Ewing	PA	63	D3
Ewings	PA	52	C2
Excelsior	PA	66	A5
Exchange Place [Jersey City]	NJ	22	C5
Exchange Street [Buffalo]	NY	46	B4
Exeter	PA	65	A3
Exeter Street [Reading]	PA	64	A5
Exmore	VA	15	B5
Exmoor	PA	62	E4
Experiment	PA	53	A5
Export [PRR Washington County]	PA	52	A6
Export [PRR Westmoreland County]	PA	49	E4
Expressrail Terminal [Port Elizabeth]	NJ	22	B6
Exton [RDG]	PA	70	E4
Exton (Woodbine) [SEPA(PRR)]	PA	70	E4
Exxon [Constable Hook]	NJ	22	B6
Exxon Chemical Plant [Pedricktown]	NJ	6	F2
Exxon Refinery [Bayway]	NJ	20	D1
EY [Columbia]	PA	64	C6
Eyer	PA	57	D3
Eyersgrove	PA	62	D1
Eyersgrove Junction	PA	62	D1
Eynon	PA	65	B1

F

Name	State	Page	Grid
F Interlocking [Washington]	DC	14	C4
F Tower [Queens]	NY	23	B3
Face Rock	PA	63	E4
Factoryville	PA	68	A3
Fagley	PA	66	B4
Fair [Trenton]	NJ	74	C2
Fair Haven	VT	29	F3
Fairbank	PA	54	C6
Fairbanks Corners	NY	36	F3
Fairbrook	PA	57	E3
Fairchance	PA	50	E4
Fairchance Transfer	PA	50	D4
Fairfax	VA	10	C5
Fairfield	CT	35	C1
Fairfield	NJ	18	E2
Fairfield	ON	36	D2
Fairfield [CSXT(WM)]	PA	63	A4
Fairfield [LVRR(RDG)]	PA	61	C4
Fairfield Auto Terminal [Curtis Bay]	MD	12	C3
Fairhope	PA	60	B3
Fairless Junction	PA	74	A3
Fairless Works	PA	74	D4
Fairless Yard	PA	74	C3
Fairmont [BLE(WARR)]	PA	49	E2
Fairmont [BPRR(P&W)]	PA	49	E2
Fairmont [LOS]	PA	63	F4
Fairmount	NY	38	B2
Fairmount Avenue [Hackensack]	NJ	22	C2
Fairmount Colliery 2	PA	58	C4
Fairplay	OH	50	A1
Fairport	NY	40	D2
Fairport	PA	60	E2
Fairton	NJ	19	B2
Fairview	NJ	22	C3
Fairview [NYC]	NY	29	A3
Fairview [RSR(BRP)]	NY	40	B4
Fairview [CSXT(LSMS) NKP]	PA	47	B6
Fairview [DH]	PA	68	B3
Fairville	NY	40	E2
Falconer	NY	43	C3
Falconer Junction	NY	43	C3
Fallen Timber	PA	57	C3
Falling Spring	PA	65	B2
Falling Waters	MD	9	F1
Falls [Philadelphia]	PA	73	A3
Falls [RBMN(LV)]	PA	65	A1
Falls Church	VA	14	A5
Falls Creek	PA	57	B1
Falls Cut Tunnel	PA	60	B3
Falls Road [Baltimore]	MD	12	B1
Falls View	ON	42	A4
Falls Village	CT	31	F4
Fallsburgh	NY	34	C1
Fallsburgh Tunnel	NY	34	C1
Fallsington	PA	74	B3
Fallston	MD	11	B2
Fallston	PA	51	C2
Falmouth	PA	63	D2
Fancher	NY	40	A1
Fanny Bartlett	NY	35	D5
Fanwood-Scotch Plains	NJ	20	B1
Far Hills	NJ	17	D4
Far Rockaway	NY	24	A6
Far Rockaway Mott Avenue	NY	24	A6
Fargo	NY	42	F3
Farleys	NY	40	F3
Farm	PA	64	C4
Farmdale	OH	48	B3
Farmdale	PA	64	D5
Farmers Valley	PA	56	C1
Farmersville	NY	43	F2
Farmingdale	NJ	18	E2
Farmingdale [LHR]	NY	27	D2
Farmingdale [LIRR]	NY	35	C3
Farmington	DE	7	D2
Farmington	NY	40	D3
Farmington	PA	69	B4
Farnham	NY	42	D4
Farnhurst	DE	6	D3
Farnworth	PA	56	A2
Farrandsville	PA	62	A1
Farrans Point	ON	36	F1
Farrell	PA	47	A3
Farwell (Drocton)	PA	56	F4
Fassett	PA	61	C1
Fawn Grove	PA	63	E4
Fayette City	PA	54	C3
Fayetteville	NY	36	C2
Fayetteville	PA	63	A3
Featherstone	VA	10	C6
Federal	PA	52	C4
Federal #2 Mine	WV	50	C4
Federal Street [Pittsburgh]	PA	53	A2
Federalsburg	MD	11	D5
Fells Point [Baltimore]	MD	12	C2
Fellwick (Camp Hill)	PA	73	A1
Felton	DE	7	E1
Felton	PA	63	D3
Feltonville	PA	72	B6
Felts Mills	NY	37	D2
Fenelton	PA	49	E2
Fenmore	PA	63	D3
Fenner	NY	44	B4
Fenstermachers	PA	69	A3
Fentonville	NY	43	D3
Fenwick	NJ	19	A1
Ferenbaugh	NY	41	E3
Ferguson	PA	55	B6
Ferguson Mine	PA	55	B6
Fern [Bordentown]	NJ	74	D4
Fern [Fernwood-Yeadon]	PA	72	D4
Fern Glen	PA	62	F2
Fern Hill	PA	70	B3
Fern Rock	PA	73	B2
Ferncliff	MD	11	B1
Ferndale	MD	12	B4
Ferndale	NY	31	A4
Ferndale [CSXT(BO) JSC]	PA	64	A2
Ferndale [RDG]	PA	67	A2
Ferney	PA	56	F4
Fernwood	NY	37	B4
Fernwood	OH	50	A1
Fernwood	PA	58	B5
Fernwood-Yeadon	PA	72	D4
Ferremont Junction	NJ	17	A2
Ferris	PA	49	D1
Ferrona	PA	47	A2
Ferry Avenue [Camden]	NJ	73	C5
Ferry Street [Buffalo]	NY	46	A4
Ferry Street [Newark]	NJ	22	A5
Feura Bush	NY	30	D4
FH Tower [Bronx]	NY	25	C4
Ficks Lock	PA	70	B2
Field (Fairfield)	PA	61	C4
Field [Greenfield]	PA	64	D4
Field [Philadelphia]	PA	73	A4
Field [Pittsburgh]	PA	53	A2
Field [PRR]	PA	61	C3
Fieldmore Springs	PA	48	E3
Fieldsboro	NJ	74	D4
Fiery Siding	MD	10	A6
Fife	PA	52	C5
Filer	PA	49	C1
Fillmore	NY	41	A1
Fillmore	PA	57	E2
Filter Plant Siding	DC	14	A4
Finderne-Manville	NJ	20	E4
Finland	PA	56	C3
Finley	NJ	19	B2
Finleyville	PA	53	A6
First Fork	PA	56	E3
Firthcliffe	NY	27	F2
Fish Creek	NY	38	D2
Fish House Junction	NJ	73	C4
Fish Island	PA	65	B5
Fisher	NJ	18	C4
Fisher	PA	49	F3
Fisher Hill	NY	29	E1
Fisher Mine	PA	49	F1
Fishers	NY	40	D2
Fishers	PA	73	B3
Fishers Hill	VA	9	D4
Fishertown	PA	60	C2
Fishing Creek	PA	63	E4
Fishkill Plains	NY	34	E1
Fishkill Village	NY	34	E2
Fishs Eddy	NY	39	F4
Fitler	PA	73	C3
Fitz Henry	PA	54	D2
Fitzgerald	NY	37	E1
Five Forks	PA	60	F4
Five Locks	PA	62	F4
Five Mile	PA	56	C2
Five Points [PRR]	PA	57	C3
Five Points [RDG]	PA	69	B4
Flagtown	NJ	18	C1
Flanders	NJ	17	C3
Flanigan Colliery	PA	59	D5
Flat Iron	NY	43	F3
Flat Rock Tunnel	PA	72	D3
Flatbush Avenue [Brooklyn]	NY	23	B4
Flatbush Avenue Tunnel [Brooklyn]	NY	23	B4
Fleetwood	NY	25	D3
Fleetwood	PA	69	A4
Fleischmanns	NY	31	B3
Fleming Summit	PA	57	B3
Flemington	NJ	18	C1
Flemington Junction	NJ	18	C1
Flemingville	NY	39	B3
Flexi-Flo Terminal [Philadelphia]	PA	73	B5
Flint	NY	40	E3
Flinton	PA	57	C3
Flo [Florence]	NJ	19	C1
Floodwood	NY	28	C4
Floral Park	NY	24	B4
Floreffe	PA	53	B6
Florence [CSAO(PRR)]	NJ	74	C4
Florence [PRSL(AC)]	NJ	19	C1
Florence	OH	50	A1
Florence Yard [Bethlemem]	PA	71	C4
Florida	NY	27	B4
Florin	PA	63	D2
Florinel	PA	64	C5
Flour	PA	63	D3
Flour Mills [Buffalo]	NY	46	B5
Flourtown	PA	73	A1
Flower	DE	7	D3
Flowing Spring	PA	57	D4
Flushing	NY	23	D3
Flushing Main Street	NY	23	D2
Fluvanna	NY	43	C3
Fly Creek	NY	38	F4
Folcroft	PA	72	D5
Foley	PA	60	B3
Foley's Siding	PA	52	D4
Follansbee	WV	50	B1
Folsom	NJ	19	C1
Folsom	PA	72	C5
Folwell	NJ	74	D6
Fombell	PA	49	C3
Fonda	NY	30	C2
Fontaine	PA	70	A2
Foot of Mountain	PA	67	A5
Foot of Ten	PA	59	C3
Foote	NY	42	C3
Footedale	PA	54	C6
Forbes Avenue [Rensselaer]	NY	32	E3
Forbes Road	PA	50	E1
Ford	DE	7	E2
Ford	NJ	16	D3
Ford [Frankford]	PA	73	C3
Ford [Norristown]	PA	72	C1
Ford City	PA	49	E3
Ford Plant [Blasdell]	NY	46	B6
Ford Plant [Edison]	NJ	20	B3
Ford Plant [Pennsauken]	NJ	73	C4
Fordham	PA	57	A2
Fordham 190th Street	NY	23	C1
Fords	NJ	20	C3
Forest	NY	28	E1
Forest [PRR]	PA	70	A2
Forest [SEPA]	PA	70	C1
Forest Castle	PA	65	A3
Forest City	PA	68	B2
Forest Grove	NJ	19	C2
Forest Hill	MD	11	B1
Forest Hill	NJ	22	A4
Forest Hill	PA	56	B4
Forest Hills	NY	23	C3
Forest Hills	PA	73	C1
Forest Lawn	NY	44	D1
Forestport	NY	37	F4
Forestville	NY	43	C1
Fork [CSAO(MGA)]	PA	50	B3
Fork [South Fork]	PA	64	B2
Forked River	NJ	18	E4
Forge [Valley Forge]	PA	72	A1
Fort	NY	37	A4
Fort Ann	NY	29	F4
Fort Belvoir	VA	10	C5
Fort Bingham	PA	62	A4
Fort Covington	NY	28	B1
Fort Dix	NJ	18	D3
Fort Drum	NY	37	D1
Fort Edward	NY	30	E1
Fort Erie	ON	46	A4
Fort Erie Spur	ON	46	A6
Fort Erie Yard [CN(GT/WAB)]	ON	46	A6
Fort Erie Yard [CP(MC/PM)]	ON	46	A5
Fort Hancock	NJ	18	F1
Fort Hill [BO WM]	PA	50	F3
Fort Hill [NS(PRR)]	PA	73	A1
Fort Hill [WM]	PA	50	F3
Fort Hunter	NY	30	C3
Fort Johnson	NY	30	C2
Fort Loudon	PA	60	E3
Fort Martin	WV	50	D4
Fort Meade	MD	11	A4
Fort Meade Junction	MD	10	D3
Fort Mifflin	PA	73	A5
Fort Montgomery	NY	26	A2
Fort Montgomery Tunnel	NY	26	A2
Fort Palmer	PA	60	A1
Fort Pitt	PA	52	C3
Fort Plain	NY	30	B3
Fort Ritchie	MD	10	B1
Fort Ticonderoga	NY	29	B4
Fort Ticonderoga Tunnel	NY	29	B4
Fort Wadsworth	NY	20	F1
Fort Washington	NY	23	B1
Fort Washington	PA	73	A1
Forty Fort	PA	65	B4
Forthton	ON	36	C2
Fortuna	PA	70	C1
Fossilville	PA	60	B3
Fossilville Gravel Pit	PA	60	B3
Foster	PA	68	A2
Foster	WV	50	A3
Foster Wheeler Junction	NY	41	C1
Foul Rift	NJ	17	B3
Founce	PA	58	A3
Foundry	NJ	74	B4
Fountain	PA	57	E2
Four Mile	NY	43	F3
Four Story Junction	NY	27	A1
Foutswell	PA	64	A3
Fowler	OH	48	A4
Fowler	PA	57	D3
Fowlerville	NY	45	F3
Fowlesburg	MD	10	D1
Fowlersville	PA	62	E2
Fox Chase [PC(PRR)]	PA	62	C4
Fox Chase [SEPA(RDG)]	PA	73	C2
Fox Ridge ADM Plant	NY	38	A2
Foxburg	PA	49	E1
Foxcroft	PA	72	C3
Frackville	PA	67	A3
Fraleighs	NY	31	E3
Francis	MD	11	A4
Franconia-Springfield	VA	10	C5
Frankford	DE	7	F4
Frankford	PA	73	C3
Frankford Arsenal	PA	73	C3
Frankford Junction	PA	73	C3
Frankfort	NY	38	F2
Franklin	MD	8	D5
Franklin	NJ	16	D1
Franklin	NY	39	F2
Franklin	PA	48	D4
Franklin City	VA	15	C3
Franklin Junction	NJ	16	D1
Franklin Junction [Ashley]	PA	65	B5
Franklin Mine	PA	58	C4
Franklin Springs	NY	38	E2
Franklin Square	OH	49	A2
Franklin Street [Reading]	PA	64	A6
Franklinville	NJ	19	B1
Franklinville	NY	43	F2
Frankston	NY	23	D3
Frankston	PA	59	D3
Frankville	MD	9	B2
Franz	PA	57	A3
Fraser [GNWR]	NY	45	E2
Fraser [OW]	NY	31	A2
Fraser	PA	69	A1
Frazer	PA	70	F4
Frazier Tunnel	MD	11	C1
Frecks	NY	43	E3
Frederick	MD	10	B2
Frederick Junction	MD	10	B2
Frederick Road [Baltimore]	MD	12	B2
Fredericktown	OH	49	B3
Fredericktown	PA	54	A5
Fredonia	NY	43	C1
Fredonia	PA	48	C4
Freedom	NY	41	A1
Freedom [NS(PRR)]	PA	49	C3
Freedom [TUV]	PA	62	A4
Freehold	NJ	18	E2
Freeland	MD	11	A1
Freeland	PA	69	A2
Freeman	NJ	73	D5
Freeman	NY	41	D3
Freeman	PA	56	C2
Freemansburg	PA	71	C4
Freemansburg Industrial Track	PA	71	C4
Freeport	NY	24	C5
Freeport	PA	49	E3
Freeport	PA	51	E2
Freeville	NY	39	B1
Freidens	PA	60	A2
French (Buchanan)	PA	48	C3
French	WV	9	D2
Frenchtown	MD	11	D1
Frenchtown	NJ	18	B1
Frenchville	PA	57	D1
Frenchville Tunnel	PA	57	D1

Freneau NJ 18 E1
Fresh Pond NY 23 C3
Fresh Pond Yard NY 23 C4
Frewsburg NY 43 C3
Freyco VA 9 F3
Frey's Grove PA 63 D2
Friendship NJ 6 E2
Friendship NY 41 A3
Friendsville MD 9 A1
Frisbie PA 67 D6
Frisco PA 51 C3
Fritz PA 62 C1
Fritztown PA 63 F1
Frog DE 7 A2
Frog Hollow WV 9 F2
Froman PA 53 A6
Front Royal VA 9 E4
Front Royal Junction VA 9 E4
Frontier Yard [Buffalo] NY 46 C4
Frost MD 8 C4
Frostburg MD 8 A2
Frostburg Tunnel MD 8 A2
Frosts PA 56 A3
Frugality PA 57 C3
Fruitland MD 15 B1
Fruitland NY 40 D2
Frush Valley PA 64 A4
Fry (Frye) PA 54 B1
Frye PA 54 B1
Fuller [PC(PRR/NYC)] PA 57 A1
Fuller [PLE(PMY)] PA 54 D3
Fullers NY 32 B4
Fullerton PA 71 A4
Fulmor PA 70 D2
Fulton MD 12 B2
Fulton NY 38 B1
Fulton [PRR] PA 66 A5
Fulton [RJCP(NYC)] PA 58 B1
Fulton Junction MD 12 B2
Fulton Terminal [Brooklyn] NY 23 A4
Fulton Tunnel PA 58 B1
Fultonville NY 30 C3
Funkstown [CSXT(BO)] MD 10 A6
Funkstown [POTED(H&F)] MD 10 B6
Furnace Road PA 57 E3
Furniss NY 37 A4
FW Tower [Buffalo] NY 46 B5

G

G&O Junction [Gouverneur] NY 36 E4
Gabriels NY 28 C3
Gaines PA 56 F2
Gaines [defect detector] PA 56 E4
Gaines Junction PA 56 F2
Gainesboro VA 9 E3
Gaineville NY 40 A4
Gaither MD 10 D2
Gaithersburg MD 10 C3
Galena [DLW] NY 38 E4
Galena [OW] NY 38 D4
Galeton PA 56 F2
Gallagerville PA 70 A3
Gallant Green MD 10 D6
Gallatin PA 54 B1
Gallatinville NY 31 E3
Gallitzin PA 59 B2
Gallitzin [defect detector] PA 59 C2
Gallitzin Tunnel PA 59 B2
Galop ON 36 E1
Galt MD 10 C1
Gambles PA 50 C2
Gambrill MD 11 A4
Ganaoque ON 36 B4
Ganaoque Junction ON 36 B4
Gang Mills NY 41 E3
Ganister PA 57 D4
Gannon MD 8 D5
Ganoga Lake PA 61 E4
Gans PA 50 D4
Gansevort NY 30 E1
Gap PA 63 F3
Gap Junction (Lehigh Gap) PA 69 E2
Gap Road PA 60 E3
Gapland MD 10 A2
Garbutt NY 45 F1
Gardeau PA 56 D3
Garden City NY 24 B4
Garden Tower [Garden City] NY 24 C4
Gardenville NY 46 C5
Gardenville Yard NY 46 C5
Gardiner NY 34 D1
Gardner [PRR Cambria County] PA 59 C6
Gardner [PRR Centre County] PA 58 D6
Gardner Avenue [New Castle] PA 51 B1
Gardners PA 63 B3
Garfield NJ 22 B2
Garfield PA 56 A2
Garland PA 48 F2
Garman PA 57 B3
Garrett PA 60 A3
Garrett Hill PA 72 C3
Garrett Park MD 10 C4
Garrett Road PA 72 D4
Garrett Slope PA 60 A3
Garrison NY 26 B1
Garrison Tunnel NY 26 B1
Garvers Ferry PA 51 E2
Garvoi PA 56 B4
Garway PA 57 B3
Garwood NJ 21 C6
Garwood Industrial Track NJ 21 C6
Garwoods NY 41 B1
Gascola PA 53 D2
Gasport NY 42 E2
Gastonville PA 53 A6
Gate [Queens] NY 23 C2
Gate PA 50 C3
Gates [MGA] PA 50 D3
Gates [PRR(KRY)] PA 56 B2
Gateway Yard OH 49 B1
Gatzmer WV 9 A3
Gawango PA 56 B1
Gay Street [Baltimore] MD 12 C2
Gaylord VA 9 F3
Gazzum PA 57 C2
GB Crossing [Blasdell] NY 46 B6
GD Tower [Glenwood] NY 25 C3
Geary PA 52 A3
Geddes Street [Syracuse] NY 36 A1
Gedney Way [White Plains] NY 25 E2
Gehman PA 69 B4
Geiger PA 60 A3
Geigertown PA 70 A2
Gemmill PA 63 D4
Gene [Geneva] NY 40 E3
General Electric Locomotive Plant [Erie] PA 47 C5
General Electric Plant [Schenectady] NY 32 B3
General Motors Plant [Linden] NJ 20 D1
General Motors Plant [Tarrytown] NY 25 C1
Genesee PA 56 E1
Genesee & Wyoming Junction NY 45 E1
Genesee Dock NY 44 C1
Genesee Dock Junction NY 44 C1
Genesee Junction NY 44 B4
Genesee Street [Buffalo] NY 46 B4
Genesee Trestle [Portageville] NY 41 B1
Geneseo NY 40 B3
Geneva NY 40 E3
Geneva PA 48 C3
Geneva Junction NY 40 E3
Genoa NY 38 A4
George PA 52 A5
George School [Newtown] PA 74 A2
Georges Creek Junction MD 8 C1
Georgetown DC 14 B4
Georgetown DE 7 E3
Georgetown MD 10 C4
Georgetown NY 38 D3
Georgetown PA 51 F3
Georgetown Junction MD 14 B3
Gerhards PA 66 B2
Germania NJ 19 D2
Germania PA 56 F2
Germans PA 69 A3
Germantown MD 10 C3
Germantown NY 31 D3
Germantown PA 73 A3
Germantown Road PA 73 A2
Germansville PA 69 B3
Germons NY 26 A6
Gerry NY 43 C3
Gerstell WV 8 A5
Getty Square Yonkers NY 25 C3
Getty Street [Paterson] NJ 22 A2
Gettysburg PA 63 B3
Gettysburg Junction PA 63 B2
Getzville NY 46 C2
Geyelin Park PA 61 D4
Ghent NY 31 E2
Gib PA 56 D4
Gibb (Gibbstown) NJ 72 D6
Gibboney PA 57 F4
Gibbstown NJ 72 D6
Gibraltar PA 70 A1
Gibson [Corning] NY 41 E3
Gibson [LIRR] NY 24 B5
Gibsonia PA 49 D3
Gibsonton PA 54 B2
Gifford NY 43 C3
Gilbert NY 40 F4
Gilbert Junction PA 56 B1
Gilberton PA 67 B3
Gilberton Breaker PA 66 C5
Gilfoyl PA 48 F3
Gillespie NJ 20 B4
Gillett PA 61 C1
Gillette NJ 21 A6
Gillintown PA 57 E2
Gilmore MD 8 A3
Gilroy Road [Hunt Valley] MD 11 A2
Ginn DE 7 A3
Gipsy PA 57 B3
Girard OH 49 A1
Girard PA 47 B6
Girard Junction PA 47 B6
Girard Manor PA 67 C2
Girard Point [Philadelphia] PA 73 A5
Girardville PA 67 A3
Girarde NY 27 D2
Girdletree MD 15 C2
Gitt's Run PA 63 C4
GJ [Ebenezer Junction] NY 46 C5
Glad Hill PA 63 A4
Gladden PA 52 B3
Glade PA 56 A2
Gladstone NJ 17 D4
Gladstone PA 72 D5
Gladwyne PA 72 D3
Glasgow DE 7 A2
Glasgow [PC(PRR)] PA 57 C3
Glasgow [RDG] PA 70 B2
Glass NJ 18 B4
Glass [Corning] NY 41 E3
Glassboro NJ 19 B1
Glassboro Industrial Track NJ 19 B1
Glassmere PA 51 C4
Glassport PA 53 B5
Glassport Transportation Center PA 53 C5
Glatfelter PA 63 D3
Gleason WV 9 B2
Glebe WV 9 C3
Glen [AMTK(PRR)] PA 70 E4
Glen [CR(PRR)] PA 51 F1
Glen [CSAO(MGA)] PA 54 B4
Glen Burn PA 68 A3
Glen Burn Colliery PA 66 A5
Glen Burnie MD 12 B4
Glen Campbell PA 59 A6
Glen Carbon PA 66 D6
Glen Cove NY 24 C1
Glen Dower PA 66 D6
Glen Easton WV 50 A3
Glen Elbe ON 36 C2
Glen Gardner NJ 17 C4
Glen Hazel PA 56 C3
Glen Hazel Junction PA 56 C3
Glen Head NY 24 C2
Glen Hope PA 57 C3
Glen Iron PA 62 B2
Glen Junction PA 62 F2
Glen Loch NY 40 D4
Glen Loch PA 70 E4
Glen Lyon PA 62 F1
Glen Mawr PA 61 D4
Glen Mills PA 72 A5
Glen Morris MD 10 D2
Glen Onoko PA 66 D3
Glen Osborne PA 52 B1
Glen Park NY 37 C2
Glen Riddle PA 72 B5
Glen Ridge NJ 22 A4
Glen Rock NJ 22 B1
Glen Rock PA 63 D4
Glen Rock-Boro Hall NJ 22 B1
Glen Rose PA 70 A3
Glen Street [Glen Cove] NY 24 C1
Glen Summit PA 69 A1
Glen Union PA 56 F4
Glen Willow PA 72 D3
Glenarden MD 10 D4
Glenarm MD 11 B2
Glenbrook CT 35 C1
Glencain PA 51 E2
Glencoe MD 11 A1
Glencoe PA 60 B4
Glendale NY 23 C3
Glendale WV 50 A3
Glendon PA 71 E3
Glendora NJ 73 C6
Glenfield NY 37 E3
Glenfield PA 52 C1
Glenham NY 34 E2
Glenmar No.1 Mine (Eureka Colliery) PA 58 B6
Glenmont NY 32 E4
Glenmoore NJ 18 C2
Glenmoore PA 70 A2
Glenndale MD 10 D4
Glenolden PA 72 D5
Glenora NY 41 E1
Glenover PA 53 C1
Glens Falls NY 30 E1
Glenshaw PA 53 A1
Glenside PA 73 B1
Glenvale ON 36 A4
Glenville PA 63 C4
Glenwillard PA 49 C4
Glenwood NJ 17 D1
Glenwood [BPRR(BRP)] NY 42 E4
Glenwood [MNC(NYC)] NY 25 C3
Glenwood [Pittsburgh] PA 53 B3
Glenwood Colliery 10 PA 59 A6
Glenwood Junction NY 34 C3
Glenwood Junction PA 53 B3
Glenworth PA 67 A6
Glidden NJ 18 E3
Gloucester NJ 73 B5
Glove CT 35 C1
Gloversville NY 30 C2
Glynden PA 48 E2
Glyndon MD 10 D2
GMLG-Super Steel Locomotive Works (Glenville) NY 32 B2
Godfrey PA 51 E2
Goff PA 49 D1
Goff Junction PA 49 D1
Goffs PA 63 F3
Golah NY 44 A6
Gold [CPPA] PA 56 E1
Gold [NS Goldsboro] PA 63 D2
Gold Bond Building Products [Florence] NJ 74 B4
Gold Mine PA 62 D4
Goldens Bridge NY 34 F3
Goldenville PA 63 B3
Goldsboro MD 11 D4
Goldsboro PA 63 D2
Golts MD 11 D2
Good [NYC] PA 57 C2
Good (Knepper) [PRR] PA 63 A3
Good Spring PA 62 E4
Good Spring Colliery PA 62 D3
Goodman Street Yard [Rochester] NY 44 C2
Goodrich Plant [Pedricktown] NJ 6 F2
Goods Corner PA 64 A1
Goodyear PA 63 B3
Goose Creek NY 23 D5
Gordon PA 66 D5
Gordon Street [Allentown] PA 71 A4
Gordonville PA 63 F3
Gore VA 9 E3
Goreham NY 40 E3
Gorgas PA 73 A2
Gorman MD 9 A3
Gorsuch MD 10 D2
Gorton PA 57 E2
Goshen NJ 19 C3
Goshen NY 27 B2
Goshen PA 63 F4
Goss Run Junction PA 58 C5
Goss Run Branch No.2 PA 58 B4
Gott MD 11 A4
Gould PA 53 A5
Gould Siding OH 50 A1
Gouldsboro PA 68 B4
Gouverneur NY 36 E4
Government Hospital [Anacostia] DC 14 C5
Gowanda NY 43 D1
Gowen PA 62 F2
Grace [Harve de Grace] MD 13 D1
Grace WV 9 C2
Gracedale Junction PA 65 C6
Graceham MD 10 B1
Graceton PA 57 A4
Grafton PA 57 E4
Graham NY 26 D6
Graham PA 58 D3
Graham Crossing PA 55 B5
Graham Tower NY 34 C2
Graham Tunnel MD 9 D1
Grahams PA 62 A4
Grahamtown MD 8 A2
Grampian PA 57 C2
Grand Canyon of Pennsylvania PA 61 A3
Grand Central Terminal [Manhattan] NY 23 B3
Grand Gorge NY 31 B2
Grand Hotel NY 31 B3
Grand Isle VT 28 F2
Grand Valley PA 48 E2
Grand View NY 25 B1
Grandview PA 56 C3
Granger NY 40 E4
Grangers PA 56 D3
Granite PA 63 B3
Granite Springs NY 34 F3
Granogue DE 6 D1
Grant PA 56 D4
Grant Avenue [Plainfield] NJ 20 A1
Grant Street Station [Pittsburgh] PA 53 A3
Grant City NY 20 F2
Grant Locomotive Works [Paterson] NJ 22 A1
Grantley PA 63 D3
Granton Junction NJ 22 C4
Grantsville MD 9 B1
Granville NY 29 F4
Granville PA 57 F4
Granville WV 50 D4
Grapeville PA 50 E1
Grasmere NY 20 F1
Grasse River Club NY 28 B4
Grasseli NJ 20 D1
Grassflats PA 57 E2
Grasslands PA 72 C4
Grassy Run Junction PA 60 A4
Grassy Sound NJ 19 C4
Graters Ford PA 70 B2
Gratztown PA 53 D6
Grave Creek WV 50 A3
Gravel Junction OH 50 A3
Gravel Place PA 16 A4
Gravers PA 73 A2
Gravesend NY 23 B5
Gravesville NY 38 F1
Gravity NY 46 D5
Gravity PA 68 C3
Graw NJ 20 C1
Gray [BO(WM)] PA 60 A2
Gray [NS(PRR)] PA 57 D3
Gray [PC(PRR)] PA 61 C3
Gray [Grays Ferry Philadelphia] PA 73 A4
Gray [RJCP(NYC)] PA 57 D1
Gray (Grays Landing) PA 50 D4
Gray Oaks NY 25 C2
Grays Landing PA 50 D4
Grays Mill PA 48 D2
Grays Yard [Sparrows Point] MD 12 D3
Graybill PA 63 C3
Graysdale PA 57 E3
Graystones MD 11 A1
Greason PA 63 B2
Great Barrington MA 31 F2
Great Belt PA 49 D3
Great Bend NY 37 D1
Great Bend PA 68 A1
Great Cacapon WV 9 E1
Great Kills NY 20 E2
Great Meadows NJ 17 C3
Great Neck NY 24 A3
Great Neck Junction [Flushing] NY 23 D3
Great Notch NJ 22 A2
Great River NY 35 D3
Great Valley NY 43 E2
Greece NY 40 C1
Green [Greenville] NJ 22 B6
Green [Greencastle] PA 60 F4
Green [Greenville] PA 47 D2
Green [Manayunk] PA 72 D3
Green [NS(LV)] PA 61 D1
Green Bush VA 15 B4
Green Fields PA 62 D4
Green Haven NY 34 F1
Green Hill PA 70 B3
Green Island NY 32 F2
Green Lane PA 70 B1
Green Lawn PA 70 A3

Name	State	Page	Grid
Green Park	PA	63	B1
Green Point	PA	62	D4
Green Pond Junction	NJ	17	D2
Green Ridge	MD	9	D1
Green Ridge	PA	65	D1
Green Ridge	WV	9	D1
Green Spring	DE	7	A3
Green Spring	WV	9	D2
Green Spring Junction	MD	11	A2
Green Springs	PA	53	C3
Green Street [Philadelphia]	PA	73	B4
Green Tree	PA	70	F4
Green Tree Tunnel	PA	52	D3
Green Valley	PA	57	A1
Greenawald	PA	69	A4
Greenbank	DE	6	C2
Greenbelt	MD	14	D3
Greenbrier	MD	10	B1
Greenbush Cemetery	NY	32	F4
Greencastle	PA	60	F4
Greendale	NY	33	B6
Greendell	NJ	17	C3
Greene	NY	39	D2
Greene Junction	PA	55	C5
Greenfield	NY	30	D2
Greenfield	PA	64	D4
Greenford	OH	49	A2
Greenhurst	NY	43	C3
Greenlawn	NY	35	C2
Greenlick Junction	PA	55	C3
Greenmount	MD	10	D1
Greenock	PA	53	D5
Greenpoint	NY	23	B3
Greenport	NY	35	C5
Green's Farms	CT	35	C1
Greensand	NJ	20	B3
Greensboro	MD	11	D4
Greensburg	PA	50	E1
Greenstone	PA	63	A4
Greenvale	NY	24	C2
Greenville	DE	6	D2
Greenville	NJ	22	B6
Greenville	PA	47	D2
Greenville	PA	48	B4
Greenville [defect detector]	PA	47	C3
Greenville Yard	NJ	22	B6
Greenwald	PA	50	F1
Greenway	NY	38	E2
Greenwich	CT	25	F2
Greenwich	NJ	19	A2
Greenwich	NY	30	F2
Greenwich Junction	NY	30	F2
Greenwich 1 & 2 Mines	PA	57	B3
Greenwich Pier	NJ	19	A2
Greenwich Yards [Philadelphia]	PA	73	B5
Greenwood	DE	7	D2
Greenwood	NY	41	C3
Greenwood 9th Avenue	NY	23	A4
Greenwood Lake	NY	34	D3
Gregg [PRR Allegheny County]	PA	52	B3
Gregg [PRR Centre County]	PA	57	F3
Gregory	MD	14	D5
Gregorytown	NY	39	F3
Greigsville	NY	45	E4
Grenloch	NJ	18	B4
Grenoble	PA	70	D2
Gretchen	PA	49	F1
Greycourt	NY	27	D3
Greystone	NY	25	C2
Greythorne	PA	63	A2
Gridleyville	NY	39	B2
Griff	NJ	19	F3
Griffis Air Force Base	NY	38	E1
Griffiths	PA	56	B2
Grimes	MD	10	A2
Grindstone	PA	54	C4
Griswold	NY	40	A3
Groffdale	PA	63	F2
Groton	NY	38	B4
Grovania	PA	62	D2
Grove [AMTK(PRR)]	MD	11	A3
Grove [BO]	MD	10	B2
Grove	NY	41	B1
Grove	PA	56	E4
Grove City	PA	49	C1
Grove North	PA	73	B1
Grove South	PA	73	B1
Grove Street [East Orange]	NJ	22	A4
Grove Street [Jersey City]	NJ	22	C5
Groveland	NY	40	C4
Grover	PA	61	C3
Groveton	PA	52	C1
Groveville Siding	NY	34	E2
Grumman	NY	24	D3
Grundy	PA	74	B4
Guernsey	PA	63	B3
Guffney	PA	53	D5
Guilderland Center	NY	30	D4
Guilford	NY	39	E2
Guilford Siding	PA	60	F3
Guilford Springs	PA	60	F3
Guiwal Mine	PA	58	D3
Gulders	PA	63	B3
Gulf Summit	NY	39	E3
Gulfport	NY	20	D1
Gulph Mills	PA	72	C2
Gum Stump	PA	57	E2
Gun Hill Road [Bronx]	NY	23	C1
Gunpow [Gunpowder River]	MD	12	F1
Gurney	PA	61	A2
Gustavus	OH	48	A3
Guth	PA	69	B3
Guy Park [Amsterdam]	NY	30	C3
Guyastua	PA	53	B1
Guyencourt	DE	6	D1
GW [Keating]	PA	56	E4
Gwyn	PA	70	C2
Gwynedd Valley	PA	70	C2
Gwynn	MD	12	B2
Gwynnbrook	MD	10	D2
GY [Greenport]	NY	35	C5
H			
H&P Junction [Bronx]	NY	25	C4
HA Tower [Conneaut Junction]	PA	48	B1
Haberman	NY	23	B3
Hack	NJ	22	B5
Hackensack	NJ	22	C2
Hackensack-Anderson Street	NJ	22	C2
Hackensack-Essex Street	NJ	22	C2
Hackett	PA	53	A6
Hackettstown	NJ	17	C3
Hacklebarney	NJ	17	C4
Hackney	PA	50	C3
Haddon Heights	NJ	73	C5
Haddonfield	NJ	73	C5
Hadley	NY	30	D1
Hadley	PA	48	C4
Hager [Hagerstown]	MD	10	A5
Hagerman	NY	35	D3
Hagerstown	MD	10	A1
Hagerstown	MD	10	A5
Hagerstown Yard [BO]	MD	10	A5
Hagerstown Yard [CSXT(WM)]	MD	10	A5
Hahntown	PA	50	E1
Hailesboro	NY	36	E4
Haines	PA	63	E4
Haines Junction	PA	65	D2
Hainesburg	NJ	16	C5
Hainesburg Junction	NJ	16	C5
Hainesport	NJ	18	C3
Halcottville	NY	31	B2
Hale Colliery 1	PA	58	B5
Hale Eddy	NY	39	E3
Halethorpe	MD	12	A3
Haleyville (Mauricetown)	NJ	19	C3
Half Acre	NY	38	A3
Halfway	NY	38	B2
Halifax	PA	62	C4
Halite	NY	40	B3
Hall	MD	11	A4
Hall [Campbell Hall]	NY	27	D2
Hall [PC(PRR)]	NY	40	E3
Hall	PA	53	D3
Hall Tower [Jamaica]	NY	23	D4
Halls [B&S]	PA	56	D2
Halls [RDG WNB]	PA	61	C4
Hallstead	PA	68	A1
Hallston	PA	49	D2
Hallton	PA	56	B4
Halltown	WV	10	A3
Hallwood	VA	15	B3
Halpine	MD	10	C4
Halsey	NJ	16	A2
Halsted	NY	31	E3
Ham [Allentown]	PA	71	B4
Hamburg	NJ	16	D1
Hamburg	NY	42	E4
Hamburg	PA	62	F4
Hamburg Street Yard [Buffalo]	NY	46	B5
Hamden	NJ	17	C4
Hamden	NY	31	A2
Hamers Mill	PA	57	D3
Hamilton	NJ	18	D1
Hamilton	VA	10	A3
Hamilton	NY	38	D3
Hamilton	PA	57	A2
Hamilton Avenue [Trenton]	NJ	74	C3
Hamilton Beach	NY	23	D5
Hamilton Township	NJ	74	D2
Hamlin	NY	40	B1
Hamlin	PA	56	C2
Hammel	NY	23	D6
Hammersley	PA	56	E3
Hammond	PA	61	B1
Hammond's	PA	56	E2
Hammondsport	NY	41	D2
Hammondsville	OH	49	A4
Hammondville	NY	29	E2
Hammonton	NJ	19	C1
Hampshire	MD	8	C6
Hampshire	WV	8	C6
Hampshire Club	WV	9	C3
Hampshire Industrial Track	MD	8	C6
Hampstead	MD	10	D1
Hampton	NJ	17	C4
Hampton Bays	NY	35	B6
Hampton Yard [Scranton]	PA	65	C2
Hamptonburgh	NY	27	D2
Hancock	MD	9	E1
Hancock	NY	39	E4
Hancock	PA	69	B4
Hancock	WV	9	E1
Hanford	NJ	17	D1
Hankins	NY	39	F4
Hanlin	PA	50	B1
Hannah	PA	57	E3
Hannastown	PA	50	E1
Hannawa	NY	28	A2
Hannibal	NY	38	A1
Hannibal	WV	50	A4
Hanover	MD	12	A4
Hanover	NJ	21	B3
Hanover	PA	63	C4
Hanover Farms	NJ	18	D4
Hanover Junction	PA	63	C3
Hansrote	WV	9	D1
Happy Creek	VA	9	E4
Harbor	NY	38	F2
Harbor (Shenks Ferry)	PA	63	E3
Harbor Bridge	PA	49	B2
Harbor Creek	PA	47	D5
Harbor Road [Arlington]	NY	20	E1
Harding	PA	65	A2
Hardys	NY	40	A4
Harewood Park	MD	12	F1
Harford	NY	39	B2
Harford Mills	NY	39	B2
Harford Road [Baltimore]	MD	12	C2
Harkness	NY	28	E3
Harlan	PA	49	F1
Harleigh Colliery	PA	66	A1
Harleigh Junction	PA	66	A1
Harlem River Yard [Bronx]	NY	23	B2
Harlingen	NJ	18	C1
Harmans	MD	11	A3
Harmer [Harmerville]	PA	53	C1
Harmerville	PA	53	C1
Harmon	NY	26	C4
Harmon Shops	NY	26	C4
Harmon Cove	NJ	22	C4
Harmonsburg	PA	48	B2
Harmony	DE	6	B3
Harmony	NJ	71	E1
Harmony	PA	49	C3
Harmony Grove	MD	10	B2
Harold Tower [Queens]	NY	23	B3
Harpers	PA	73	C2
Harpers Ferry	WV	10	A2
Harpursville	NY	39	D3
Harriet	NY	46	A2
Harriman	NY	27	E4
Harrington	DE	7	E2
Harrington Park	NJ	25	B2
Harris (Butler Junction)	PA	51	D2
Harris [Harrisburg]	PA	64	C2
Harris Terminal Warehouse [West Collingswood]	NJ	73	B5
Harrisburg	PA	63	C1
Harrisburg	PA	64	C2
Harrisburg Fuel Station	PA	64	C1
Harrisburg Yard	PA	64	C2
Harrison [ERIE]	NJ	22	A4
Harrison [NJT(DLW)]	NJ	22	A5
Harrison [PATH(H&M)]	NJ	22	A5
Harrison	NY	25	E2
Harrison	PA	60	A2
Harrison	WV	9	B2
Harrison City	PA	50	E1
Harrison Shops	NJ	22	B5
Harrison Valley	PA	56	F1
Harrisville	NY	37	E1
Harrisville	PA	49	D1
Harrowsmith	ON	36	A3
Harsimus Cove	NJ	22	C5
Hartfield	NY	43	B2
Hartford	NJ	18	C3
Hartford	OH	48	B4
Hartley	PA	60	C3
Hartly	DE	7	A4
Hartman	PA	63	E2
Hartranft	PA	70	C2
Hartsdale	NY	25	D2
Hartstown	PA	48	B3
Hartwell	NY	28	D3
Hartwick	NY	38	F4
Hartwick Seminary	NY	30	A4
Hartwood	NY	34	B2
Harvard	NY	39	F3
Harvey Breaker	PA	65	B4
Harvey Junction	PA	65	B4
Harveys Lake	PA	61	F4
Harwick	PA	53	B1
Harwood Junction	PA	66	A1
Harwood Mines	PA	66	A2
Harwood Road	PA	66	A2
Haskell	NJ	17	E2
Haskill	PA	48	F4
Hasleton Yard	OH	49	B1
Hastings (Hastings-on-Hudson)	NY	25	C2
Hastings	PA	59	C4
Hastings Junction (Garway)	PA	57	B3
Hastings-on-Hudson	NY	25	C2
Hastings No.7 Mine	PA	59	C5
Hatboro	PA	70	D2
Hatch (Fish House Junction)	NJ	73	C4
Hatfield	PA	70	C1
Haucks	PA	67	D3
Haucks Junction	PA	67	D3
Hauto	PA	66	C3
Hauto Coal Storage	PA	66	C3
Hauto Tunnel	PA	66	C4
Hauto Yard	PA	66	C3
Haverford	PA	72	C3
Haverstraw	NY	26	B4
Haverstraw Tunnel	NY	26	B5
Havre de Grace	MD	11	C1
Havre de Grace	MD	13	D1
Hawk	NY	38	A1
Hawk Mountain Tunnel	NY	39	E4
Hawk Run	PA	58	D3
Hawkins	PA	53	C3
Hawkins Colliery 3	PA	58	C4
Hawkins Point	MD	12	D4
Hawley	PA	68	C3
Hawleys	NY	39	F3
Haworth	NJ	22	D1
Hawstone (Narrows)	PA	62	A4
Hawthorne	NJ	22	A1
Hawthorne	NY	26	D6
Hawthorne	PA	49	F2
Hayden [Ashland]	MD	11	C4
Haynes	NY	39	D1
Hays	PA	53	B3
Haysville	PA	52	C1
Hayts Corners	NY	40	F4
Hayville	NJ	19	C1
Hazel	NY	31	A4
Hazel Dell	DE	6	D3
Hazel Kirk	PA	54	A1
Hazel Street [Wilkes-Barre]	PA	65	B5
Hazelhurst	PA	56	C2
Hazelton Mills	PA	56	B1
Hazelwood	PA	53	B3
Hazle Brook	PA	66	C1
Hazle Brook Tunnel	PA	66	C1
Hazle Creek Junction	PA	66	C1
Hazlet	NJ	18	E1
Hazleton	PA	62	F2
Hazleton	PA	66	A1
Hazleton Junction	PA	66	A3
HB Tower [Baltimore]	MD	12	B2
Head of Grape	PA	67	A4
Headerson	NY	38	F3
Heathcote	NY	25	D2
Heathville	PA	49	F1
Heaton	PA	70	D2
Hebron	MD	15	B1
Heckman	PA	60	F1
Hecks	PA	63	C1
Hecla	NY	38	E2
Hecla [RDG]	PA	62	F3
Hecla [PRR]	PA	55	D2
Hecla Park	PA	57	F2
Hector	NY	41	F1
Hegarty Branch	PA	57	C3
Heidrick	PA	49	F1
Heidrick Scales	PA	49	F1
Heilwood	PA	57	B4
Heislerville	NJ	19	C3
Helen	NJ	20	B2
Helen	PA	54	D5
Helena	NY	28	B1
Hell Gate Bridge	NY	23	B2
Hellam	PA	63	D3
Hellers Church	PA	63	F2
Hellertown	PA	71	C4
Hellman Dale	PA	63	E1
Helmetta	NJ	18	D2
Helmstetter's Curve	MD	8	C1
Helvetia	PA	57	B2
Hemlock	NY	40	C3
Hemlock [PRR Northumberland County]	PA	62	D2
Hemlock [PRR Warren County]	PA	56	A1
Hempfield [PRR]	PA	50	E1
Hempfield [RDG]	PA	64	D6
Hempfield Junction	PA	50	E1
Hempstead	NY	24	C4
Hempstead Crossing	NY	24	C4
Hempstead Gardens	NY	24	B4
Henderson	MD	11	D4
Henderson [LEFC]	PA	49	F1
Henderson [NS(PRR)]	PA	72	C2
Henderson [RDG]	PA	72	C2
Henderson Mine No.1	PA	52	B5
Hendersonville	PA	52	B5
Hendlers [defect detector]	PA	65	D5
Hendricks	PA	70	B1
Henlein	PA	47	D3
Henley	PA	47	D3
Henrietta	NY	44	C4
Henrietta	PA	60	D1
Henrietta No.6 Mine	PA	58	C5
Henry	OH	50	A1
Henry	WV	9	A3
Henry Street [Elmira]	NY	41	F3
Henry's Bend	PA	48	E3
Henrys Mill	PA	56	A3
Henryton	MD	10	D2
Hepburnville	PA	61	B4
Hepler	PA	49	F2
Herbert	MD	10	D6
Hercules	DE	6	C2
Hercules	NY	34	A4
Hercules Cement [Stockertown]	PA	71	D1
Herkimer	NY	30	A2
Herman	PA	49	D3
Herminie	PA	50	E1
Herminie #2	PA	50	E1
Hermon	NY	36	F3
Herndon	PA	62	C3
Herndon	VA	10	B4
Herr [Pittsburgh]	PA	53	A2
Herrick	OH	50	A2
Herrick Center	PA	68	B2
Herrings	NY	37	D1
Herrville	PA	63	E3
Hershey	PA	63	D1
Heshbon	PA	57	A4
Hess	NJ	20	D2
Hess	PA	63	F3
Heston	OH	49	A3
Heuvelton	NY	36	E2
Heverly	PA	57	C3
Hewitt	NJ	17	E2
Hewitt	PA	71	E4
Hewlett	NY	24	B5
Heyden	NJ	20	C3
Hiawatha	NY	39	B3
Hibernia	NJ	21	A1
Hibernia	NY	31	E4
Hickling	NY	41	E3
Hickman	DE	7	D2
Hickman	PA	52	C4
Hickory	PA	50	C1
Hickory No.1 Mine	PA	57	C2

Hickory Run PA 69 A2
Hickox PA 56 E1
Hicks Ferry PA 62 F1
Hicks Run PA 56 D4
Hicksville NY 24 D3
Hickton PA 50 B1
Hidecker NY 43 E3
Higgins (Creighton) PA 51 E4
High [Matawan] NJ 18 E1
High Bridge MD 11 A4
High Bridge NJ 17 C4
High Bridge NY 23 B1
High Dry Siding PA 56 C2
High Falls NY 31 C4
High Peak PA 63 D4
High View NY 34 C2
High View Tunnel NY 34 C1
Highfield MD 10 B1
Highhouse PA 50 D3
Highland NY 34 C4
Highland [LV] PA 69 A2
Highland [SEPA(PRR)] PA 73 A2
Highland Avenue [Marcus Hook] PA 72 B6
Highland Avenue [Orange] NJ 21 D4
Highland Falls NY 26 B1
Highland Mills NY 27 E3
Highlands NJ 18 F1
Highpoint NJ 19 F1
Highspire PA 63 C2
Hightstown NJ 18 D2
Hill [Reading] PA 64 A5
Hill [RJCP(CR)] PA 57 D2
Hill Crest VA 9 E3
Hill Industrial Track [Harrisburg] PA 64 D2
Hill Street [Ashley] PA 65 B6
Hillards NJ 19 E1
Hillburn NY 34 D3
Hillcrest NJ 74 C2
Hillcrest PA 73 A2
Hillen Junction [Baltimore] MD 12 C2
Hillen Station [Baltimore] MD 12 C2
Hilliard PA 49 D1
Hillman PA 59 A4
Hills PA 52 C5
Hillsboro MD 11 D4
Hillsboro PA 60 B2
Hillsdale NJ 25 A2
Hillsdale NY 31 F2
Hillsdale PA 65 C4
Hillsgrove PA 61 D3
Hillside NJ 22 A5
Hillside NY 23 D3
Hillside [MSL] PA 49 B2
Hillside [PRR Lawrence County] PA 49 B2
Hillside [PRR Westmoreland County] PA 50 F1
Hillside [PSN] PA 56 C3
Hillside Colliery 3 PA 57 B3
Hillside Junction [Avoca] PA 65 C3
Hillside Shops NY 23 D3
Hilltop PA 69 C4
Hilton NY 40 B1
Hiltons NJ 18 F1
Himrod NY 40 E4
Himrod Junction NY 40 E4
Himrods NY 40 E4
Hinkles PA 66 D2
Hinckley NY 38 F1
Hinsdale NY 43 F3
Hip PA 64 C1
Hiwa NY 38 B2
HK Tower [Ohio Pyle] PA 50 F3
HM [Mahaffey] PA 59 B5
HO Tower [Hancock] WV 9 E1
Hoard WV 50 D4
Hoardley PA 68 C3
Hobart NY 31 B2
Hobbs MD 11 D5
Hobbs (Bardane) WV 9 F2
Hoblitzell PA 60 B3
Hoboken NJ 17 F4
Hoboken [NJT(DLW)] NJ 22 C5
Hoboken [WS] NJ 22 C5
Hoboken Yard NJ 22 C5
Hockessin DE 6 B2
Hoffman [CPA] MD 8 B2
Hoffman [WM-GV] MD 10 D1
Hoffman NJ 18 D2
Hoffman PA 62 B4
Hoffmans NJ 17 C4
Hoffmans NY 32 A1
Hoffmanville MD 10 D1
Hog Island PA 72 D6
Hohokus NJ 17 E3
Hokendauqua PA 71 A3
Hokes PA 63 C4
Holabird MD 12 D3
Holban Yard [Queens] NY 24 A4
Holcomb NY 40 D3
Holden PA 49 F1
Holland NJ 18 B1
Holland [LIRR] NY 23 D6
Holland [NS(PRR)] NY 42 F4
Holland PA 70 D2
Holland Patent NY 38 E1
Holley NY 40 B2
Holliday PA 61 B1
Hollidaysburg PA 59 D3
Hollidaysburg Car Shop PA 59 D3
Hollins MD 12 B1
Hollis NY 24 A4
Holly DE 6 E1
Holly Oak DE 6 E2
Holm (Holmes) NY 34 F2
Holmes NY 34 F2
Holmes [BO] PA 72 C5
Holmes [Holmesburg Junction] PA 73 C3
Holmesburg PA 73 C3
Holmesburg Junction PA 73 C3
Holmesville NY 39 E1
Holsopple PA 60 B2
Holtsville NY 35 D2
Holtwood PA 63 E3
Home NJ 19 C2
Home [CSAO(MGA)] PA 50 C3
Home [NS(BRP)] PA 57 A3
Homer [Altoona] PA 59 D1
Homer City PA 57 A4
Homeland MD 12 B1
Homer NY 38 B4
Homestead PA 53 B3
Homestead Tube Mill [Pittsburgh] PA 53 B3
Homestead Yard PA 53 B3
Hometown PA 66 A4
Homewood [NS(PRR) Allegheny County] PA 53 B2
Homewood [NS(PRR) Beaver County] PA 51 B4
Honeoye Falls NY 44 C6
Honesdale PA 68 C3
Honey Brook PA 70 A2
Honey Creek PA 57 F3
Honey Grove PA 63 A1
Hoods Mill MD 10 D2
Hook [Marcus Hook] PA 72 B6
Hooker PA 49 D2
Hooks PA 47 C4
Hooley PA 57 F3
Hoopeston PA 73 A1
Hoosick NY 30 F3
Hoosick Falls NY 30 F3
Hoosick Junction NY 30 F3
Hooverhurst PA 57 B3
Hooversville PA 60 B2
Hop Bottom Siding PA 68 A2
Hopatcong Junction NJ 17 A1
Hope [Hopewell Junction] NY 34 E1
Hopedale OH 50 A1
Hopeton VA 15 B4
Hopewell MD 15 B3
Hopewell NJ 18 C1
Hopewell [HBTM] PA 60 D2
Hopewell [LOS] PA 63 F4
Hopewell Junction NY 34 E1
Hopp PA 61 F3
Horatio PA 57 A2
Horeb Church OH 50 A3
Horn [Hornell] NY 41 C2
Horn [PRR] PA 48 E2
Horn [Sunbury] PA 66 A6
Horn Springs PA 69 C3
Hornell NY 41 C2
Hornerstown NJ 18 D3
Horningford PA 57 F4
Horning (Mine 4) PA 53 A4
Horrell PA 57 D4
Horseheads NY 41 F3
Horseheads Industrial Track NY 41 F3
Horseshoe NY 29 B1
Horseshoe Curve PA 59 B2
Horton NJ 17 D3
Horton Run PA 59 A6
Hosensack PA 69 B4
Hosetter PA 50 F2
Hostler PA 57 E3
Houghton NY 41 A2
Housatonic MA 31 F2
Houseville PA 49 D3
Houston DE 7 E2
Houston PA 52 B6
Houston Junction PA 48 C4
Houtzdale PA 58 B5
Howard [NYC] PA 57 F2
Howard [PRR Allegheny County] PA 53 B3
Howard [PRR Cameron County] PA 56 D3
Howard Beach-JFK Airport NY 23 D4
Howard Junction PA 56 C1
Howard Street Tunnel [Baltimore] MD 12 B2
Howards NY 29 F1
Howardville MD 12 A1
Howell NJ 18 E2
Howell PA 63 C2
Howells NY 27 A1
Howellville PA 72 A2
Howes Cave NY 30 C4
Howland PA 56 A3
Howland Hook NY 20 E1
Hoyts NY 43 E1
Hoytsville PA 61 B3
HS Tower [Hastings] NY 25 C2
Hubbard OH 49 B1
Hubbardsville NY 38 E3
Hubbardtown NY 39 B3
Huber Breaker PA 65 B6
Hublersburg PA 57 F2
Hudson NY 33 B5
Hudson (Manhattan Transfer) NJ 22 B5
Hudson Avenue-Englewood NJ 22 D1
Hudson Falls NY 30 E1
Hudson Junction [Campbell Hall] NY 27 D2
Hudson Junction [Chester] NY 27 C3
Hudson Junction [Hudson] NY 33 C6
Hudson Tunnels NJ 22 C4
Hudson Upper NY 33 B6
Hudson Yard [Phillipsburg] NJ 71 E2
Hudson Yard [Wilkes-Barre] PA 65 C4
Hudsondale PA 66 C2
Huey PA 49 E1
Huffnagle PA 70 D1
Hughes PA 60 C2
Hughes Park PA 72 C2
Hughesville MD 10 D6
Hughesville NJ 71 F4
Hughesville PA 61 D4
Huguenot [OW] NY 34 C2
Huguenot [SIRT(SIRY)] NY 20 E2
Hulings PA 56 E4
Hull PA 56 E3
Hulton PA 53 C1
Humaston NY 38 D1
Humbert PA 50 F3
Humboldt PA 66 A2
Hume NY 41 A1
Hummel PA 60 D1
Hummelstown PA 63 D1
Humphrey NY 43 F2
Humphrey PA 55 D1
Hundred WV 50 B4
Hunker PA 55 B2
Hunlock Creek PA 62 F1
Hunt [Huntingdon] PA 57 E4
Hunt [Philadelphia] PA 73 B3
Hunt Valley MD 11 A2
Hunter NJ 22 A5
Hunter NY 31 C2
Hunter [PC(PRR)] PA 48 E3
Hunter [RDG] PA 62 D3
Hunter VA 10 C4
Hunters Run PA 63 B2
Hunterspoint Avenue [Queens] NY 23 B3
Huntingdon PA 57 E4
Huntingdon Avenue [Baltimore] MD 12 B2
Huntingdon Industrial Track PA 57 E4
Huntingdon Valley PA 73 C1
Huntington NY 35 C2
Huntley PA 56 D4
Huntley's PA 56 C4
Hunts Point NY 23 C1
Huntsdale PA 63 B2
Huntsman NJ 73 A6
Huntsville MD 14 D4
Huntsville NJ 17 C3
Hurd NJ 17 D3
Hurley NY 31 D4
Hurlock MD 11 D6
Huron PA 50 D3
Hursley (Stockton) MD 15 C2
Husband PA 60 A2
Huskin PA 60 B2
Huskin 3, 4 & 6 Mines PA 60 B2
Husted NJ 19 B2
Husted NY 31 E3
Huston PA 50 F3
Hutchins PA 56 C2
Hutchinson NJ 71 F1
Hutchinson Mine PA 55 A1
Hutton MD 9 A2
HX [Harmons Cove] NJ 22 B4
Hyatt NY 36 E4
Hyattsville MD 14 D4
Hyde MD 11 B2
Hyde [PSN] PA 56 B4
Hyde [RJCP(BRP/NYC)] PA 58 A2
Hyde Park NY 31 D4
Hyde Park PA 51 F3
Hydetown PA 48 E2
Hydro Spur [Niagara Falls] ON 42 B3
Hyland PA 52 C5
Hyndman PA 60 B4
Hyndsville NY 30 B4
Hyner PA 56 F4
Hyper-Humus (Warbasse Junction) NJ 16 B2

I

Icedale PA 70 A2
Idamar PA 57 A3
Idaville PA 63 B3
Idlewood PA 52 D3
Ifield PA 50 D3
Ijamsville MD 10 B2
Ilion NY 38 F2
Imler PA 60 C2
Imperial PA 52 A2
Index NY 38 F4
Indian Camp PA 57 A2
Indian Castle NY 30 A2
Indian Creek PA 55 D6
Indian Head MD 10 C6
Indian Head PA 50 F3
Indian Head Junction MD 10 D6
Indian River DE 7 F3
Indian River Power Plant DE 7 F3
Indian Road [Pembroke] NY 42 F3
Indiana PA 57 A4
Indianola PA 49 D4
Indianola Branch Junction PA 53 B1
Indiantown Gap PA 62 D4
Indigo Tunnel MD 9 E1
Industry NY 44 A5
Industry PA 49 B3
Ingalls NY 38 B1
Ingersoll-Rand Plant [Phillipsburg] NJ 71 F2
Inghams NY 30 A2
Ingleby PA 62 A2
Inglehart MD 11 A4
Inglenook PA 62 C4
Ingram PA 52 D2
Inkerman PA 65 C4
Instanter PA 56 C3
Interlaken NY 40 F4
International Bridge [Fort Erie] ON 46 A4
International Junction [Buffalo] NY 46 B3
Intersection PA 63 C4
Interstate Industrial Park [Glendora] NJ 73 C6
Inverness NY 45 E3
Inwood [LIRR] NY 24 A6
Inwood [Manhattan] NY 23 B1
Inwood [KV] PA 57 F4
Inwood [RDG] PA 62 D4
Inwood WV 9 F2
Iona NJ 19 B1
Iona Island NY 26 B2
Ionia NY 40 C3
Iowa PA 57 A1
Ira NY 38 A2
Irish NY 37 D1
Iron (Iron Hill) MD 6 A4
Iron Bridge [BO] PA 55 C3
Iron Bridge [WNF] PA 51 E1
Iron City PA 56 A3
Iron Hill MD 6 A4
Iron Ridge PA 63 C3
Iron Works [Troy] NY 32 F3
Irona NY 28 E1
Irondale NY 29 A1
Irondale OH 49 A4
Ironia NJ 17 D3
Ironshire MD 15 D1
Ironstone PA 70 B1
Ironton NY 28 B1
Ironton PA 69 F4
Ironville NY 29 F2
Iroquois ON 36 E1
Iroquois PA 62 C4
Irvin Junction PA 53 B4
Irvin Works PA 53 B5
Irvine Mills NY 43 E3
Irvineton PA 48 F2
Irving NY 43 D1
Irving PA 62 E4
Irvington NJ 22 A5
Irvington NY 25 C1
Irvona PA 57 C3
Irwin PA 50 E1
Irwintown PA 56 B4
Isabella [MGA] PA 54 B6
Isabella [RDG] PA 70 A2
Ischua NY 43 F2
Iselin NJ 20 C2
Iselin PA 49 F4
Island NJ 22 B2
Island [Norristown] PA 72 C1
Island Avenue [Pittsburgh] PA 52 D2
Island Heights NJ 18 E4
Island Park NY 24 B6
Isle [NS Carlisle] PA 63 B2
Isle [NS Pittsburgh] PA 52 D2
Isle [WARR] PA 49 C2
Isle La Motte VT 28 F1
Islip NY 35 D3
Itaska NY 39 C2
Ithaca NY 39 A1
Ivy City [Washington] DC 14 C4
Ivy Ridge (Glen Willow) PA 72 D3
Ivy Rock PA 72 C2
Ivyland PA 70 D2

J

J Tower [Monongahela Junction] PA 53 C4
J&B Junction [Mt. Jewett] PA 56 C2
J&L Furnaces [Pittsburgh] PA 53 A3
J&L Steel Works [Donora] PA 54 C1
J&L Steel Works [Pittsburgh] PA 53 A3
J&L Tunnel [Pittsburgh] PA 53 A3
Jack DE 7 E2
Jacks [Mount Union] PA 60 E1
Jack's Mountain PA 63 A4
Jacks Run Dock PA 52 D2
Jackson MD 13 E1
Jackson PA 47 C6
Jackson Avenue [Jersey City] NJ 22 B5
Jackson Center PA 48 C4
Jackson Corners NY 31 E3
Jackson Junction MD 8 A3
Jackson Summit PA 61 C1
Jackson's Wharf [Baltimore] MD 12 C2
Jacksonville [NB] PA 71 B2
Jacksonville [RDG] PA 69 A3
Jacksonville Mine Junction PA 49 F4
Jacobs PA 60 E1
Jacobs Creek PA 54 D2
Jacobs Ferry PA 54 B6
Jacobs Mill PA 63 C3
Jacobsburg PA 71 D1
Jamaica NY 23 D4
James City PA 56 B3
James Street [Middletown] NY 27 A2
Jamesburg NJ 18 D2
Jamesport NY 35 B5
Jamestown NY 43 C3
Jamestown PA 47 C1
Jamesville NY 38 C3
Jamieson PA 56 E3
Jamison PA 48 F3
Jamison City PA 61 E4
Jamison Road NY 42 E3
Jamisonville PA 49 D2
Janesville PA 58 A6
Java Center NY 42 F4
Jay Street [Brooklyn] NY 23 A3
Jay Street [Rochester] NY 44 B3
Jay Tower [Jamaica] NY 23 D4
Jayville NY 37 F1
JD [Depew] NY 46 D4
JD (Alexandria Junction) [Hyattsville] MD 14 D3

JG [Jamesburg] NJ 18 D2
J G Brill Plant [Philadelphia] PA 72 D5
Jeanette PA 50 E1
Jeansville PA 66 A2
Jeb PA 63 D2
Jeddo PA 66 C1
Jeddo No.7 Breaker PA 66 B1
Jeff PA 72 D4
Jefferson MD 10 B2
Jefferson NJ 19 B1
Jefferson [BO(P&W)] PA 49 E1
Jefferson [RDG] PA 62 F4
Jefferson [AJCY(LSMS)] OH 48 A2
Jefferson [NS(PRR)] OH 50 A1
Jefferson Avenue [Grant City] NY 20 F2
Jefferson Colliery PA 58 D3
Jefferson Junction PA 68 B1
Jenkin PA 73 B2
Jenkins (Jenkins Junction) PA 65 D4
Jenkins Junction PA 65 D4
Jenkintown-Wyncote PA 73 B2
Jenner PA 60 A2
Jennings MD 9 B1
Jessup MD 10 D3
Jessup PA 65 B1
Jermyn PA 68 B3
Jerome PA 60 A2
Jerome WV 9 D1
Jerome Junction PA 60 B2
Jersey NJ 73 C4
Jersey Avenue [New Brunswick] NJ 20 A4
Jersey City [CNJ/RDG/BO] NJ 22 C5
Jersey City [ERIE/NYSW] NJ 22 C5
Jersey City [PRR] NJ 22 C5
Jersey Mills PA 61 A4
Jersey Shore PA 62 B1
Jersey Shore Junction PA 62 B1
Jersey Yard [Philadelphia] PA 73 A4
Jerseytown PA 62 D1
Jewell NY 38 D1
Jewell PA 52 D5
Jewettville NY 42 E4
Jim Run PA 50 F3
Jim Thorpe PA 69 A2
Jim Thorpe (Mauch Chunk) PA 69 E1
Jo Jo Junction PA 56 B2
JO Tower [Woodlawn] NY 25 C4
Joanna PA 70 A2
Joanna Heights PA 70 A2
Jobstown NJ 74 D6
Jocelyn PA 49 E1
John Hopkins Hospital [Baltimore] MD 12 C2
Johnetta PA 51 F2
Johnson [Binghamton] NY 36 A3
Johnson [MNJ(MU)] NY 34 C2
Johnson WV 9 C3
Johnson Avenue [Brooklyn] NY 23 B3
Johnson City NY 36 A3
Johnsonburg NJ 17 C3
Johnsonburg NY 40 A4
Johnsonburg PA 56 C3
Johnsons OH 48 A4
Johnsonville NY 30 F3
Johnsonville [DLW] PA 16 B6
Johnsonville [LNE] PA 16 A6
Johnston Avenue [Jersey City] NJ 22 C5
Johnstown NY 30 C2
Johnstown PA 60 B1
Johnstown PA 64 A1
Johnsville PA 70 D2
Joint Stock Yard [Pittsburgh] PA 53 A2
Joller PA 60 E2
Jones MD 11 A4
Jones Hill MD 14 D4
Jones Mill PA 50 F2
Jones Point NY 26 B3
Jonestown PA 62 D4
Joppa MD 13 A3
Jordan NY 38 A2
Jordanville NY 38 F3
Josephine PA 57 A4
Josephtown PA 49 B3
Joyce MD 11 B4
JS [Deer Park] NY 35 C3
JS Tower [Van Courtlandt] NY 25 C4
JU [Bethlehem] PA 71 B4
JU Cabin [Swartswood Junction] NJ 16 A2
Judges Chambers PA 50 C2
Julian PA 57 E2
Juliustown NJ 18 D3
Jumbo Bridge NJ 6 F2
Junction Amesville Branch No.2 PA 58 B5
Junction Amesville Branch No.3 PA 58 B4
Junction Bear Run Branch PA 59 A4
Junction Beaver Branch PA 58 C5
Junction Betz Branch PA 58 A5
Junction Beulah Branch PA 58 B5
Junction Big Run Branch PA 58 C4
Junction Brady Run Branch PA 59 A5
Junction Burley Branch PA 58 B3
Junction Ednie Branch PA 58 C5
Junction Glen Campbell Branch PA 59 A6
Junction Goss Run Branch No.2 PA 58 B4
Junction Goss Run Branch No.3 PA 58 B4
Junction Graham Branch PA 58 D3
Junction Graham Branch No.2 PA 58 D3
Junction Horton Run Branch PA 59 A6
Junction Janesville Branch PA 58 A6
Junction Keister Branch PA 54 D5
Junction Lancaster Branch PA 66 A5
Junction Lantzy Branch PA 59 B5
Junction Leskie Branch PA 58 C5
Junction Little Muddy Run Branch PA 58 A5
Junction Luther Branch PA 59 C6
Junction Mapleton Branch No.1 PA 59 D4
Junction Mapleton Branch No.2 PA 58 D4
Junction Mapleton Branch No.3 PA 58 C4
Junction McCoys Run Branch PA 59 A5
Junction Morea Branch PA 67 B3
Junction Morewood Branch PA 55 C3
Junction Morgan Run Branch PA 58 B3
Junction Moshannon & Clearfield Branch PA 58 C4
Junction Muddy Run Branch PA 58 A5
Junction No.1 [Carnegie] PA 52 C3
Junction Osceola Branch PA 58 C4
Junction Paketa Branch PA 51 D4
Junction Patton No.1 Branch PA 59 D5
Junction Patton No.3 Branch PA 59 D5
Junction Patton No.4 Branch PA 59 D5
Junction Scoonmaker Branch PA 55 C3
Junction Scottdale Branch PA 55 D3
Junction Smoke Run Branch PA 58 A5
Junction Sterling Branch PA 59 C5
Junction Stevens Branch PA 57 C4
Junction Stonerville Branch PA 55 C3
Junction Tarr Branch PA 55 B2
Junction Trout Run Branch PA 58 C4
Junction Vulcan Branch PA 58 A5
Juneau PA 57 B2
Juniata PA 59 D1
Juniata Bridge PA 63 C1
Juniata Furnace PA 62 B4
Juniata Locomotive Shop [Altoona] PA 59 D1
Juniata Terminal [Philadelphia] PA 73 B3
Juniper [Philadelphia] PA 73 B4
Junius NY 40 E3
Jutland NJ 17 B4
JW [Johnstown] PA 64 A1

K

K Tower [Washington] DC 14 C4
K&T Industrial Track [Frankford] PA 73 B3
Kaaterskill NY 31 D2
Kaaterskill Junction NY 31 C2
Kaighns Point [Camden] NJ 73 B5
Kalb (DeKalb Junction) NY 36 E3
Kalb [Norristown] PA 72 C1
Kalurah NY 37 F1
Kamm PA 48 C2
Kane NY 37 C2
Kane PA 56 B2
Kanesholm PA 56 B2
Kanona NY 41 D2
Kanty PA 47 C6
Kapp PA 62 C2
Karen No.1 Mine PA 57 C3
Karner NY 32 E2
Karns PA 51 D3
Karns City PA 49 E2
Karter NY 37 E1
Karthaus PA 57 E1
Karthaus Tunnel PA 57 E1
Kase [Sunbury] PA 66 A6
Kasoag NY 37 C4
Kasson PA 56 C2
Kast Bridge NY 38 F2
Kato PA 57 E1
Katonah NY 34 F3
Kaufmann [BO] PA 50 F3
Kaufmann [PRR] PA 60 F3
Kaufmann Run PA 64 A3
Kaylor PA 49 E2
Kayuta NY 37 F4
KD Tower [Punxsutawney] PA 57 A2
Kean PA 56 D2
Keansburg NJ 18 E1
Kearney PA 60 D2
Kearny [CNJ] NJ 22 B5
Kearny [NS(ERIE)] NJ 22 B4
Kearny Junction NJ 22 B5
Keasbeys NJ 20 C3
Keating PA 56 E4
Keating Summit PA 56 D2
Keedysville MD 10 A2
Keefer PA 66 B6
Keenes NY 36 D4
Keeney's NY 31 B3
Keepawa NY 29 A2
Keeseville NY 28 F3
Keffers PA 62 E4
Kehley Run Junction PA 67 C2
Keim NJ 74 B5
Keisters PA 49 D2
Keller (Buckeyestown) MD 10 B2
Keller VA 15 B4
Kellettville PA 48 F3
Kelley PA 52 D3
Kellogg NY 46 B6
Kellogg PA 61 E2
Kellog's Industrial Track [Amsterdam] NY 30 C3
Kelly MD 12 B4
Kelly PA 51 F1
Kelly Island WV 9 F2
Kelly-Springfield MD 8 C2
Kellys NY 32 A3
Kelly's Corners NY 31 B2
Kelton PA 70 A4
Kemps MD 10 A1
Kempton PA 69 A3
Kempton Junction WV 9 A3
Kempton Mine MD 9 A3
Ken PA 60 F3
Kendala NY 40 F4
Kendall MD 9 A1
Kendall NY 40 B1
Kendall PA 52 B1
Kendall Grove VA 15 A6
Kendrick PA 58 B5
Kenilworth NJ 21 D6
Kenilworth PA 70 B2
Kenilworth WV 49 B4
Kenmore Yard NY 46 A3
Kennard PA 47 D1
Kennedy NJ 71 F3
Kennedy NY 43 D3
Kennedysville MD 11 C3
Kennerdell PA 48 D4
Kennerdell Tunnel PA 48 D4
Kennett Road [Wilmington] DE 6 D2
Kennett Square PA 6 B1
Kenneys PA 70 A2
Kenny Yard [Port Perry] PA 53 C3
Kensico Cemetary NY 26 D6
Kensington MD 10 C4
Kensington NY 23 B5
Kensington [Philadelphia] PA 73 B4
Kent NJ 71 E3
Kent PA 49 F4
Kent Avenue [Brooklyn] NY 23 B3
Kenton DE 7 A4
Kenvil NJ 17 A2
Kenwood NY 38 D2
Kenwood PA 51 C2
Kenwood Junction NY 32 E4
Kenwood Yard NY 32 E4
Keplers Mill PA 71 E2
Kepner PA 69 A3
Kepples Siding PA 51 D1
Kerhonkson NY 31 C4
Kerneysville WV 9 F2
Kernstown VA 9 E3
Kerrmoor PA 57 C2
Kerry NY 39 E3
Kershong NY 40 E4
Kesler Tunnel MD 9 D1
Keswick Grove NJ 18 E4
Ketner PA 56 C3
Keuka Mills NY 40 E4
Kew Gardens NY 23 D3
Key OH 50 A3
Keymar MD 10 C1
Keyport NJ 20 D4
Keyser PA 65 C1
Keyser WV 8 A6
Keyser Junction MD 8 A6
Keystone PA 60 A4
Keystone Cement [Bath] PA 71 B2
KG (Ashtabula) OH 48 A1
Kiamensi DE 6 C3
Kiefers MD 9 D2
Kier PA 55 A4
Kilbourne PA 56 F2
Kildare NY 28 B4
Killawog NY 39 C2
Kimberton PA 70 B2
Kimmel [BO(BRP)] PA 57 A3
Kimmel [EBT] PA 60 E2
Kimmelton PA 60 A2
Kinderhook NY 33 D3
King [NS(CR)] PA 63 B2
King [RJCP(PRR)] PA 57 C3
King [White Marsh Junction] PA 72 C1
King Manor PA 72 C2
King of Prussia PA 72 B2
Kings NY 30 D2
Kings ON 36 B4
Kings Bridge NY 25 C4
Kings Bridge Freight Station NY 25 C4
Kings Creek MD 15 B2
Kings Ferry NY 40 F4
Kings Highway [Brooklyn] NY 23 B5
Kings Mills PA 63 C1
Kings Park NY 35 C2
Kings Park State Hospital NY 35 D2
Kings Station NY 30 E2
Kingsbridge Road [Mount Vernon] NY 25 D4
Kingsdale PA 63 B4
Kingsland NJ 22 B3
Kingsland Junction NJ 22 B4
Kingsland Tunnel NJ 22 B4
Kingsley PA 68 A2
Kingston MD 15 B2
Kingston NJ 18 D2
Kingston NY 31 D4
Kingston NY 34 A3
Kingston ON 36 A4
Kingston [LIGV] PA 50 F1
Kingston [LS(DLW) LV] PA 65 B4
Kingston Point NY 34 B4
Kingston Tunnel NY 34 A4
Kingsville OH 48 A1
Kingsville PA 49 F1
Kingwood NJ 18 B1
Kinkora NJ 74 C4
Kinlock PA 51 D4
Kinslers NY 38 A3
Kinsman OH 48 A3
Kintigh Power Plant NY 42 F1
Kinzer PA 63 F3
Kinzua PA 56 B1
Kinzua Bridge PA 56 C2
Kinzua Junction PA 56 C1
Kinzua Viaduct PA 56 C2
Kipp's NY 27 C2
Kipp's Run PA 62 D2
Kirk (Kirkwood) DE 7 A2
Kirkham MD 11 C5
Kirkland PA 70 E4
Kirkville NY 38 C2
Kirkville Junction NY 38 C2
Kirkwood DE 7 A2
Kirkwood NJ 73 D6
Kirkwood NY 39 D3
Kishacoquillas PA 57 F3
Kisiner PA 63 E4
Kiski (Kiskiminetas Junction) PA 51 E2
Kiskiminetas Junction PA 51 E2
Kis-Lyn PA 62 F2
Kissena NY 23 D3
Kitchawan NY 26 D4
Kitner PA 57 B4
Kittaning PA 49 E3
Kittaning Point PA 59 B2
Kladder PA 60 C1
Klapperthall Junction PA 64 B6
Klawitter NY 43 E3
Kline PA 48 E4
Klineís Grove PA 66 B5
Klondike MD 8 A3
Knapps NY 28 A2
Knapps Creek NY 43 F3
Knapps Meadow MD 8 A3
Kneass PA 62 C3
Kneedler PA 70 C2
Knepper PA 63 A3
Knickerbocker PA 70 F4
Knobley Farm WV 9 B2
Knobley Tunnel [BO] WV 8 C3
Knobley Tunnel [CSXT(WM)] WV 8 D2
Knobmont Yard WV 8 C2
Knowlesville NY 40 A1
Knowlton [CPPA] PA 56 D2
Knowlton [PRR] PA 72 B6
Knox PA 48 E4
Knox Spur PA 48 F4
Knoxdale PA 57 A1
Knoxville MD 10 A2
Knoxville PA 61 A1
KO [Ronkonkoma] NY 35 D2
KO Junction PA 47 D1
Kobuta PA 49 B3
Kodak Park [Rochester] NY 44 B2
Kodak Distribution Center [Rochester] NY 44 B2
Koh-I-Moor Junction PA 67 A3
Konwenhoven NY 23 B5
Kopp [Koppel] PA 51 B3
Koppel PA 51 B4
Korb Siding PA 57 C2
Kortright Station NY 31 A1
Kraft PA 69 B4
Kratz PA 70 B1
Kreamer PA 62 C3
Krebs [PC(NYC)] PA 58 A2
Krebs [RDG] PA 67 B2
Kremis PA 48 C4
Krings PA 64 A2
Kriegbaum MD 8 C1
Krumrine PA 57 E3
Kulps PA 62 D3
Kunkletown PA 69 B2
Kushequa PA 56 C2
Kutztown PA 69 A4
KW [Secaucus] NJ 22 C5
KW Yard [Rockville] PA 64 C1
KY Junction [Kremis] PA 48 C4
Kyle NJ 20 E4
Kylers Corners PA 56 C4
Kyserike NY 31 C4

L

LA Cabin [Albany] NY 32 E4
La Grange NY 34 F1
La Jose PA 57 C3
La Jose Junction PA 57 B3
La Plata MD 10 D6
La Plume PA 68 A3
La Salle NY 46 A1
La Vale MD 8 C2
Lab [Rensselaer] NY 32 E4
Labelle PA 54 A5
Lace [Wallaceton] PA 58 C2
Lacey NJ 18 E4
Lacey (Laceyville) PA 61 F2
Lacey VA 14 A5
Laceyville PA 61 F2
Lack WV 50 C4
Lackawanna Plant [Bethlehem Steel] NY 46 B6
Lackawanna-South Park NY 46 B5
Lackawaxen PA 68 D3
Lacona NY 37 C3
Laddenburg PA 61 E3
Ladiesburg MD 10 C1
Lafargeville NY 36 C4
Lafayette [EL(DLW)] NJ 16 B2
Lafayette [LV] NJ 28 C5
Lafayette PA 56 B2
Lahaska PA 70 D1
Laird PA 49 E2
Lake MD 11 A2
Lake NY 27 C4
Lake (Lakewood) NY 43 C3
Lake [Columbia] PA 64 C6
Lake Ariel PA 68 C3
Lake Ariel Junction PA 68 C3
Lake Avenue [Arlington] NY 20 E1
Lake Avenue [Blasdell] NY 46 B6
Lake Bonaparte NY 37 E1
Lake Carey PA 61 F3
Lake City PA 47 B6
Lake Clear Junction NY 28 C4
Lake George NY 29 E4
Lake Grinnell NJ 16 C2
Lake Hopatcong [CNJ] NJ 17 A1
Lake Hopatcong [NJT] NJ 17 D3

Lake House NY 38 F3
Lake Junction NJ 17 A1
Lake Katrine NY 31 D3
Lake Kushaqua NY 28 D3
Lake Lynn PA 50 D4
Lake Mahopac NY 34 F2
Lake Placid NY 28 D4
Lake Ridge NY 39 A1
Lake Shore NY 40 E1
Lake View MD 10 B2
Lake View NJ 22 B2
Lake View NY 42 D4
Lakehurst NJ 18 E3
Lakehurst Naval Air Station NJ 18 E3
Lakemont NY 41 E1
Lakeview NY 24 B5
Lakeview PA 47 C6
Lakeview Power Plant NY 37 B4
Lakeville CT 31 F3
Lakeville NY 40 C3
Lakeville PA 48 D2
Lakewood NJ 18 E3
Lakewood NY 43 C3
Lakewood PA 68 C1
Lalor Street [Trenton] NJ 74 C3
Lamar PA 62 A2
Lambert PA 54 B6
Lambertville NJ 18 C2
Lamb's Creek PA 61 B2
Lambsons MD 11 D3
Lamington NJ 17 C4
Lamoke Mountain PA 61 D2
Lamokin PA 72 B6
Lamond DC 14 C3
Lanark Colliery 1 PA 58 C5
Lancashire No.25 Mine PA 59 C5
Lancaster [defect detector] NY 42 E3
Lancaster [DLWR(DLW)] NY 42 E3
Lancaster [NS(ERIE)] NY 46 D4
Lancaster PA 63 E2
Lancaster PA 64 D4
Lancaster Mines PA 66 A5
Lancaster Junction PA 63 E2
Land [Vineland] NJ 19 C2
Land [Lansdale] PA 70 C2
Landaff MD 11 C5
Landenberg PA 6 A2
Landenberg Junction DE 6 C3
Landia NY 24 D2
Landingville PA 67 C6
Landis [Vineland] NJ 19 C2
Landis PA 63 D1
Landisburg PA 63 B1
Landisville NJ 19 C2
Landisville PA 63 E2
Landith DE 6 E2
Landon PA 54 C3
Landover MD 14 D4
Landrus PA 61 B2
Landsdown NJ 17 C4
Landstreet PA 60 B2
Lane NJ 22 A6
Lane (Bierler's) PA 62 A1
Lane [CR(PRR)] PA 51 D2
Lane's Mills PA 56 B4
Lanesboro PA 68 B1
Lanesville NY 31 C3
Lang [Langhorne] PA 74 A3
Lang WV 50 A3
Langdondale PA 60 D2
Langeloth Mine PA 50 B1
Langdon DC 14 C4
Langdon MD 15 B2
Langdon [ERIE] PA 65 C3
Langdon [PRR] PA 47 C6
Langhorne [CSXT/SEPA(RDG)] PA 74 A4
Langhorne [NS(PRR)] PA 74 A3
Lanoka NJ 18 E4
Lansdale PA 70 C2
Lansdowne MD 12 B3
Lansdowne ON 36 C3
Lansdowne PA 72 D4
Lansford PA 66 C4
Lansing NY 38 A4
Lansingburg NY 32 F1
Lantzy PA 59 C5
Laona NY 43 C2
Lap MD 8 C1
Lapham's Mills NY 28 F3
Laporte PA 61 D4
Laquin PA 61 D3
Larabee PA 56 D1
Larchmont NY 25 E3
Lardin PA 50 D3
Large PA 53 B5
Larimer PA 50 E1
Larrabees Point VT 29 B4
Larry's Creek PA 61 B4
Larue PA 63 D4
Last Run Colliery No. 1 PA 59 A4
Latimer OH 48 A4
Latrobe PA 50 F1
Lattimer Mines PA 66 B1
Lauder MD 8 D5
Laughlin OH 49 B3
Laughlin Junction PA 53 B3
Laurel DE 7 E3
Laurel MD 10 D4
Laurel NY 35 B5
Laurel [MPA] PA 63 D4
Laurel [Reading] PA 64 A4
Laurel Brook MD 11 B2
Laurel Hill [CSXT(RDG)] PA 73 A3
Laurel Hill [PRR] PA 55 A6
Laurel House NY 31 D2
Laurel Junction PA 67 D2
Laurel Race Track MD 10 D4
Laurel Run PA 65 C5
Laurel Run [defect detector] PA 65 C6
Laurel Run #2 Mine PA 57 C4
Laurel Springs NJ 73 D6
Laurel Summit PA 60 A2
Laurelton NY 24 A5
Laurens NY 39 F1
Laurys PA 69 F4
Lavallette NJ 18 F3
Lavenia PA 55 A4
Laverock PA 73 A2
Lawn [NS(RDG)] PA 64 A6
Lawn [PC(PRR)] PA 63 D2
Lawn View PA 56 D3
Lawndale PA 73 B2
Lawrence NJ 74 D1
Lawrence NY 24 A6
Lawrence Junction PA 51 B1
Lawrenceville NJ 74 D1
Lawrenceville [CKMR] NY 31 D2
Lawrenceville [WCOR(NYC/ERIE)] NY 41 E3
Lawsonham PA 49 E2
Lawtons NY 43 D1
Layton PA 55 A4
Le Búuf PA 48 D1
Le Enfant DC 14 C5
Le Gore MD 10 C1
Le Roy NY 45 D1
Lead [Island Park] NY 24 B6
Leadenhall Street [Baltimore] MD 12 B3
Leahigh MD 12 A1
Leahigh Yard MD 12 A1
Leak Run PA 53 D2
Leaman PA 63 F3
Leaman Place PA 63 F3
Leaming NJ 19 D4
Leatherwood PA 49 F2
Lebanon NJ 17 C4
Lebanon NY 38 D4
Lebanon PA 63 E1
Lebanon Center NY 31 F1
Lebanon Springs NY 31 F1
Lecato (Oak Hall) VA 15 C3
Leckrone PA 50 D3
Ledgewood NJ 17 D3
Lee PA 62 F1
Leech [Leechburg] PA 51 F3
Leechburg PA 51 F3
Leeds NY 33 A5
Leeds ON 36 C4
Leeland MD 11 A5
Lee's NY 30 F3
Lees Crossroads PA 63 A2
Leesburg NJ 19 C3
Leesburg PA 49 C1
Leesburg VA 10 B3
Leesport PA 62 F4
Leetonia OH 49 A2
Leets (Leetsdale) PA 49 C4
Leetsdale PA 49 C4
Lefevre PA 63 B4
Leflin PA 65 C4
Lehigh Gap PA 69 E2
Lehigh Valley Junction NY 40 F3
Lehighton [CNJ] PA 69 E1
Lehighton [NS-RBMN(LV)] PA 69 F1
Lehmasters PA 60 E3
Leibigs Lane NJ 20 D2
Leicester NY 40 B4
Leith PA 50 E3
Leland No.10 Mine PA 58 B6
Lemont PA 57 F3
Lemont Furnace PA 50 E3
Lemoyne [PC(PRR)] PA 64 C2
Lemoyne [RDG] PA 64 C3
Lenape PA 70 B3
Lenhartsville PA 69 A4
Lenkers PA 62 C4
Lenni PA 72 A5
Lennig NJ 19 E4
Lenola NJ 73 D4
Lenover PA 63 F3
Lentz MD 10 B1
Leola PA 63 F2
Leolyn PA 61 C3
Leon OH 48 B2
Leonard PA 58 A1
Leonardo NJ 18 F1
Leonard's Grove PA 60 F1
Leonardsville NY 38 E3
Leonia NJ 22 D2
Lerchs PA 71 B2
Leslie MD 11 C1
Leslie Run PA 69 A2
Lester PA 72 D6
Letterkenny Army Depot PA 60 F3
Levanna NY 40 F4
Levans Mill PA 64 D5
Leviston PA 66 B2
Levittown-Tullytown PA 74 B4
Lewes DE 7 F2
Lewis [Lewistown] PA 57 F4
Lewis Run [BRP] PA 56 C1
Lewis Run [BWP] PA 56 C1
Lewis Run [E&RV] PA 56 D3
Lewis Run [ERIE] PA 56 C1
Lewis Run Junction PA 52 D3
Lewisburg NJ 17 D2
Lewisburg PA 62 C2
Lewisburg Penitentiary PA 62 C2
Lewiston NY 42 B2
Lewiston Freight Station NY 42 B2
Lewistown MD 10 B1
Lewistown NJ 18 D3
Lewistown PA 57 F4
Liberty NY 31 A4
Liberty PA 56 D2
Liberty Corners NY 34 C3
Liberty Grove MD 13 A1
Liberty/Park Terminal [Baltimore] MD 12 B2
Library PA 53 A5
Library Junction PA 52 D5
Lick Island PA 56 E4
Light [Trenton] NJ 74 C3
Light Street PA 62 E2
Ligonier PA 50 F2
Liller Run WV 9 B2
Lilly PA 59 A3
Lilly Coal Mine PA 59 A3
Lilly Run Branch Junction PA 54 B5
Lily Dale NY 43 C2
Lima NY 40 C3
Lime Bluff PA 61 D4
Lime Kiln MD 10 B2
Lime Lake NY 43 F1
Lime Ridge PA 62 E2
Lime Rock CT 31 F4
Lime Rock NY 45 E1
Lime Rock PA 63 E2
Limecrest NJ 16 B2
Limerick NY 37 C1
Limerick PA 70 B2
Limestone NY 43 E3
Limestone PA 49 F1
Limestone WV 8 A6
Limestone Tipple PA 49 E3
Linchester MD 11 D5
Lincoln MD 10 D4
Lincoln NJ 20 B2
Lincoln NY 25 C4
Lincoln City DE 7 E2
Lincoln Colliery PA 62 E4
Lincoln Hill PA 50 C2
Lincoln Park NJ 21 C1
Lincoln Park NY 44 B3
Lincoln University PA 70 A4
Lincolndale NY 34 F3
Lincolnville PA 48 D2
Linden NJ 20 D1
Linden NY 45 A3
Linden PA 61 B4
Linden VA 9 F4
Linden Hall PA 57 F3
Linden Junction NJ 20 D1
Linden Street [Allentown] PA 71 A4
Lindenhurst NY 35 C3
Lindenwold NJ 73 D6
Linder PA 66 A4
Lindley NY 41 E3
Lindley PA 73 B3
Lindsey PA 57 A2
Lineboro MD 10 D1
Linesville PA 48 B2
Linfield PA 70 B2
Link PA 70 C1
Link Belt PA 70 C1
Linkwood MD 11 D6
Linn PA 54 C4
Linndale PA 62 B2
Linntown PA 62 C2
Linore PA 56 D3
Linthicum MD 12 B4
Linwood MD 10 C1
Linwood NJ 19 D2
Linwood NY 45 D3
Lion Fine Coal Plant [Hazleton] PA 66 B1
Lisbon NY 36 E2
Lisbon OH 49 A3
Lisle NY 39 C2
Lister Avenue [Newark] NJ 22 B5
Listie PA 60 A3
Litchfield NY 39 A3
Lititz PA 63 E2
Little Britain NY 27 E1
Little Cacapon WV 9 D2
Little Falls NJ 21 D2
Little Falls NY 30 A2
Little Ferry NJ 22 C3
Little Ferry Junction NJ 22 C3
Little Ferry Yard NJ 22 C3
Little Gap PA 69 B3
Little Genesee NY 41 A3
Little Neck NY 24 A3
Little Orleans MD 9 E1
Little Rapids NY 29 A2
Little Run Junction PA 69 E3
Little Silver NJ 18 F2
Little Valley NY 43 E2
Little York NY 38 B4
Littlestown PA 63 B4
Littleton WV 50 B4
Liveright PA 58 A1
Livermore PA 49 F4
Liverpool NY 38 B2
Liverpool PA 62 C4
Livingston NY 22 B6
Livingston Manor NY 31 A4
Livonia NY 40 C3
Lizard Creek Junction PA 69 D2
Llanerch PA 72 C4
Llanfair PA 60 B1
Llewellyn NJ 21 D4
Llewellyn Crossing PA 67 A5
Lloyd MD 11 A4
Lloyd NJ 18 E1
Lloydell PA 60 B1
Lloydville PA 57 C3
Lobb No.1 Mine PA 58 B4
Loch Lomond Junction PA 58 D3
Loch Raven MD 11 A2
Lock Haven PA 62 A1
Lock No.3 [Monongahela River] PA 53 B6
Locke NY 38 A4
Locke Valley PA 60 E2
Lockport NY 42 E2
Lockport [CNJ] PA 69 F3
Lockport [PRR] PA 60 A1
Lockport Junction NY 42 E2
Locksley PA 72 A5
Lockwood NY 39 A3
Lockwood OH 48 A3
Locust [Locust Valley] NY 24 C1
Locust [NS(BRP)] PA 57 A2
Locust [Philadelphia] PA 73 A4
Locust Gap PA 66 B5
Locust Gap Junction PA 66 B5
Locust Grove MD 10 B2
Locust Grove NJ 73 D5
Locust Manor NY 23 D4
Locust Point [Baltimore] MD 12 C3
Locust Summit PA 66 C5
Locust Valley NY 24 C1
Locustdale PA 66 C5
Lodi NJ 22 B2
Lodi NY 40 F4
Lodi Junction NJ 22 C2
Logan PA 73 B3
Logan's Ferry PA 53 D1
Logansport PA 51 F1
Loganton PA 62 B2
Lofty PA 67 D2
Lofty Tunnel PA 67 D2
Loleta PA 56 A4
Lonaconing MD 8 A3
Lonaconing Junction MD 8 A3
Lonaconing Junction Mine MD 8 A3
Lone Star Cement [Nazareth] PA 71 C2
Loner Siding MD 9 E1
Long [Lewistown] PA 57 F4
Long Beach NY 24 B6
Long Branch NJ 18 F2
Long Bridge [Washington] DC 14 B5
Long Bridge NJ 17 C3
Long Bridge PA 50 F1
Long Eddy NY 39 F4
Long Green MD 11 B2
Long Island City NY 23 B3
Long Point VA 15 C3
Long Valley NJ 17 C3
Long Valley PA 61 D2
Long Valley Station PA 61 D2
Longacre PA 69 A3
Longbrook PA 61 D4
Longfellow PA 57 F4
Longport NJ 19 E4
Longsdorf PA 63 A2
Longview PA 53 A4
Loomis Park PA 65 A6
Loon Lake NY 28 D3
Loop PA 59 D3
Loop Run PA 57 E1
Lopez PA 61 E3
Lorane PA 64 B6
Lorberry Junction PA 62 E4
Lordville NY 39 F4
Loreley MD 11 B2
Loretto MD 15 B2
Lorraine NJ 21 D6
Lorreto Road PA 57 C4
Lorton VA 10 C5
Losh's Run PA 62 C4
Lost Creek PA 67 A3
Lothair MD 14 B1
Lottsville PA 48 F1
Lotus PA 52 B2
Louderville WV 50 B3
Loudon Park MD 12 B3
Lounsberry NY 39 B3
Love Point MD 11 B4
Lovell PA 48 E1
Lovett PA 60 B1
Low Phos PA 54 C6
Low Phos Branch Junction PA 54 C6
Lowber PA 53 D6
Lowellville OH 49 B2
Lower Askem PA 65 A6
Lower Hackensack NJ 22 C5
Lower Hillville PA 49 E2
Lower Jamesburg NJ 18 D2
Lower Squankum NJ 18 E3
Lower St. Clair PA 67 B5
Lowerne NY 25 C4
Lowman NY 41 F3
Lownders (Renix) MD 8 B4
Lowville NY 37 E3
Loyalhanna No.6 Mine PA 60 B2
Loyalsock PA 61 C4
Loyalton PA 62 D4
Loyer MD 10 B2
Loy's MD 10 B1
Loysville PA 63 A1
LTV Coke Ovens [Pittsburgh] PA 53 B3
Lucas PA 53 B3
Lucaston NJ 18 B4
Lucasville PA 49 D2
Lucerne Junction PA 57 A4
Lucerne Mines PA 57 A4
Lucinda PA 48 F4
Luciusboro PA 57 A4

Luckett PA 59 A3
Lucknow PA 64 C1
Ludlam Street [Sea Isle City] NJ 19 D4
Ludlow NJ 17 B4
Ludlow NY 25 C3
Ludlow PA 56 B2
Ludlowville NY 39 A1
Luellen PA 50 C2
Luke MD 8 C6
Lum [Columbiana] OH 49 A2
Lumber PA 57 C2
Lumberton NJ 18 C3
Lundlines NY 37 F1
Lurgan PA 63 A2
Lushbaugh PA 56 E3
Luthersburg PA 57 B1
Lutherville MD 11 A2
Lutzville PA 60 C3
Luzerne [LV] PA 65 B4
Luzerne [MGA] PA 54 A5
Luzon NY 31 B4
LV [Lovett] PA 60 B1
Lycoming NY 37 B4
Lykens PA 62 D4
Lykens Steel [Swedeland] PA 72 C2
Lyman Run PA 56 F2
Lyman's Mill PA 56 E3
Lyn ON 36 D3
Lyn Junction ON 36 D3
Lynbrook NY 24 B5
Lynces Junction PA 48 B3
Lynch MD 11 C3
Lynch PA 56 A3
Lyndall PA 70 A2
Lyndhurst NJ 22 B3
Lyndhurst Draw NJ 22 B3
Lyndonville NY 42 F1
Lyon Mountain NY 28 D2
Lyons NJ 17 D4
Lyons NY 40 E2
Lyons PA 69 A4
Lyons Falls NY 37 E3
Lyons Junction NY 40 E2
Lyons' Siding NJ 17 D4
Lynn [LV] PA 61 F2
Lynn [Roslyn] PA 73 B1
Lynnport PA 69 A3
Lystra MD 11 A2
Lytle PA 67 A5

M

M&H Junction
(Penn Haven Junction) PA 69 A2
MA [Woodbourne] PA 74 B3
Macedon NY 40 D2
Machias NY 43 F2
Machipongo VA 15 A5
Mackeyville PA 62 A2
Maclay Street [Harrisburg] PA 64 C2
Macopin NJ 17 D2
Macungie PA 69 B4
Madawaska NY 28 C3
Madeira Hill PA 59 A4
Madera PA 58 A5
Madge PA 56 B3
Madison NJ 21 B4
Madison Street [Troy] NY 32 F2
Madley PA 60 B3
Madrid NY 36 F2
Magee PA 48 F2
Magnolia MD 13 A4
Magnolia NJ 73 C6
Magnolia WV 9 D1
Mahaffey PA 57 B2
Mahaffey [RJCP(NYC)] PA 59 B4
Mahaffey [PRR] PA 59 B5
Mahaffey Junction PA 59 B5
Mahanoy PA 62 B4
Mahanoy City PA 67 B3
Mahanoy Plane PA 67 A3
Mahanoy Tunnel Station PA 67 C3
Mahantango PA 62 C4
Maher #4 Mine PA 51 F3
Mahoning [CR(PRR)] PA 47 D3
Mahoning [PSR(PS)] PA 47 D4
Mahoningtown [BO] PA 51 A1
Mahoningtown [PLE] PA 51 B1
Mahoningtown [PRR] PA 51 B1
Mahoning PA 49 F2
Mahopac NY 34 F2
Mahopac Falls NY 34 F2
Mahopac Mines NY 34 F2
Mahwah NJ 17 E2
Maiden Creek PA 69 A4
Maidsville WV 50 D4
Main Avenue [Vineland] NJ 19 C2
Main Street [Buffalo ERIE] NY 46 B3
Main Street [Buffalo INT] NY 46 A4
Main Street [Buffalo NYC] NY 46 B3
Main Street [Watertown] NY 37 C2
Main Street [Lewistown] PA 57 F4
Main Street [Norristown] PA 72 C1
Main Street [Wilkes Barre] PA 65 B5
Main Street Station [Rochester] NY 44 C3
Mainville PA 62 E2
Maitland ON 36 D2
Maitland PA 62 A3
Maizeville PA 67 A3
Malaga NJ 19 C2
Malba NY 23 D2
Malden-on-Hudson NY 31 D3
Mallory NY 38 C1
Mallorytown ON 36 C3
Malone NY 28 C1
Malone Junction NY 28 C1
Maltby NJ 19 D3
Maltby PA 65 B4
Maltby Colliery PA 65 B4
Malvern PA 70 F4
Malverne NY 24 B5
Mamakating NY 34 C1
Mamaroneck NY 25 E3
Mamaroneck Avenue
White Plains] NY 25 E1
Mammoth PA 55 D2
Man NJ 18 C4
Man PA 50 C3
Manahawkin NJ 19 E1
Manasquan NJ 18 F3
Manayunk PA 72 D3
Manayunk East PA 72 D3
Mance PA 60 B3
Manchester NY 40 D3
Manchester Bridge NY 34 E1
Manhasset NY 24 B2
Manhasset Viaduct NY 24 B3
Manhattan PA 61 A2
Manhattan Beach NY 23 B6
Manhattan Beach Junction NY 23 B5
Manhattan Transfer NJ 22 B5
Manhattanville Yard NY 23 B1
Manheim [defect detector] NY 30 A2
Manheim PA 63 E2
Manilla PA 60 A4
Manitou NY 26 B2
Manlius NY 38 C3
Mann OH 48 A3
Mannington NJ 19 A1
Manns Choice PA 60 C3
Mannville NY 37 C3
Manor [NS(PRR)
Lancaster County] PA 64 C6
Manor [PRR
Westmoreland County] PA 50 E1
Manorville NY 35 A6
Manorville PA 49 E3
Manown PA 54 B1
Mansel PA 60 D1
Mansfield PA 61 B2
Mansfield Street [Belvidere] NJ 17 B3
Mantoloking NJ 18 F3
Mantua Terminal [Thorofare] NJ 73 A6
Manumuskin NJ 19 C3
Manunka Chunk NJ 16 C6
Manunka Chunk Tunnel NJ 16 C6
Manver PA 57 B3
Manville NJ 20 E4
Mapes NY 41 B3
Maple NJ 22 B1
Maple NY 38 B1
Maple PA 54 B2
Maple Creek Mine PA 54 B1
Maple Grove MD 10 D1
Maple Shade NJ 73 D4
Maple Springs NY 43 C3
Maple View NY 37 B4
Mapleton [CNYS} NY 38 A3
Mapleton [NYC] NY 42 E2
Mapleton PA 60 E1
Mapleton No.5 Mine PA 58 D4
Mapleville MD 10 A1
Maplewood NJ 21 D5
Maplewood NY 44 B4
Maplewood PA 68 B3
Mar (Martin) PA 50 D4
Marathon NY 39 C1
Marble Hill NY 25 C4
Marbletown NY 40 E2
Marcellus NY 38 B3
March [defect detector] OH 48 A2
Marcus Hook PA 6 F1
Marcy NY 38 E2
Mardela Springs MD 11 D6
Marengo PA 57 E3
Margaret PA 49 F3
Margaretville NY 31 B3
Margate City NJ 19 E4
Marguerite PA 55 D1
Maria Furnace PA 63 A4
Marianna PA 50 C3
Marienville PA 56 A3
Marietta PA 63 D2
Marietta Industrial Track PA 63 D2
Marietta Junction PA 64 D5
Marietto NY 38 B3
Marilla NY 42 F3
Mariner's Harbor NY 20 E1
Marion MD 15 B2
Marion [Jersey City] NJ 22 C5
Marion NY 40 E2
Marion PA 60 F3
Marion Center PA 57 A3
Mark [Philadelphia] PA 73 B4
Market East [Philadelphia] PA 73 B4
Markham VA 9 F4
Markhams NY 43 D2
Marklesburg PA 60 D1
Markleton PA 50 F3
Marksboro NJ 17 C3
Markwood WV 9 B2
Marlboro MD 11 A5
Marlboro NJ 18 E2
Marlborough NY 34 E1
Marley MD 11 A3
Marlton NJ 18 C4
Marquis OH 49 A2
Marr MD 10 D5
Marriottsville MD 10 D2
Mars PA 49 D3
Mars Hill PA 63 F3
Marsh Creek PA 61 A2
Marsh Hill Junction PA 61 C3
Marsh Run PA 64 D3
Marshall WV 50 A4
Marshall Mine PA 52 B2
Marshallton DE 6 C3
Marshburg PA 56 B1
Marshland PA 61 A2
Marshville NY 36 F3
Martensia NY 40 D3
Martha [Manhattan] NY 23 B1
Martha PA 57 E3
Martic Forge PA 63 E3
Martin [CSAO(MGA)] PA 50 D4
Martin [PRR] PA 63 C3
Martin Airport MD 12 E1
Martindale NY 31 E2
Martindale PA 60 C1
Martins NJ 19 E1
Martins Creek NJ 71 E1
Martins Creek Junction PA 69 C3
Martins Ferry OH 50 A2
Martins Siding VA 15 A5
Martinsburg NY 37 E3
Martinsburg PA 60 D1
Martinsburg WV 9 F2
Martinsburg Junction PA 60 D1
Martinsville NY 46 B1
Martisco NY 38 B2
Martville NY 38 A1
Marvindale PA 56 C2
Marwood PA 49 D3
Marydel MD 11 D3
Maryland NY 30 A4
Maryland Junction WV 8 D2
Marysville PA 64 C1
Mason MD 10 D6
Mason-Dixon PA 60 F4
Masontown PA 50 D3
Masonville NJ 18 C3
Maspeth NY 23 B3
Massapequa NY 35 C3
Massapequa Park NY 35 C3
Massena NY 28 A1
Massey MD 11 D3
Massey NY 37 C2
Mast Hope [defect detector] PA 68 D3
Masten PA 61 C3
Mastic NY 35 A6
Mastic-Shirley NY 35 A6
Mat (Mather) PA 50 C3
Matawan NJ 18 E1
Mather PA 50 C3
Mathies Mine PA 53 A6
Matsonford (Conshohocken Road) PA 72 C2
Mattawana (McVeytown) PA 57 F4
Mattawoman MD 10 D6
Matteawan NY 26 C1
Mattern PA 57 E3
Mattern Junction PA 57 E3
Matthew's Summit PA 60 D1
Mattituck NY 35 B5
Mauch Chunk PA 69 E1
Mauch Chunk Junction PA 67 D2
Maugansville MD 10 A1
Mauk PA 57 A2
Maurertown VA 9 D4
Maurice River NJ 19 C3
Mauricetown NJ 19 C3
Mausdale PA 62 D2
Maxim (Lower Squankum) NJ 18 E3
Maxon Road [Schenectady] NY 32 C2
Maxwell PA 54 A5
May NJ 19 C1
Maybrook NY 27 D1
Mayburg PA 48 F3
Mayes PA 57 C3
Mayetta NJ 19 E1
Mayfield NY 30 C2
Mayfield PA 68 B3
Mayport PA 49 F2
Mays Landing NJ 19 D2
Mays Mills NY 40 E4
Mayview PA 52 C5
Mayville NY 43 B2
Maywood NJ 22 C2
Maywood NY 39 E2
MC (Martins Creek Junction) PA 69 C3
McAbee PA 53 D1
McAdams PA 52 A4
McAdoo PA 66 A2
McAfee NJ 17 D2
McAuley PA 62 E2
McBride PA 49 D3
McCalls PA 63 E3
McCalls Ferry PA 63 E3
McCalmont PA 56 A2
McCarthy MD 10 D4
McCartney PA 57 C3
McClainville OH 50 A3
McClintock PA 48 E3
McClure PA 62 B3
McConnellstown PA 57 E4
McConnellsville NY 38 D1
McCoole MD 8 A6
McCormick Road [Hunt Valley] MD 11 A2
McCoy PA 56 F3
McCracken PA 50 C2
McCulloch PA 60 F3
McDaniel MD 11 B5
McDonald NY 28 C3
McDonald PA 52 A4
McDonald Mine PA 52 A4
McDonalds "Y" PA 48 F3
McDonaldton PA 60 B3
McDonogh MD 11 A2
McDougall NY 40 F3
McElhatten PA 62 A1
McEwansville PA 62 C1
McGareys PA 57 A1
McGarveys PA 59 C2
McGees PA 59 B4
McGinnis MD 10 D1
McGraw NY 39 C1
McGraw Yard [Rahway] NJ 20 C1
McGraws NY 41 C3
McGuire Air Force Base NJ 18 D3
McGurgin Tunnel PA 50 B1
McIntyre NY 31 E4
McIntyre PA 49 F4
McKean PA 51 E3
McKeansburg PA 67 D6
McKee PA 60 C1
McKee City NJ 19 D2
McKees Rocks PA 52 D2
McKeesport PA 53 C4
McKeever NY 37 F3
McKeages PA 57 B3
McKelvey Siding PA 60 A2
McKenzie MD 8 C3
McKenzie Collieries 1 & 2 PA 58 B5
McKinley PA 56 B3
McKinney PA 61 C4
McKinney NY 39 A1
McKnightstown PA 63 B3
McLaughlin PA 53 D2
McLean NY 39 B1
McLeans PA 70 B1
McMechan WV 50 A3
McMinns Summit PA 57 B1
McMurray PA 52 D5
McNeill WV 9 C3
McPherson MD 11 A3
McSherry PA 63 C4
McVey PA 57 F4
McVeytown PA 57 F4
McWilliams PA 49 F2
MDTA Shops (Leahigh Yard) MD 12 A1
Meadow Brook NY 27 F2
Meadow Brook Colliery PA 58 C3
Meadow Lands PA 50 C2
Meadowbrook NY 24 C4
Meadowbrook PA 73 B1
Meadows NJ 22 B5
Meadows Maintenance Center
[Kearny] NJ 22 B5
Meadows Yard [Frankford] PA 73 C3
Meadville PA 48 C3
Meadville Junction PA 48 B3
Meadville Yard PA 48 C3
Mears VA 15 B3
Mechanics Grove PA 63 F3
Mechanicsburg PA 63 C2
Mechanicsville MD 14 C1
Mechanicville NY 30 E3
Medford MD 10 C1
Medford NJ 18 C4
Medford NY 35 D2
Medford Junction NJ 18 C3
Media PA 72 B5
Medina NY 42 F2
Medix Run PA 56 D4
Medo (Big Meadow Run) PA 54 B5
Mehoopany PA 61 F3
Meiser PA 62 C3
Melcroft PA 50 F2
Melfa VA 15 B4
Mellenville NY 33 D5
Mellinger PA 63 E3
Melrea PA 52 B2
Melrose MD 10 D1
Melrose NJ 18 C4
Melrose [BM] NY 30 E3
Melrose [MNC(NYC)] NY 23 C1
Melrose PA 60 D2
Melrose Junction NY 23 C1
Melrose Park PA 73 B2
Melsena Colliery PA 59 A5
Melvale MD 12 B1
Memphis NY 38 B2
Menands NY 32 E3
Menantico NJ 19 C2
Mendenhall PA 70 B3
Mendham NJ 17 D4
Mendon NY 44 D5
Menges Mill PA 63 C3
Menlo (Menlo Park) NJ 20 C2
Menlo Park NJ 20 C2
Meno NY 28 C3
Mensch PA 62 D2
Menzies PA 57 F3
Mercer PA 48 C4
Mercer Junction PA 48 C4
Mercer Pike PA 48 C3
Mercer Road PA 49 D2
Mercersburg PA 60 E3
Mercersburg Junction PA 60 E3
Merchantville NJ 73 C4
Meredith PA 57 B1
Merharg PA 49 D3
Merillion Avenue [Mineola] NY 24 B4
Merion PA 72 D3
Merrick NY 24 D5
Merrickville NY 39 F2
Merrifield NY 38 A4
Merrill [PRR] PA 49 B3
Merrill [PSN] PA 56 C4

Merriman NY 28 F4
Merritt 7 CT 35 C1
Merrittstown PA 54 C5
Mertztown PA 69 B4
Meshoppen PA 61 F3
Messengerville NY 39 C1
Messick DE 7 E3
Messmore PA 50 D3
Mesta PA 53 B3
Metal Service Plant [Apollo] PA 51 F4
Metcalf NY 38 A1
Metcalf PA 51 D3
Met-Edison Power Plant [Portland] PA 16 C5
Metro Park NJ 20 C2
Metropolitan Avenue [Maspeth] NY 23 B3
Metropolitan Freight Station [Elizabeth] NJ 22 A6
Metropolitan Grove MD 10 C3
Mettler NJ 18 D1
Metuchen NJ 20 B2
Mexico MD 8 D3
Mexico NY 37 B4
Mexico PA 62 A4
Meyer Road [West Seneca] NY 46 C5
Meyers MD 11 A4
Meyersdale PA 60 A4
MG Tower PA 59 C2
MHMRR Junction [Wharton] NJ 17 A1
Mickleton NJ 18 A4
Mickleys PA 71 A3
Mid Penn Mine PA 58 A5
Middle Creek PA 60 A3
Middle Granville NY 29 F4
Middle Falls NY 30 E2
Middle Lehigh Colliery PA 67 C3
Middle River MD 12 E1
Middle Run Junction PA 50 D3
Middle Tunnel NY 26 B2
Middle Valley NJ 17 C4
Middleburg MD 10 C1
Middleburg NY 30 C4
Middleburg PA 62 C3
Middlebury PA 61 B2
Middlebush NJ 18 D1
Middleport NY 42 F2
Middleport PA 67 C4
Middlesex NJ 20 F4
Middlesx NY 40 D4
Middlesex PA 63 B2
Middletown DE 7 A3
Middletown MD 10 B2
Middletown [NJT(NYLB)] NJ 18 E1
Middletown [PRSL(AC)] NJ 19 D3
Middletown NY 34 C2
Middletown [ERIE MNJ OW] NY 27 A2
Middletown [MNC] NY 27 B1
Middletown PA 63 D2
Middletown VA 9 E4
Middleville NY 38 F2
Midland MD 8 A3
Midland [Beaver County] PA 49 B3
Midland [Washington County] PA 52 B6
Midland Park NJ 17 E3
Midlothian MD 8 A2
Midlothian Junction MD 8 A2
Midsteel [Midland] PA 49 B3
Midvale NJ 17 E2
Midvale [CSAO(PRR)] PA 73 A3
Midvale [LWV] PA 65 C4
Midvale [WM] PA 63 A4
Midvale Colliery [Goss Run] PA 58 B4
Midvale Colliery [McCartney] PA 57 C3
Midway [Monmouth Junction] NJ 18 D2
Midway [NS(PRR)] PA 63 E4
Midway [PC(PRR)] PA 52 A4
Midway [RDG(COR)] PA 63 E1
Mifflin PA 62 A4
Mifflin Crossroads PA 62 E2
Mifflin Junction PA 53 B4
Mifflin Mine No.2 PA 53 C4
Mifflinsburg PA 62 C2
Mifflinville PA 62 E2
Milan PA 61 D1
Mildred PA 61 E3
Milesburg PA 57 F2
Milesville PA 54 C1
Milford DE 7 E2
Milford NJ 18 B1
Milford NY 30 A4
Milford Mill MD 12 A1
Military Ocean Terminal [Bayonne] NJ 22 B6
Mill DE 7 F3
Mill [Camden] NJ 73 B5
Mill (Lansing) NY 39 A1
Mill Creek [BO(BRP)] PA 56 B4
Mill Creek [defect detector] PA 57 E4
Mill Creek [EL(ERIE)] PA 61 B1
Mill Creek Junction PA 67 B5
Mill Hall PA 62 A1
Mill Hall Junction PA 62 A1
Mill Haven PA 56 B4
Mill Neck NY 24 D1
Mill Rift PA 68 E4
Mill Rock OH 49 B3
Mill Village PA 48 D1
Millards PA 63 D1
Millbank PA 50 F1
Millbourne Mills PA 72 D4
Millbrook NY 31 E4
Millburn NJ 21 C5
Millen WV 9 D2
Miller WV 9 F1
Miller Farm PA 48 E3
Miller Place NY 35 D2
Miller Run PA 60 B2
Miller's MD 10 D1
Millers NY 42 F1
Millers [EL(ERIE)] PA 48 D2
Millers [LNE LV] PA 69 A3
Millers Mills NY 38 F3
Millersburg PA 62 C4
Millerstown PA 62 B4
Millersville MD 11 A4
Millerton PA 61 C1
Milleson WV 9 C2
Millham Junction NJ 74 D2
Millham Yard NJ 74 D2
Milliken Power Plant (Lake Ridge) NY 39 A1
Millikens PA 58 C1
Millington MD 11 D3
Millington NJ 17 D4
Millmont [BO] PA 72 C6
Millmont [PRR] PA 62 B2
Millport NY 41 F2
Millport PA 56 D1
Mills PA 56 F1
Millsboro DE 7 F3
Millsboro PA 54 A5
Millstone Junction NJ 20 A3
Milltown NJ 20 A4
Milltown PA 53 D1
Millvale Yard [Pittsburgh] PA 53 A2
Millville NJ 19 C2
Millville PA 62 D1
Millville WV 10 A3
Millway PA 63 E2
Millwood NY 26 D4
Millwood PA 50 F1
Milmay NJ 19 C2
Milnersville PA 66 A1
Milnor PA 60 F4
Milo NY 40 E4
Milo Mills NY 40 E4
Milroy PA 57 F3
Milton DE 7 E2
Milton NY 34 E1
Milton PA 62 C2
Milton Interchange PA 62 C2
Mina PA 56 E2
Mine 1&2 [Cooleys] PA 53 A4
Mine 3 [Bennicoal] PA 52 D4
Mine 4 [Horning] PA 53 A4
Mine 5 [Horning] PA 53 A4
Mine 6 [Bruceton] PA 53 A5
Mine Brook NJ 17 D4
Mine Hill NJ 16 D1
Mine Hill Gap PA 67 A5
Mine No.8 PA 52 D5
Minefield MD 11 B1
Mineola NY 24 B4
Mineral WV 8 A6
Mineral Point PA 60 B1
Mineral Spring Yard [Buffalo] NY 46 B5
Mineral Spring PA 58 B1
Miners Mills PA 65 C4
Miners Village PA 63 E1
Minersville [CBL] PA 64 A1
Minersville [PRR] PA 67 A5
Minersville [RBMN(RDG)] PA 67 A5
Minetto NY 37 A4
Mineville NY 29 E1
Mingo PA 70 F1
Mingo Junction OH 50 A1
Minnehaha NY 37 F3
Minnequa PA 61 C2
Minnick MD 13 D1
Minnowbrook NY 29 A3
Minoa NY 36 D1
Minooka PA 65 C2
Minooka Junction PA 65 C2
Minotola NJ 19 C2
Minson NJ 73 C4
Mintzers PA 67 D3
Miquon PA 72 D2
Mirrer Transfer Yard [Passaic Junction] NJ 22 B2
Mitchell Field NY 24 C4
Mitzpah NJ 19 C2
Mix Run PA 56 D4
MJ [Florence] NJ 74 C5
M-K Locomotive Shops [Mountaintop] PA 69 A1
MO [Cresson] PA 59 A2
MO [Mott Haven] NY 23 B1
Mobil [Paulsgrove] NJ 72 D6
Mocanaqua PA 62 F1
Model City NY 42 C2
Modena NY 34 D1
Modena PA 70 A3
Moffet MD 9 E1
Mogees PA 72 C1
Mohawk [defect detector] NY 30 B3
Mohawk [WS] NY 30 A2
Mohawk View NY 32 E1
Mohawk Yard [Schenectady] NY 32 C2
Mohrsville PA 62 F4
Moira NY 28 B1
Molino PA 62 F4
Molly PA 62 C2
Mon Valley Works [Braddock] PA 53 C3
Mona [defect detector] PA 70 A1
Monaca PA 49 C3
Monarch PA 55 B6
Monessen [CSXT(PMY)] PA 54 B2
Monessen [WE(PWV)] PA 54 C2
Monks NJ 17 E2
Monkton MD 11 A1
Monmouth Beach NJ 18 F2
Monmouth Junction NJ 18 D2
Monmouth Park NJ 18 F2
Monocacy [RDG] PA 70 A1
Monocacy [PC(PRR)] PA 70 A2
Monongahela PA 54 B1
Monongahela Junction PA 53 C4
Monroe NJ 16 C1
Monroe NY 27 D4
Monroe PA 51 D1
Monroeton PA 61 E2
Monroeville NJ 19 B1
Monrovia MD 10 C2
Monsanto Plant [Center Square] NJ 6 F1
Monsey NY 34 E4
Mont Alto PA 63 A3
Mont Alto Park PA 63 A3
Montana PA 66 D4
Montandon PA 62 C2
Montauk NY 35 D5
Montcalm Landing (Fort Ticinderoga) NY 29 B4
Montchanin DE 6 D2
Montclair-Bay Street NJ 22 A3
Montclair Heights NJ 22 A3
Montclair-Walnut Street NJ 22 A3
Montelius PA 66 C5
Montello PA 63 F1
Monteola NY 37 D3
Monterey NY 36 F4
Montezuma NY 38 A2
Montford Avenue Yard [Baltimore] MD 12 C2
Montgomery NY 34 D2
Montgomery PA 62 C1
Montgomeryville PA 49 E2
Monticello NY 34 B1
Montour Falls NY 41 F2
Montour Junction [MTR-BO] PA 53 A6
Montour Junction [MTR-PLE] PA 52 C1
Montour Mine #1 PA 52 A4
Montour Mine #4 PA 52 C5
Montour Mine #9 PA 52 A4
Montour Mine #10 PA 53 A5
Montoursville PA 61 C4
Montrose NY 26 B3
Montrose ON 42 A4
Montrose PA 68 A2
Montvale NJ 25 A1
Montville NJ 21 B1
Monty [defect detector] PA 62 C1
Monument PA 57 F1
Monview [defect detector] PA 50 D4
Monvue PA 50 D4
Moodna Viaduct NY 27 F2
Mooers NY 28 E1
Mooers Forks NY 28 E1
Moon Run PA 52 C2
Moon Run Mine PA 52 C2
Moones Mill PA 57 D4
Moons NY 43 C2
Moore DE 7 E2
Moore NJ 74 A1
Moore PA 72 C5
Moorefield WV 9 B4
Moores NJ 19 B3
Moores Mills NY 34 F1
Moores Mills PA 63 B2
Mooresburg PA 62 D2
Moorestown NJ 73 D4
Moorhead PA 47 D5
Moosic [LWV] PA 65 C3
Moosic [STLH(DH)] PA 65 B3
Morado PA 51 B4
Moraine NY 41 C1
Morantown MD 8 B1
Moravia NY 38 A4
Moravia PA 51 B2
Morea PA 67 B3
Morea Junction (Laurel Junction) PA 67 D2
Moreland NY 41 F2
Morestein PA 70 E4
Morewood PA 55 C3
Morgan MD 10 C2
Morgan NJ 20 D4
Morgan [PRR Allegheny County] PA 52 C4
Morgan [PRR Delaware County] PA 72 B6
Morgan Fork PA 56 F3
Morgan Hill PA 52 B4
Morgan Run PA 58 B3
Morgan Run Junction WV 50 D4
Morgans Mills NY 28 D3
Morgantown WV 50 D4
Morgantown Power Plant MD 14 B1
Morganville NJ 18 E2
Morganza PA 52 C6
Moritz NY 43 F3
Morrell PA 60 D1
Morrellville PA 64 A1
Morris NJ 73 C4
Morris [Morrisville] PA 74 C3
Morris [BFC] PA 57 F2
Morris [ERIE] PA 61 B3
Morris Heights NY 23 B1
Morris Junction [Morris] NJ 73 C4
Morris Junction [Port Morris] NJ 17 D3
Morris Junction PA 67 B4
Morris Mine PA 52 A5
Morris Park [Bronx] NY 23 C1
Morris Park Shops [Queens] NY 23 D4
Morris Plains NJ 21 A3
Morris Run PA 61 C2
Morrisana 168th Street NY 23 C1
Morrisburg ON 36 F1
Morrisdale PA 58 D2
Morrison PA 56 B2
Morrison's MD 8 D5
Morrison's Cove Junction PA 59 D3
Morrisonville NY 28 E2
Morristown NJ 21 A4
Morristown NY 36 D3
Morrisville PA 74 C3
Morrisville NY 38 D3
Morrisville Yard PA 74 C3
Morse NY 38 C1
Morsemere NJ 22 D3
Mortimer NY 44 B4
Morton NY 40 B1
Morton-Rutledge PA 72 C5
Mortonville PA 70 A3
Moscow PA 68 B4
Moselem PA 69 A4
Moser Run Junction PA 50 D3
Mosgrove PA 47 C5
Moshannon PA 58 C4
Moshannon Mine PA 59 D5
Mosher NY 28 B2
Moss Creek Junction PA 59 C6
Mostoller PA 60 B2
Motters MD 10 C1
Mott Haven NY 23 B1
Mott Haven Yard NY 23 B1
Mottville NY 38 A3
Moundsville WV 50 A3
Mount [Mountville] PA 64 D6
Mount Airy NJ 18 C1
Mount Alverno PA 72 B6
Mount Arab NY 28 B4
Mount Braddock PA 55 B6
Mount Carbon PA 67 B6
Mount Carmel PA 62 E3
Mount Carmel PA 66 C5
Mount Carmel Junction (Alaska) PA 66 B5
Mount Clare PA 70 F2
Mount Eagle PA 57 F2
Mount Hermon PA 50 C2
Mount Holly NJ 18 C3
Mount Holly Springs PA 63 B2
Mount Hope NY 25 C2
Mount Hope PA 55 A6
Mount Ivy NY 26 A4
Mount Kisco NY 34 F3
Mount Marion NY 31 D3
Mount Morris NY 40 B4
Mount Olive NJ 17 C3
Mount Pleasant NY 26 D6
Mount Pleasant PA 55 C3
Mount Ross NY 31 E3
Mount Savage MD 8 B1
Mount Savage Junction MD 8 D1
Mount St. Vincent NY 25 C4
Mount Storm Power Plant WV 9 A3
Mount Union PA 60 E1
Mount Upton NY 39 E2
Mount Vernon NY 25 D4
Mount Vernon West NY 25 C3
Mount Wilson MD 11 A2
Mount Wolf PA 63 D2
Mountain Avenue-Montclair NJ 22 A3
Mountain Dale NY 34 C1
Mountain Grove PA 62 E2
Mountain House Station NY 31 D2
Mountain Lake Park MD 9 A2
Mountain Lakes NJ 21 B2
Mountain Springs PA 61 E4
Mountain Station [Orange] NJ 21 D4
Mountain Top PA 65 C6
Mountain View NJ 21 D2
Mountaindale PA 57 C3
Mountainhome PA 69 C1
Mountainview NY 28 D2
Mountainville NY 27 F2
Mountville PA 64 D6
Mowry PA 57 D1
Moyer PA 55 C4
Moyers PA 62 E4
Moylan-Rose Valley PA 72 B5
Moyston PA 57 D4
MPA Shops [Baltimore] MD 12 B2
MQ Tower [Campbell Hall] NY 27 C2
MR [Manorville] NY 35 A6
MS Tower [Corry] PA 48 E1
Mt. Airie PA 59 B5
Mt. Airy MD 10 C2
Mt. Airy PA 73 A2
Mt. Airy Junction MD 10 C2
Mt. Airy Tunnel MD 10 C2
Mt. Arlington NJ 17 A1
Mt. Bethel [LNE] PA 16 B5
Mt. Bethel [NS(DLW)] PA 16 B6
Mt. Calvert MD 11 A5
Mt. Calvery NJ 19 D2
Mt. Clare 'A' Yard [Baltimore] MD 12 B2
Mt. Clare Shops [Baltimore] MD 12 B2
Mt. Cuba DE 6 C2
Mt. Dallas PA 60 D3
Mt. Ephraim NJ 73 C5
Mt. Etna PA 57 D4
Mt. Governor Dick PA 63 E2
Mt. Gretna PA 63 E2
Mt. Hope NJ 17 B1
Mt. Hope [KV] PA 57 F3
Mt. Hope [RDG(COR)] PA 63 E2
Mt. Jefferson PA 66 D3
Mt. Jewett PA 56 C2
Mt. Joy PA 63 D2
Mt. McGregor NY 30 E1
Mt. Pisquah PA 66 D3
Mt. Pleasant DE 7 A2
Mt. Pleasant NY 31 C3

Name	State	Page	Grid
Mt. Pleasant	PA	63	A1
Mt. Pocono	PA	69	C1
Mt. Riga	NY	31	F3
Mt. Royal [Baltimore]	MD	12	B2
Mt. Royal	NJ	18	B4
Mt. Savage	MD	9	C1
Mt. Sterling	PA	50	D3
Mt. Tabor	NJ	21	A2
Mt. Vernon Mines	PA	55	D3
Mt. Vision	NY	38	F4
Mt. Washington	MD	12	B1
Mt. Winans	MD	12	B3
Mud Run	PA	69	A2
Muddy Creek Forks	PA	63	E4
Muddy Run Junction	PA	58	A6
Muhlenburg	PA	64	A5
Muir	PA	62	D4
Muirheid	NJ	18	C1
Muirkirk	MD	10	D4
Mule Shoe	PA	59	B3
Mulford	NJ	16	B3
Mullica Hill	NJ	19	B1
Mullikin	MD	11	A4
Mullin	PA	55	C3
Mumford	NY	45	E1
Muncy	PA	62	C1
Muncy Valley	PA	61	D4
Munhall	PA	53	B3
Munhall Wharf	PA	53	C3
Munnsville	NY	38	D3
Munson [DH]	PA	68	B3
Munson [PC(NYC)]	PA	57	D2
Munster	PA	57	C4
Murdock	PA	60	A3
Murphy	NJ	19	C1
Murray	PA	62	D4
Murray Hill	NJ	21	B6
Murray Hill	NY	23	D2
Murray Mine	PA	61	E3
Murrysville	PA	49	E4
Murvale	ON	36	A4
Musconetong Tunnel	NJ	17	B4
Muse	PA	52	B5
Muse Junction	PA	52	B5
Muskee Siding	NJ	19	C3
Musser	PA	57	E3
Mutual	PA	55	D1
MV Tower [Mount St. Vincent]	NY	25	C4
Myers [CNYS]	NY	38	A4
Myers [LV]	NY	39	A1
Myers Plant	PA	55	C2
Myerstown	PA	63	E1
Myersville	MD	10	B2
Myobeach	PA	61	F3

N

Name	State	Page	Grid
NA Tower [Martinsburg]	WV	9	F2
NAX (North Alexandria)	VA	14	B6
Naaman	DE	6	F1
Nacco	OH	50	A3
Nadine	PA	53	C2
Nag	PA	60	B2
Naginey	PA	57	F3
Nancy	PA	60	F2
Nansen	PA	56	B3
Nanticoke	PA	65	A6
Nanty Glo	PA	57	B4
Nanty Glo Mine	PA	57	B4
Nanuet	NY	26	A6
Nanuet Junction	NY	26	A6
Napanoch	NY	31	C4
Napeague Beach	NY	35	D5
Napier	NY	43	F2
Napier	PA	60	C3
Naples	NY	40	D4
Narbeth	PA	72	D3
Narco	PA	60	E2
Narrows	MD	11	B4
Narrows [Narrowsburg]	NY	34	A1
Narrows	PA	62	A4
Narrows Creek	PA	57	B1
Narrowsburg	NY	34	A1
Narvon	PA	63	F2
Nashua	PA	49	B1
Nashville	PA	63	C3
Nassau	DE	7	F2
Nassau [SIRT(SIRY)]	NY	20	D3
Nassau [Princeton Junction]	NJ	18	D2
Nassau Boulevard	NY	24	B4
Nassau Lake	NY	30	E4
Nassau Tower [Mineola]	NY	24	B4
Nassawadox	VA	15	A5
National	PA	52	B5
National Capital Trolley Museum [Wheaton]	MD	10	D4
National Docks [Jersey City]	NJ	22	C5
National Hill	PA	52	C4
National Mine No.2	PA	52	B5
National Mine No.3	PA	52	B5
Natrona	PA	51	D3
Natrum	WV	50	A4
Natural Bridge	NY	37	E1
Natural Dam	NY	36	E4
Nav (White Plains)	MD	10	D6
Naval Research Laboratory [Shepherd]	DC	14	C6
Naval Shipyard [Philadelphia]	PA	73	A5
Navarro	PA	71	A2
Nave [Jersey City]	NJ	22	C5
Navy Siding	VA	14	A5
Navy Yard [Washington]	DC	14	C5
Nay Aug Tunnel	PA	65	D2
Nazareth	PA	71	D2
Nazareth Cement	PA	71	D2
Nazareth Junction (Northampton Junction)	PA	71	C2
NC Tower [Hagerstown]	MD	10	A5
NE Junction [Niobe]	NY	43	C3
Neabsco	VA	10	C6
Nealy	PA	49	C2
Nebo	PA	50	F2
Nebraska	PA	48	F3
Neck Road [Brooklyn]	NY	23	B6
Neely Town	NY	27	D1
Neelyton	PA	60	F2
Neffs	OH	50	A3
Neffs Run	MD	8	A3
Negley	OH	49	B3
Ne-ha-sa-ne	NY	29	A1
Nelson	NY	37	F3
Nelson	PA	61	B1
Nelson Run	PA	56	E3
Nemacolin	PA	50	D3
Nepara Park	NY	25	C2
Nepperhan	NY	25	C3
Neptune Yard [Bradley Beach]	NJ	18	F2
Nescopeck	PA	62	E2
Nescopeck Pass	PA	62	F1
Nesh [Neshaminy]	PA	73	D1
Neshaminy [CSXT(RDG)]	PA	73	D1
Neshaminy [PC(PRR)]	PA	70	D2
Neshaminy Falls	PA	73	D1
Neshanic	NJ	18	C1
Neshannock Falls	PA	49	C1
Nesquehoning	PA	66	D3
Nesquehoning Breaker	PA	66	D3
Nesquehoning Junction	PA	66	D3
Netcong	NJ	17	C3
Netherwood	NJ	20	B1
Neversink	PA	64	B6
Neville (P&OV Junction)	PA	52	C2
Neville Island	PA	52	C1
New Albany	PA	61	E3
New Alexandria	OH	50	A1
New Alexandria	PA	50	F1
New Baltimore	NY	33	B2
New Berlin	NY	38	E4
New Berlin	PA	62	C2
New Berlin Junction	NY	39	E2
New Berlinsville	PA	70	B1
New Bethlehem	PA	49	F2
New Bloomfield	PA	62	B4
New Boston	PA	67	B3
New Boston Junction	PA	67	C3
New Bremen	NY	37	E2
New Brighton	NY	22	B6
New Brighton	PA	51	C2
New Britain	PA	70	C1
New Brunswick	NJ	20	A3
New Canaan	CT	35	C1
New Carrollton	MD	10	D4
New Castle	DE	6	D4
New Castle	PA	49	B2
New Castle	PA	51	B1
New Castle [AMTK (BO Mahoningtown)]	PA	51	A1
New Castle Junction	PA	51	B1
New Castle Yard	PA	51	B1
New Centerville	PA	72	B2
New Church	VA	15	C3
New City	NY	26	A5
New Columbia	PA	62	C2
New Cumberland	PA	64	D3
New Cumberland	WV	49	B4
New Dorp	NY	20	F2
New Egypt	NJ	18	D3
New Florence	PA	60	A1
New Florence Branch	PA	60	A1
New Freedom	PA	63	D4
New Galilee	PA	51	A4
New Geneva	PA	50	D4
New Germantown	PA	63	A1
New Hamburg	NY	34	E1
New Hampton	NJ	17	C4
New Hampton	NY	27	A2
New Hartford	NY	38	E2
New Haven	NY	37	B4
New Hempstead	NY	26	A5
New Holland	PA	63	F2
New Hope	PA	70	D1
New Hyde Park	NY	24	B4
New Jersey Zinc Franklin Plant	NJ	16	D1
New Jersey Zinc Ogdensburg Mine	NJ	16	C2
New Jersey Zinc Palmerton Smelter	PA	69	E2
New Kensington	PA	51	C4
New Kingston	PA	63	B2
New Lebanon	NY	31	F1
New Lisbon	NJ	18	D3
New Lots Avenue [Brooklyn]	NY	23	C4
New Lyme	OH	48	A3
New Market	NJ	20	A2
New Martinsville	WV	50	A4
New Midway	MD	10	C1
New Milford	NY	34	C3
New Milford	PA	68	A1
New Millport	PA	57	C2
New Mines	PA	62	E3
New Oxford	PA	63	B3
New Paltz	NY	31	D4
New Park	PA	63	D4
New Philadelphia	PA	67	C5
New Portage Junction	PA	59	C3
New Portage Tunnel [Gallitzin]	PA	59	B2
New Providence	NJ	21	B5
New Providence	PA	63	F3
New Ringgold	PA	62	F3
New Rochelle	NY	25	D4
New Salem	PA	54	C6
New Salisbury	OH	49	A4
New Scotland	NY	30	D4
New Stanton	PA	55	B1
New Village	NJ	17	B4
New Waterford	OH	49	B2
New Wilmington	PA	49	C1
New Windsor	MD	10	C1
New Windsor	NY	26	B1
New Woodstock	NY	38	C3
New Yard [Bayway]	NJ	22	A6
New York	NY	35	A3
New York Mills	NY	38	E2
New York Museum of Transportation	NY	44	B5
Newall	PA	61	E4
Newark [AMTK(PRR)]	DE	6	A4
Newark [CSXT(BO)]	DE	6	A3
Newark [SEPA]	DE	6	A4
Newark	MD	15	C2
Newark	NJ	17	E4
Newark	NJ	22	A5
Newark	NY	40	E2
Newark Airport [CNJ]	NJ	22	A6
Newark Airport [NJT]	NJ	22	A5
Newark Bay Bridge	NJ	22	A6
Newark Heights	NJ	21	D5
Newark Junction	NJ	22	A5
Newark Transfer	NJ	22	B5
Newark Valley	NY	39	B2
Newberry Junction [Williamsport]	PA	61	B4
Newberry Yard [Williamsport]	PA	61	B4
Newbridge	DE	6	D2
Newburgh	NY	26	C1
Newburgh Junction	NY	27	E4
Newcastle	PA	67	A5
Newcomer	PA	50	D3
Newell	WV	49	B4
Newell Yard	PA	54	B3
Newfield	NJ	19	C2
Newfield	NY	39	A2
Newfield	PA	56	F1
Newfield Junction	PA	56	F1
Newfoundland	NJ	17	D2
Newhouse	OH	49	A3
Newington	VA	10	C5
Newkirk	NJ	19	B1
Newkirk	NY	28	A4
Newkirk	PA	62	F3
Newlonsburg	PA	49	E4
Newport	DE	6	C3
Newport	NJ	19	B3
Newport	NY	38	F2
Newport [PRR Lawrence County]	PA	51	B2
Newport [PRR Perry County]	PA	62	B4
Newton	NJ	16	A2
Newton	PA	48	E2
Newton Falls	NY	37	F1
Newton-Hamilton	PA	60	F1
Newton Hook	NY	33	B4
Newtonville	NJ	19	C2
Newtown [SEPA(RDG)]	PA	74	A2
Newtown [URR]	PA	53	C3
Newtown Junction	PA	73	B3
Newtown Square	PA	72	B3
Newville	PA	63	A2
NG Cabin [Colonie]	NY	32	F2
Niagara Falls	NY	42	B3
Niagara Falls [CN/VIA(GT) NSCT]	ON	42	B3
Niagara Falls [CP/CSXT(MC/PM)]	ON	42	B4
Niagara Falls Yard [CSXT(NYC)]	NY	42	B3
Niagara Falls Yard [EL(ERIE)]	NY	42	C3
Niagara Junction	NY	46	D4
Niagara-on-the-Lake	ON	42	B1
Nice [Nicetown]	PA	73	A3
Nicetown	PA	73	B3
Nichola	PA	49	E2
Nichols [EL(DLW)]	NY	39	B3
Nichols [WAG(B&S)]	NY	41	D3
Nicholson	MD	11	C3
Nicholson	PA	68	A3
Nicholson Tunnel	PA	68	A3
Nick [Manhattan]	NY	23	B2
Nilan	PA	50	D4
Nile	NY	41	A3
Niles	OH	49	A1
Niles	PA	48	D4
Niles Valley	PA	61	B2
Nineveh	NY	39	D3
Niobe	NY	43	C3
Nisbet	PA	61	B4
Niskayuna	NY	32	D1
Nitro	PA	49	F2
Nittany	PA	57	F2
Niver Junction	PA	60	A3
Niverton	PA	60	A4
Niverville	NY	33	D2
Nixon	NJ	20	C3
Nixon	NY	43	B2
NJ&NY Junction	NJ	22	B3
NK [Newark Junction]	NJ	22	A5
No.6 Breaker [Summit Hill]	PA	66	C3
No.7 Junction [Inkerman]	PA	65	D4
No.7 Tipple	PA	60	D2
No.8 Breaker [Lansford]	PA	66	B4
No.14 Breaker [Arlington]	PA	62	F3
Noble	PA	73	B1
Noblestown	PA	52	B3
Nobody	NY	34	A1
Noel	PA	57	C4
Nolton	PA	50	C2
Nora Breaker	PA	66	C5
Nordmont	PA	61	D4
Norfolk	NY	36	F2
Norma	NJ	19	B2
Norman	PA	57	A1
Noroton Heights	CT	35	C1
Norris [Norristown]	PA	72	C1
Norris Tunnel	PA	54	D3
Norristown	PA	72	C1
Norristown Transportation Center	PA	72	C1
Norry [Northumberland]	PA	66	A6
North 3rd Street [Brooklyn]	NY	23	B3
North Abrams	PA	72	B1
North Alexander	NY	45	A2
North Alexandria	VA	14	B6
North Allens [defect detector]	PA	61	C4
North Arlington	NJ	22	B4
North Avenue [Baltimore]	MD	12	B2
North Avenue [New Rochelle]	NY	25	D3
North Baker	PA	56	F4
North Bangor	PA	16	A6
North Barnesboro	PA	59	B4
North Bay	NY	38	D1
North Beach Haven	NJ	19	E1
North Bend [NS(PRR)]	PA	56	F4
North Bend [SRRR]	PA	56	F3
North Bergen	NJ	22	C4
North Bessemer	PA	53	D2
North Boston	NY	42	E4
North Boyles	PA	62	C3
North Branch	MD	8	D3
North Branch	NJ	17	C4
North Branch	WV	9	A3
North Branch Industrial Track	MD	8	D3
North Broad Street [Philadelphia]	PA	73	B3
North Brookfield	NY	38	E3
North Buffalo Junction	NY	46	A3
North Chatham	NY	31	E1
North Chittenango	NY	38	C2
North Clarion Junction	PA	48	F4
North Claymont	DE	6	F1
North Cohocton	NY	41	D1
North Collins	NY	42	D4
North Cornwall	PA	63	E1
North Creek	NY	29	D3
North Croghan	NY	37	E1
North Croton	NY	26	C4
North Driftwood	PA	56	D4
North Drury	PA	56	F4
North East	PA	47	D5
North Eldred	PA	56	D1
North Elizabeth	NJ	22	A6
North Elwyn	PA	72	B5
North Evans	NY	42	D4
North Fair	PA	62	C1
North Fair Haven	NY	38	A1
North Ferrisburg	VT	28	F4
North Ferry (Fox Chase)	PA	62	C4
North Fish	NJ	18	C4
North Fork [PRR]	PA	62	A1
North Fork [PSN]	PA	56	C3
North Fox Chase	PA	73	C2
North Germantown	NY	31	D3
North Glenside	PA	73	A1
North Hackensack	NJ	22	C2
North Harford	NY	39	B1
North Hawthorne	NJ	22	A1
North Hero	VT	28	F2
North Hills (North Glenside)	PA	73	A1
North Hoosick	NY	30	F3
North Hornell	NY	41	C2
North Ilion	NY	38	F2
North Jackson	OH	49	A1
North Java	NY	42	F4
North Kean	PA	56	D2
North Keating	PA	56	E4
North Lansing	NY	38	A4
North Lawrence	NY	28	B2
North Le Roy	NY	45	D1
North Lica	NJ	19	D1
North Lima	OH	49	A2
North Linthicum	MD	12	B4
North Long Branch	NJ	18	F2
North Lucas (Lucaston)	NJ	18	B4
North Macedon	NY	40	D2
North McKees Rocks	PA	52	C2
North Memphis	NY	38	B2
North Miller	PA	62	C4
North Mountain	WV	9	F1
North Newark	NJ	22	A4
North Newark	NY	40	E2
North Oakland	PA	49	D2
North Olean	NY	43	F3
North Ore	PA	73	A1
North Penn Junction [Philadelphia]	PA	73	B3
North Petersburg	NY	30	F3
North Philadelphia	PA	73	B3
North Pine Grove	PA	62	E4
North Pittston	PA	65	B3
North Point	MD	12	E3
North Point	PA	57	A2
North Pomo (Pomona)	NJ	19	D2
North Port Byron	NY	38	A2
North Possum Point	VA	10	C6
North Pownal	VT	30	F3
North Race	NJ	73	C5
North Rahway	NJ	20	C1
North Reading	PA	64	A5
North River	NY	29	D3
North Rose	NY	40	F2
North Sewickley	PA	51	C3
North Spencer	NY	39	A2
North St. Johns	PA	62	F2
North Star Junction	PA	52	A2
North Star Mine	PA	52	A2
North Stephentown	NY	30	F4
North Tonawanda	NY	46	A2

Name	State	Page	Grid
North Tonawanda Junction	NY	46	B2
North Towanda	PA	61	E2
North Vineland	NJ	19	C2
North Wales	PA	70	C2
North Warren	PA	56	A1
North Weedsport	NY	38	A2
North White Plains	NY	25	D1
North Wildwood	NJ	19	C4
North Wins (Ancora)	NJ	19	C1
North Woodbury	NJ	73	B6
Northbrook	PA	70	B3
Northeast	MD	11	D1
Northern Junction [North Bergen]	NJ	22	C4
Northfield	NJ	19	D2
Northfield	NY	39	F2
Northfield Tunnel	NY	39	F2
Northampton	PA	71	A3
Northampton Junction	PA	71	C2
Northland Avenue [Buffalo]	NY	46	B4
Northport	NY	35	C2
Northport Junction	NY	35	C2
Northport Village	NY	35	C2
Northumberland	NY	30	E2
Northumberland	PA	66	A6
Northvale	NJ	25	B2
Northville	NY	30	C1
Northwest Junction	PA	68	B3
Nortons	NY	43	C2
Norwich	NY	39	E1
Norwich	PA	56	D2
Norwood	NJ	25	B2
Norwood	NY	36	F2
Norwood	PA	72	D5
Nostrand Avenue [Brooklyn]	NY	23	B4
Notch Cliff	MD	11	B2
Notre Dame	MD	12	B1
Nottingham	PA	63	F4
Noxen	PA	61	F3
NP [Ashtabula]	OH	48	A1
NS Tower	PA	55	A4
Nuangola	PA	62	F1
Nunda	NY	40	B4
Nunda Junction	NY	40	B4
Nunnery	PA	63	A4
Nursery Road [Baltimore]	MD	12	B4
Nutley	NJ	22	A3
Nutley-Franklin Avenue	NJ	22	A3
Nutley-Walnut Street	NJ	22	B3
Nutt Avenue [Phoenixville]	PA	70	F2
NY [Portage]	PA	60	B1
NY&RB Junction [Rockaway Beach]	NY	23	D6
Nyack	NY	26	B6
Nylon	DE	7	D3
O			
Oak	MD	13	D2
Oak	PA	53	A3
Oak Corners	NY	40	E3
Oak Grove	DE	7	D3
Oak Grove	PA	50	C2
Oak Grove	VA	10	B4
Oak Island	NJ	22	A5
Oak Island Junction	NJ	22	B5
Oak Hall	PA	57	F3
Oak Hall	VA	15	C3
Oak Hill	PA	53	C3
Oak Point	NY	23	C2
Oak Ridge	NJ	17	D2
Oak Ridge	PA	49	F2
Oak Summit	NY	31	E4
Oak Tree	NJ	20	B2
Oak Tree	PA	57	A3
Oakbourne	PA	70	B3
Oakdale	NY	35	D3
Oakedale	PA	52	B3
Oakeola	PA	72	D5
Oakfield	NY	40	A2
Oakfield	OH	48	A4
Oakington	MD	13	D2
Oakland	MD	9	A2
Oakland [NYSW]	NJ	17	E2
Oakland [PRSL(WJS)]	NJ	19	B1
Oakland [OW]	NY	34	B2
Oakland [PRR]	NY	40	B4
Oakland [PRR]	PA	47	B3
Oakland [PSR(PS)]	PA	49	F2
Oakleigh	MD	11	A2
Oakley	DE	7	E2
Oaklyn	NJ	73	C5
Oakmont	WV	9	B2
Oakmont	PA	53	C1
Oaks	PA	72	A1
Oaksville	NY	38	F4
Oakvale	NY	36	D3
Oakville	PA	63	A2
Oakville	VA	14	B6
Oakwood	NY	38	A3
Oakwood Heights	NY	20	E2
Obi	NY	41	A3
Occidental Chemical [Florence]	NJ	74	B5
Ocean	MD	8	A3
Ocean Avenue [Brooklyn]	NY	23	B5
Ocean City	MD	15	D1
Ocean City	NJ	19	D3
Ocean Gate	NJ	18	E4
Ocean Heights	NJ	19	D3
Ocean View	NJ	19	D4
Oceanport	NJ	18	F2
Oceanside	NY	24	B5
Oceanville	NJ	19	E2
Octoraro	MD	13	A1
Odell	PA	49	D3
Odenton	MD	11	A4
Odessa	NY	41	F2
O'Donnell	PA	57	B1
Oella	MD	10	D3
Ogden	PA	72	A6
Ogdens	NY	39	F3
Ogdensburg	NJ	16	D2
Ogdensburg	NY	36	E2
Ogdensburg Mine	NJ	16	C2
Ohio Pyle	PA	50	E3
Ohio Street Yard [Buffalo]	NY	46	B5
Oil City	PA	48	E3
Okonoko	WV	9	D2
Old Bridge	NJ	18	E1
Old Chatham	NY	31	E1
Old Court	MD	12	A1
Old Ferry	PA	62	B4
Old Forge	NY	37	F3
Old Forge [J&S]	PA	60	D1
Old Forge [RBMN(DLW)]	PA	65	B3
Old Fort	PA	57	F3
Old Greenwich	CT	35	B1
Old Holbrook	NY	35	D2
Old Home Works	PA	50	D3
Old Maid's Lane	NJ	18	C4
Old Penn Haven	PA	69	A2
Old Port	PA	62	A4
Old Stone Tunnel	NY	43	D2
Old Town	NY	20	F1
Oldman	NJ	6	F2
Oldtown	MD	9	D1
Olean	NY	43	F3
Oleopolis	PA	48	E3
Oliphant Furnace	PA	50	E3
Olivers Mills	PA	65	C5
Olmsted	PA	56	E2
Olney [Reading]	PA	64	A5
Olney [SEPA(RDG)]	PA	73	B3
Olyphant	PA	65	A1
Omal	OH	50	A4
Onativia	NY	38	C3
Onchiota	NY	28	D3
Onco	OH	50	A3
Ondawa	NY	30	E2
Oneida	NY	38	D2
Oneida [BLE]	PA	49	D2
Oneida [LV]	PA	67	C1
Oneida Castle	NY	38	D2
Oneida Junction	PA	66	A2
Oneonta	NY	39	F1
Onley	VA	15	B4
Onoville	NY	43	D3
Ontario	NY	40	D1
Ontario	PA	50	C2
Ontario Center	NY	40	D1
Ontelaunee	PA	64	A4
Option	PA	53	A4
Oradell	NJ	22	C1
Oramel	NY	41	A2
Oran	NY	38	C3
Oranda	VA	9	E4
Orange	NJ	21	D4
Orange Farm	NY	27	B3
Orangeburg	NY	25	B1
Orangeville	MD	12	C2
Orangeville	OH	47	A1
Orangeville	PA	62	E1
Orbisonia	PA	60	E2
Orchard	NJ	73	D5
Orchard Park	NY	42	E4
Orchard Siding	WV	8	A6
Ordway	NY	29	D3
Ore Bank	PA	63	A3
Ore Docks [Buffalo]	NY	46	A5
Ore Hill	PA	60	C1
Oreland	PA	73	A1
Oreminea	PA	60	D1
Orfley	NJ	18	F3
Orient	PA	54	C6
Oriskany	NY	38	E2
Oriskany Falls	NY	38	E3
Orleans	NY	40	E3
Orleans Road	WV	9	E1
Ormrod	PA	69	F4
Ormsbee Road	PA	48	E1
Ormsby Junction	PA	56	C2
Orphanage[Sunbury]	PA	66	B6
Orr's Mill	NY	27	F2
Orrtanna	PA	63	A3
Orrton-Richwood	PA	64	B6
Orson	PA	68	B2
Orston	NJ	73	C5
Orviston	PA	57	F1
Orwell	VT	29	F2
Orwig	PA	63	D4
Orwigsburg	PA	67	C6
Osage	NJ	73	D6
Osborn	PA	50	F1
Osborn Street [Johnstown]	PA	64	A2
Osborne	MD	13	D2
Oscar	PA	49	F3
Oscawanna	NY	26	B4
Oscawanna Tunnel	NY	26	B4
Osceola [NYC]	PA	61	A1
Osceola [P&S]	PA	58	C4
Osceola [WAG(B&S]	PA	61	A1
Osceola Junction	PA	58	C4
Osceola Mills	PA	58	C4
Osgood	PA	47	D1
Osgood Viaduct	PA	47	D1
Ossining	NY	26	C5
Ostend	PA	57	B2
Osterburg	PA	60	C2
Ostrander	PA	56	B1
Oswayo	PA	56	E1
Oswegatchie	NY	37	F1
Oswego	NY	37	A3
Oswego	NY	37	A4
Otego	NY	39	F2
Otis	NY	44	B2
Otis Junction [CKMR]	NY	31	D2
Otis Junction [DH(CHAT)]	NY	28	F2
Otis Summit	NY	31	D2
Otisville	NY	34	C2
Otisville Tunnel	NY	34	C2
Ottawa	PA	62	D1
Otter Lake	NY	37	F3
Otter Point	MD	13	B3
Otto	PA	62	C3
Outcalt	NJ	18	D2
Outcrop	PA	50	D4
Outer Station [Reading]	PA	64	A5
Outwood	PA	62	E4
Overbrook	DE	7	F2
Overbrook	PA	72	D4
Overlook	PA	63	E2
Ovid	NY	40	F4
OW Shops [Middletown]	NY	27	A1
OW Tower [Tarrytown]	NY	25	C1
Owasco Lake	NY	38	A3
Owego	NY	39	B3
Owens	DE	7	E2
Owens-Corning Plant [Magnolia]	NJ	73	C6
Owings	MD	11	A5
Owings Mill	MD	10	D2
Owl's Head	NY	28	C2
Owings Mill	MD	11	A2
Oxford	MD	11	C5
Oxford [ERIE]	NY	27	D3
Oxford [NYSW(DLW)]	NY	39	D1
Oxford [OW]	NY	39	D1
Oxford	ON	36	D1
Oxford	PA	63	F4
Oxford Furnace	NJ	16	D6
Oxford Road [Philadelphia]	PA	73	C3
Oxford Tunnel	NJ	16	D6
Oyster Bay	NY	24	D1
Ozone Park	NY	23	D4
P			
P&D Junction [Summit]	NJ	21	B5
P&N No.1 Mine	PA	57	C1
P&OV Junction [North McKees Rocks]	PA	52	C2
PA Siding	PA	48	B1
Pacific Avenue [Jersey City]	NJ	22	C5
Pack [Torrance]	PA	50	F1
Packer Marine Terminal [Philadelphia]	PA	73	B5
Packer No.2 Mine	PA	67	A3
Packer No.3 Mine	PA	67	A3
Packer No.4 Mine	PA	67	A3
Packer No.5 Mine	PA	67	A3
Packerton (Packerton Junction)	PA	69	E1
Packerton Junction	PA	69	E1
Packeta Branch Junction	PA	51	D4
Paddlefords	NY	40	D3
Paddy Mountain	PA	62	A3
Padonia	MD	11	A2
Paeonian Springs	VA	10	A3
Page	PA	60	D1
Paine	PA	56	C4
Paint	PA	64	B3
Paint Creek	PA	64	A3
Paint Creek Branch	PA	64	B3
Paint Mills	PA	48	F4
Painted Post	NY	41	E3
Painter	VA	15	B5
Paintsville	PA	62	A3
Pal [Palermo]	NJ	19	D3
Palanka	PA	52	A6
Palatine	NJ	19	B2
Palatine Bridge	NY	30	B3
Palenville	NY	31	D2
Palermo	NJ	19	D3
Palisades Park	NJ	22	D2
Palm	PA	69	B4
Palmer	PA	50	F1
Palmer Falls	NY	30	E1
Palmer Mine	PA	54	B6
Palmer's Summit	NY	43	E3
Palmersville	PA	56	C2
Palmerton	PA	69	E2
Palmyra	NJ	73	D3
Palmyra	NY	40	D2
Palmyra	PA	63	D1
Palo Alto	PA	67	B5
Pamassus	PA	51	C4
Pamelia	NY	37	C2
Panama	NY	43	B3
Pancake	WV	9	C3
Pancoast	NJ	19	C2
Pandrol Jackson Shops [East Syracuse]	NY	36	C1
Panther	PA	57	E1
Panther Hollow Tunnel [Pittsburgh]	PA	53	B2
Paoli	PA	72	A2
Paper Mill [CR(PRR RDG)]	PA	62	E2
Paper Mill [SEPA(RDG)]	PA	73	C1
Paramont	MD	10	A1
Pardee	PA	62	B2
Pardoe	PA	48	C4
Paris	NY	38	E3
Park	NJ	21	B4
Park	NY	39	A2
Park (Luckett)	PA	59	A3
Park [Park Junction Philadelphia]	PA	73	A4
Park [Parkesburg]	PA	70	A3
Park Avenue Tunnel [Manhattan]	NY	23	B2
Park Head	MD	9	F1
Park Hill	NY	25	C3
Park Place [LV]	PA	67	C2
Park Place [OW]	PA	65	C1
Park Ridge	NJ	25	A1
Parkdale	NJ	19	D1
Parker	PA	49	E1
Parker Ford	PA	70	B2
Parkers	NY	42	F2
Parkesburg	PA	70	A3
Parkers (Parkers Glen)	PA	68	D3
Parkers Glen	PA	68	D3
Parkers Landing	PA	49	E1
Parkertown	NJ	19	E1
Parkside	NY	23	C3
Parksley	VA	15	B4
Parksville	NY	31	A4
Parkton	MD	11	A1
Parkview	PA	72	D4
Parkville	NJ	18	B4
Parkville	NY	23	B5
Parkville Junction	NY	23	B5
Parkwood	PA	49	F4
Parlett	OH	50	A1
Parlin	NJ	20	C4
Parish	NY	37	C4
Parrish	OH	48	B1
Parrish	PA	56	A3
Parryville	PA	69	F2
Parshall Branch Junction	PA	50	D3
Parsons	PA	65	C5
Parsonsburg	MD	15	C1
Pasadena	MD	11	A3
Pasadena	NJ	18	D4
Pascack Junction (NJ&NY Junction)	NJ	22	B3
Passaic [NJT(DLW)]	NJ	22	B3
Passaic [NS(ERIE)]	NJ	22	B2
Passaic [NYSW]	NJ	22	B2
Passaic Junction	NJ	22	B2
Passaic Park	NJ	22	B3
Passmore	PA	58	C3
Patapsco [PRR]	MD	12	A4
Patapsco [WM]	MD	10	D1
Patapsco Avenue [Baltimore]	MD	12	B3
Patchen	PA	59	A6
Patchin	NY	42	E4
Patchogue	NY	35	D3
Paterson	NJ	22	A2
Paterson Broadway	NJ	22	A1
Paterson City	NJ	22	A1
Paterson Junction	NJ	22	A2
Paterson-Market Street	NJ	22	A1
Paterson-River Street	NJ	22	A1
Patt	MD	15	B1
Pattenburg	NJ	17	B4
Patterson	NY	34	F2
Patterson Creek	WV	8	D3
Patterson Park Yard [Baltimore]	MD	12	C2
Patterson Street [St. Clair]	PA	67	B5
Pattersonville	NY	30	D3
Patton	NJ	17	B4
Patton	PA	57	C3
Patton	PA	59	D5
Patton Branch No.2	PA	59	D5
Patton Colliery No.1	PA	59	D5
Pattons	MD	15	B1
Patuxent	MD	11	A4
Patuxent Naval Air Test Center	MD	14	D1
Paul [Baltimore]	MD	12	B2
Paul [Paulsboro]	NJ	72	D6
Paul	NY	37	A3
Paul	PA	50	D4
Paul Smithís	NY	28	C3
Paulding	NJ	19	B1
Paulin's Kill Viaduct	NJ	16	C5
Pauls	NY	38	A3
Paulsboro	NJ	72	D6
Pavilion	NY	45	C3
Pavilion Center	NY	45	C3
Pavonia	NJ	22	C5
Pavonia Junction [Camden]	NJ	73	C4
Pavonia Yard [Camden]	NJ	73	C4
Paw Paw	WV	9	D2
Pawl [Pawling]	NY	34	F1
Pawling	NY	34	F1
Pawling	PA	62	C3
Paxinos	PA	62	D2
Paxtang	PA	64	D2
Paxton Street Industrial Track [Harrisburg]	PA	64	D2
Paxtonville	PA	62	B3
Payne	PA	49	C2
Paynesville	NY	41	B3
PD [Port Reading]	NJ	20	D2
PD Tower [Patchogue]	NY	35	D3
Peach Bottom [MPA]	PA	63	E4
Peach Bottom [NS(PRR)]	PA	63	E4
Peach Glen	PA	63	B3
Peahala	NJ	19	E1
Peakville	NY	39	F4
Peale	PA	57	E2
Peapack	NJ	17	D4
Pearl	NY	32	E4
Pearl Creek	NY	45	C4
Pearl River	NY	25	A1
Pearre	MD	9	E1
Pearson Yard	WV	9	F2
Pebble Dell	PA	56	A3
Pecan	PA	48	D4
Peck	PA	60	D1
Pecksport	NY	38	D3
Peckville	PA	65	B1
Peconic	NY	35	B5
Peddie Ditch	NJ	22	A5
Pedricktown	NJ	6	F2

Location	State	Page	Grid
Peekskill	NY	26	B3
Peerless #1 Mine	PA	57	C3
Peermont	NJ	19	D4
Pelham	NY	25	D4
Pelham Bay	NY	23	D1
Pelham Manor	NY	25	D4
Pelham Parkway [Bronx]	NY	23	C1
Pelhamwood	NY	25	D4
Pellettown	NJ	16	B1
Pells (Addison Junction)	NY	29	B4
Pelton Road [Warwick]	NY	34	C3
Pemberton	NJ	18	C3
Pembroke	NY	42	F3
Pembroke	PA	72	D4
Pembroke Center	NY	42	F3
Pen Argyl	PA	16	A5
Pen Argyl	PA	69	C2
Pen Argyl Junction	PA	16	A5
Pen-Mar	MD	10	B1
Penbryn	NJ	18	C4
Pencoast	PA	57	B1
Pencoyd	PA	73	A3
Pendleton Center	NY	42	E2
Penfield [BO(B&S)]	PA	56	C4
Penfield [PSR(PRR)]	PA	56	C4
Penfield [SEPA(PHWN)]	PA	72	D4
Penllyn	PA	70	C2
Penn [Philadelphia]	PA	73	A4
Penn [Pittsburgh]	PA	53	A2
Penn [Westmoreland County]	PA	50	E1
Penn Cave	PA	57	F2
Penn-Dixie No.4	PA	71	C2
Penn-Dixie No.5	PA	71	C2
Penn-Dixie No.6	PA	71	C2
Penn Haven Junction	PA	69	A2
Penn-Mary Yard [Baltimore]	MD	12	C3
Penn-Walt Chemical [Cornwells Heights]	PA	73	D2
Penn-Walt Chemical [Thorofare]	NJ	73	A6
Penn-Warner Industrial Park [Morrisville]	PA	74	C3
Penn Station [Baltimore]	MD	12	B2
Penn Station [Manhattan]	NY	23	A3
Penn Station [Newark]	NJ	22	A5
Penn Yan	NY	40	E4
Pennbrook	PA	70	C2
Pennellvillle	NY	38	B1
Pennhurst	PA	70	B2
Pennington	NJ	74	C1
Pennington	PA	57	D3
Pennmont	PA	53	A6
Penns Grove	NJ	19	A1
Penns Neck	NJ	18	D2
Pennsauken	NJ	73	C4
Pennsauken Industrial Park	NJ	73	C4
Pennsburg	PA	70	B1
Pennsdale	PA	61	C4
Pennside	PA	48	B2
Pennsville	PA	55	C4
Pennsylvania Colliery	PA	66	B5
Pennsylvania Collieries 1 & 2	PA	59	A6
Pennsylvania Collieries 5 & 6	PA	58	C5
Pennsylvania Furnace	PA	57	E3
Pennsylvania Glass Sand [Bridgeport]	PA	57	E4
Pennsylvania No.16 Mine	PA	59	A1
Pennsylvania No.22 Mine	PA	59	B6
Pennsylvania Nos. 3 & 8 Mines	PA	64	B2
Pennsylvania Railroad Museum [Strasburg]	PA	63	F3
Pennsylvania Trolley Museum [Arden]	PA	50	C2
Penny Bridge	NY	23	B3
Penrose [Philadelphia]	PA	73	A5
Penrose Yard [Philadelphia]	PA	73	A5
Penobscot	PA	65	C6
Penowa	PA	50	B1
Penryn Park	PA	63	E2
Penton	NJ	19	A1
Pentress	WV	50	C4
Pepatcon	NY	31	A3
Pepco	MD	10	B3
Pepco [Alexandria]	VA	14	B6
Pepper Road [Hunt Valley]	MD	11	A2
Pequannock	NJ	21	D1
Pequea	PA	63	E3
Pequest	NJ	16	D6
Per Se	PA	57	E2
Percivals	NY	43	E3
Perdix	PA	63	C1
Perkasie	PA	70	C1
Perkins	WV	50	A3
Perkinsville	NY	41	C1
Perkintown	NJ	6	F2
Perkiomen Junction	PA	72	A1
Perkiomenville	PA	70	B1
Perlee	MD	11	C4
Perry [Perryville]	MD	13	E1
Perry	NY	40	B4
Perry (Thompson)	PA	53	C4
Perry Bluff	PA	47	B6
Perryman	MD	13	C3
Perryopolis	PA	54	D3
Perrys	NY	40	A4
Perrysburg	NY	43	D1
Perryville	MD	11	C1
Perryville	NJ	38	D3
Persia	NY	43	D2
Perth	ON	36	D3
Perth Amboy	NJ	20	C3
Perth Amboy Junction	NJ	20	C1
Perth Amboy Yard	NJ	20	D3
Peru	NY	28	E3
Perulack	PA	60	F1
Peruville	NY	39	B1
Pete	PA	50	C3
Peters Creek	PA	53	B5
Petersburg	NJ	19	D3
Petersburg	NY	30	F3
Petersburg	PA	57	E4
Petersburg	WV	9	B4
Petersburg Junction	NY	30	F3
Peth	NY	43	E3
Petroleum	NJ	20	D1
Petroleum Center	PA	48	E3
Petrolia	NY	41	B3
Petrolia	PA	49	E2
Pettits	NJ	20	B3
Petty Island [Camden]	NJ	73	B4
Pew	PA	49	F1
Phelan	PA	49	F2
Phelps	NY	40	E3
Phelps Junction	NY	40	E3
Phil [Philadelphia]	NY	37	D1
Phil [Philadelphia]	PA	73	A5
Philadelphia	NY	37	D1
Philadelphia	PA	70	C3
Philadelphia	PA	73	A4
Philadelphia Electric Power Plant [Eddystone]	PA	72	C6
Philadelphia Industrial Park	PA	73	D2
Philadelphia International Airport	PA	72	D6
Philipse Manor	NY	26	C6
Philipsburg	PA	58	D3
Philipston	PA	49	E2
Phillips [NYC]	PA	61	A1
Phillips [PC(PRR)]	PA	55	A6
Phillips Plant	MD	8	A2
Phillips Street [Jersey City]	NJ	22	C5
Phillipsburg	NJ	17	B4
Phillipsburg	NJ	71	E3
Philmont	NY	31	E2
Philmont	PA	73	C1
Philson	PA	60	B4
Phoenicia	NY	31	C3
Phoenix	MD	11	A2
Phoenix	NJ	20	C4
Phoenix	NY	38	B1
Phoenix Steel [Claymont]	DE	6	F1
Phoenixville	PA	70	B2
Phoenixville	PA	70	F2
Picatinny	NJ	17	D3
Pickering	PA	70	B2
Picture Rock	PA	61	D4
Pidgeon Street [Queens]	NY	23	B3
Pier 40 [Philadelphia]	PA	73	B4
Pier 122 [Philadelphia]	PA	73	B5
Pier 124 [Philadelphia]	PA	73	B5
Pierce	PA	53	A5
Pierce Road	NY	30	E3
Piercefield	NY	28	B4
Piedmont	WV	8	D6
Pierrepont Manor	NY	37	C3
Piermont	NY	25	B1
Piermont Landing	NY	25	C1
Piffard	NY	45	F4
Pigeon (Atlas Point)	DE	6	D3
Pike	MD	10	B5
Pike [Reading]	PA	64	A5
Pike [RJCP(CR)]	PA	58	D1
Pikes Crossing	NY	42	D4
Pikesville	MD	12	A1
Pilgrim State Hospital	NY	35	C2
Pilot	MD	11	C1
Pindell	MD	11	A5
Pine [CR(NYC)]	PA	61	A3
Pine [NS(PRR)]	PA	62	B1
Pine Aire	NY	35	C3
Pine Avenue Industrial Track [Niagara Falls]	NY	42	B4
Pine Beach	NJ	18	E4
Pine Bush	NY	34	D1
Pine City	NY	41	F3
Pine Creek	PA	53	B1
Pine Creek Railroad [Allaire State Park]	NJ	18	E3
Pine Crest	NJ	18	D4
Pine Flats	PA	57	B3
Pine Forge	PA	70	B1
Pine Furnace	PA	49	F2
Pine Grove	DE	7	E1
Pine Grove [LOS]	PA	63	F4
Pine Grove [RDG]	PA	62	E4
Pine Grove Furnace	PA	63	B3
Pine Grove Mills	PA	57	E3
Pine Hill	NY	31	B3
Pine Island	NY	27	A4
Pine Island Junction	NY	27	A4
Pine Lane	NJ	18	C3
Pine Plains	NY	31	E3
Pine Run Branch	PA	57	C3
Pine Valley	NJ	18	B4
Pine Valley	NY	41	F2
Pine Valley	OH	50	A2
Pine View	PA	62	F1
Pinelawn	NY	35	C3
Pinesburg	MD	9	F1
Piney Fork	OH	50	A2
Pinkerton	PA	50	F3
Pinkerton Tunnel	PA	50	F3
Pinola	PA	60	F3
Pinto	MD	8	C3
Piper	PA	57	E1
Pitcairn	PA	53	D3
Pitman	NJ	19	B1
Pitt [Pittsburgh]	PA	53	A2
Pitts	PA	61	B2
Pittsburgh	PA	49	D4
Pittsburgh	PA	53	A2
Pittsburgh & Lehigh Junction	NY	45	E1
Pittsfield	NY	38	E4
Pittsfield	PA	48	F2
Pittsford	NY	44	D4
Pittsford [defect detector]	NY	44	C4
Pittston	PA	65	B3
Pittston Junction	PA	65	B3
Pittston Yard (Coxton Yard)	PA	65	A3
Pittstown	NJ	17	B4
Pittsville	MD	15	C1
Pixley	NY	41	B3
Plain [Plainfield]	NJ	20	A1
Plainfield	NJ	20	A1
Plainfield	PA	60	F3
Plainfield	WV	50	A3
Plains	PA	65	C4
Plains Junction	PA	65	C4
Plainsboro	NJ	18	D2
Plainsville	PA	65	C4
Plandome	NY	24	B2
Plane #4	MD	10	C2
Planebrook	PA	70	E4
Plank	NJ	22	B5
Plantation	VA	15	A6
Platea	PA	47	B6
Plattsburgh	NY	28	F2
Plauderville	NJ	22	B2
Pleasant Gap	PA	57	F2
Pleasant Gap Junction	PA	57	F2
Pleasant Mount	PA	68	B2
Pleasant Plains	NY	20	D3
Pleasant Point	NY	37	B4
Pleasant Valley	NJ	17	D4
Pleasant Valley	NY	31	E4
Pleasant Valley	PA	69	C4
Pleasantview	PA	62	A4
Pleasantville	NJ	19	E3
Pleasantville	NY	26	D5
Plum Creek	PA	53	D2
Plumadore	NY	28	D2
Plumville	PA	57	A3
Plymouth [EL(DLW)]	PA	65	B5
Plymouth [Plymouth Meeting]	PA	72	D1
Plymouth Industrial Track [Oreland]	PA	73	A1
Plymouth Junction [DH EL(DLW)]	PA	65	B5
Plymouth Junction [SEPA(PRR)]	PA	72	C2
Plymouth Meeting	PA	72	D1
Plymouth Meeting [defect detector]	PA	70	D2
PN [Oak Island Junction]	NJ	22	B5
Pocantico Hills	NY	26	D6
Pocomoke	MD	15	C2
Pocono Lake	PA	69	B1
Pocono Summit	PA	69	C1
Pocopson	PA	70	B3
Pogue	PA	60	E2
Pohick	VA	10	C5
Point (Back River Junction)	MD	12	D2
Point Airy	NJ	19	B1
Point Bridge [Pittsburgh]	PA	53	A3
Point Chautauqua	NY	43	B2
Point Hill	WV	50	B2
Point Lookout	NY	24	C6
Point Marion	PA	50	D4
Point of Rocks	MD	10	B3
Point Phillip	PA	69	C3
Point Pleasant Beach	NJ	18	F3
Point View	PA	57	D4
Poland	MD	8	D6
Poland	NY	38	F1
Poland	PA	50	D4
Poland #3	PA	50	D4
Poland Mines	PA	50	D4
Polk	PA	48	D4
Polk Junction	PA	48	D4
Pomerania	NJ	19	D2
Pomeroy	PA	70	A3
Pomfret	NY	43	B2
Pomona	NJ	19	D2
Pomona	NY	26	A5
Pompton Junction	NJ	17	E3
Pompton Lakes	NJ	17	E2
Pompton Plains	NJ	17	E3
Pond [Fresh Pond]	NY	23	C3
Pond Bank	PA	63	A3
Pond Creek Junction	PA	69	A2
Pond Eddy	PA	68	D3
Pond Hill	PA	62	F1
Ponders Siding	DE	7	E2
Poolville	NY	38	E4
Poorman Side	PA	57	E1
Pope	MD	14	B1
Popes Creek	MD	14	B1
Poplar	MD	13	C2
Port [Trenton]	NJ	74	D2
Port [Freeport]	NY	24	D4
Port [Port Homer]	OH	49	A4
Port [Bridgeport]	PA	54	B4
Port [Newport]	PA	62	B4
Port [Washington Boro]	PA	63	E3
Port Allegany	PA	56	D2
Port Bowkley	PA	65	C4
Port Byron	NY	38	A2
Port Carbon	PA	67	B5
Port Chester	NY	25	F2
Port Clinton	PA	62	F4
Port Covington	MD	12	C3
Port Crane	NY	39	C3
Port Deposit	MD	13	A2
Port Elizabeth [Newark]	NJ	22	B6
Port Elizabeth [PRSL(WJSL)]	NJ	19	C3
Port Ewen	NY	34	A4
Port Gibson	NY	40	E2
Port Henry	NY	29	F1
Port Homer	OH	49	A4
Port Indian	PA	72	B1
Port Ivory	NY	20	E1
Port Jefferson	NY	35	D2
Port Jersey	NJ	22	C6
Port Jervis	NY	34	B2
Port Kennedy	PA	72	B1
Port Kent	NY	28	F3
Port Leyden	NY	37	E3
Port Matilda	PA	57	E3
Port Monmouth	NJ	18	E1
Port Morris	NJ	17	D3
Port Morris	NY	23	C2
Port Morris Yard	NY	23	C2
Port Murray	NJ	17	C4
Port Newark	NJ	22	B6
Port Norris	NJ	19	C3
Port of Albany	NY	32	E4
Port Perry	PA	53	C3
Port Perry Tunnel	PA	53	C3
Port Providence	PA	72	A1
Port Reading	NJ	20	D2
Port Reading Junction	NJ	20	E4
Port Republic	NJ	19	E2
Port Richmond	NY	20	E1
Port Richmond	PA	73	B4
Port Royal [NS(PRR)]	PA	62	A4
Port Royal [PLE(PMY)]	PA	54	D2
Port Tobacco	MD	10	D6
Port Vue	PA	53	C4
Port Washington	NY	24	B2
Portage [defect detector]	NY	41	B1
Portage [defect detector]	PA	60	B1
Portageville	NY	41	B1
Portal [Kearny]	NJ	22	B4
Porter	DE	7	A2
Porter Avenue [Buffalo]	NY	46	A4
Porter Run	PA	59	C4
Porters	PA	63	C4
Portland	NY	43	B2
Portland	PA	16	B5
Portland Avenue [Rochester]	NY	44	C2
Portland Mills	PA	56	B4
Portlandville	NY	30	A4
Portside	NJ	22	A6
Portville	NY	43	F3
Portway	NY	41	C1
Possum Point	VA	10	C6
Post [Painted Post]	NY	41	E3
Post Creek	NY	41	E2
Post Road [defect detector]	NY	33	D1
Post Road Crossing	NY	33	D1
Potomac (Pinto)	MD	8	C3
Potomac	WV	8	C3
Potomac Landing [Alexandria]	VA	14	B6
Potomac Manor	WV	9	B2
Potomac Yard [Alexandria]	VA	14	B6
Potsdam	NY	36	F2
Potter Brook	PA	56	F1
Pottersville	NJ	17	C4
Pottersville	PA	49	C2
Potts Run	PA	58	A3
Pottsgrove	PA	62	D2
Pottstown	PA	70	B2
Pottsville	PA	62	F3
Pottsville	PA	67	B5
Pottsville Junction	PA	67	B5
Pouch Terminal [Clifton]	NY	20	F1
Poughkeepsie	NY	34	E1
Poughkeepsie	NY	34	C4
Poughkeepsie Bridge	NY	34	B4
Poughkeepsie Industrial Track	NY	34	C4
Poughkeepsie Junction	NY	34	C4
Poughquag	NY	34	F1
Powell	PA	61	D2
Powell's Creek	VA	10	C6
Powys	PA	61	B4
Powhatan	OH	50	A3
Poyntelle	PA	68	B2
Prattsburg	NY	41	D1
Preble	NY	38	B4
Preisser	PA	57	B4
Prentisvale	PA	56	C1
Prescott	ON	36	E2
Prescottville	PA	57	B1
Presho	NY	41	E3
President	PA	48	E3
President Street Station [Baltimore]	MD	12	C2
Presswood	PA	61	E2
Presto	PA	52	C4
Preston	MD	11	D5
Preston Park	PA	68	C1
Pratts Hollow	NY	38	D3
Prescott	PA	63	E1
Prices	MD	11	D3
Primos	PA	72	C5
Primrose	PA	52	A4
Prince [CSXT(PRR)]	MD	11	A5
Prince (Principio)	MD	13	E1
Prince Street [Lancaster]	PA	64	D4
Princes Bay	NY	20	D3
Princeton	NJ	18	C2
Princeton	PA	49	C2
Princeton Junction	NJ	18	D2
Princess Anne	MD	15	B2
Principio	MD	13	E1
Priscilla Nos.1 & 2 Mines	PA	64	B2
Probst's Mill	PA	62	A1
Procter	WV	50	A4
Produce Yard [Pittsburgh]	PA	53	A2
Promised Land	NY	35	D5
Prompton	PA	68	C3
Prospect	NJ	18	A4

Name	State	Page	Grid
Prospect	PA	72	B6
Prospect [PC(PRR)]	NY	43	B2
Prospect [PC(RWO)]	NY	38	F1
Prospect Junction	NY	38	F1
Prospect No.2 Mine	PA	58	B4
Prospect Park [CNJ]	PA	71	D3
Prospect Park [SEPA]	PA	72	C5
Prospect Plains	NJ	18	D2
Prospect Street [Sea Isle City]	NJ	19	D4
Prosser	NY	43	F3
Protection	NY	42	F4
Protectory	PA	72	A1
Providence	MD	11	D1
Providence	PA	65	D1
PRR Junction [Mayville]	NY	43	B2
PT (Eastport)	NY	35	A6
PU [Patton]	PA	59	D5
Pulaski	NY	37	C4
Pulaski	PA	49	B1
Pullen	PA	69	C4
Pulvers	NY	31	E2
Pumphrey	MD	12	B4
Punxsutawney	PA	57	A2
Purcellville	VA	10	A3
Purchase Line	PA	57	B3
Purdy's	NY	34	F3
Pureland Business Park	NJ	18	A4
Purex [Bristol]	PA	74	B5
Pusher Siding	PA	56	F1
Putnam	NY	29	F3
Putnam Junction	NY	26	D1
Putneyville	PA	49	F2
PW Interlocking [Pinelawn]	NY	35	C3
PW&S Junction [Somerset]	PA	60	A3
Pylesville	MD	11	B1
Pymatuning	PA	47	B1
Pyrites	NY	36	F3
Q Tower [Hyndman]	PA	60	B4
QN Tower [Washington]	DC	14	C4
Quakake	PA	66	A3
Quaker Bridge	NY	43	D3
Quaker Falls	PA	49	B2
Quaker Ridge	NY	25	D3
Quakers Knob	PA	50	B1
Quakertown	PA	69	C4
Quality Pine Hill Mines 1 & 2	PA	60	A3
Quantico	VA	10	C6
Quarry	MD	13	B2
Quarry Junction	PA	16	A6
Quarryville	NJ	17	D1
Quarryville	PA	63	F3
Queen [Plainfield]	NJ	20	A1
Queen	PA	60	C2
Queen Anne	MD	11	D4
Queen Junction	PA	49	D2
Queen Lane [Germantown]	PA	73	A3
Queens	ON	36	A4
Queens Run	PA	62	A1
Queens Tower [Queens Village]	NY	24	A4
Queens Village	NY	24	A4
Queenston	ON	42	B2
Queenston Quarry	ON	42	B2
Queenstown	MD	11	C4
Quemahoning Junction	PA	60	A2
Queponco (Newark)	MD	15	C2
Quincy	OH	50	A3
Quincy	PA	63	A4
Quinsonia	PA	60	F3
Quinton	NJ	19	A2
Quogue	NY	35	B6
R (Jamesport)	NY	35	B5
Raburn-Fair Lawn	NJ	22	B1
Race	NJ	73	C5
Race Street [Philadelphia]	PA	73	A4
Raceway Spur [Elizabeth]	NJ	22	A6
Radbourn	NY	39	A2
Rade (Radebaugh)	PA	50	E1
Radebaugh	PA	50	E1
Radis [Radison]	NY	38	B2
Radison	NY	38	B2
Radix	NJ	19	C1
Radnor	PA	72	C3
Ragan	DE	6	D3
Rager's Summit	PA	62	A3
Rahns	PA	70	B2
Rahway [CSAO(CNJ)]	NJ	20	D1
Rahway [NJT(PRR)]	NJ	20	C1
Rahway Bridge	NJ	20	D1
Railroaders Memorial Museum [Altoona]	PA	59	D2
Rainbow	NY	28	D3
Rainbow Lake	NY	28	C3
Rainey	PA	55	B5
Raineys	OH	50	A2
Ralph	PA	54	B6
Ralphton	PA	60	A2
Ralston	NJ	17	D4
Ralston	PA	61	C3
Ram [Ithaca]	NY	39	A1
Ramapo	NY	34	D3
Ramblers	NY	23	D4
Ramey	PA	58	B5
Ramsey	NJ	17	E2
Ramsey	PA	61	B4
Ramseytown	PA	57	A1
Ran	NJ	73	D3
Rancks	PA	63	F2
Rand	PA	53	B4
Randall	NY	30	B3
Randall	WV	50	D4
Randallsville	NY	38	D3
Randle	MD	10	D4
Randolph	NJ	17	D3
Randolph	NY	43	D3
Randolph	PA	60	A2
Randolph #2 Mine	PA	57	A3
Randolph Tunnel	WV	9	D1
Randy	PA	65	A2
Rankin	PA	53	B3
Rankin Furnaces	PA	53	B3
Ranshaw Washery	PA	66	A5
Ransom	PA	65	A2
Ransomville	NY	42	D1
Ranson	WV	9	F3
Rappahannock	PA	67	A3
Raquette Lake	NY	29	B2
Rare [South Amboy]	NJ	20	C3
Raricks	PA	67	A1
Raritan	NJ	18	D1
Raritan Center Industrial Park	NJ	20	B3
Raritan Junction	NJ	20	C3
Raritan River Bridge	NJ	20	C3
Raritan River Railroad Junction	NJ	20	C3
Rasselas	PA	56	C3
Rassmussens Siding	MD	10	C6
Rathbone	NY	41	D3
Rathbun	PA	56	C3
Rathmel	PA	57	B1
Rattling Run	PA	62	D4
Raubs Mill	PA	62	B3
Rausch Creek	PA	62	E4
Rausch Gap	PA	62	D4
Rausch's	PA	62	F3
Raven Rock	NJ	18	B1
Raven Run	PA	67	A3
Ravena	NY	33	B1
Ravensworth	VA	10	C5
Rawlings	MD	8	B4
Rawson	NY	41	A2
Ray	NY	40	A3
Ray	PA	58	B2
Ray Brook	NY	28	D4
Rayard	PA	57	A1
Raymilton	PA	48	D4
Raymond	PA	56	E1
Raymondville	NY	36	F1
Rea	PA	50	B1
Read [Wilmington]	DE	6	D3
Read Valley	NJ	18	C1
Readers	PA	69	C2
Reading	PA	64	A5
Reading	PA	70	A1
Reading Center	NY	41	E2
Reading Junction	PA	60	B2
Reading Mines	PA	60	A2
Reading No.3 Mine	PA	60	B2
Reading Shops [Reading]	PA	64	A5
Reading Terminal [Philadelphia]	PA	73	B4
Rectortown	VA	9	F4
Red Bank	NJ	18	F2
Red Bank [BFC]	PA	57	E3
Red Bank [CR(PRR)]	PA	49	E2
Red Creek	NY	40	F1
Red Hill	MD	10	B1
Red Hill	PA	70	B1
Red Hook	NY	31	D3
Red House [ERIE PRR]	NY	43	E3
Red House [BPRR(BRP)]	NY	43	E3
Red Lion	PA	63	D3
Red Onion	NY	27	B1
Red Raven	PA	53	C1
Red Rock	PA	56	C1
Red Stone Junction	PA	50	E3
Redden	DE	7	E3
Redd's Mill	PA	54	A2
Redington	PA	71	D3
Reduction	PA	54	D1
Redwood	NY	36	D4
Reed [NS(NKP)]	OH	48	A1
Reed [PRR]	OH	50	A1
Reed [PWV]	OH	50	A1
Reed	PA	62	D2
Reed Colliery No.1	PA	59	C6
Reed Crossing	NJ	18	C4
Reed Mine	PA	49	F1
Reeder	PA	70	D1
Reeds Road	PA	70	A2
Reedson	WV	10	A2
Reedsville	PA	57	F3
Reedy	PA	47	D3
Reega	NJ	19	D2
Reels Mill	MD	10	B2
Reese	PA	57	D4
Reesedale	PA	47	D3
Reeves	NJ	18	C4
Reevesdale	PA	67	D3
Reformatory Extension [Carteret]	NJ	20	D2
Refton	PA	63	E3
Regan Junction	PA	57	B4
Regis	NY	37	D2
Rego Park	NY	23	C3
Rehoboth	DE	7	F3
Rehoboth	PA	54	C2
Reids Grove	MD	11	D6
Reidsburg	PA	49	F1
Reilly	PA	48	D1
Reiner	PA	62	D4
Reinolds	PA	63	F1
Reissing	PA	52	B4
Reistertown Plaza [Baltimore]	MD	12	A1
Reitz [PRR]	PA	60	B2
Reitz [PSR(PS)]	PA	56	B4
Reitz 3 & 4 Mines	PA	60	B2
Reitz 5 Mine	PA	64	A3
Reitz Junction	PA	60	B2
Relay	MD	12	A3
Relee	VA	14	B5
Relius	NY	38	A3
Rembrandt	PA	57	A3
Remoh	PA	57	A4
Remsen	NY	38	F1
Rene Mont	PA	62	F3
Renfrew	PA	49	D3
Reniff	NY	39	A3
Renix	MD	8	B4
Rennerdale	PA	52	C3
Reno	PA	48	D3
Renovo	PA	56	F4
Rensselaer	NY	32	E4
Rensselaer Falls	NY	36	E3
Rensselaer Shop	NY	32	E4
Renton	PA	49	E4
Renwick	NY	39	A1
Repaupo	NJ	18	A4
Republic	NY	35	C3
Republic	PA	54	B5
Republic Hill	PA	71	D3
Reservoir	PA	60	D1
Reservoir	WV	8	A6
Resources Terminal [Secaucus]	NJ	22	C4
Retort	PA	58	D5
Retreat	PA	62	F1
Retsof	NY	45	E4
Retsof Junction	NY	45	F4
Revell	MD	11	B4
Revloc	PA	57	B4
Rew City	PA	56	C1
Reynolds	PA	62	F3
Reynoldsdale	PA	60	C2
Rexford	PA	61	A2
Rexis	PA	57	B4
Rexville	NY	41	C3
Reybold	DE	7	A2
Reynolds	NY	30	E3
Reynoldsville	PA	57	B1
RG Tower [Philadelphia]	PA	73	A4
Rheems	PA	63	D2
Rheims	NY	41	D2
Rhinebeck	NY	31	D4
Rhinecliff	NY	34	B4
Rhoades	PA	57	E2
Rhodesdale	MD	11	D6
Ribolds	PA	49	D3
Rice (Rices)	NY	37	C2
Rices	NY	37	C2
Rices Landing	PA	54	A6
Riceville	NY	43	E1
Riceville	PA	48	D2
Rich (East X)	NY	40	E3
Rich [Gouverner Junction]	NY	36	E4
Rich Valley	PA	56	D3
Richard Street [Girardville]	PA	66	D5
Richards (Richards Yard)	PA	71	D3
Richards Yard	PA	71	D3
Richburg	NY	41	A3
Richey	PA	48	E4
Richfield Junction	NY	38	E3
Richfield Springs	NY	38	F3
Richford	NY	39	B2
Richland	NJ	19	C2
Richland	NY	37	C4
Richland	PA	63	E1
Richlandtown	PA	69	C4
Richmond	MA	31	F2
Richmond	PA	60	E3
Richmond Furnace	MA	31	F2
Richmond Hill	NY	23	D4
Richmond Summit	MA	31	F1
Richmond Valley	NY	20	D3
Richmondville	NY	30	B4
Richville	NY	36	E3
Richwood	PA	64	B6
Rick [Pedricktown]	NJ	6	F2
Rickenbach	PA	64	A4
Ricketts	PA	61	E4
Riddlesburg	PA	60	D2
Riddleton	NJ	19	A1
Riders	NY	31	E1
Riderwood	MD	11	A2
Ridge [Clearfield County]	PA	59	B5
Ridge [Strawberry Ridge]	PA	62	D1
Ridge #8 Mine	PA	57	C3
Ridge Avenue [Philadelphia]	PA	73	A4
Ridgedale	WV	9	C2
Ridgedale Industrial Campus [Hanover]	NJ	21	B3
Ridgefield	NJ	22	C3
Ridgefield Park	NJ	22	C3
Ridgeland	NY	44	C4
Ridgeley Yard	WV	8	D2
Ridgely	MD	11	D4
Ridgeway	ON	42	D3
Ridgeway	PA	56	B3
Ridgeway	WV	9	F3
Ridgewood	NJ	17	E3
Ridgewood Junction	NJ	22	B1
Ridley Park	PA	72	C5
Riegelsville	NJ	71	E4
Riegelsville	PA	71	E4
Riker Yard [Punxsutawney]	PA	57	B2
Rilltown	PA	50	E1
Rimerton	PA	47	C3
Rimersburg	PA	49	E2
Ring	DE	7	E2
Ringdale	PA	61	E3
Ringgold	PA	57	A2
Ringlands	PA	50	C3
Ringoes	NJ	18	C1
Ringtown	PA	67	A2
Ringwood	NJ	17	E2
Ringwood Junction	NJ	17	E2
Rio Grande	NJ	19	C4
Ripley	NY	43	B2
Ripley [defect detector]	NY	43	A2
Rippleton	NY	38	C3
Rippon (Featherstone)	VA	10	C6
Rippon	WV	9	F3
Risher Mine	PA	53	B4
Rising Junction	MA	31	F2
Rising Springs	PA	57	F3
Rising Sun	MD	11	C1
Risley	NJ	19	C2
Ritchie	MD	10	D5
Ritchie	PA	56	F4
Riters	NJ	18	C4
Rittenhouse Gap	PA	69	B4
Ritter	WV	9	C2
Ritts	PA	49	E1
River	MD	12	D2
River [Raritan River Bridge]	NJ	20	C3
River [CSXT(CR)]	NY	37	D1
River [LV]	NY	38	B4
River	OH	49	A4
River [Linden]	PA	61	B4
River [Miquon]	PA	72	D2
River [Philadelphia]	PA	73	A3
River Edge	NJ	22	C1
River Forks	NY	38	E3
River Junction	NY	41	B1
River Road [Camden]	NJ	73	B4
River Street [Wilkes-Barre]	PA	65	B5
River Valley	PA	53	C1
Riverbridge Industrial Center [Chester]	PA	72	C6
Riverdale	MD	14	D3
Riverdale	NY	25	C4
Rivergate	NY	36	D4
Riverhead	NY	35	B5
Riverside	CT	35	B1
Riverside [CSAO(PRR)]	NJ	73	D3
Riverside [EL(ERIE)]	NJ	22	A4
Riverside [NYSW]	NJ	22	A1
Riverside	NY	29	D3
Riverside	PA	64	A2
Riverside [Bethlehem]	PA	71	B4
Riverside [JSC]	WV	8	C3
Riverside Junction	NY	43	E3
Riverside Junction	PA	65	A1
Riverside Park Tunnel [Manhattan]	NY	23	B2
Riverside Yard [Baltimore]	MD	12	C3
Riverton	NJ	73	D3
Riverton	PA	53	C4
Riverton Junction	VA	9	E4
Riverview [PRR Clearfield County]	PA	58	A1
Riverview [PRR Washington County]	PA	54	A1
Riverview [PRR York County]	PA	63	D2
Rixford	PA	56	C1
RO [Alexandria]	VA	14	B5
Roa Hook Tunnel	NY	26	B2
Roach	PA	48	E1
Road	DE	7	A2
Roadrailer Switch [Rutherford]	PA	63	D1
Roaring Brook	PA	61	C3
Roaring Creek	PA	62	D2
Roaring Springs	PA	60	D1
Rob [Bordentown]	NJ	74	D4
Robanna	NJ	19	C1
Robbins	DE	7	E2
Robbins	PA	53	D5
Robbinsville	NJ	18	D2
Robert Moses Power Plant	NY	42	B3
Roberts [BO]	MD	8	C2
Roberts (Tighman) [MDDE(PRR)]	MD	11	D3
Roberts	PA	60	A3
Robertsdale	PA	60	D2
Robesonia	PA	63	F1
Robindale [defect detector]	PA	60	A1
Robinson	MD	11	A4
Robinson	PA	49	B2
Robinson Street [North Tonawanda]	NY	46	A2
Robinwood	NY	29	A1
Rochelle Park	NJ	22	B2
Rochester	NY	40	C2
Rochester	NY	44	C3
Rochester	PA	49	C3
Rochester & Genesee Valley Railroad Museum	NY	44	A5
Rochester Junction	NY	44	C6
Rochester Mills	PA	57	A3
Rock (Canal)	MD	13	A1
Rock [CSXT(RWO)]	NY	37	C2
Rock [NYC(RWO)]	NY	37	E1
Rock [NS(CR)]	PA	61	E2
Rock [NS(RDG)]	PA	72	D3
Rock [PRR]	PA	67	B3
Rock [RDG]	PA	62	E4
Rock Cabin	PA	61	F4
Rock City	NY	43	F3
Rock Creek	OH	48	A2
Rock Cut	NY	32	E3
Rock Cut	PA	56	C2
Rock Enon Springs	VA	9	E3
Rock Glen	NY	40	A4
Rock Glen	PA	62	F2
Rock Junction	PA	65	D2
Rock Point	PA	51	B3
Rock Rift	NY	39	F3
Rock Run	MD	13	A2
Rock Stream	NY	41	E1
Rock Tavern	NY	27	D1
Rockaway	NJ	17	B1
Rockaway Junction	NY	23	D3

Rockaway Park Beach 116 Street NY 23 D6
Rockdale NY 39 E2
Rockdale [BLE] PA 49 D3
Rockdale [PRR] PA 72 B5
Rockdale [SNY] PA 61 C3
Rockhill PA 70 C1
Rockhill Furnace PA 60 E2
Rockland DE 6 D1
Rockland MD 11 A2
Rockland PA 48 D4
Rocklyn PA 70 A2
Rockmere PA 48 E3
Rockport PA 69 A2
Rocks MD 11 B1
Rocks WV 9 C2
Rockton PA 57 C1
Rockview PA 57 F2
Rockville MD 10 C4
Rockville NY 41 A2
Rockville PA 64 C1
Rockville Center NY 24 B5
Rockwalking MD 15 B1
Rockwells Mills NY 39 E1
Rockwood PA 60 A3
Rockwood Junction PA 60 A3
Rocky [Rockville Center] NY 24 C5
Rocky Glen PA 65 C3
Rocky Hill NJ 18 D1
Rocky Point NY 35 A5
Rocky Ridge MD 10 C1
Rocky Ridge PA 60 E2
Rod [Himrod] NY 40 E4
Roddy PA 62 B4
Roddy's PA 60 B4
Rodman PA 60 C1
Roebling NJ 74 C4
Rogers MD 11 A2
Rogers [DH] NY 28 E3
Rogers [NYC(RWO)] NY 37 E2
Rogers [NS(PRR)] OH 49 A4
Rogers [OHPA(YS)] OH 49 A3
Rogers Avenue [Baltimore] MD 12 A1
Rogers Locomotive Works [Paterson] NJ 22 A1
Rogers Mill PA 50 F3
Rogerstown PA 55 B5
Rogues Harbor NY 39 A1
Rohrerstown PA 64 C4
Rohrersville MD 10 A2
Rohrns & Haas [Bristol] PA 74 B5
Rohrns & Haas [Croydon] PA 74 A5
Rolfe PA 56 C3
Roll PA 57 D1
Roller MD 10 D1
Rolling Road (Ravensworth) VA 10 C5
Roman PA 63 E4
Rome NY 38 E2
Rome OH 48 A3
Romer PA 57 B4
Rommell PA 60 D2
Romney WV 9 C2
Romney Junction WV 9 C2
Romulus NY 40 F4
Ronco PA 50 D3
Rondaxe NY 29 A3
Roneys Point WV 50 B2
Ronk PA 63 F3
Ronkonkoma NY 35 D2
Ronkonkoma Yard NY 35 D2
Rook PA 52 D3
Rooseveltown NY 28 B1
Roots NY 37 C1
Roots PA 57 D4
Rose Point PA 49 C2
Rosebank NY 20 F1
Roseby Rock WV 50 A3
Roscoe NY 31 A4
Roscoe PA 54 C3
Rose [Altoona] PA 59 D1
Rose [Brookville] PA 57 A1
Rosebud PA 57 C3
Rosecran's NY 30 E4
Rosedale MD 12 D2
Rosedale NJ 19 C1
Rosedale NY 24 A5
Roseland NJ 21 C3
Roselle Park NJ 21 D6
Roselle-Roselle Park NJ 21 D6
Rosemont OH 49 A1
Rosemont PA 72 C3
Rosendale NY 31 D4
Rosenhayn NJ 19 B2
Roseto PA 16 A6
Roseton NY 34 E1
Rosevelt NJ 18 E2
Roseville Avenue [Newark] NJ 22 A4
Rosiere NY 37 B1
Roslyn NY 24 B3
Roslyn PA 73 B1
Ross DE 7 D3
Ross Crossing NY 41 B1
Ross Farm PA 60 F1
Ross Mills NY 43 C3
Ross Run PA 48 F3
Ross Siding PA 61 A4
Ross Yard PA 53 B2
Rossburg NY 41 A1
Rossiter PA 57 B2
Rossiter Junction PA 57 B2
Rosslyn PA 52 D3
Rosslyn VA 14 B5
Rossmans NY 33 C4
Rossmoyne PA 64 C3
Rossmoyne [defect detector] PA 63 C2
Rosston PA 49 E3
Rossville MD 12 D1
Rothruck PA 54 D5
Rothsville PA 63 E2
Rotterdam Junction NY 32 A1
Roulette PA 56 D2
Round Bay MD 11 A4
Round Hill VA 10 A3
Round Island PA 56 E4
Round Lake NY 30 E3
Round Pond NY 28 D3
Round Top PA 63 B4
Roup PA 53 B2
Rouses Point NY 28 F1
Rouses Point Junction NY 28 F1
Rouseville PA 48 E3
Rowayton CT 35 C1
Rowe Street-Bloomfield NJ 22 A4
Rowena PA 60 B2
Rowland PA 73 D2
Rowlandsville MD 13 A1
Rowles PA 57 C2
Rowley PA 52 C5
Roxburg NJ 71 F1
Roxbury MD 10 A1
Roxbury [ME(CNJ)] NJ 17 A2
Roxbury [Netcong] NJ 17 C3
Roxbury NY 31 B2
Roxton PA 70 D2
Roy (Royalton) PA 63 D2
Royal PA 54 D5
Royal Oak MD 11 C5
Royalton PA 63 D2
Royce NJ 18 D1
Royer PA 57 D4
Royersford PA 70 F1
Roystone PA 56 A2
Ruffsdale PA 55 B2
Rugby NY 23 C5
Rulon Road NJ 18 A4
Rumbaugh PA 55 D2
Rummerfield PA 61 E2
Runyon NJ 20 B4
Rupert PA 62 E2
Rupert VT 30 F1
Rural Ridge PA 53 B1
Rush NY 44 B6
Rushford NY 41 A2
Rushland PA 70 D1
Rushton PA 58 D4
Rushville NY 40 D4
Russel MD 14 D4
Russel Power Plant [Charlotte] NY 44 B1
Russell PA 56 A1
Russell City PA 56 B3
Russelldale WV 9 C3
Russelton PA 49 D4
Russia NY 28 E2
Rustic PA 58 D1
Ruth [CR(PRR)] PA 55 C5
Ruth [Rutherford] PA 63 C2
Rutherford NJ 22 B3
Rutherford PA 63 C1
Rutherford Junction NJ 22 B3
Rutherton PA 62 B2
Ruthford PA 60 B1
Ruxton MD 11 A2
Rycot PA 70 D1
Rydal PA 73 B1
Ryde PA 57 F4
Rye NY 25 F2
Ryers PA 73 C2
Rynd Farm PA 48 E3

S

S&M Junction PA 50 D4
SA Tower [Sand Patch] PA 60 A4
Sabatts NY 29 B1
Sabillasville MD 10 B1
Sabinsville PA 61 A1
Sabula PA 57 C1
Sacandaga NY 30 C1
Sackets Harbor NY 37 C2
Sackett PA 56 B3
Saco PA 68 B4
Saddle River NJ 22 B3
Saegers PA 62 C1
Saegersville Quarry PA 69 D3
Saegertown PA 48 C2
Safe Harbor PA 63 E3
Sag Harbor NY 35 C5
Sagamore [BO] PA 50 F3
Sagamore [BO(B&S)] PA 57 A3
Saginaw [defect detector] PA 63 D2
Sagon Junction PA 66 B5
Sailors Snug Harbor NY 22 B6
Saint Martin MD 15 D1
Saint Marys PA 56 C3
Sal [Waverly] NY 39 A3
Salamanca NY 43 E3
Salem NJ 19 A2
Salem NY 30 F2
Salem OH 49 A2
Salem PA 48 C3
Salem Yard [Woodbury] NJ 73 B6
Salida PA 53 A4
Salix PA 60 B1
Salford PA 70 B1
Salina PA 49 E4
Salinesville OH 49 A3
Salisbury CT 31 F3
Salisbury MD 15 B1
Salisbury Center NY 30 A2
Salisbury Junction PA 60 A4
Salisbury Mills NY 27 E2
Salisbury Plains NY 24 C4
Salisbury Viaduct PA 60 A3
Salmon River NY 28 F2
Salona PA 62 A1
Salt Point NY 31 E4
Saltillo PA 60 E2
Salts [Saltsburg] PA 49 F4
Saltsburg PA 49 F4
Saltsburg Tunnel PA 49 F4
Saltvale NY 40 A4
Salunga PA 63 E2
Sam [Chambersburg] PA 60 F3
Sample Run PA 57 A3
Samson PA 47 C6
Sanatoga PA 70 B2
Sanborn NY 46 D1
Sanborn OH 48 A2
Sand NJ 18 F2
Sand Patch PA 60 A4
Sand Patch Tunnel PA 60 A4
Sandfords NJ 22 B5
Sandts Eddy PA 71 E1
Sandusky NY 43 F1
Sandy PA 56 D3
Sandy Creek PA 53 C2
Sandy Hill PA 73 A1
Sandy Hook MD 10 A2
Sandy Lake PA 48 C4
Sandy Lick PA 51 D1
Sandy Ridge PA 58 D5
Sandy Run [HBTM] PA 60 D2
Sandy Run [LV] PA 69 A2
Sanford Junction PA 58 D3
Sanitaria Springs NY 39 D3
Santa Clara NY 28 B2
Santee PA 71 C3
Sarah Furnace PA 49 E2
Saranac Inn NY 28 C4
Saranac Lake NY 28 D4
Saranac Lake Junction NY 28 D4
Saratoga Springs NY 30 E2
Sardinia NY 43 F1
Sardinia Junction NY 43 F1
Sarver PA 51 D1
Satterfield PA 61 E3
Saucon [Bethlehem] PA 71 C4
Saugerties NY 31 D3
Saunders Range MD 11 A3
Sauquoit NY 38 E3
Savage MD 10 D3
Savage Industrial Track MD 10 D3
Savan PA 57 A3
Savannah NY 40 F2
Savannah Avenue [Margate City] NJ 19 E4
Savona NY 41 D2
Sawmill [Norristown] PA 72 C1
Sawyer NY 46 A3
Sawyer PA 56 C1
Saxonburg PA 49 D3
Saxton PA 60 D2
Saybrook PA 56 A2
Saylorsburg PA 69 C2
Saylorsburg Junction PA 69 C2
Sayre PA 61 D1
Sayreville NJ 20 B4
Sayreville Junction NJ 20 C4
Sayville NY 35 D3
Scale PA 62 A1
Scales PA 57 B3
Scalp Level PA 64 B3
Scarborough NY 26 C5
Scarsdale NY 25 D2
Scenery Hill PA 50 C2
Schaffer MD 9 A2
Schaghticoke NY 30 E3
Schell WV 9 A2
Schenectady NY 30 D3
Schenectady NY 32 B2
Schenevus NY 30 A4
Schenley [BO] [Pittsburgh] PA 53 B3
Schenley [KJR(PRR)] PA 51 E2
Schodack Center NY 30 E4
Schodack Junction NY 33 C1
Schodack Landing NY 33 C1
Schoenberger PA 57 D3
Schoharie NY 30 C4
Schoharie Junction NY 30 C4
Scholes NY 41 B2
School House PA 57 E2
Schulyer [defect detector] NY 38 F2
Schuyler PA 62 D1
Schulyer Junction [NYC] NY 38 F2
Schulyer Junction [S&S] NY 30 E2
Schulyer Lake NY 38 F4
Schulyerville NY 30 E2
Schuylkill [Philadelphia] PA 73 A4
Schuylkill Avenue [Reading] PA 64 A5
Schuylkill Haven PA 67 B6
Schweibinzville PA 50 F3
Schwenksville PA 70 B2
Scio NY 41 B3
Sciota NY 28 E1
Scoke (Schaghticoke) NY 30 E3
Scot Branch PA 66 B5
Scotch [Scotch Plains] NJ 21 C6
Scotch Valley PA 62 E2
Scotia PA 57 E3
Scotia [defect detector] NY 32 B2
Scotia-Glenville Industrial Park NY 32 B2
Scotia Naval Supply Depot NY 32 B2
Scotia Yard NY 32 B2
Scotland PA 60 F3
Scott PA 52 B2
Scott Glen PA 57 A4
Scott Haven PA 53 D6
Scott Mine PA 52 B2
Scottdale PA 55 C3
Scottsville NY 44 A5
Scranton PA 65 C2
Scranton PA 68 B3
Scudders Falls NJ 74 B2
Scully Yard PA 52 C2
Sea DE 7 D3
Sea Breeze NY 44 D1
Sea Cliff NY 24 C1
Sea Girt NJ 18 F3
Sea Isle City NJ 19 D4
Sea Isle Junction NJ 19 D3
Seaboard NJ 22 B4
Seabrook MD 10 D4
Seabrook NJ 19 B2
Seaford DE 7 D3
Seaford NY 24 D5
Seagirt Marine Terminal [Baltimore] MD 12 C3
Sears PA 73 B3
Seaside NY 23 D6
Seaside Heights NJ 18 F3
Seaside Park NJ 18 F4
Seaview NJ 19 D3
Seawall [Curtis Bay] MD 12 C3
Seat Pleasant MD 14 D5
Secane PA 72 C5
Secaucus Road NJ 22 C4
Secaucus Transfer NJ 22 B4
Security MD 10 B5
Security Junction MD 10 A6
Sedgwick PA 73 A2
Sedgwick Avenue [Bronx] NY 23 B1
Seeley Creek NY 41 F3
Seeleyville PA 68 C3
Seiple PA 71 A3
Seitzland PA 63 D4
Seitzville PA 63 D3
Selbyville DE 7 F4
Selinsgrove PA 62 C3
Selinsgrove Junction PA 62 C3
Selkirk NY 30 D4
Selkirk PA 48 E2
Sell PA 63 C4
Sellersville PA 70 C1
Seminary Yard [Alexandria] VA 14 B6
Seneca Army Depot NY 40 F4
Seneca Castle NY 40 E3
Seneca Falls NY 40 F3
Seneca Mills NY 40 E4
Seneca River NY 38 A2
Seneca Street [Buffalo] NY 46 B5
Seneca Yard [Lackawanna] NY 46 B6
Sennett NY 38 A3
SEPA Shops [Frazer] PA 70 F4
SEPA Shops [Overbrook] PA 72 D4
SEPA Shops [Paoli] PA 72 A2
SEPA Shops [Wayne Junction] PA 73 B3
Sergeant PA 56 B3
Serviss Junction NJ 20 B4
Setauket NY 35 D2
Seven Bridges PA 56 E2
Seven Stars PA 67 B6
Severence NY 44 A5
Severn MD 11 A3
Severn Stars PA 63 B3
Severna Park MD 11 A4
Severna Run MD 11 A3
Severnside MD 11 B4
Seward NY 30 B4
Seward PA 60 A1
Sewaren NJ 20 D2
Sewell MD 13 B3
Sewell NJ 18 B4
Sewells Point NJ 19 C4
Sewickley PA 52 B1
Seyfert PA 64 B6
Seymour WV 8 C3
SF [Gallitzin] PA 59 B2
SF [Sunbury] PA 66 A6
SG (Sheridan) PA 64 A1
SG Cabin [Colonie] NY 32 E3
SH [South Schenectady] NY 32 B3
Shade Creek PA 64 B3
Shade Creek Branch PA 64 B3
Shade Gap PA 60 E2
Shadeland PA 48 B2
Shadyside OH 50 A3
Shadyside PA 53 B2
Shaffer PA 57 B1
Shaft No.1 Station PA 57 B1
Shafton PA 50 E1
Shamokin PA 66 A5
Shamokin Dam PA 66 A6
Shamrock [BO] PA 60 A3
Shamrock [NS(RDG)] PA 69 B4
Shamrock [SVRR(PRR)] PA 62 D2
Shamrock Branch Junction PA 54 C6
Shamrock Works PA 54 C6
Shandaken NY 31 C3
Shaner PA 53 D5
Shanleys NY 28 B2
Shannon OH 50 A2
Shannon PA 49 E2
Shannon Smokeless Mine PA 58 D1
Shark NJ 18 F2
Sharktown PA 57 B3
Sharon MD 11 B1
Sharon NJ 18 D2
Sharon PA 47 A3
Sharon PA 48 B4
Sharon Hill PA 72 D5
Sharon Springs NY 30 B3

Name	State	Page	Grid
Sharon Station	NY	31	F4
Sharon Steel [Sharon]	PA	47	A3
Sharp	NJ	74	D5
Sharp [Sharpsburg]	PA	53	B2
Sharps Hill	DE	7	E3
Sharpsburg Yard	PA	53	B2
Sharpsville	PA	47	A2
Sharret's	MD	10	C1
Shavertown (Andes Junction)	NY	31	A3
Shaw (Shawsville)	PA	57	D1
Shaw	WV	9	B2
Shaw Junction	PA	49	B2
Shaw Mines	PA	60	A4
Shawmont	PA	72	D2
Shawmut	PA	56	B4
Shawnee	PA	62	A4
Shaws	NY	39	D3
Shaws	PA	48	C3
Shawsville	PA	57	D1
Shawsville Tunnel	PA	57	D1
Shea [Flushing]	NY	23	C3
Shea Stadium (Worlds Fair) [Flushing]	NY	23	C3
Sheepshead Bay	NY	23	B6
Shedaker	NJ	74	A5
Sheds	NY	38	C3
Sheffield	MA	31	F3
Sheffield	PA	56	A2
Sheffield Junction	PA	56	A3
Sheffer	PA	63	D4
Shekomeko	NY	31	E4
Shelburne	VT	28	F3
Sheldrake Springs	NY	40	F4
Shell [Thorofare]	NJ	73	A6
Shell Tower [New Rochelle]	NY	25	D4
Shelly	PA	69	C4
Shelocta	PA	49	F3
Shenandoah	PA	67	B3
Shenandoah Junction	PA	67	A3
Shenandoah Junction	WV	9	F2
Shenango	PA	47	D3
Shenks Ferry	PA	63	E3
Shenorock	NY	34	F3
Shepherd	DC	14	C6
Shepherd	MD	10	D5
Shepherd Junction [Washington]	DC	14	C5
Shepherdstown	WV	10	A2
Sheppard	MD	11	A2
Sheppton	PA	67	C1
Sherburne	NY	38	E4
Sherburne Four Corners	NY	38	D4
Sheridan	NY	43	C1
Sheridan [NS(RDG)]	PA	63	E1
Sheridan [PRR]	PA	64	A1
Sherman	NY	43	B3
Sherman Avenue Industrial Track [Camden]	NJ	73	C4
Shermansville	PA	48	B3
Sherriff	PA	56	A3
Sherrill	NY	38	D2
Sherwood	PA	57	B1
Shickshinny	PA	62	F1
Shindle	PA	62	A3
Shingle House	PA	56	D1
Shingles Street Yard [McKees Rocks]	PA	52	D2
Shinhopple	NY	39	F3
Shinn Hollow	NY	34	C2
Shinnecock Hills	NY	35	B5
Shintown	PA	56	F4
Ship [Shippensburg]	PA	63	A2
Ship Bottom	NJ	19	F1
Ship Road	PA	70	E4
Ship Yard [South Camden]	NJ	73	B5
Shippensburg	PA	63	A2
Shippenville	PA	48	E4
Shippingport	PA	49	B4
Shire Oaks	PA	53	B6
Shiremanstown	PA	63	C2
Shirley [CSXT(BO)]	PA	49	C3
Shirley [EBT]	PA	60	E1
Shirley Siding	PA	57	C2
Shirlington	VA	14	A5
Shoaf	PA	50	D3
Shocks (Shocks Mills)	PA	63	D2
Shocks Mill	PA	63	D2
Shoe [Clearfield]	PA	58	A1
Shoemakersville	PA	62	F4
Shohola	PA	68	D3
Shomo Yard [Hagerstown]	MD	10	A6
Shongo [PRR]	NY	43	E3
Shongo [WAG(B&S)]	NY	41	B3
Shoo Fly (Fort Hill)	PA	50	F3
Shoofly Tunnel	PA	50	F3
Shops [Stroudsburg]	PA	16	A4
Shore [Frankford]	PA	73	B3
Shoreham	NY	35	A5
Shoreham	VT	29	F2
Short Creek	WV	50	A2
Short Hills	NJ	21	C5
Short Lane	MD	13	C2
Short Mountain	PA	62	D4
Short Run	PA	61	C3
Shortsville	NY	40	D3
Shoup	PA	55	D1
Showell	MD	15	D1
Shrader	PA	57	F3
Shrein [Lancaster]	PA	64	D4
Shreiners	PA	64	C4
Shrewsbury	NJ	18	F2
Shrewsbury	PA	63	D4
Shrewsbury Road	NJ	18	D2
Shumans	PA	62	E2
Shunpike	NY	31	E4
Shurtleff	NY	28	B4
Shusan	NY	30	F2
Sibley Junction	PA	65	B2
Sickletown	NJ	19	C1
Sideburn	VA	10	C5
Sidell	PA	48	F4
Sidley	PA	70	F3
Sidney	NY	39	E2
Sidney	PA	59	A4
Siegfried	PA	71	A2
Sieglersville	PA	69	B3
Sierks	NY	40	A3
Signal Junction	OH	49	A3
Sills Crossing	NY	38	A4
Silver Brook	PA	66	A3
Silver Brook Junction	PA	66	A3
Silver Creek	NY	43	C1
Silver Lake	NJ	22	A4
Silver Lake	NY	40	B4
Silver Lake Junction	NY	40	A4
Silver Spring	MD	14	B3
Silver Springs	NY	40	A4
Silverbrook	DE	6	D2
Silverbrook	PA	66	A3
Silverly	PA	48	E4
Silvernails	NY	31	E3
Silverside	DE	6	E1
Silverton	PA	67	A6
Simkins	VA	15	A6
Simons	OH	48	B3
Simpson [BBK]	PA	56	C2
Simpson [MGA]	PA	54	B5
Simpson [OW]	PA	68	B3
Sincel	WV	9	A3
Sinclair	PA	50	E1
Sinclairville	NY	43	C2
Singac	NJ	21	D2
Singerly	MD	11	D1
Sink [Sinking Spring]	PA	63	F1
Sinking Spring	PA	63	F1
Sinnemahoning	PA	56	E4
Sinns	PA	53	C5
Sinns Industrial Track	PA	53	C5
Sinsheim	PA	63	C4
Sipesville	PA	60	A2
Sir John's Run	WV	9	E1
Sisson	NY	36	F2
Sitka	PA	55	B5
Sittler	PA	69	A3
Sizerville	PA	56	D3
SK Yard [East Buffalo]	NY	46	B4
Skaneateles	NY	38	A3
Skaneateles Falls	NY	38	A3
Skaneateles Junction	NY	38	A2
Skensowane	NY	29	A3
Skillman	NJ	18	C1
Skinners [defect detector]	NY	34	A1
Skinners Eddy	PA	61	F2
Skinners Falls	NY	34	A1
Slate Hill	NY	34	C2
Slate Junction	PA	69	F2
Slate Run [CR(NYC)]	PA	61	A3
Slate Run [MPA]	PA	63	E4
Slate Valley	PA	69	F3
Slatefield	PA	71	A1
Slateford Junction	PA	16	B5
Slatington	PA	69	E3
Slaughter	DE	7	A4
Sleds Point	MD	12	C4
Sleepy Creek	WV	9	F1
Slickville	PA	49	E4
Sligo	PA	49	E1
Slingerlands	NY	30	D4
Sloam	PA	65	C4
Sloan	WV	9	C3
Sloatsburg	NY	34	D3
Slope [Altoona]	PA	59	C2
Smalley	NJ	18	C3
Smethport	PA	56	C2
Smicksburg	PA	49	F2
Smiley	PA	50	D3
Smith	MD	11	A3
Smith	NY	37	E4
Smith	PA	49	F4
Smithboro	NY	39	B3
Smithdale	PA	53	D6
Smithfield	OH	50	A1
Smithfield	PA	50	D4
Smithfield Street [Pittsburgh]	PA	53	A3
Smiths	PA	63	C4
Smiths Basin	NY	29	F4
Smiths Ferry	PA	49	B3
Smiths Landing	NJ	19	E3
Smiths Mills	NY	43	D1
Smith's Run	PA	56	C2
Smithsburg	MD	10	B1
Smithton	PA	54	D2
Smithtown	NY	35	D2
Smithville	NJ	18	C3
Smithville	PA	63	E3
Smithville Flats	NY	39	D2
Smock	PA	54	D5
Smoke Run	PA	58	A5
Smyrna	DE	7	A3
Smyrna	NY	38	D4
Smyser	PA	63	D3
Snediker	PA	61	C1
Snow [Clearfield]	PA	58	A1
Snow Hill	MD	15	C2
Snow Junction	NY	38	F1
Snow Shoe	PA	57	E2
Snow Shoe Intersection	PA	57	F2
Snowden	PA	53	A6
Snyder	NY	39	B2
Snyder Avenue Yard [Philadelphia]	PA	73	B5
Snyders	PA	69	A3
Snydersburg	PA	48	F4
Snydertown	PA	62	D2
SO Tower [South Fork]	PA	64	B2
Soaptown	OH	49	A1
Sodus	NY	40	E1
Sodus Center	NY	40	E2
Sodus Point	NY	40	E1
Solar Mine	PA	52	A2
Soldier Run	PA	57	B1
Solomans Gap	PA	65	B6
Solon	NY	39	C1
Solsville	NY	38	E3
Solvay	NY	36	A1
Somerdale	NJ	73	C6
Somerfield	PA	50	F4
Somers	PA	54	C2
Somers Point	NJ	19	D3
Somerset	NJ	74	B2
Somerset	PA	60	A3
Somerton	PA	73	D1
Somerville	NJ	20	E4
Somers Lane	PA	61	B1
Sonestown	PA	61	D4
Sonman	PA	60	C1
Sonyea	NY	40	B4
Soperton	ON	36	C2
Sorrento	MD	11	A2
Souderton	PA	70	C1
Sours Mills	PA	71	D1
South Altoona	PA	59	C2
South Ambler	PA	73	A1
South Amboy	NJ	18	E1
South Amsterdam	NY	30	C3
South Avoca	PA	65	B3
South Avon	NY	45	F3
South Baker (Ferney)	PA	56	F4
South Bay	NY	38	D2
South Beach	NY	20	F1
South Berlin	NY	30	F4
South Bethlehem	NY	30	D4
South Bombay	NY	28	B1
South Bound Brook	NJ	20	F4
South Boyles (Herndon)	PA	62	C3
South Branch	PA	61	E2
South Bridgeton	NJ	19	B2
South Byron	NY	40	B2
South Cairo	NY	31	D2
South Cambridge	NY	30	F2
South Camden	NJ	73	B5
South Carnegie	PA	52	D3
South Carolina Avenue [Atlantic City]	NJ	19	F4
South Chester	PA	72	C6
South Clyde	NY	40	F2
South Columbia	NY	38	F3
South Corinth	NY	30	D1
South Cumberland	MD	8	D2
South Danville	PA	62	D2
South Dayton	NY	43	D2
South Dennis	NJ	19	C3
South Driftwood	PA	56	D4
South Duquesne	PA	53	C4
South Edmeston	NY	38	E4
South Eldred	PA	56	D1
South Elizabeth	NJ	21	D6
South Elwyn	PA	72	B5
South Emporium	PA	56	D3
South Fair	PA	62	C2
South Farmingdale	NY	35	C3
South Farwell	PA	56	F4
South Ferry (Clarks Ferry)	PA	63	C1
South Fish	NJ	19	C1
South Fork	PA	64	B2
South Fort Erie	ON	46	A4
South Fort Plain	NY	30	B3
South Fox Chase	PA	73	C2
South Hamburg	PA	62	F4
South Gaines	PA	61	A2
South Gilboa	NY	31	B1
South Glassboro	NJ	19	B1
South Gloucester	NJ	73	B5
South Greenfield	NY	23	B5
South Greensburg	PA	50	E1
South Hartwick	NY	38	F4
South Heights	PA	49	C4
South Hero	VT	28	F2
South Junction	NY	28	F2
South Kearny	NJ	22	B5
South Keating (Cooks Run)	PA	56	E4
South Kortright	NY	31	A2
South Lakewood	NJ	18	E3
South Lansing	NY	39	A1
South Lee	MA	31	F2
South Lica	NJ	19	D1
South Lima	NY	40	C3
South Linden	PA	61	B4
South Little Falls	NY	30	A2
South Livonia	NY	40	C4
South Lucas (Reed Crossing)	NJ	18	C4
South Machias	NY	43	F2
South Miller	PA	62	C4
South Millville (Menantico)	NJ	19	C2
South Montrose	PA	61	F2
South Mountain	PA	63	F1
South New Berlin	NY	39	E1
South Norwalk	CT	35	C1
South Nyack	NY	25	B1
South Oil City	PA	48	E3
South Olean	NY	43	F3
South Orange	NJ	21	D5
South Ore	PA	73	A1
South Owego	NY	39	B3
South Palmyra	NY	40	D2
South Paterson	NJ	22	A2
South Pemberton	NJ	18	C3
South Philipsburg	PA	58	D4
South Pittston	PA	65	B3
South Plainfield	NJ	20	B2
South Plainfield Yard	NJ	20	B2
South Pomo	NJ	19	D2
South Race	NJ	73	C5
South Red Bank	PA	49	E2
South Richards [defect detector]	PA	71	D3
South River	NJ	20	B4
South Schenectady [CSXT(WS)]	NY	32	B3
South Schenectady [STLH(DH)]	NY	32	A3
South Scranton	PA	65	C2
South Seaville	NJ	19	D3
South Side	PA	63	E4
South Side Crossing	NY	23	B3
South Side Junction [Pittsburgh]	PA	53	A3
South Siding	NY	36	F4
South Street [Brocton]	NY	43	C2
South Street [Wilkes-Barre]	PA	65	C5
South Unadilla	NY	39	E2
South Utica	NY	38	E2
South Vineland	NJ	19	C2
South Wales	NY	42	E4
South West Junction	PA	50	E1
South Westville	NJ	73	B6
South Wilkes-Barre	PA	65	B5
South Williamsport	PA	61	C4
South Wins (Winslow Junction)	NJ	19	C1
South Witmer Branch	PA	57	C3
South Woodstown	NJ	19	B1
Southampton	NY	35	C5
Southampton	PA	70	D2
Southampton Campus/LIU	NY	35	B5
Southfields	NY	34	D3
Southold	NY	35	B5
Southport	CT	35	C1
Southview	PA	52	A5
Southwood	DE	6	B2
Sowash	PA	50	E1
Sox	PA	61	E2
Spa Spring	NJ	20	C2
Spangler	PA	59	B5
Spangler No.3 Mine	PA	59	C5
Sparkill	NY	25	B1
Sparks	MD	11	A1
Sparrow (Sparrowbush)	NY	34	B2
Sparrowbush	NY	34	B2
Sparrows Point	MD	12	D3
Sparrows Point Mill [Bethlehem Steel]	MD	12	E3
Sparta	NJ	16	C3
Sparta Junction [new]	NJ	16	C2
Sparta Junction [old]	NJ	16	B2
Spartanburg	PA	48	E2
Speeceville	PA	63	C1
Speedwell	PA	50	F2
Spellmans	NY	28	F2
Spencer	NY	39	A3
Spencerport	NY	40	B2
Spencerville	ON	36	D1
Speonk	NY	35	A6
Spielman	MD	10	A1
Spotswood	NJ	18	D1
Sprakers	NY	30	B3
Spray Beach	NJ	19	E1
Spring [Boiling Spring]	PA	63	B2
Spring [Chestnut Hill]	PA	73	A2
Spring [Falling Spring]	PA	65	B2
Spring Brook	NY	46	D5
Spring City	PA	70	F1
Spring Creek	PA	48	E1
Spring Gap	MD	9	C1
Spring Garden	PA	67	B6
Spring Garden Junction	PA	67	C6
Spring Garden Street [Philadelphia]	PA	73	B4
Spring Glen	NY	34	C1
Spring Grove	NY	28	B3
Spring Grove	PA	63	C3
Spring Lake	NJ	18	F3
Spring Meadow	PA	59	C3
Spring Mill	PA	72	D2
Spring Mount	PA	70	B1
Spring Street Yard [Reading]	PA	64	A5
Spring Valley	NY	26	A6
Springboro	PA	48	B2
Springbrook	PA	68	B4
Springdale	CT	35	C1
Springdale	NJ	73	D5
Springdale	PA	53	D1
Springdell	PA	70	A3
Springfield	MD	11	A4
Springfield	NJ	21	C5
Springfield	PA	47	B6
Springfield	VA	10	C5
Springfield	WV	9	C2
Springfield #5 Mine	PA	57	C3
Springfield Gardens	NY	24	A5
Springfield Junction	NY	24	A5
Springhill Junction	PA	58	D3
Springside	NJ	74	B5
Springton	PA	70	A2
Springtown	NJ	71	F3
Springtown	PA	69	C4
Springvale	PA	63	D3
Springville	NY	43	E1
Springville	PA	61	F2
Springville Junction	NY	43	E1
Springwater	NY	40	C4
Sproul	PA	60	C1
Spruce	PA	57	E1

Spuce Creek PA 57 D4
Spruce Hill PA 62 A4
Spuyten Duyvil NY 25 B4
SR [Susquehanna] PA 68 B1
SRO [Alexandria] VA 14 B5
St. Albans NY 24 A4
St. Benedict PA 59 C5
St. Charles PA 49 F2
St. Clair PA 67 B5
St. Clairsville OH 50 A2
St. Clairsville Junction OH 50 A2
St. Davids ON 42 A3
St. Davids [SEPA(PRR)] PA 72 B2
St. Davids [PHWN] PA 72 B3
St. Denis MD 12 A3
St. George NY 22 C6
St. George PA 48 D4
St. George's MD 10 D2
St. Helena MD 12 D3
St. James MD 10 A1
St. James NY 35 D2
St. Joe PA 49 D2
St. Johns PA 62 F2
St. Johns Park [Manhattan] NY 23 A3
St. Johnsville NY 30 B2
St. Josephs NY 34 B1
St. Leonard PA 74 A3
St. Lu PA 57 B3
St. Martins PA 73 A2
St. Michael PA 60 B1
St. Michaels MD 11 C5
St. Nicholas PA 67 B3
St. Nicholas Breaker [new] PA 67 A5
St. Nicholas Breaker [old] PA 67 B3
St. Peters PA 70 A2
St. Petersburg PA 49 E1
St. Regis Falls NY 28 B2
St. Vincent PA 50 F1
St. Xavier PA 50 F1
Staatsburg NY 31 D4
Stackhouse PA 62 F1
Stadium [Villanova] PA 72 C3
Stafford NY 45 C1
Staffordville NJ 19 E1
Stalbird NY 36 F3
Stam [Stamford] CT 35 C1
Stamburgh PA 50 E3
Stamford CT 35 C1
Stamford NY 31 B1
Stamford [CN(GT)] ON 42 A4
Stamford [NYC(MC)] ON 42 A3
Stan [Pulaski] NY 37 C4
Standard PA 55 C2
Standing Stone PA 61 E2
Standish NY 28 D2
Stanfordville NY 31 E4
Stanhope OH 48 B3
Stanhope PA 62 E4
Stanley MD 9 E1
Stanley NY 40 E3
Stanley PA 57 B2
Stannards NY 41 B3
Stanton DE 6 C3
Stanton NJ 18 C1
Stanton [EBT] PA 60 F2
Stanton [PSR(PS)] PA 57 A1
Stanton [SEPA(RDG)] PA 73 A2
Stanton [WPE] PA 65 A2
Stanwick Avenue [Moorestown] NJ 18 C3
Staple Bend Tunnel PA 64 B1
Stapleton NY 20 F1
Star Brick PA 48 F2
Star City WV 50 D4
Star Farm Beach VT 28 F3
Star Junction PA 54 D4
Star Rock PA 63 E3
Starford PA 57 B3
Starkey NY 41 E1
Starlight PA 68 C1
Starner PA 63 B3
Starr [EBT] PA 60 F2
Starr [NYC] PA 48 E2
Starr Farm NY 43 C2
Starrucca PA 68 B1
Starrucca Viaduct PA 68 B1
Startzman MD 10 A5
State [Harrisburg] PA 64 C2
State College PA 57 E3
State Hospital [Poughkeepsie] NY 31 D4
State Hospital [Wingate] NY 34 F1
State Line CT 31 F3
State Line MA 31 F2
State Line NY 43 A2
State Line PA 60 B4
State Line Junction NY 41 F3
State Line Tunnel NY 31 F2
State Line Tunnel PA 50 B1
State Road DE 6 C4
State School [NS(LHR)] NY 34 D3
State School [PC(NYC)] NY 31 E4
State Street Station [Rochester] NY 44 C2
Staten Island Junction NJ 21 D6
Station Square [Pittsburgh] PA 53 A3
Stauffer Chemical [Morrisville] PA 74 C3
Stautsburg NJ 18 C1
Ste. Agnes PQ 28 C1
Steamburg NY 43 D3
Steamtown National Historic Site [Scranton] PA 65 C2
Steel [Bethlehem] PA 71 B4
Steel [RJCP(CI-PRR)] PA 57 B4
Steel [SEPA] PA 73 B1
Steelton PA 64 D3
Steeple Chase NY 23 D6
Steiners PA 58 D3
Stell PA 64 C2
Stellaville NY 36 F3
Stelton NJ 20 B2
Stemmer's Run MD 12 D2
Stephens City VA 9 E4
Stephensburg NJ 17 C3
Stephenson VA 9 F3
Stephentown NY 30 F4
Stepney MD 13 C2
Sterling [LV-PC(RWO)] NY 38 A1
Sterling [NS(ERIE)] NY 34 D3
Sterling VA 10 B4
Sterling Forest NY 34 D3
Sterling Mine NY 34 D3
Sterling Mine PA 58 B5
Sterling No.1 Mine PA 59 C5
Sterling No.10 Mine PA 59 D4
Sterling Run PA 56 D4
Sterlingville NY 37 D1
Steuben PA 71 C2
Steubenville OH 50 A1
Stevens NJ 74 B5
Stevens NY 43 E3
Stevens PA 63 F2
Stevens Point PA 68 B1
Stevenson MD 11 A2
Stevenson PA 61 E3
Stevensville MD 11 B4
Stevensville ON 42 D3
Stewart Manor NY 24 B4
Stewarton PA 50 E3
Stewarts OH 50 A3
Stewarts PA 66 B3
Stewartstown PA 63 D4
Stewartsville NJ 71 F2
Steyer MD 9 A3
Stickpile Tunnel MD 9 D1
Stier (Johnsonville) PA 16 A6
Stiles NY 38 B2
Stiles PA 57 B4
Stiles Street Yard [Linden] NJ 20 D1
Still Pond MD 11 C3
Stilleys Siding PA 53 A5
Stillwater NJ 17 C2
Stillwater NY 29 D2
Stillwater PA 62 E1
Stillwater Junction NY 30 E3
Stirling NJ 21 A6
Stissing NY 31 E4
Stissing Junction NY 31 E4
Stittville NY 38 E2
Stock [Oak Island] NJ 22 A5
Stock Yard [Buffalo] NY 46 B4
Stockbridge MA 31 F2
Stockdale PA 54 C3
Stockertown PA 71 D1
Stockholm NJ 17 D2
Stockley DE 7 E3
Stockport [EL(ERIE)] NY 39 E4
Stockport [PC(NYC)] NY 33 C4
Stockport Centre NY 33 C4
Stockton MD 15 C2
Stockton NJ 18 B1
Stockton PA 66 B1
Stoke Park PA 71 C3
Stone Gap PA 63 C1
Stone Harbor NJ 19 D4
Stone Siding PA 62 A2
Stoneboro PA 48 C4
Stonebreaker MD 10 A2
Stonebridge PA 60 F3
Stoneham PA 56 A2
Stoneham Mill PA 56 A2
Stonerville PA 55 B3
Stoney [NS(CR)] PA 63 C1
Stoney [PRR] PA 63 D3
Stoney Creek Yard [Marcus Hook] PA 72 B6
Stoney Point [defect detector] NY 26 B3
Stony PA 48 C3
Stony Brook NY 35 D2
Stony Brook PA 63 D3
Stony Brook Junction NY 43 E3
Stony Clove NY 31 C3
Stony Creek NY 29 D4
Stony Hollow NY 31 D3
Stony Point NY 26 B4
Stony Point PA 48 C3
Stony River WV 9 A3
Stony Run MD 12 A4
Stoops Ferry PA 52 B1
Storage PA 52 C1
Stormstown PA 57 E3
Stormville NY 34 F1
Stottsville PA 70 A3
Stottville NY 33 C5
Stoughton PA 60 A2
Stover PA 57 D3
Stoverdale PA 63 D2
Stowe PA 70 B2
Stoystown PA 60 B2
Strafford PA 72 B2
Straight PA 56 C3
Straight Creek PA 56 C3
Strangleford PA 60 A1
Strasburg PA 63 F3
Strasburg VA 9 E4
Strasburg Junction VA 9 E4
Stratford CT 35 D1
Stratford NJ 73 D6
Strattonville PA 49 F1
Straw Bridge PA 63 D4
Strawberry Ridge Power Plant PA 62 D1
Strawbridge PA 61 D4
Strecker MD 9 B2
Street MD 11 B1
Street Road PA 70 D2
Strickler PA 63 D3
Stringer OH 50 A2
Stringtown PA 53 D5
Stronach PA 57 C2
Stroudsburg PA 16 A4
Stroudsburg PA 69 C2
Stroughs NY 36 C4
Stroup PA 56 C4
Strubles PA 57 E3
Strum PA 50 D4
Struthers PA 56 A2
Stuart Tunnel WV 9 D1
Studa PA 50 B1
Stull PA 61 F4
Sturgeon PA 52 B4
Stuyvesant NY 33 B3
Stuyvesant Falls NY 33 C3
Suburban Station [Philadelphia] PA 73 B4
Succasuna NJ 17 D3
Sudan PA 54 A2
Sudbrook MD 12 A1
Sudlersville MD 11 D3
Suedberg PA 62 E4
Suffern NY 34 D4
Sugar (Sugar Loaf) NY 27 C4
Sugar Camp PA 57 E1
Sugar Creek [NS(ERIE)] PA 48 D3
Sugar Creek [NS(LV)] PA 61 E2
Sugar Hill PA 56 B4
Sugar Loaf NY 27 C4
Sugar Notch PA 65 B6
Sugar Notch Gap PA 65 B6
Sugar Run PA 56 B1
Sugar Run Junction PA 56 B1
Sulgar PA 57 B1
Sullivan NY 38 D2
Sulphur Springs [PC(PRR)] PA 60 C3
Sulphur Springs [SRW] PA 62 B4
Summerdale NY 43 B2
Summerdale PA 73 B3
Summerfield MD 11 B2
Summerhill PA 64 B2
Summerson PA 56 D4
Summerville [BLE] PA 48 B1
Summerville [PSR(LEFC PRR)] PA 49 F1
Summit [NJT(DLW)] NJ 21 C5
Summit [NYSW] NJ 17 D2
Summit [APRR] PA 59 A3
Summit [BNYP(KERR)] PA 56 C1
Summit [BO] PA 60 A3
Summit [LNE] PA 71 B1
Summit [NS(PRR Cambria County)] PA 60 B1
Summit [PRR Centre County] PA 58 D5
Summit [PRR Lancaster County] PA 63 F3
Summit [RDG] PA 62 E4
Summit Hill PA 66 C4
Summit Park NY 26 A5
Summit Park PA 52 D5
Summit Point WV 9 F3
Summit Switch PA 65 C3
Summitville NY 34 C1
Summitville OH 49 A3
Sumner PA 53 B1
Sun Colliery PA 66 B5
Sun Oil [Naaman] DE 6 F1
Sun Oil [Philadelphia] PA 73 A5
Sunbrook PA 59 C3
Sunbury PA 66 A6
Sunnybrook PA 73 A1
Sunnyside MD 10 D4
Sunnyside NY 33 C3
Sunnyside Junction [Queens] NY 23 C2
Sunnyside Restoration NY 25 C1
Sunnyside Yard [Queens] NY 23 B3
Sunset Hills VA 10 B3
Superior No.1 Mine PA 59 A5
Suplee PA 70 A2
Surf NJ 19 F1
Surveyor PA 57 D1
Suscon PA 68 A4
Suspension Bridge NY 42 B3
Suspension Bridge Yard [DLWR(LV)] NY 42 B3
Suspension Bridge Yard [EL(ERIE)] NY 42 B4
Susquehanna [LOS] PA 63 E4
Susquehanna [NS(ERIE)] PA 68 B1
Susquehanna Bridge PA 58 D1
Susquehanna Moveable Bridge [Perryville] MD 13 D1
Susquehanna Transfer [Secaucus] NJ 22 C4
Sussex NJ 17 D2
Sussex Junction (Lewisburg) NJ 17 D2
Sussex Junction [Netcong] NJ 17 C3
Suter PA 53 D6
Sutton PA 49 F1
Swain NJ 19 C4
Swains NY 41 B1
Swamp Creek PA 56 C3
Swan Creek MD 13 D2
Swanton MD 9 B2
Swanville PA 47 C6
Swart PA 50 C3
Swarthmore PA 72 C5
Swartswood NJ 16 A2
Swartswood Junction NJ 16 A2
Swartwood NY 39 A2
Swatara PA 62 E3
Swatara Junction PA 62 E3
Swede NJ 18 A4
Swedeland PA 72 C2
Sweden Valley PA 56 E2
Swedesboro NJ 18 A4
Swedesford Road PA 70 E4
Sweets NY 38 E4
Swengel PA 62 B2
Swissmont PA 56 C3
Swissvale PA 53 B3
Switch Back PA 66 A3
Switch No.9 MD 8 B1
Syberton PA 59 A2
Sycamore [Buffalo] NY 46 B4
Sycamore PA 50 C3
Sydenham ON 36 A3
Sygan PA 52 C4
Sykes PA 56 D2
Sykesville MD 10 D2
Sykesville PA 57 B2
Sylmar MD 11 C1
Sylvan Beach NY 38 D2
Sylvan Junction NY 38 D2
Sylvan Lake NY 34 F1
Syosset NY 24 D2
Syracuse NY 38 C2
Syracuse [DLW] NY 36 A1
Syracuse [NYC] NY 36 B1
Syracuse Intermodal Center NY 36 A1
Syracuse Junction NY 36 A1
Syracuse University NY 36 B2

T

Tablers WV 9 F2
Tabor PA 73 B3
Tabor Junction PA 73 B3
Taconic CT 31 F3
Tacony PA 73 C3
Tadd PA 71 C2
Tadmor PA 71 C2
Tag PA 50 B4
Tahawus NY 29 D1
Takoma Park DC 14 C3
Talcville NY 36 E4
Tallman NY 34 D4
Tally Ho PA 56 B2
Talmadge Hill CT 35 C1
Tamanend PA 67 D2
Tamaqua PA 62 F3
Tambine PA 56 C3
Tangas PA 62 A1
Tank PA 62 F2
Tanners NY 31 E3
Tannersville NY 31 C2
Tannersville PA 69 C2
Tannery MD 10 D1
Tannery PA 69 A2
Tanneytown MD 10 C1
Tappan NY 25 B1
Tara PA 63 D1
Tarbel NY 38 A4
Tarentum PA 51 D3
Tarport PA 56 C1
Tarr PA 55 C2
Tarrytown NY 25 C1
Tasker DE 6 D4
Tasley VA 15 B4
Tatamy PA 71 D2
Tatesville PA 60 D2
Taughannock Falls NY 39 A1
Taylor NJ 73 D3
Taylor NY 45 E2
Taylor PA 57 F3
Taylor Yard [Scranton] PA 65 C2
Taylorstown PA 50 B2
Teaneck NJ 22 C2
Teegarden OH 49 A3
Tekene Junction NY 28 D3
Telford PA 70 C1
Temple PA 64 A4
Temple Tunnel PA 54 A2
Temple University [Philadelphia] PA 73 B4
Templeton PA 47 D4
Ten Mile Run Junction PA 54 A5
Tenneco Chemical [Burlington] NJ 74 B5
Tennent NJ 18 E2
Tennessee Avenue [Atlantic City] NJ 19 F4
Term DE 6 D3
Terra Cotta DC 14 C4
Terrace [Buffalo] NY 46 A4
Terrace Park NY 36 D3
Teterboro-Williams Avenue NJ 22 C2
Texaco [Westville] NJ 73 B6
Texas MD 11 A2
The Glen NY 29 D3
The Hunt PA 72 B3
The Raun NY 23 D5
Thendara NY 37 F3
Theresa NY 36 D4
Thiells NY 26 A4
Thomas [CSXT(PSO)] PA 52 C6
Thomas [PRR] PA 62 B2
Thomas WV 9 A3
Thomas Fork WV 50 D4
Thomas Mill PA 59 D4
Thomas Viaduct MD 12 A4
Thomastons PA 67 A5
Thomastons Colliery PA 67 A5
Thomasville PA 63 C3
Thompson DE 6 A3
Thompson MD 11 C6
Thompson [BKRR(GJ)] NY 30 E2
Thompson [NYC] NY 40 E3
Thompson [DH/ERIE] PA 68 B1
Thompson [Dusquene] PA 53 C4
Thompson [Thompsontown] PA 62 B4
Thompson No.1 Mine PA 54 B6
Thompson No.2 Mine PA 54 B6

Place	State	Page	Grid
Thompson Point	NJ	72	C6
Thompson Ridge	NY	34	D1
Thompsontown	PA	62	B4
Thompsonville	PA	52	C5
Thorn	PA	49	D2
Thornton	PA	70	A3
Thornton Junction	PA	47	B6
Thornwood	NY	26	D6
Thorofare	NJ	73	A6
Three Bridges	NJ	18	C1
Three Mile Bay	NY	37	B1
Three River Point	NY	38	B2
Three Springs	PA	60	E2
Throop	NY	38	A3
Throop	PA	65	D1
Thrush	WV	9	C2
Thurlow Yard [Marcus Hook]	PA	72	B6
Thurman	NY	29	D4
Thurmont	MD	10	B1
Tiadaghton	PA	61	A2
Ticonderoga	NY	29	F2
Ticonderoga [AMTK]	NY	29	B4
Ticonderoga [STLH(DH)]	NY	29	A4
Ticonderoga Junction	NY	29	A4
Tidedale	PA	57	A4
Tidioute	PA	48	F2
Tiffany	PA	68	A2
Tifft Yard [CSXT(LV) Buffalo]	NY	46	B5
Tifft Yard [NS(NKP) Lackawanna]	NY	46	B5
Tighman	MD	11	D3
Tilly Foster	NY	26	D1
Tillys	PA	70	B2
Tiltonville	OH	50	A2
Timblin	PA	49	F2
Timonium	MD	11	A2
Tin Bridge	PA	61	C2
Tioga [EL(ERIE)]	PA	61	B1
Tioga [Philadelphia]	PA	73	B3
Tioga Center	NY	39	B3
Tioga Junction	PA	61	B1
Tioga Marine Terminal [Philadelphia]	PA	73	C4
Tioga Street [Philadelphia]	PA	73	B3
Tiona	PA	56	A2
Tionesta	PA	48	E3
Tippencanoe	PA	54	D5
Tipton	PA	57	D3
Titus (Klapperthall Junction)	PA	64	B6
Titus Power Plant	PA	64	B6
Titusville	NJ	74	B1
Titusville	PA	48	E3
Tivoli	NY	31	E3
Tivoli (Essick)	PA	61	D4
Toby	PA	56	C4
Tobyhanna	PA	69	C1
Tobyhanna Army Depot	PA	69	B1
Todd	PA	60	E1
Toddsville	NY	38	F4
Tolna (Sheffer)	PA	63	D4
Tomb	PA	61	B4
Tome [Port Deposit]	MD	13	B2
Tomhicken	PA	62	F2
Tomkins	PA	61	B1
Tomkins Cove	NY	26	B3
Tomlin	NJ	18	A4
Tompkinsville	NY	20	F1
Toms (Strangleford)	PA	60	A1
Toms Brook	VA	9	D4
Tom's River	NJ	18	E4
Tomson	PA	66	B6
Tonawanda	NY	46	B2
Tonawanda Island	NY	46	A2
Tonawanda Junction	NY	46	B2
Topton	PA	69	B4
Tor (Toronto)	OH	49	B4
Toronto	OH	49	B4
Torpedo	PA	48	E2
Torrance	PA	50	F1
Torresdale	PA	73	D2
Totowa	NJ	22	A2
Tottenville	NY	20	D3
Toughkenamon	PA	6	A1
Towaco	NJ	21	C1
Towanda	PA	61	E2
Tower City	PA	62	D4
Tower Hill	NJ	20	E1
Tower Hill	NY	22	B6
Town Line	NY	42	E3
Town [Hagerstown]	MD	10	A5
Town	PA	69	B4
Town Creek	MD	9	D2
Towners	NY	34	F2
Townley	NJ	21	D6
Townsbury	NJ	17	C3
Townsend	DE	7	A3
Townsend	VA	15	A6
Townsends Inlet	NJ	19	D4
Townshend	MD	10	D6
Towson	MD	11	A2
Towson Heights	MD	11	A2
Tracey	NJ	18	E2
Tracktowne	PA	63	D3
Traff [Trafford]	PA	53	D4
Trafford	PA	53	D4
Trail	NJ	73	C3
Trainer	PA	72	B6
Tranquility	NJ	17	C3
Transfer	PA	47	B1
Transit	NY	46	D2
Transit Bridge	NY	41	A2
Trap Rock	PA	70	A2
Trap Rock	VA	10	B4
Trappe	MD	11	C5
Trauger	PA	55	D1
Travis Con-Ed Power Plant	NY	20	D2
Traymore	PA	70	D2
Treasury Building [Washington]	DC	14	B5
Trees Mills	PA	49	E4
Treichler	PA	69	F3
Tremley	NJ	20	D1
Tremont [PLE(PMY)]	PA	54	C3
Tremont [RBMN(RDG)]	PA	62	E3
Tremont 177th Street	NY	23	C1
Trent [West Trenton]	NJ	74	C2
Trenton	NJ	18	C2
Trenton	PA	67	C2
Trenton Falls	NY	38	F1
Trenton Industrial Track	NJ	74	C2
Tresckow	PA	66	B2
Treverton	PA	62	D3
Trevose	PA	73	D1
Trexler	PA	69	A3
Trexlertown	PA	69	B4
Tribes Hill	NY	30	C3
Triconda	NY	30	E2
Tridelphia	WV	50	A2
Trindle Spring	PA	63	C2
Tripoli	PA	69	A3
Trobe [Latrobe]	PA	50	F1
Trough Creek	PA	60	D1
Trout	MD	9	B2
Trout Run	PA	61	B4
Troutman	PA	49	D2
Trowbridge	PA	61	C1
Troy	NY	32	F2
Troy	PA	61	C2
Trucksville	PA	65	B4
Truman	PA	56	D3
Trumansburg	NY	39	A1
Trunkeyville	PA	48	F3
Truxall	PA	49	E4
Truxton	NY	38	C4
Try Street Yard [Pittsburgh]	PA	53	A3
Tryonville	PA	48	D2
Trythall	PA	70	A2
Tuckahoe	MD	11	D4
Tuckahoe	NJ	19	D3
Tuckahoe	NY	25	D3
Tuckerton	NJ	19	E1
Tuckerton	PA	64	A4
Tucquan	PA	63	E3
Tully	NY	38	C3
Tullytown	PA	18	C3
Tulp [Reading]	PA	64	A5
Tulphocken	PA	73	A3
Tumble Falls	NJ	18	B1
Tunkhannock	PA	61	F3
Tunkhannock Viaduct	PA	68	A3
Tunnel	NY	39	D2
Tunnel [CR (PRR Cambria County)]	PA	59	C6
Tunnel [NS (PRR Huntingdon County)]	PA	57	E4
Tunnel [RBMN(CNJ)]	PA	69	A1
Tunnelton	PA	49	F4
Tupper Lake	NY	28	B4
Tupper Lake Junction	NY	28	B4
Turbett	PA	62	A4
Turbotville	PA	62	D1
Turkey City	PA	49	E1
Turner	MD	12	D3
Turner	PA	48	B3
Turners	MD	11	C5
Turnpike	PA	63	D4
Turrell's Mill	PA	61	E4
Turtle Point	PA	56	D1
Tuscarora	MD	10	B3
Tuscarora	NY	40	B4
Tuscarora [PRR]	PA	62	B4
Tuscarora [RDG]	PA	67	D4
Tuscarora Pump Station	PA	60	E1
Tuscarora Wye	NY	46	D1
Tusten	PA	68	D3
Tuxedo	NY	34	D3
Twenty-First (Keyser Junction)	MD	8	A6
Twin Arch	MD	10	C2
Twin Lakes	CT	31	F3
Twin Mountain	WV	9	B3
Twin Oaks	PA	72	B6
Twin Ponds	NY	28	D2
Twin Rocks	PA	57	B4
Two Lick	PA	57	A4
Tyburn Yard [Morrisville]	PA	74	C3
Tyler [BO(B&S)]	PA	56	C4
Tyler [LV]	PA	61	F2
Tyler [PC(PRR)]	PA	56	C4
Tylerdale	PA	50	C2
Tylerdale Connecting Railroad Junction	PA	50	C2
Tylersburg	PA	48	F4
Tyrell	OH	48	A4
Tyrone	PA	57	D3

U

Place	State	Page	Grid
U [Grand Central Terminal Manhattan]	NY	23	B3
Udell	PA	55	C1
Uhlers	PA	71	E1
UK	NY	43	E3
Ulster	PA	61	D2
Ulster Park	NY	31	D4
Ulysses	PA	56	F1
UN [Gallitzin]	PA	59	A2
UN [New Castle Yard]	PA	51	B2
Unadilla	NY	39	E2
Uncas Road	NY	29	A2
Underwood's	PA	56	A2
Unicorn	PA	63	F3
Union (Perth Amboy Junction)	NJ	20	C1
Union	NY	26	A6
Union Beach	NJ	18	E1
Union Bridge	MD	10	C1
Union Carbide [South Bound Brook]	NJ	20	F4
Union City	PA	48	D1
Union Crossing [Baltimore]	MD	12	C2
Union Grove	NY	31	A3
Union Hall Street [Jamaica]	NY	23	D4
Union Hill	NY	40	D2
Union Furnace	PA	57	D4
Union Junction [Baltimore]	MD	12	C2
Union Junction [Bessemer]	PA	53	C3
Union Landing	NJ	73	D3
Union Market Terminal [Washington]	DC	14	C4
Union Mills	PA	57	F4
Union No.1	MD	8	B1
Union Road [West Seneca]	NY	46	C5
Union Springs	NY	40	F3
Union Station [Albany]	NY	32	E4
Union Station [Alexandria]	VA	14	B6
Union Station [Atlantic City]	NJ	19	F4
Union Station [Erie]	PA	47	C6
Union Station [Troy]	NY	32	F2
Union Station [Washington]	DC	14	C5
Union Station [Wilkes-Barre]	PA	65	C5
Union Street [Pottsville]	PA	67	B5
Union Township	NJ	21	D6
Union Tunnel [Baltimore]	MD	12	C2
Unionbury	NJ	21	D5
Uniondale	PA	68	B2
Unionport	OH	50	A1
Uniontown	PA	50	E3
Unionville [CSXT(WS)]	NY	30	D4
Unionville [MNJ(MU)]	NY	34	C3
Unionville	PA	57	E2
United	PA	55	D1
Unity	PA	53	D2
Unity Junction	PA	53	D1
Universal	PA	53	D2
University [Washington]	DC	14	C4
University City [Philadelphia]	PA	73	A4
University Heights	NY	23	C1
US Pipe [Stevens]	NJ	74	B5
Upland	PA	72	B6
Upper Bangor	PA	16	A6
Upper Bay [Newark]	NJ	22	B5
Upper Colver	PA	57	B4
Upper Hillville	PA	49	E2
Upper Lehigh	PA	69	A2
Upper Lehigh Junction	PA	69	A2
Upper Marlboro	MD	11	A5
Upper Middletown	PA	54	D5
Upper Montclair	NJ	22	A3
Upsal	PA	73	A3
Upton	NJ	18	D4
Upton	NY	35	A6
Urey	PA	59	A5
Urquhart	PA	61	F4
Ursina	PA	50	F4
US Naval Weapons Laboratory [Dahlgren]	VA	14	A1
Uscan	ON	28	B1
Ushers	NY	30	E3
Utahville	PA	57	C3
Utica	NY	38	F2
Utica	PA	48	D3

V

Place	State	Page	Grid
Vail	NJ	16	C5
Vail	PA	57	D3
Vail Mills	NY	30	C2
Vails Gate	NY	27	F1
Vails Gate Junction	NY	27	F1
Valatie	NY	33	D2
Valcour	NY	28	F2
Vale	MD	11	B1
Vale	PA	51	C2
Vale Summit	MD	8	B2
Valencia	PA	49	D3
Valentines	NJ	20	C3
Valhalla	NY	25	D1
Valier	PA	57	A2
Valley [CNJ]	NJ	17	B4
Valley [Oak Island]	NJ	22	A5
Valley [Coatesville]	PA	70	A3
Valley [Philadelphia]	PA	72	D4
Valley Brick	PA	51	C4
Valley Camp	PA	51	D4
Valley Cottage	NY	26	B6
Valley Falls	NY	30	E3
Valley Falls	PA	73	C1
Valley Forge	PA	72	A1
Valley Junction	NY	34	C2
Valley Junction [Reading]	PA	64	A5
Valley Junction [WM]	PA	63	C4
Valley Mills	NY	38	D2
Valley Store	PA	70	F4
Valley Stream	NY	24	B5
Valley Tower [Valley Stream]	NY	24	B5
Valley Works	PA	55	C4
Vallonia	OH	50	A3
Valois	NY	41	F1
Van [Brooklyn]	NY	23	B4
Van	PA	48	E4
Van Bibber	MD	13	A3
Van Buren	NY	43	C1
Van Courtlandt	NY	25	C4
Van Deusenville	MA	31	F2
Van Dorn Street Intermodal Terminal [Alexandria]	VA	14	A6
Van Emmans	PA	52	C5
Van Etten	NY	39	A3
Van Etten Junction	NY	39	A3
Van Hoesen	NY	33	D1
Van Housen	PA	56	F2
Van Meter	PA	54	D2
Van Mine	PA	58	C2
Van Nest Shops [Bronx]	NY	23	C1
Van Nostrand Avenue [Jersey City]	NJ	22	B5
Van Nostrands	NY	41	B1
Van Ormer	PA	57	C3
Van Vleet	NY	41	D3
Van Voohis	PA	54	A2
Van Voohis	WV	50	D4
Van Wagners	NY	31	D4
Vance	PA	50	C2
Vance	WV	9	C2
Vance Mill Junction	PA	55	A6
Vanclevesville	WV	9	F2
Vandalia	NY	43	E3
Vanderbilt	PA	55	B5
Vanderbilt Avenue [Brooklyn]	NY	23	B4
Vanderbilt Avenue [Niagara Falls]	NY	42	B3
Vandergrift	PA	51	F3
Vanderveer Park	NY	23	B5
Vandling	PA	68	B3
Vandyke	DE	7	A3
Vandyke	PA	62	B4
Vang Junction	PA	60	A2
Vankirk [PMY]	PA	53	C6
Vankirk [PRR(WAW)]	PA	50	C2
Vanport	PA	49	B3
Vanscoyoc	PA	58	D6
Vardo	MD	10	A6
Varick	NY	40	E3
Varna	NY	39	A1
Varysburg	NY	40	A4
Vaucluse	VA	9	E4
Venango	PA	48	C2
Venice Center	NY	38	A4
Venice Industrial Track	PA	72	D3
Ventnor	NJ	19	E4
Vera Cruz	PA	69	B4
Verbank	NY	34	F1
Vermontville	NY	28	D3
Vern	MD	11	A3
Vern	NY	36	E4
Vernon	NJ	17	D2
Vernon	NY	38	D2
Verona	NJ	21	D3
Verona	NY	38	D2
Verona	PA	53	C1
Versailes	PA	53	C5
Vestaburg	PA	54	A4
Vestal	NY	39	C3
Vexit Junction	PA	66	B1
Viaduct [PC(NYC Centre County)]	PA	57	E2
Viaduct [PSR (NYC Jefferson County)]	PA	57	A1
Viaduct Junction [Cumberland]	MD	8	D2
Vicksburg	PA	62	C2
Victor	NY	40	D3
Victor No.19 Mine	PA	58	D1
Victoria	PA	50	F3
Victoria Park	ON	42	B4
Victory	PA	47	D3
Victory Mill	NY	30	E2
Vienna	MD	11	D6
Vienna	NJ	17	C3
Vienna	NY	38	D1
Vienna [BO]	PA	50	B2
Vienna [MTR]	PA	52	A5
Vienna [NW(PWV)]	PA	52	A5
Vienna	VA	10	C4
Villanova	PA	72	C3
Villanova Junction	PA	72	C3
Vincentown	NJ	18	C4
Vine [CSXT(BO) Philadelphia]	PA	73	A4
Vine [SEPA Philadelphia]	PA	73	B4
Vineland	NJ	19	C2
Vinemont	PA	63	F1
Vineyard	PA	57	F4
Vintage	PA	63	F3
Vintondale	PA	57	B4
Vintondale No.6 Mine	PA	57	B4
Viola	DE	7	A4
Virginia	PA	65	C2
Virginia	WV	50	B1
Virginia Avenue [Cumberland]	MD	8	D2
Virginia Avenue Junction [Washington]	DC	14	C5
Virginia Avenue Tunnel [Washington]	DC	14	C5
Virginia Inland Port	VA	9	E4
Virginia Mills	PA	63	A4
Virginville	PA	69	A4
Vista (Fort Ritchie)	MD	10	B1
Vista	PA	53	D6
Vliettown	NJ	17	C4
Vly Summit	NY	30	F2
VO Tower [Mount Vernon]	NY	25	C3
Volant	PA	49	C1
Volkswagen Plant [Mount Pleasant]	PA	55	C2
Volomite	PA	49	F2
Voorhees	NJ	20	A3
Voorheesville	NY	30	D4
Voorheesville Junction	NY	30	D4
Vosburg	NY	41	A3
Vosburg	PA	61	F3
Vowinckle	PA	48	F4
Vreeland Avenue [Paterson]	NJ	22	B2
Vulcan	PA	67	C3
Vulcanite	NJ	71	E3

W

Place	State	Page	Grid
W [South Fork]	PA	64	B2
W&N Junction [Newfoundland]	NJ	17	D2
W&W Junction [Winchester]	VA	9	E3

Wabash Station [Pittsburgh] PA 53 A3
Waddington NY 36 F1
Waddle PA 57 E3
Wadesville VA 9 F3
Wadhams NY 28 F4
Wadsworth Junction NY 44 A6
Wading River NY 35 A5
Wagner PA 62 A3
Wagner Tower [Rosslyn] PA 52 D3
Wagners MD 12 D4
Wagners [POTED(H&F)] MD 10 A1
Wagners Point MD 12 C3
Wago Junction PA 63 D2
Wagontown PA 70 A3
Wahlville PA 49 C3
Wainscott NY 35 C5
Waite Street [Paterson] NJ 22 A1
Waites Crossing NY 43 C1
Wakefield NY 25 C4
Walbert PA 69 B4
Walden [Erie County] NY 46 C4
Walden [Orange County] NY 34 D1
Waldo [Jersey City] NJ 22 C5
Waldorf MD 10 D6
Waldwick NJ 17 E2
Wales [South Wales] NY 42 E4
Walford PA 49 B2
Walk [Norwalk] CT 35 C1
Walker MD 11 A1
Walker NY 40 B1
Walker [PSR(PS)] PA 51 E2
Walker [RJCP(CR)] PA 58 C2
Walkers Mills PA 52 C3
Walkersville MD 10 B2
Walkill NY 34 D1
Walkton PA 69 B3
Wall NJ 18 F2
Wall [Lebanon] PA 63 E1
Wallace NY 41 D1
Wallace PA 53 A6
Wallace Junction PA 47 B6
Wallaceton PA 58 C2
Waller VA 10 C6
Wallbrook Junction MD 12 B2
Wallingford PA 72 B5
Wallington NY 40 E2
Wallman MD 9 A2
Wallner PA 69 B4
Walnut [Reading] PA 64 A5
Walnut Bend PA 48 E3
Walnut Hill PA 50 E3
Walnut Hills PA 73 C2
Walnutport PA 69 E3
Walsall PA 64 A3
Walston MD 15 C1
Walston PA 57 A2
Walters PA 71 D2
Waltersburg PA 54 D5
Walton NY 39 F3
Walton [RJCP(NYC)] PA 57 D1
Walton [WAG(B&S)] PA 56 F2
Waltonville PA 63 D2
Waltz PA 55 B1
Walworth NY 40 D2
Wampsville NY 38 D2
Wampum PA 51 B3
Wampum Junction PA 51 B3
Wana Junction PA 50 C4
Wanakena NY 29 A1
Wanamaker PA 69 A3
Wanamaker Yard PA 72 C6
Wanaque NJ 17 E2
Wandin PA 57 B3
Wane PA 50 C3
Wanheta PA 62 B4
Wantage NJ 17 D1
Wantagh NY 24 D5
Wapocomo WV 9 C2
Wappinger Creek NY 34 E1
Wapwallopen PA 62 F1
War [Warren] OH 48 A4
Warbasse Junction NJ 16 B2
Warble PA 62 A4
Ward [Wilmington] DE 6 D3
Ward Road [North Tonawanda] NY 46 A1
Wardensville WV 9 D4
Wardour MD 11 B4
Waretown NJ 18 E4
Waretown Junction NJ 18 E4
Waring MD 10 C3
Warm [Warminster] PA 70 D2
Warminster PA 70 D2
Warner PA 74 C3
Warner Sand & Gravel PA 74 C4
Warners NJ 20 D1
Warners NY 38 B2
Warnock's WV 8 C6
Warren OH 48 A4
Warren PA 48 F2
Warren Glen NJ 71 F4
Warren Point NJ 22 B1
Warren Road [Cockeysville] MD 11 A2
Warren Street [Trenton] NJ 74 C2
Warrensburg NY 29 E4
Warrenton OH 50 A2
Warrior Run [CNJ] PA 65 A6
Warrior Run [LV] PA 65 A6
Warrior Run [PRR] PA 62 C1
Warrior's Mark PA 57 D3
Warroquier No.1 Mine PA 58 A1
Warsaw NY 40 A4
Warrington NJ 16 C5
Warrior Ridge PA 57 E4
Warwick NY 34 C3
Warwick PA 70 A2
Warwood WV 50 A2
Washington DC 10 D4
Washington DC 14 C4
Washington NJ 17 B4
Washington PA 50 C2
Washington Boro PA 63 E3
Washington Boulevard [Baltimore] MD 12 B3
Washington Crossing NJ 74 B1
Washington Grove MD 10 C3
Washington Hunt NY 41 B1
Washington Industrial Track NJ 17 B4
Washington Lane PA 73 A2
Washington Mills NY 38 E2
Washington Mines PA 54 D4
Washington Street [Cambridge] MD 11 C6
Washington Union Station DC 14 C5
Washingtonville NY 27 E2
Washingtonville OH 49 A2
Wassaic NY 31 E4
Wat [Watsontown] PA 62 C1
Watchung Avenue-Montclair NJ 22 A3
Water (Waterboro) NY 43 D3
Water PA 47 A3
Water Gap PA 16 B4
Water Plug PA 62 B4
Water Station MD 8 A3
Water Street PA 57 D4
Water Street Trap Rock PA 57 D4
Water Valley NY 42 E4
Water Witch NJ 18 F1
Waterboro NY 43 D3
Waterbury MD 11 A4
Waterford NJ 19 C1
Waterford (West Waterford) NY 32 F1
Waterford PA 48 D1
Waterford Junction NY 32 F1
Waterloo MD 10 D3
Waterloo NJ 17 C3
Waterloo NY 40 F3
Waterloo PA 60 F1
Watervliet NY 32 F2
Watermill NY 35 C5
Waterport NY 40 A1
Waterson PA 49 F1
Watersville MD 10 C2
Watertown NY 37 C2
Watertown Junction NY 37 C2
Waterville NY 38 E3
Waterville PA 61 A4
Watessing Avenue [Bloomfield] NJ 22 A4
Watkins [Watkins Glen] NY 41 F2
Watkins Glen NY 41 F2
Watrous PA 56 F2
Watson Farm PA 56 A3
Watsontown PA 62 C1
Watt PA 55 B6
Watts [NS (Gettysburg Junction)] PA 63 B2
Watts [PRR] PA 63 D2
Watts Flats NY 43 C3
Waugh Chapel MD 11 A4
Wawa PA 72 A5
Wawarsing NY 31 C4
Wawaset PA 70 B3
Waverly NY 39 A3
Waverly Yard [Newark] NJ 22 A5
Wayco OH 50 A1
Wayland NY 41 C1
Waymart PA 68 C3
Wayne [CSAO(NYG)] NJ 21 D1
Wayne [NJT(DLW)] NJ 21 A3
Wayne [PHWN] PA 72 B3
Wayne [SEPA(PRR)] PA 72 B2
Wayne [SEPA(RDG)] PA 73 B3
Wayne Junction PA 73 B3
Wayne Park Hospital NJ 21 A3
Waynecastle PA 60 F4
Wayneport NY 40 D2
Wayneport Junction NY 40 D2
Waynesboro PA 63 A4
Waynesboro Junction PA 60 F3
Waynesburg PA 50 C3
Wayville NY 30 E2
WB Tower [Brunswick] MD 10 A3
WB&H Junction PA 66 A1
WC [Waldwick] NJ 17 E2
WC (West Salamanca) NY 43 E3
WD [Lyons] NY 40 E2
Weatherly PA 66 C2
Weaver [PC(PRR)] PA 54 A2
Weaver [SRW] PA 62 B4
Weavers PA 67 A5
Weaversville PA 71 B3
Weaver's Old Stand PA 55 C1
Webb Farms (West Hibernia) NY 31 E4
Webster NY 40 D2
Webster PA 54 C1
Webster Avenue [New Rochelle] NY 25 D4
Websters NY 38 D3
Websters Crossing NY 40 C4
Wedgewood NY 41 F2
Weedsport NY 38 A2
Weedsport PA 56 B1
Weedville PA 56 C4
Weehawken [ERIE] NJ 22 C4
Weehawken [WS/OW] NJ 22 C4
Weehawken Tunnel NJ 22 C4
Wegee OH 50 A3
Wehrum PA 57 B4
Weidman NY 28 B
Weigh Scales PA 62 D3
Weiker PA 62 B2
Weirton WV 49 B4
Weirton Junction WV 50 B1
Wiessport PA 69 F1
Wiessport [defect detector] PA 69 F2
Welch PA 60 B3
Weldon NJ 16 D3
Welham MD 12 B4
Well PA 54 A4
Wellendorf PA 56 C3
Wells PA 57 A3
Wells Bridge NY 39 F2
Wells Creek PA 60 A3
Wellsboro PA 61 B2
Wellsboro Junction PA 61 B2
Wellsburg NY 41 F3
Wellsburg WV 50 B1
Wellsville NY 41 B3
Wellsville OH 49 A4
Wellsville Siding NY 41 B3
Welshdale PA 57 C3
Welton WV 9 B4
Welton Tunnel WV 8 D2
Wemple NY 30 E4
Wende NY 42 F3
Wenonah NJ 18 B4
Wenonah Falls PA 61 D4
Wentworth Avenue [South Beach] NY 20 F2
Wernersville PA 63 F1
Wertz PA 57 D4
Wesley MD 15 C2
Wesley NY 41 A2
Wesleyville PA 47 C6
West 1st Street [Oswego] NY 37 A3
West 2nd Street [Bayonne] NJ 22 B6
West 3rd Street [Bethlehem] PA 71 C4
West 8th Street [Bayonne] NJ 22 B6
West Aikin (Aikin) MD 13 E1
West Albany NY 32 E3
West Alexander PA 50 B2
West Aliquippa PA 49 C3
West Amity PA 50 C3
West Annapolis MD 11 B4
West Ansonia PA 61 A2
West Arlington NJ 22 B4
West Athens NY 33 B5
West Austintown OH 49 A1
West Avalon MD 12 A3
West Baltimore [CSXT(BO)] MD 12 B3
West Bellevue PA 52 D1
West Berlin NJ 18 C4
West Branch PA 59 B5
West Brown (West Brownsville Junction) PA 54 B4
West Brownsville PA 54 B4
West Brownsville Junction PA 54 B4
West Cambridge NY 30 F2
West Candor NY 39 A2
West Carthage NY 37 D2
West Catasauqua PA 71 A3
West Chazy NY 28 F1
West Chester PA 70 B3
West Chester Junction NJ 17 A1
West Clarksville NY 41 A3
West Cold Spring MD 12 B1
West Collingswood NJ 73 C5
West Columbia PA 54 C2
West Conshohocken PA 72 C2
West Conway PA 49 C3
West Coplay PA 71 A3
West Cornwall CT 31 F4
West Craigville NY 27 D3
West Creek NJ 19 E1
West Cressona Yard PA 67 B6
West Cumbo WV 9 F1
West Danby NY 39 A2
West Darlington PA 49 B3
West Davenport NY 31 A1
West Davis (Woodstock) MD 10 D2
West Earle NJ 18 E2
West Economy PA 49 C4
West Edmeston NY 38 E4
West Elizabeth PA 53 B6
West Ellwood Junction PA 51 B4
West End [Secaucus] NJ 22 C5
West End [Woodbury] NJ 73 A6
West End [Pittsburgh] PA 52 D2
West End [RDG] PA 62 E3
West End [SRRR] PA 56 F3
West Englewood NJ 22 C2
West Falls NY 42 E4
West Falls Church VA 10 C4
West Falls Yard [Philadelphia] PA 73 A3
West Farm Junction [Bronx] NY 23 C1
West Feltonville PA 72 A6
West Ford City PA 49 E3
West Grove PA 70 A4
West Haddonfield NJ 73 C5
West Hall NY 27 C1
West Hamburg PA 62 F4
West Harbor (Safe Harbor) PA 63 E3
West Haverstraw [CSXT(WS)] NY 26 B4
West Haverstraw [NJNY] NY 26 A4
West Hazleton PA 66 A1
West Hempstead NY 24 B4
West Henrietta NY 44 B5
West Hibernia NY 31 E4
West Hickory PA 48 F3
West Homestead Yard PA 53 B3
West Hood (Morgan) MD 10 C2
West Hump [Cumberland] MD 8 D2
West Hurley NY 31 D3
West Kendall NY 40 A1
West Keyser WV 8 D6
West Kittaning PA 49 E3
West Kodak Park NY 44 B2
West Laurel PA 64 A4
West Lebanon PA 49 F4
West Leechburg PA 51 F3
West Leesport PA 62 F4
West Liberty [B&S] PA 57 B1
West Liberty [WE(WSB)] PA 53 A3
West Lincoln Park NJ 21 C1
West Manayunk PA 72 D3
West Merchantville NJ 73 C4
West Meyersdale PA 60 A4
West Middlesex PA 47 B4
West Milton PA 62 C2
West Mohrsville PA 62 F4
West Monessen PA 54 B2
West Monroe NY 38 C1
West Monterey PA 49 E2
West Moorestown NJ 73 D4
West Morrisville PA 74 C3
West Mosgrove PA 47 C5
West Moshannon PA 58 B5
West Nanticoke PA 65 A5
West New Brighton NY 20 F1
West New Kensington PA 51 C4
West Newburgh NY 26 B1
West Newton PA 54 D1
West Norwood NJ 25 B2
West Notch NY 41 A3
West Nunda NY 40 B4
West Nyack NY 26 B6
West Ocean City MD 15 D1
West Oneonta NY 39 F1
West Orange NJ 21 D4
West Overbrook PA 72 D4
West Overton PA 55 C3
West Park NY 31 D4
West Patterson NY 34 F2
West Pawlet VT 29 F4
West Pawling NY 34 F1
West Penn PA 69 A3
West Pike PA 56 F2
West Pilot MD 11 C1
West Pitt [Pittsburgh] PA 53 A2
West Pittsburg PA 51 B2
West Pittsfield MA 31 F1
West Pittston PA 65 A3
West Pittston Junction PA 65 A3
West Plane MD 10 C2
West Point NY 26 B1
West Point OH 49 A3
West Point PA 70 C2
West Point Marion PA 50 D4
West Point Tunnel NY 26 B1
West Portal NJ 17 B4
West Portland NY 43 B2
West Reel MD 10 B2
West Richmondville NY 30 B4
West River NY 40 D4
West Rock MD 13 A1
West Romney WV 9 C2
West Rupert VT 30 F1
West Salamanca NY 43 E3
West Salisbury PA 60 A4
West Sand NJ 18 E3
West Side [Jersey City] NJ 22 B5
West Singerly MD 11 D1
West Secaucus NJ 22 B4
West Shoemakersville PA 62 F4
West Somerset NY 42 E1
West Sparta NY 40 C4
West Springfield PA 48 B1
West Stam [Stamford] CT 35 C1
West Stockbridge MA 31 F2
West Summit NJ 21 B5
West Tarentum PA 51 C4
West Trenton NJ 74 B2
West Trenton Yard NJ 74 C2
West Union PA 50 C3
West Valley NY 43 E2
West Valley Falls NY 30 E3
West Van Bibber MD 13 A3
West Vernon PA 48 C3
West View NJ 22 C2
West Virginia Central Junction WV 8 C6
West Waterford NY 32 F1
West Wheeling OH 50 A2
West Williamsfield OH 48 B3
West Willow PA 63 E3
West Winfield NY 38 F3
West Winfield PA 49 E3
West Yard [Oswego] NY 37 A3
West Yard [Wilmington] DE 6 D2
West York PA 63 C3
West Yough Transfer PA 55 C5
Westbury NY 24 C3
Westchester NY 23 C1
Westchester Avenue [Bronx] NY 23 C1
Westcolang Park PA 68 D3
Westdale NY 37 D4
Westernport MD 8 D6
Westfield NJ 21 C6
Westfield NY 43 B2
Westfield PA 61 A1
Westford PA 48 B3
Westhampton NY 35 B6
Westinghouse Air Brake Co. [East Pittsburgh] PA 53 D3
Westinghouse Electric Co. [East Pittsburgh] PA 53 C3
Westinghouse Electric Co. [Eddystone] PA 72 C6
Westinghouse Electric Co. [South Philadelphia] PA 72 D6
Westland PA 52 A6
Westland Mine PA 52 A5
Westline PA 56 B2

Westminster MD 10 D1
Westmont NJ 73 C5
Westmont PA 63 E1
Westmoreland PA 73 A3
Weston NJ 20 E4
Weston PA 61 D2
Westover MD 15 B2
Westover PA 57 C3
Westport CT 35 C1
Westport MD 12 B3
Westport NY 28 F4
Westport PA 56 E4
Westtown NY 34 C3
Westtown PA 70 B3
Westville NJ 73 B6
Westwood NJ 25 A2
Westwood NY 24 B5
Westwood Junction PA 67 A6
Westwood Switch PA 67 A5
Wetham PA 56 F4
Wetherill Junction PA 67 B4
Wetmore PA 56 B2
Weverton MD 10 A2
Weymouth NJ 19 C2
Whaley Lake NY 34 F2
Whaleysville MD 15 D1
Whallonsburgh NY 28 F4
Wharton NJ 17 A1
Wharton PA 56 E3
Wheat Road NJ 19 C2
Wheatfield [defect detector] NY 46 D1
Wheatfield PA 57 A4
Wheatland NY 45 F1
Wheatland PA 47 A3
Wheatville NY 40 A2
Wheeler NY 41 D2
Wheelers NY 40 D3
Wheelerville PA 61 C3
Wheeling WV 50 A2
Wheeling-Pittsburgh Steel [Monessen] PA 54 B2
Whippany NJ 21 B3
Whippany Railway Museum NJ 21 B3
Whitaker PA 63 E4
White MD 10 D4
White PA 49 F4
White Bear PA 70 A2
White Bridge NY 40 C4
White Bridge PA 57 D4
White Church NY 39 B2
White Cottage Tunnel PA 50 B4
White Creek NY 30 F3
White Deer PA 62 C1
White Deer Furnace PA 62 C1
White Gravel PA 56 B2
White Hall MD 11 A1
White Haven PA 69 A2
White Hill PA 64 C3
White House NJ 17 C4
White Lake NJ 17 C2
White Marsh MD 12 E1
White Marsh PA 73 A1
White Marsh Junction PA 72 C1
White Mill PA 57 B4
White Mills PA 68 C3
White Oak MD 11 D3
White Oak PA 63 E2
White Plains MD 10 D6
White Plains NY 25 D1
White Plains Shops NY 25 E1
White Plains Westchester Avenue NY 25 E1
White Post VA 9 F4
White Rock PA 63 F4
White Spring PA 63 C1
White Valley PA 49 E4
Whiteboro NJ 19 C4
Whiteford MD 11 B1
Whitehall NY 29 F4
Whitehall Tunnel PA 53 A4
Whitehall Yard NY 29 F4
Whitehead NJ 19 B3
Whites [CNYS] NY 38 A3
Whites [PRR] NY 44 A4
Whites Crossing PA 68 B3
Whites Mills NY 39 C1
Whitesboro NY 38 E2
Whitestone NY 23 D2
Whitestone Junction NY 23 D3
Whitestone Landing NY 23 D2
Whitesville NJ 18 E3
Whitesville NY 41 C3
Whitford PA 70 D4
Whiting PA 57 D1
Whitings NJ 18 E4
Whitmier NY 43 B2
Whitney PA 50 F2
Whitney Point NY 39 C2
Whitsett Junction PA 54 D3
Whitsons NY 26 D5
Wick OH 48 A3
Wick Haven PA 54 D2
Wickham Avenue [Middletown] NY 27 A2
Wicopee NY 26 C1
Wide Water VA 10 C6
Widnoon PA 49 F2
Wierwood VA 15 A5
Wiggan PA 67 B3
Wigton PA 58 D4
Wikatunk NJ 18 E2
Wilawana PA 61 D1
Wilburtha NJ 74 B2
Wilburton PA 66 C4
Wilcox NY 34 C3
Wilcox PA 56 B3
Wildcat Tunnel MD 11 C1
Wildwood NJ 19 C4
Wildwood [CSXT(P&W)] PA 49 D4
Wildwood [PSN] PA 56 C3
Wildwood Crest NJ 19 C4
Wildwood Junction NJ 19 C4
Wildwood Springs PA 59 A2
Wilkes-Barre PA 65 C5
Wilkes-Barre PA 68 A4
Wilkes Street Tunnel [Alexandria] VA 14 B6
Wilkins NJ 18 C4
Wilkinsburg PA 53 B2
Wiley PA 63 D4
Willada PA 52 B2
Willard PA 61 B2
Willard State Hospital NY 40 F4
Willards MD 15 C1
Willards NY 39 D2
Willets NY 40 F4
William WV 9 A3
William Penn PA 67 A3
Williams [BO] PA 60 B3
Williams [CR(RDG)] PA 72 D1
Williams Bridge NY 25 C4
Williams Grove PA 63 C2
Williams Mill PA 56 B1
Williams Tunnel PA 63 E4
Williams Valley Junction PA 62 D4
Williamsburg MD 11 D6
Williamsburg PA 57 D4
Williamson NY 40 D1
Williamson PA 60 F3
Williamson School PA 72 B5
Williamsport MD 10 A1
Williamsport PA 61 C4
Williamstown NJ 19 C1
Williamstown NY 37 C4
Williamstown [Williamstown Junction] NJ 18 C4
Williamstown PA 62 D4
Williamstown Junction NJ 18 C4
Williamsville NY 46 C3
Willock PA 53 A4
Willoughby MD 11 C4
Willow Brook NY 31 E4
Willow Creek NY 39 A1
Willow Grove PA 73 B1
Willow Grove Yard [Pittsburgh] PA 53 A2
Willow Point NY 39 C3
Wills Creek PA 60 B3
Willsboro NY 28 F4
Willsboro Tunnel NY 28 F3
Willseyville NY 39 B2
Wilmer PA 70 F2
Wilmerding PA 53 D3
Wilmerding [defect detector] PA 53 C3
Wilmington DE 6 D2
Wilmington DE 7 B1
Wilmington Junction PA 49 C1
Wilmington Shops DE 6 E2
Wilmore PA 60 B1
Wilna NY 37 D2
Wilsmere Yard [Wilmington] DE 6 C3
Wilson MD 9 A2
Wilson NY 42 E1
Wilson [NYC] PA 49 F1
Wilson [PRR] PA 53 B5
Wilson WV 9 A3
Wilson Creek PA 60 A3
Wilson Creek Branch PA 60 A3
Wilson Run PA 57 C3
Wilt [Wilton] CT 35 C1
Wilton CT 35 C1
Wilton NJ 18 C4
Wilton NY 30 E1
Wilton Kent Road CT 35 C1
Wilton Point CT 35 C1
Wimmers PA 68 B4
Win [Winfield] NY 23 C3
Winans MD 12 A3
Winburne PA 57 D2
Winchells NY 31 E3
Winchester [BE(M&DC)] MD 11 C4
Winchester [BLA(BASL)] MD 11 B4
Winchester NY 46 C5
Winchester VA 9 E3
Wind [Wayne Junction] PA 73 B3
Wind Gap PA 16 A5
Wind Gap Junction PA 16 A5
Windber PA 64 B3
Windfall PA 56 C1
Windfall Connection [East Salamanca] NY 43 E3
Windsor NJ 18 D2
Windsor NY 39 D3
Windsor Beach NY 44 C1
Wine [Wilmington] DE 6 D2
Wine MD 10 D5
Winfield NY 23 C3
Winfield PA 62 C2
Winfield Junction PA 51 D1
Wing NJ 74 C1
Wing [East Pittsburgh] PA 53 C3
Wingdale NY 34 F1
Wingdale-Halem Valley (State Hospital) NY 34 F1
Wingerton PA 60 F4
Winlack PA 56 A4
Wins [Baldwinsville] NY 38 B2
Winslow NJ 19 C1
Winslow PA 57 B2
Winslow Junction NJ 19 C1
Winterburn PA 57 C1
Winterset PA 57 B4
Winterthur DE 6 D1
Winterton NY 34 C2
Winthrop NY 28 A2
Winthrop PA 50 F1
Winton PA 65 B1
Winton Junction PA 65 D2
Wirt NY 41 A3
Wisner NY 34 D3
Wissahickon PA 73 A3
Wissinoming PA 73 C3
Wistar PA 56 E4
Wister PA 73 B3
Withington NJ 18 D2
Witmer PA 63 F2
Witte PA 69 C4
WJ [Mahaffey] PA 59 B4
WK [Allentown] PA 71 A4
Wolcott NY 40 F2
Woleben NY 43 B2
Wolf Creek NY 29 D1
Wolf Pond NY 28 D2
Wolf Run NY 43 D3
Wolfert NJ 18 A4
Wolfsburg PA 60 C2
Wolverton PA 62 D2
Womelsdorf PA 63 F1
Wood [Edgewood] MD 13 A4
Wood (Woodbridge Junction) NJ 20 D3
Wood [Norwood] NY 28 A2
Wood [Woodside] NY 23 C3
Wood [CSAO(MGA)] PA 50 C3
Wood (Homewood) PA 51 B4
Wood [Woodbourne] PA 74 B3
Wood Run PA 54 B3
Woodard NY 38 B2
Woodberry MD 12 B1
Woodbine MD 10 C2
Woodbine NJ 19 C3
Woodbine [MPA] PA 63 E4
Woodbine [PRR] PA 70 E4
Woodbine Junction NJ 19 C3
Woodbourne PA 74 A3
Woodbourne Yard PA 74 A3
Woodbridge NJ 20 C2
Woodbridge VA 10 C6
Woodbridge Junction NJ 20 D3
Woodbrook MD 12 B1
Woodbury NJ 73 B6
Woodbury NY 27 F3
Woodbury Heights NJ 18 B4
Woodbury Viaduct NY 27 F3
Woodcliff Lake NJ 25 A1
Woodcrest NJ 73 C5
Wooddale DE 6 C2
Woodensburg MD 10 D2
Woodgate NY 37 F4
Woodhaven NY 23 C4
Woodhaven Junction NY 23 D4
Woodland NY 25 D1
Woodland WV 50 A4
Woodland PA 58 B1
Woodland No.2 Mine PA 59 B6
Woodlane NJ 74 C6
Woodlane PA 72 D2
Woodlawn MD 13 B2
Woodlawn NY 25 C4
Woodmansie NJ 18 D4
Woodmere NY 24 A6
Woodmont PA 70 D2
Woodmont Club MD 9 E1
Woodridge NJ 22 B3
Woodridge NY 34 C1
Woodrow PA 50 B1
Woodruff WV 50 B4
Woodruffs NJ 19 B2
Woodruffs NY 40 C3
Woodruffs Gap NJ 16 C2
Woods NY 29 A2
Woods Branch DE 7 E3
Woods Falls NY 28 E1
Woods Mill NY 38 A4
Woods Run PA 52 D2
Woodsboro MD 10 C1
Woodside DE 7 A4
Woodside NJ 22 A4
Woodside NY 23 C3
Woodside PA 62 C4
Woodstock MD 10 D2
Woodstock PA 63 A3
Woodstown NJ 19 B1
Woodvale [EBT] PA 60 D2
Woodvale [PRR] PA 56 C2
Woodville MD 10 D6
Woodville [NYPA] PA 56 E1
Woodville [PRR/PCY] PA 52 C4
Woodville Junction PA 52 C4
Woodward Avenue [North Buffalo] NY 46 A3
Woodworth OH 49 A2
Woodworth PA 48 B1
Woolgin NY 43 B2
Wopsononock PA 59 C1
Worcester NY 30 A4
Works [Altoona] PA 59 D1
World Trade Center [Manhattan] NY 23 A3
Worlds Fair [Flushing] NY 23 C3
Wortendyke NJ 17 E3
Worth PA 60 A4
Worthington NY 25 D2
Worthington PA 49 E3
Worton MD 11 C3
Woytych MD 11 A4
Wray's Hill PA 60 E2
Wright NY 29 F2
Wrights NJ 20 B4
Wrights PA 56 D2
Wrightstown NJ 18 D3
Wrightsville PA 63 D3
WS Tower [East Butler] PA 49 D2
Wurlitzer NY 46 B1
Wurtenburg PA 51 C3
Wurtsboro NY 34 C1
WX Cabin [Waterlviet] NY 32 F2
Wyalusing PA 61 E2
Wyandanch NY 35 C3
Wyckoff NJ 17 E2
Wycombe PA 70 D1
Wydel DE 7 B4
Wye [New Portage Junction] PA 59 C3
Wye [Rockville] PA 64 C1
Wye Mills MD 11 C4
Wyebrook PA 70 A2
Wykagyl NY 25 D3
Wylandville PA 50 C2
Wylie PA 53 C5
Wyndmoor PA 73 A2
Wynn PA 58 A3
Wynnfield Avenue [Philadelphia] PA 72 D4
Wynnewood PA 72 D3
Wynnewood Road PA 72 C3
Wyoanna PA 65 A1
Wyomanock NY 31 F1
Wyoming DE 7 B4
Wyoming NY 45 C4
Wyoming PA 65 A3
Wyoming Avenue [Philadelphia] PA 73 B3
Wyoming Street [Hazleton] PA 66 A1
Wyomissing Junction PA 64 A5
Wyside PA 56 E4
Wysox PA 61 E2

X

XC Crossing [Lake Mahopac] NY 34 F2
XG Tower [Conneaut Junction] PA 48 B1
XO Tower [Mechanicville] NY 30 E3
XW [Paterson] NJ 22 A2

Y

Y Interlocking [Sayville] NY 35 D3
Yale NY 40 E3
Yaphank NY 35 A6
Yard [Wilmington] DE 6 D3
Yard A [Queens] NY 23 B3
Yardley PA 74 B2
Yardville NJ 18 D2
Yatesboro PA 49 F3
Yatesville [LV RDG] PA 67 B3
Yatesville [STLH(DH)] PA 65 D4
YD [Corning] NY 41 E3
YD [Hagerstown] MD 10 A5
Yeagertown PA 57 F3
Yeatman PA 6 A2
Yellow Brook NJ 18 E2
Yellow Creek OH 49 A4
Yellow Spring PA 62 D4
Yellow Springs MD 10 B2
Yerkes PA 70 B2
Yoder PA 60 A3
Yoe PA 63 D3
Yonkers NY 25 C3
York [GNWR] NY 45 E3
York [NYC] NY 36 E4
York [PRR] NY 45 F3
York PA 63 D3
York Farm Junction PA 67 A5
York Furnace PA 63 E3
York Haven PA 63 D2
York Junction PA 66 A2
York Road PA 63 C4
York Run PA 50 D3
Yorklyn DE 6 C1
Yorkship NJ 73 B5
Yorkshire NY 43 F1
Yorktown NJ 19 B1
Yorktown Heights NY 26 D3
Yorkville OH 50 A2
Yosts NY 30 B3
Youngdale PA 62 A1
Youngs NY 39 E2
Youngstown NY 42 B1
Youngstown OH 49 A1
Youngstown Test Site NY 42 C1
Youngsville PA 48 F2
Youngwood PA 55 C1
Younts PA 60 C2
Yukon PA 55 A1

Z

Zaners PA 62 E1
Zediker PA 50 C2
Zehners PA 62 F3
Zelienople PA 49 C3
Zenith PA 62 F2
Zeno PA 49 D3
Zepp MD 12 B3
Zieglersville PA 70 B1
Zimmerman PA 60 A2
Zion [CRPA] PA 57 F2
Zion [WPE] PA 65 A3
Zionsville PA 69 B4
Zoo Tower [Philadelphia] PA 73 A4
Zucksville PA 71 D2
Zumbro PA 60 F3
Zurich NY 40 E2